To the friend who drew *D.Gray-man* with me… Thank you for drawing great backgrounds. Thank you for the fun memories. The manga we promised to someday draw together still remains, but I will definitely draw it someday. When I do, I will dedicate it to you. So just wait.

—Katsura Hoshino

Shiga Prefecture native Katsura Hoshino's hit manga series *D.Gray-man* has been serialized in *Weekly Shonen Jump* since 2004. Katsura's debut manga, "Continue," appeared for the first time in *Weekly Shonen Jump* in 2003.

Katsura adores cats.

D.GRAY-MAN

VOL. 25
SHONEN JUMP ADVANCED
Manga Edition

STORY AND ART BY
KATSURA HOSHINO

English Adaptation/Lance Caselman
Translation/John Werry
Touch-up Art & Lettering/Susan Daigle-Leach
Design/Matt Hinrichs
Editor/Gary Leach

D.GRAY-MAN © 2004 by Katsura Hoshino. All rights reserved.
First published in Japan in 2004 by SHUEISHA Inc., Tokyo. English translation rights arranged by SHUEISHA Inc.

The stories, characters and incidents mentioned in this publication are entirely fictional.

Printed in the U.S.A.

Published by VIZ Media, LLC
P.O. Box 77010
San Francisco, CA 94107

10 9 8 7 6 5 4 3 2 1
First printing, May, 2017

www.viz.com

www.shonenjump.com

SHONEN JUMP ADVANCED MANGA EDITION

D.Gray-man

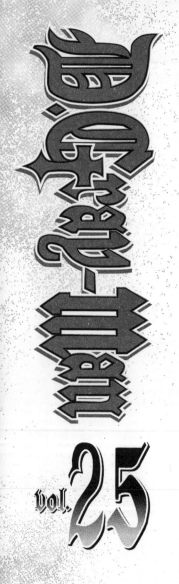

vol. 25

STORY & ART BY

Katsura Hoshino

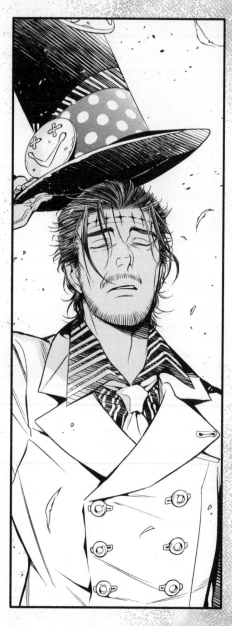

D.Gray-man
CHARACTERS

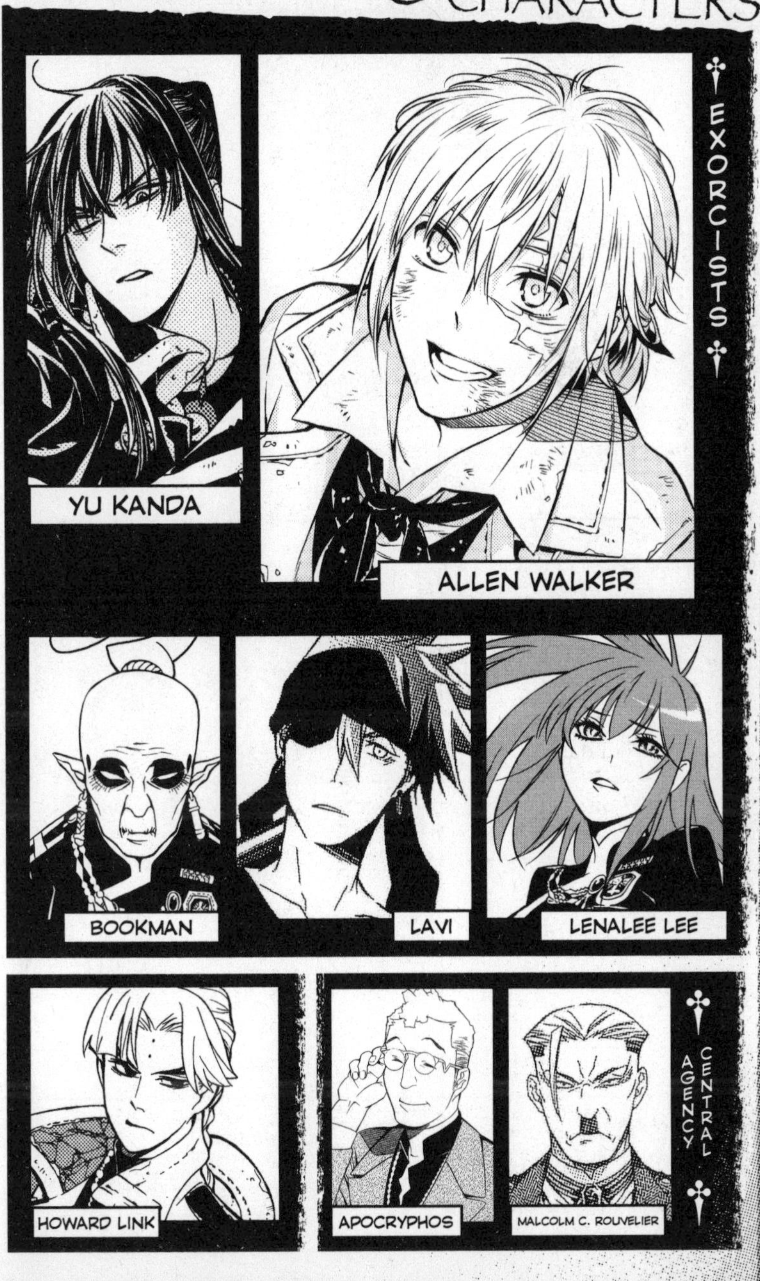
EXORCISTS
ALLEN WALKER
YU KANDA
LENALEE LEE
LAVI
BOOKMAN
CENTRAL AGENCY
MALCOLM C. ROUVELIER
APOCRYPHOS
HOWARD LINK

NEA
(THE FOURTEENTH)

CROSS MARIAN

MANA WALKER

MANA D.
CAMPBELL

JOHNNY GILL

WAIZURII

TYKI MIKK
(JOIDO)

THE MILLENNIUM EARL

THE
NOAH
CLAN

SHERIL
(DEZAIASU)

ROAD CAMELOT

FIIDORA

JASDEVI

S T O R Y

IT ALL BEGAN CENTURIES AGO WITH THE DISCOVERY OF A CUBE CONTAINING AN APOCALYPTIC PROPHECY FROM AN ANCIENT CIVILIZATION AND INSTRUCTIONS IN THE USE OF INNOCENCE, A CRYSTALLINE SUBSTANCE OF WONDROUS SUPERNATURAL POWER. THE CREATORS OF THE CUBE CLAIMED TO HAVE DEFEATED AN EVIL KNOWN AS THE MILLENNIUM EARL BY USING THE INNOCENCE. NEVERTHELESS, THE WORLD WAS DESTROYED BY THE GREAT FLOOD OF THE OLD TESTAMENT. NOW, TO AVERT A SECOND END OF THE WORLD, A GROUP OF EXORCISTS WIELDING WEAPONS MADE OF INNOCENCE MUST BATTLE THE MILLENNIUM EARL, HIS SERVANTS THE NOAH, AND HIS LEGIONS OF DEMONIC DESTRUCTION, THE AKUMA.

ALLEN CONTINUES HIS TRANSFORMATION INTO NEA, THE FOURTEENTH. THE INNOCENCE APOCRYPHOS ATTEMPTS TO FUSE WITH HIM AND A FIERCE BATTLE ENSUES. BUT ALLEN IS JUDGED TO BE A NOAH AND EXPELLED FROM THE BLACK ORDER. RATHER THAN TURN AGAINST HIS FRIEND, JOHNNY LEAVES THE ORDER AND, IN THE COMPANY OF KANDA, SETS OUT TO FIND ALLEN. BUT THEY SOON ENCOUNTER A FORCE OF NOAH AND A FAR DEADLIER FOE—THE MILLENNIUM EARL HIMSELF!

D.GRAY-MAN
Vol. 25

CONTENTS

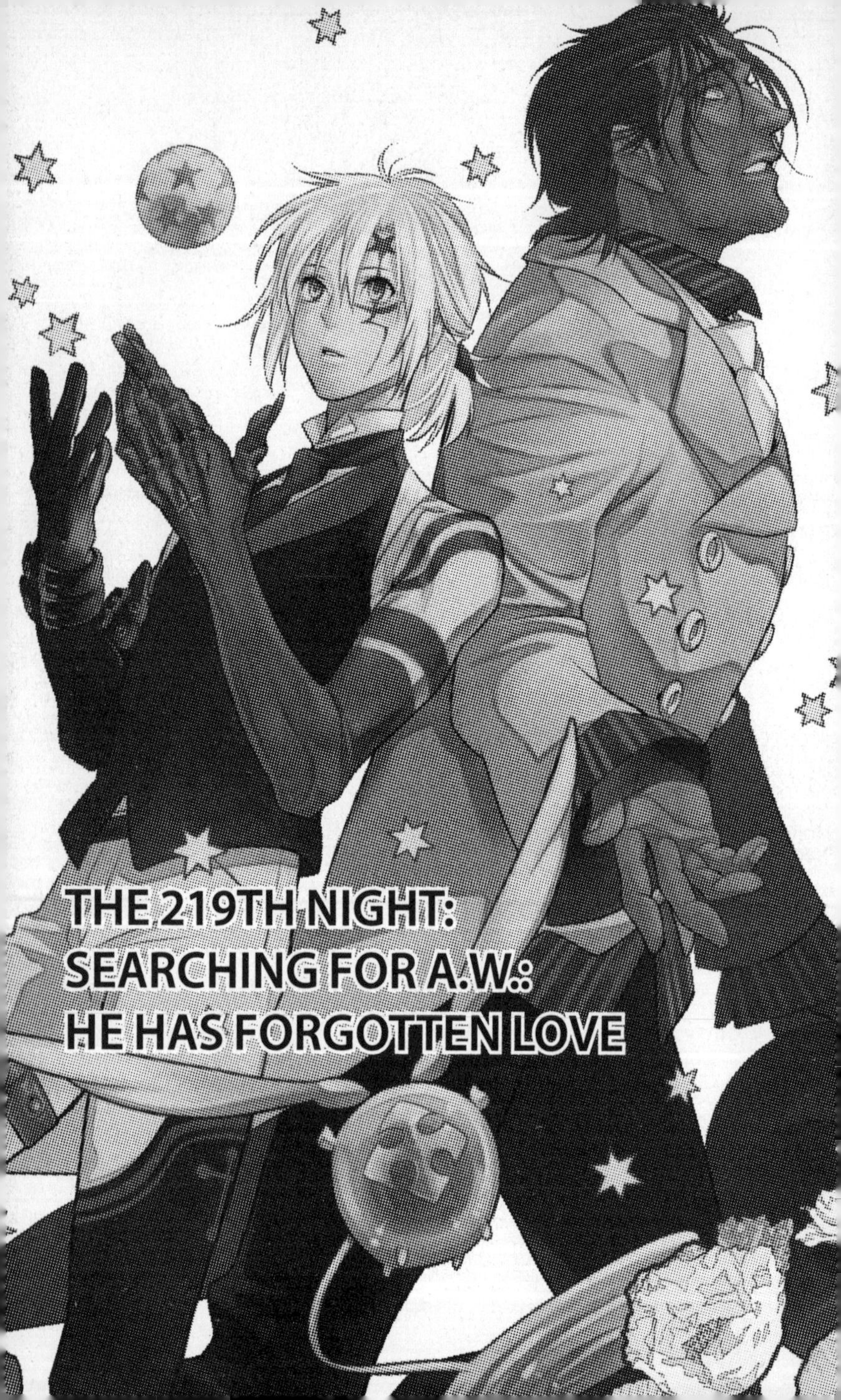
THE 219TH NIGHT:
SEARCHING FOR A.W.:
HE HAS FORGOTTEN LOVE

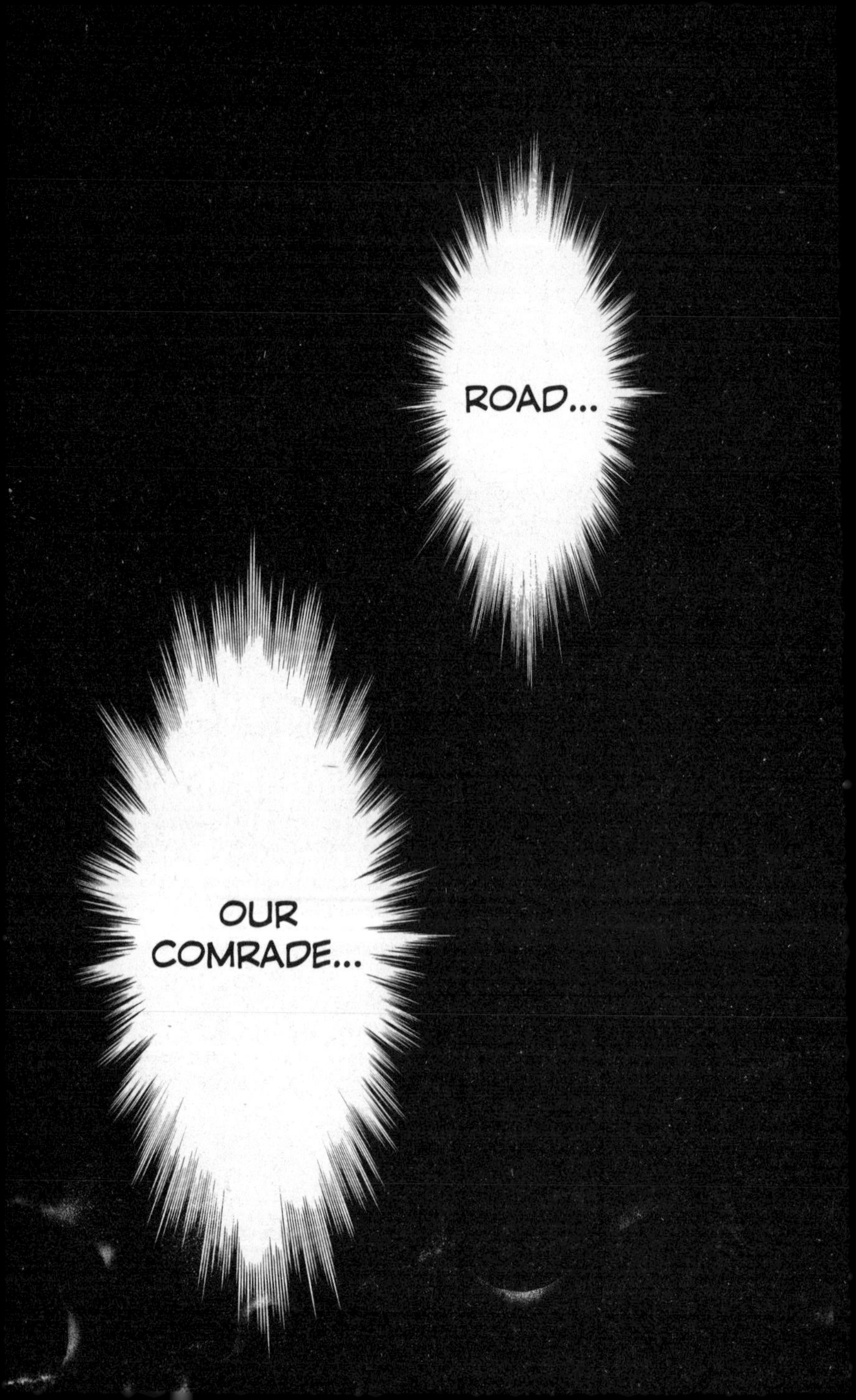
ROAD...
OUR COMRADE...

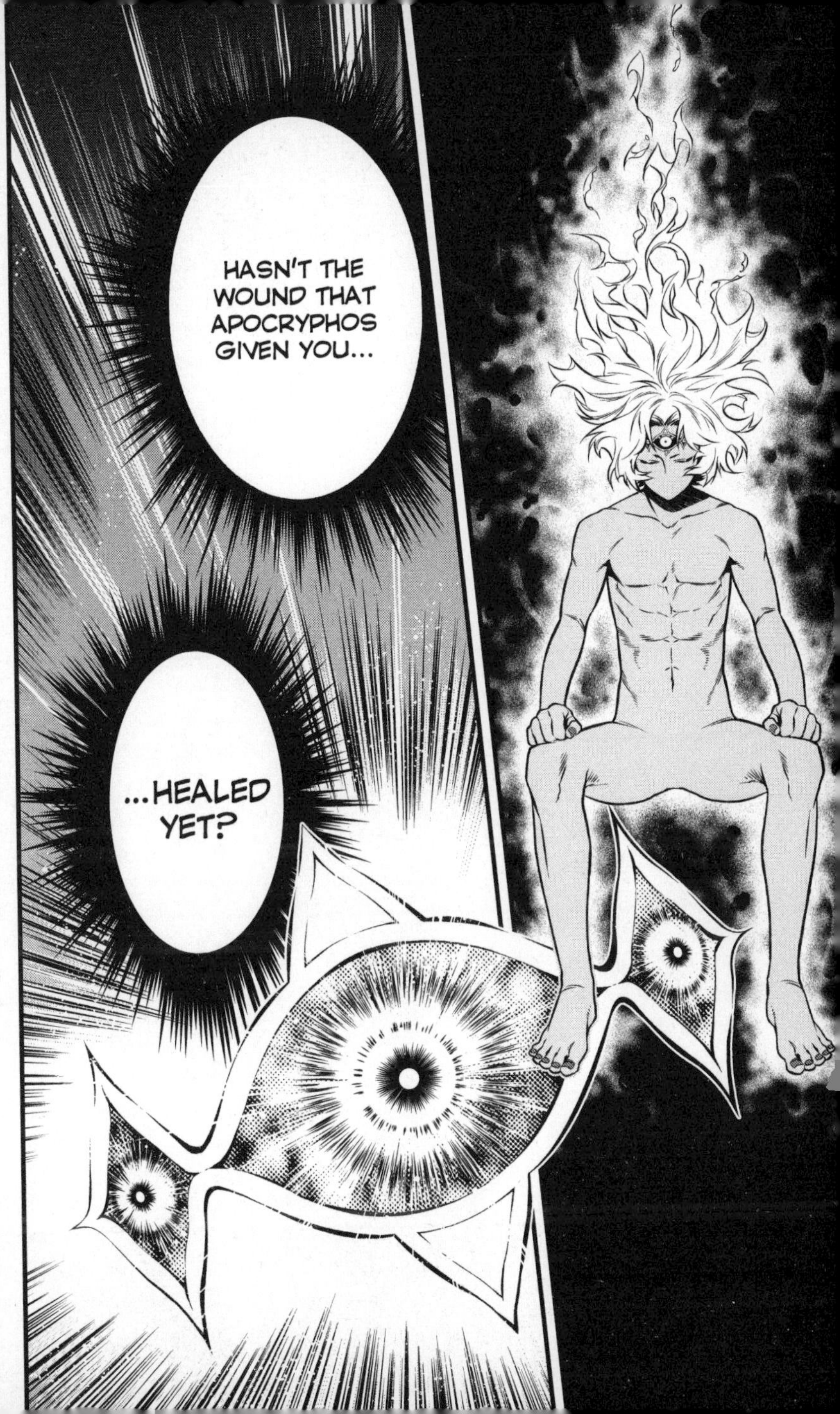
HASN'T THE WOUND THAT APOCRYPHOS GIVEN YOU...
...HEALED YET?

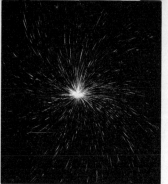

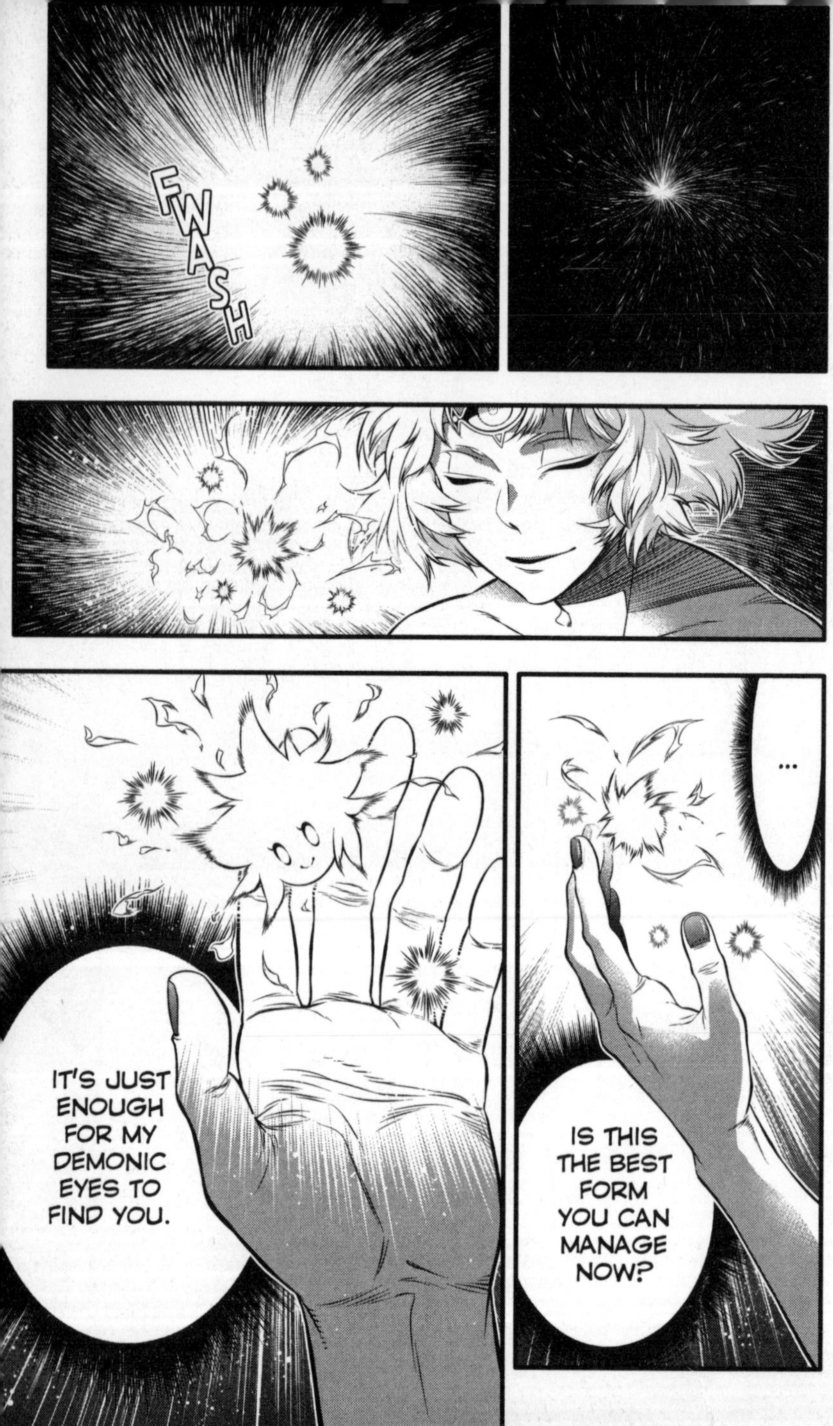
FWASH
...
IS THIS THE BEST FORM YOU CAN MANAGE NOW?
IT'S JUST ENOUGH FOR MY DEMONIC EYES TO FIND YOU.

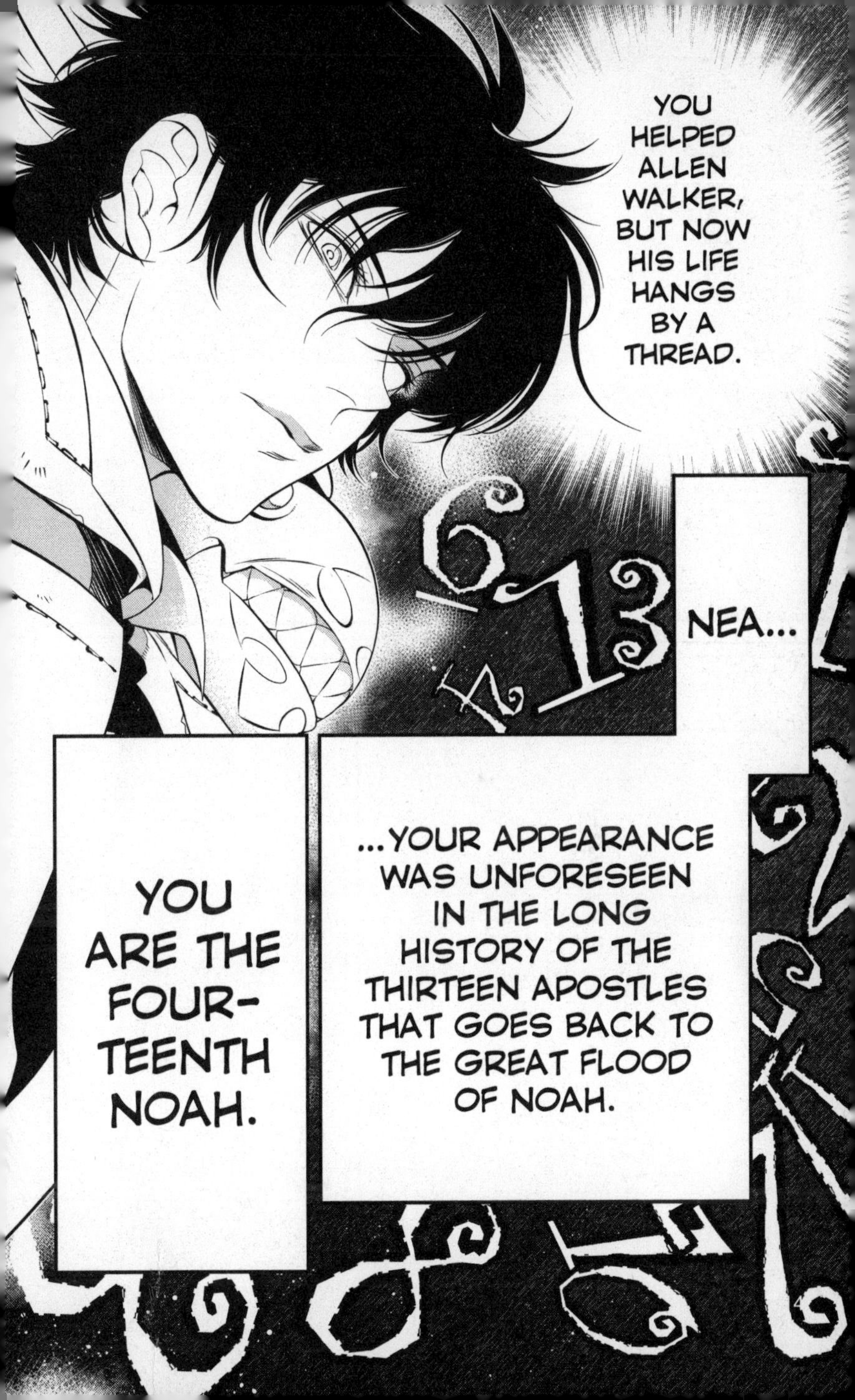
YOU HELPED ALLEN WALKER, BUT NOW HIS LIFE HANGS BY A THREAD.
NEA...
...YOUR APPEARANCE WAS UNFORESEEN IN THE LONG HISTORY OF THE THIRTEEN APOSTLES THAT GOES BACK TO THE GREAT FLOOD OF NOAH.
YOU ARE THE FOURTEENTH NOAH.

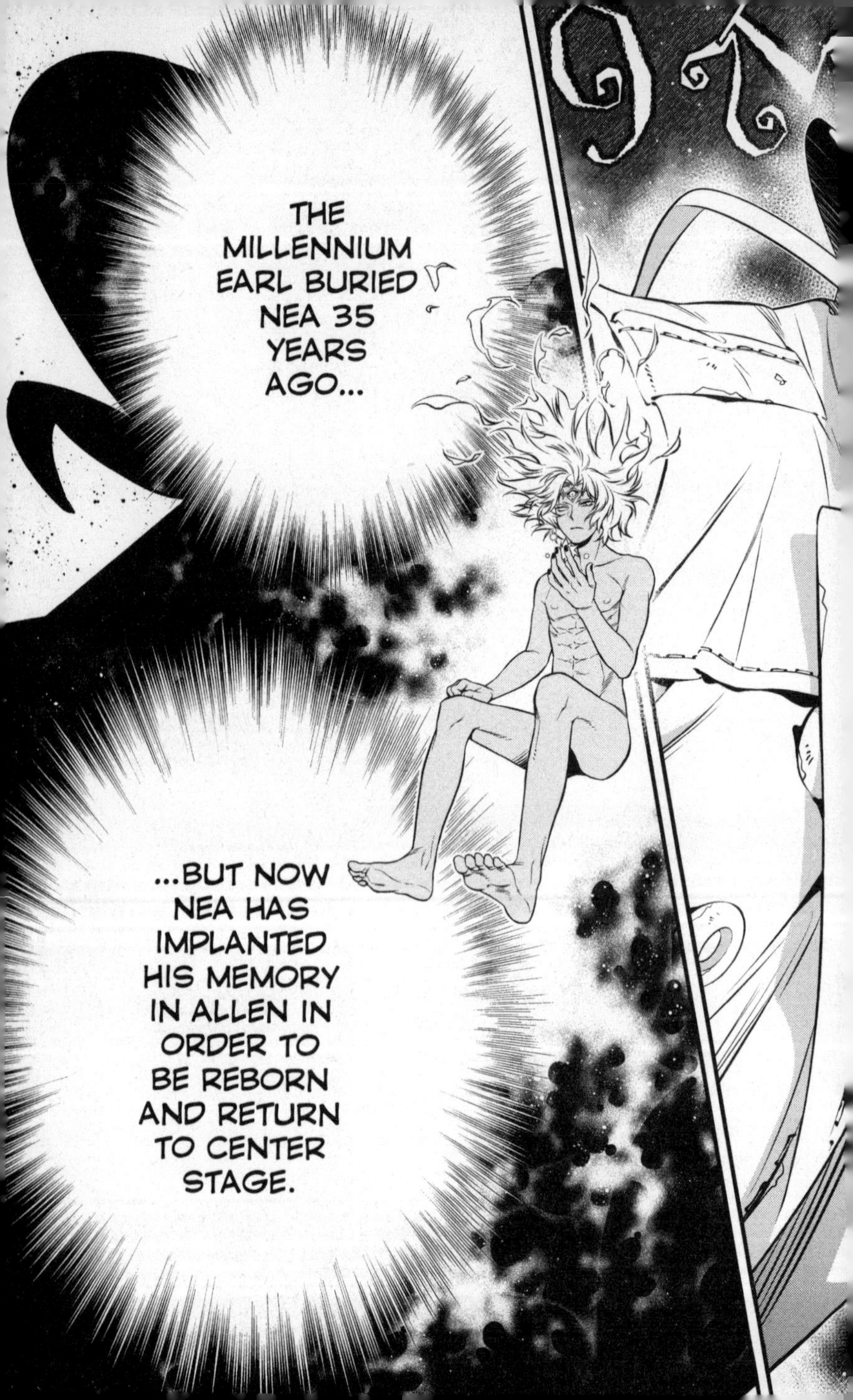
THE MILLENNIUM EARL BURIED NEA 35 YEARS AGO...
...BUT NOW NEA HAS IMPLANTED HIS MEMORY IN ALLEN IN ORDER TO BE REBORN AND RETURN TO CENTER STAGE.

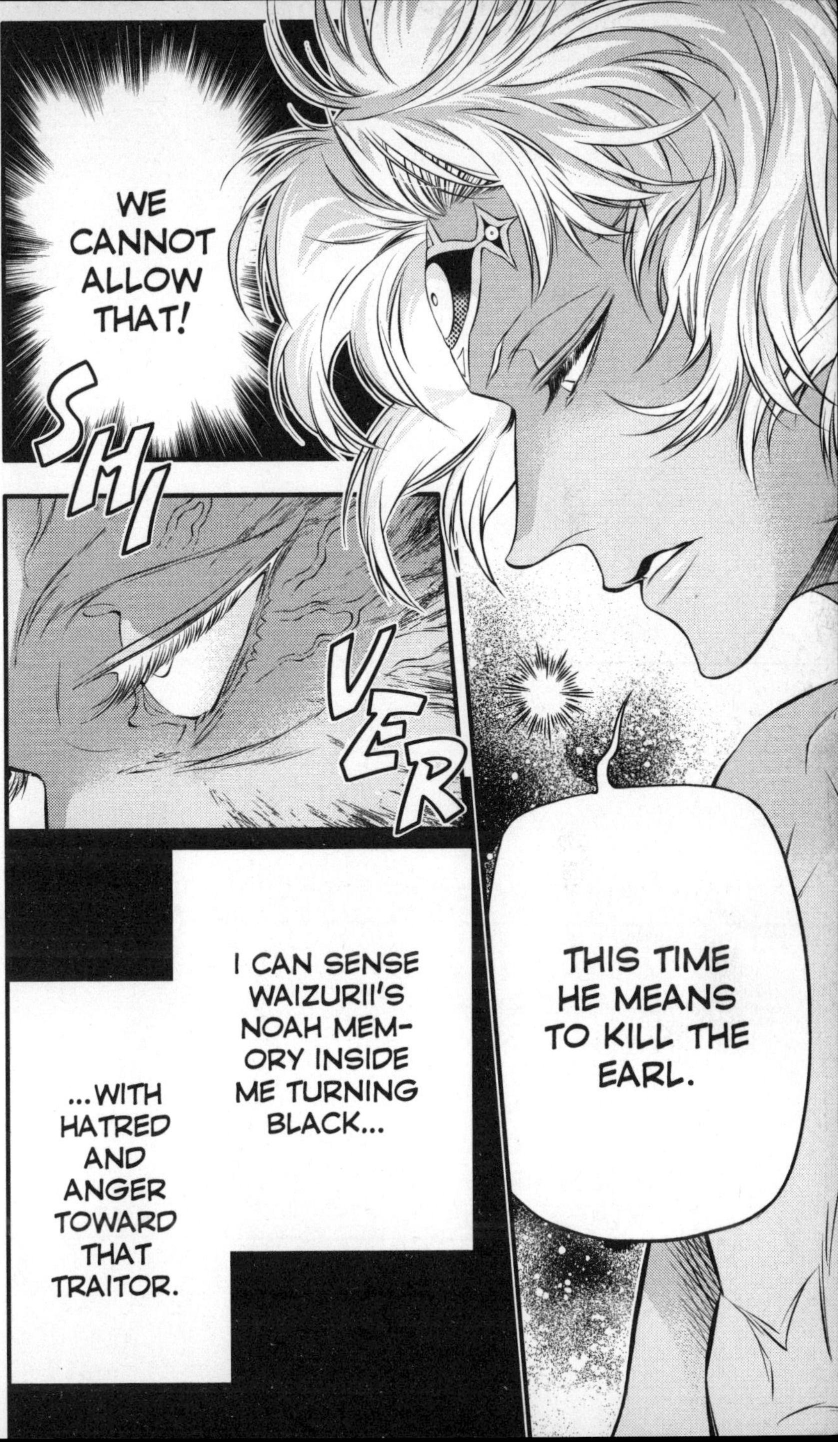
WE CANNOT ALLOW THAT!
SHIVER
THIS TIME HE MEANS TO KILL THE EARL.
I CAN SENSE WAIZURII'S NOAH MEMORY INSIDE ME TURNING BLACK...
...WITH HATRED AND ANGER TOWARD THAT TRAITOR.

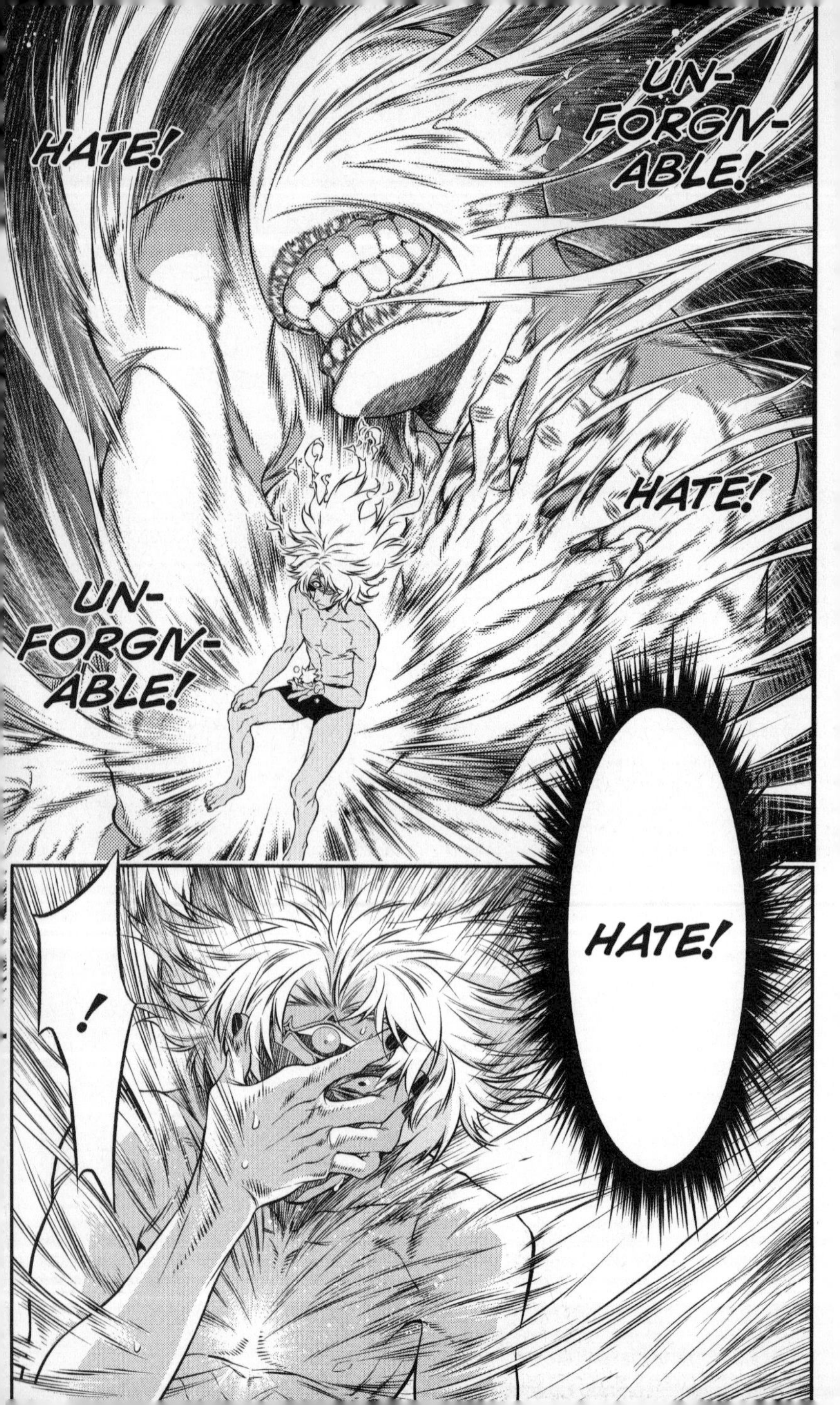
UN-FORGIV-ABLE!
HATE!
HATE!
UN-FORGIV-ABLE!
HATE!
!

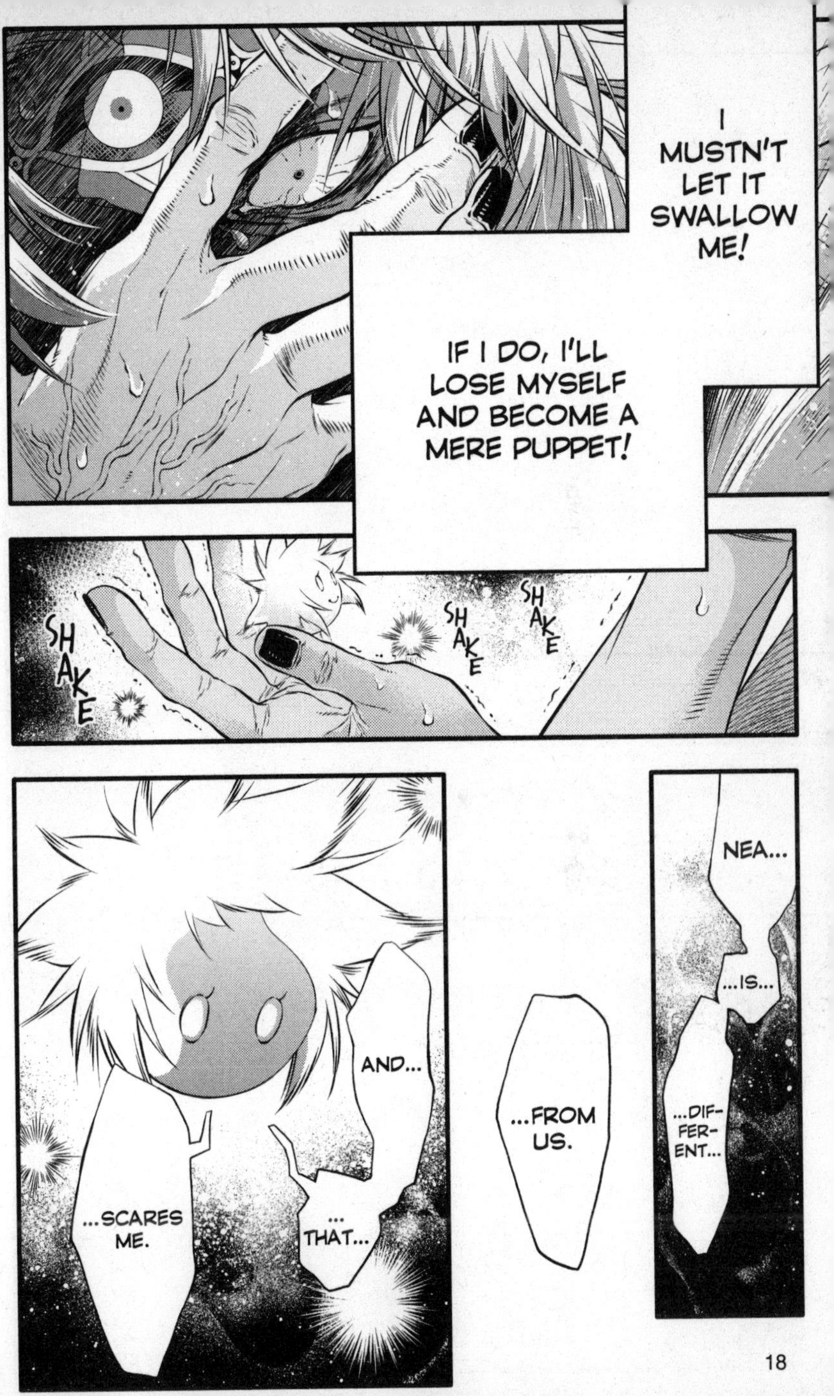
I MUSTN'T LET IT SWALLOW ME!
IF I DO, I'LL LOSE MYSELF AND BECOME A MERE PUPPET!
SHAKE
SHAKE
SHAKE
NEA...
...IS...
...DIF-FER-ENT...
...FROM US.
AND...
...THAT...
...SCARES ME.

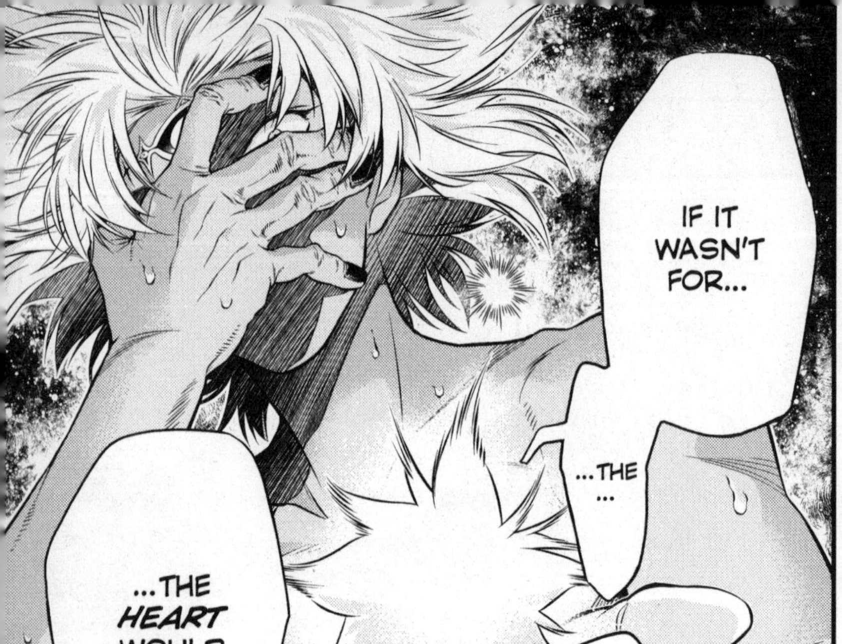
IF IT WASN'T FOR...
...THE ...
...EARL ...
...THE *HEART* WOULD DESTROY...
...US.
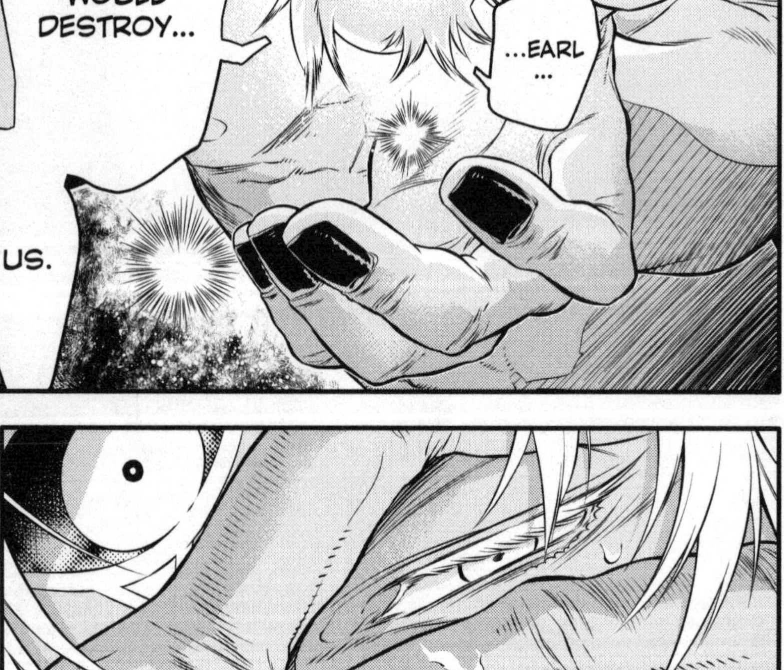

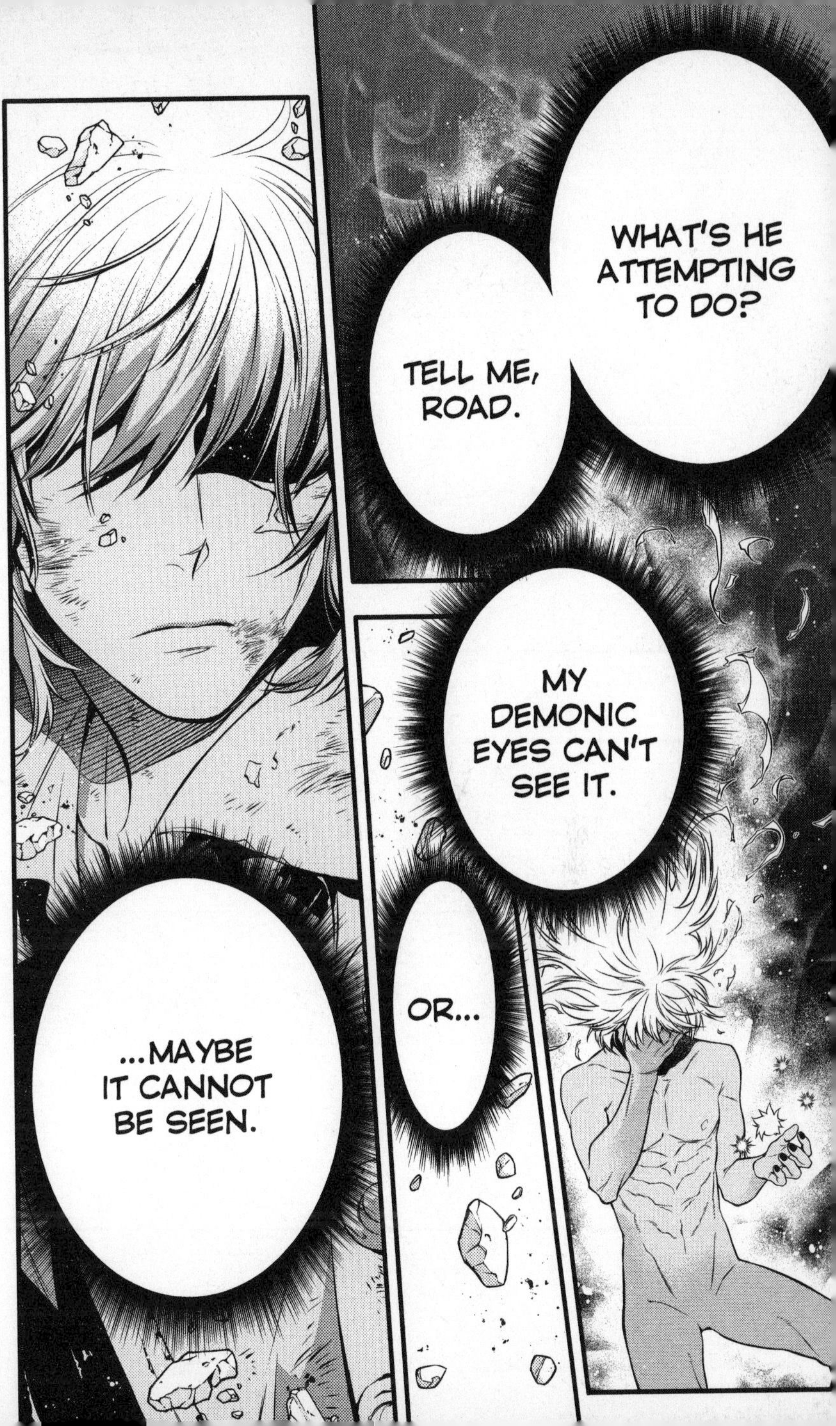
WHAT'S HE ATTEMPTING TO DO?
TELL ME, ROAD.
MY DEMONIC EYES CAN'T SEE IT.
OR...
...MAYBE IT CANNOT BE SEEN.

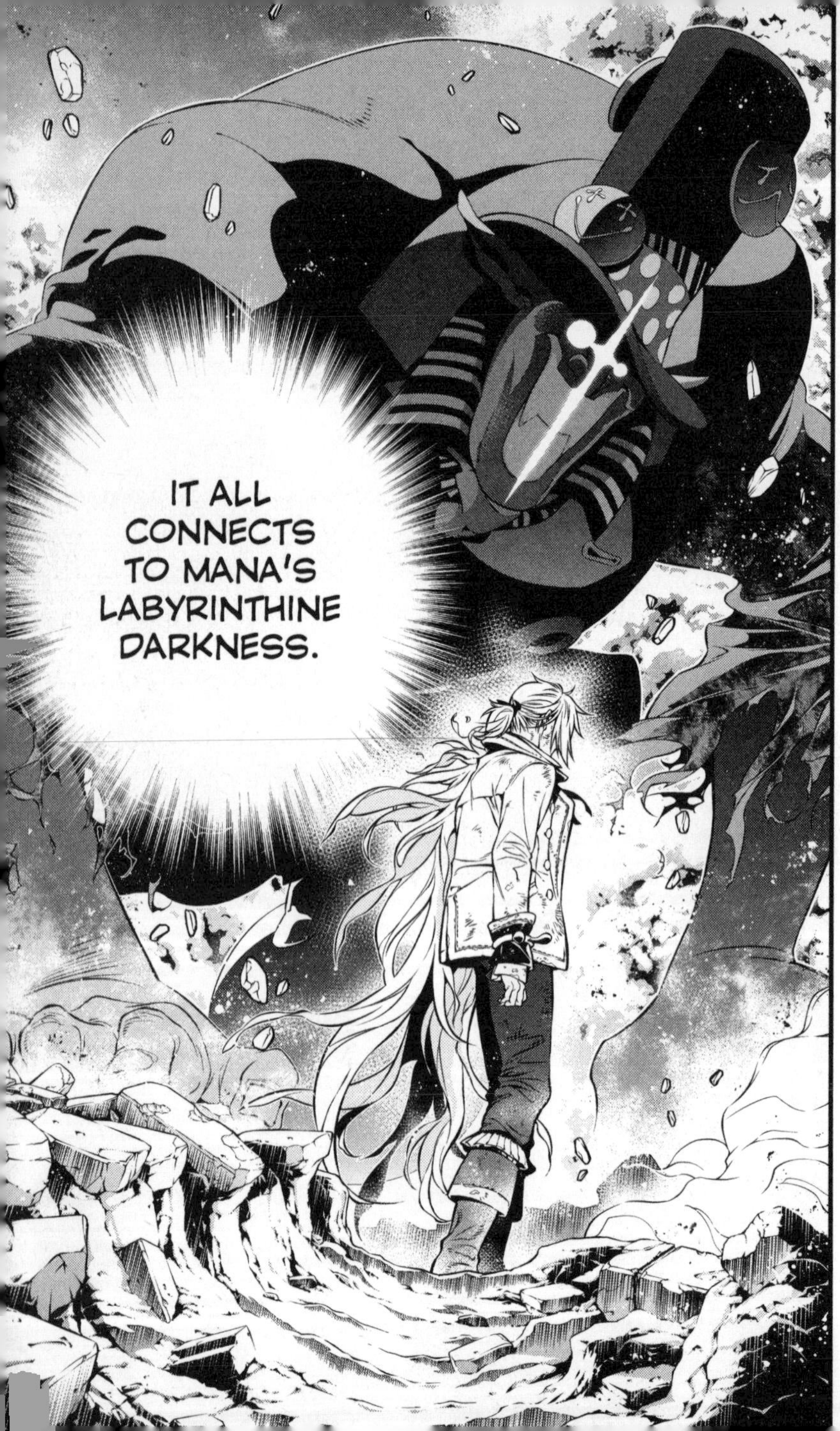
IT ALL CONNECTS TO MANA'S LABYRINTHINE DARKNESS.

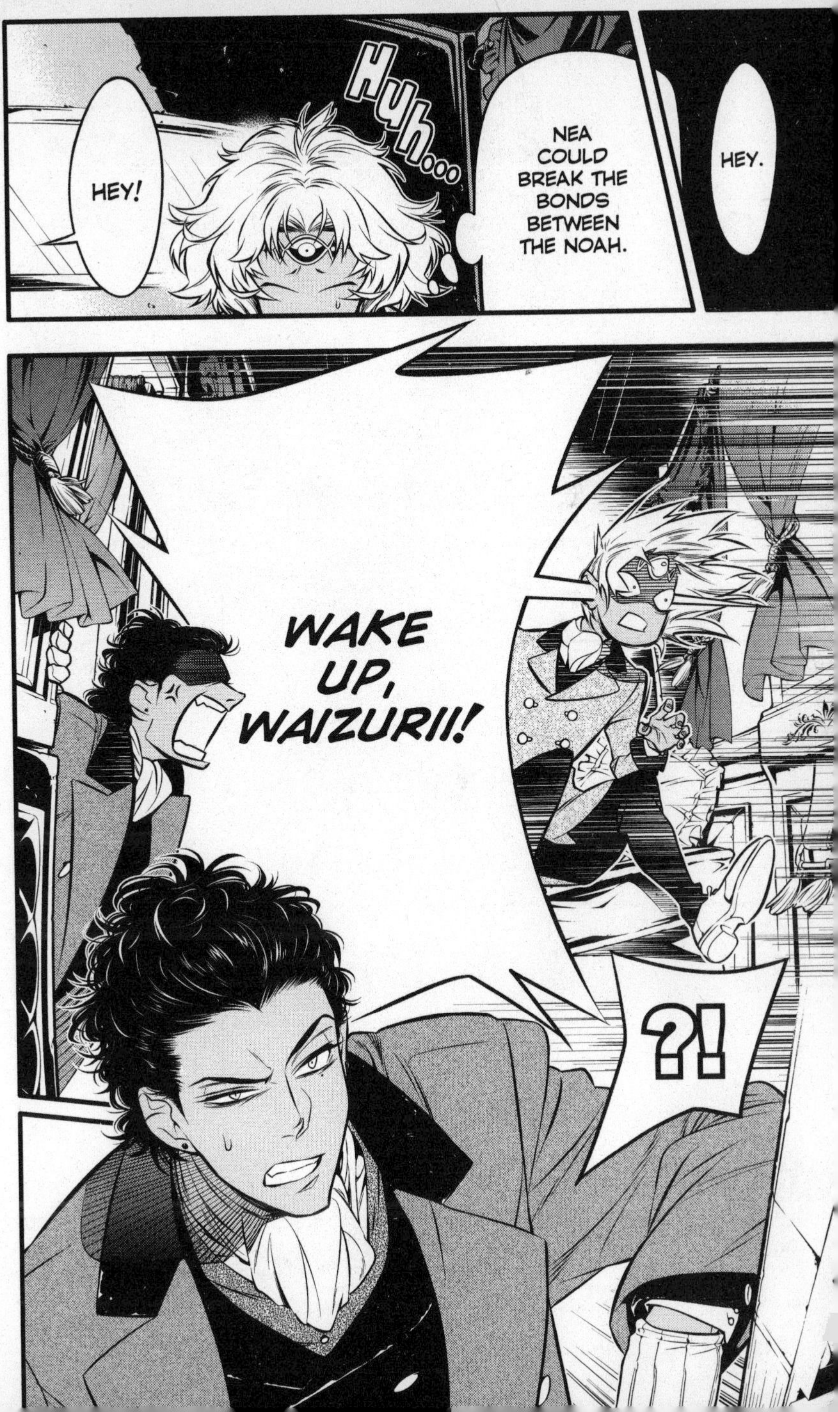
HEY.
NEA COULD BREAK THE BONDS BETWEEN THE NOAH.
Huhooo
HEY!
WAKE UP, WAIZURII!
?!

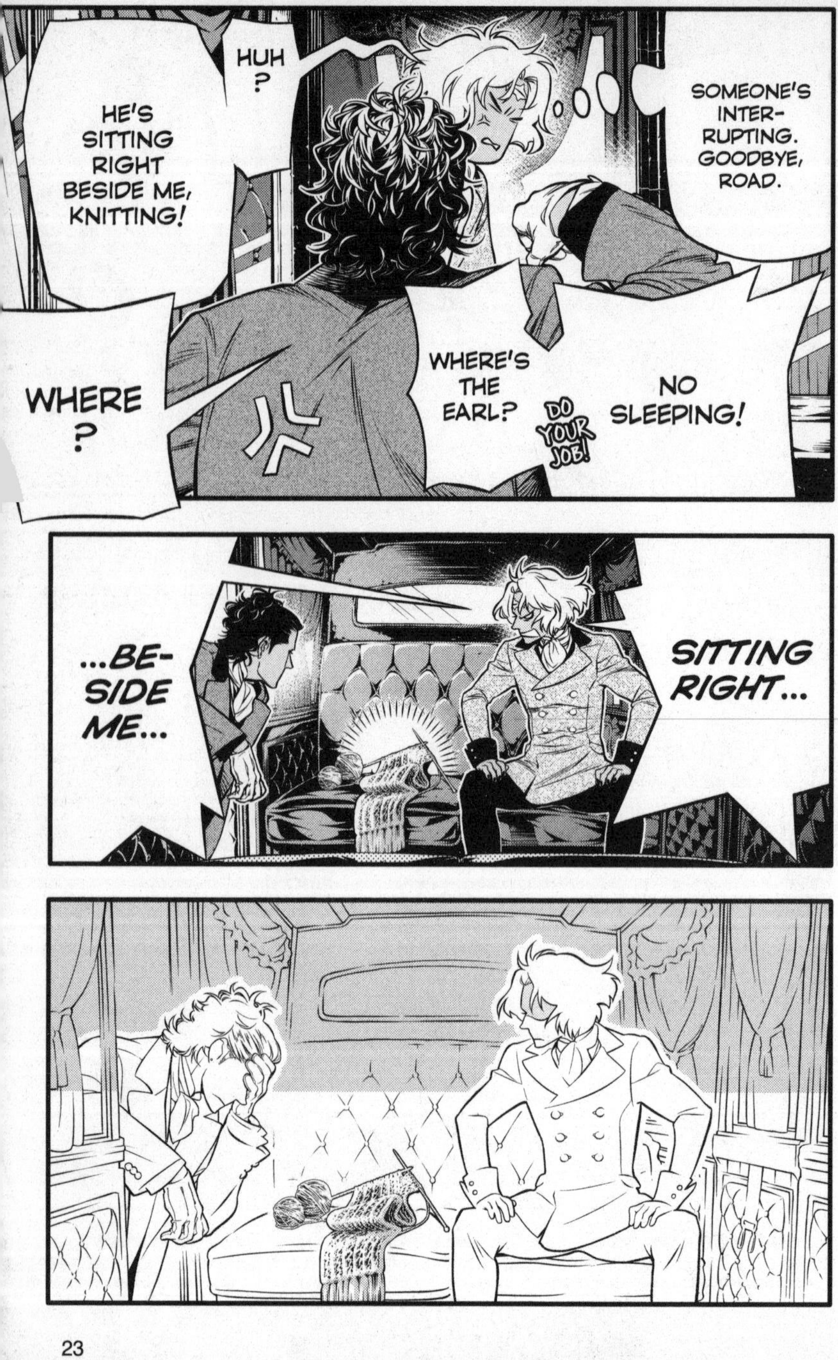
SOMEONE'S INTER-RUPTING. GOODBYE, ROAD.
HUH?
HE'S SITTING RIGHT BESIDE ME, KNITTING!
NO SLEEPING!
DO YOUR JOB!
WHERE'S THE EARL?
WHERE?
SITTING RIGHT...
...BE-SIDE ME...

IT'S MY FAULT FOR TRUSTING YOU!

EARRRL

NOOOOO!

IT'S FROM THE TWINS. THEY'VE CAUGHT...

skrik skrik

skrik

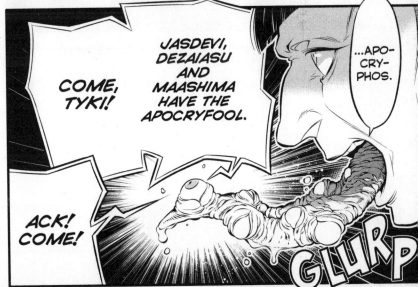

JASDEVI, DEZAIASU AND MAASHIMA HAVE THE APOCRYFOOL.

COME, TYKI!

...APO-CRY-PHOS.

ACK! COME!

GLURP

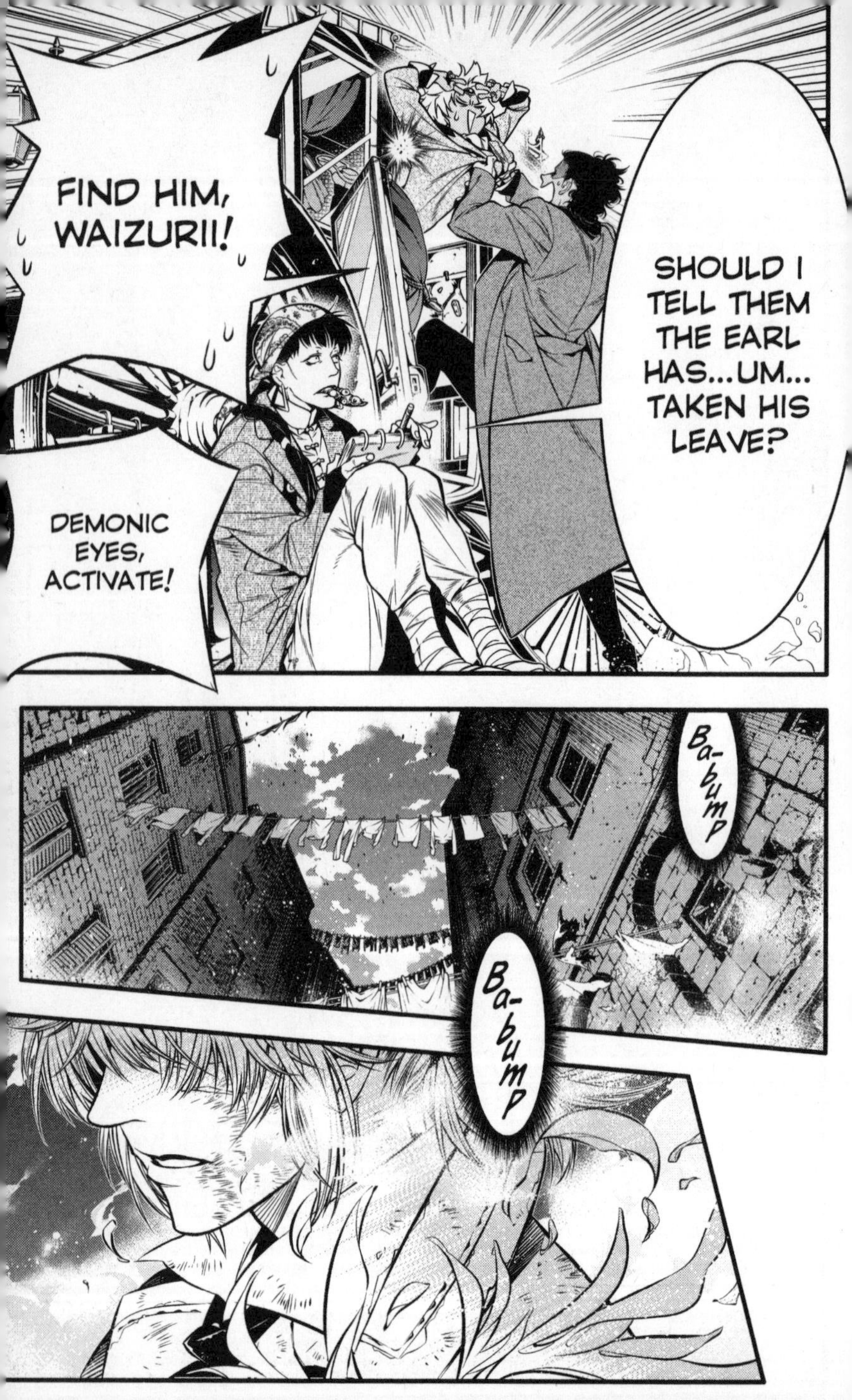
SHOULD I TELL THEM THE EARL HAS...UM... TAKEN HIS LEAVE?
FIND HIM, WAIZURII!
DEMONIC EYES, ACTIVATE!
Ba-bump
Ba-bump

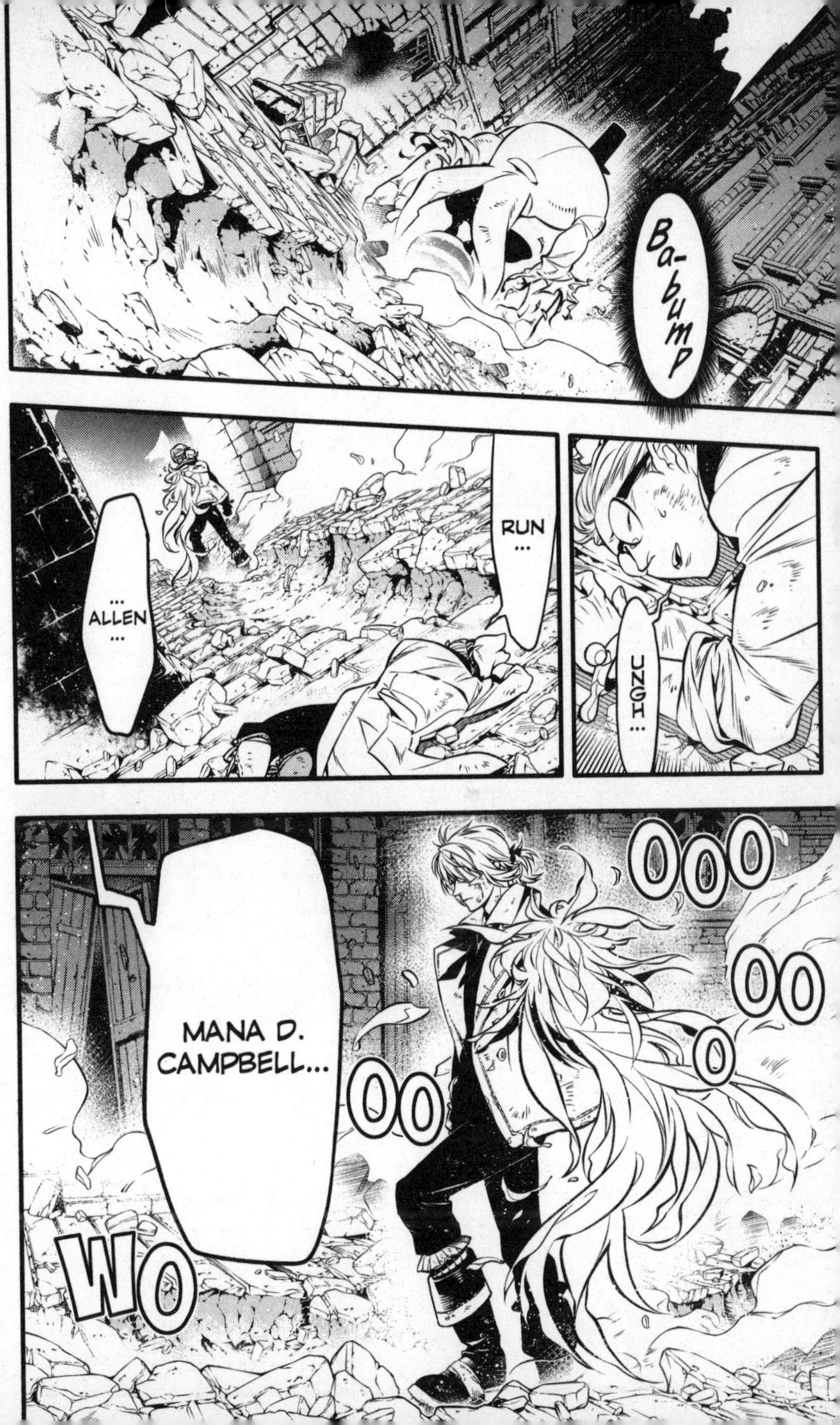
Ba-bump
UNGH...
RUN...
...ALLEN...
MANA D. CAMPBELL...
WOOOOOOOOO

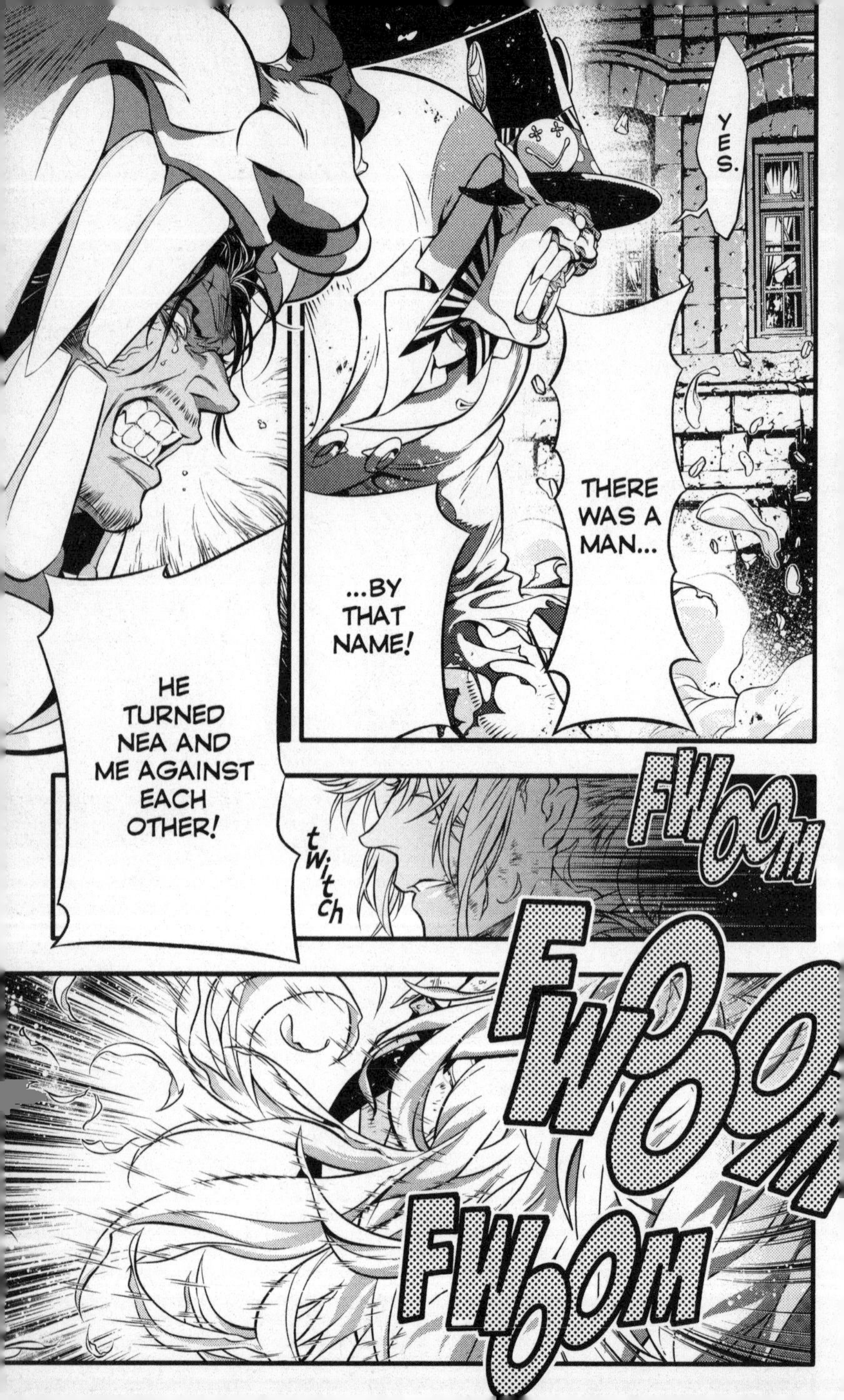
YES.
THERE WAS A MAN...
...BY THAT NAME!
HE TURNED NEA AND ME AGAINST EACH OTHER!
twitch
FWOOM
FWOOM
FWOOM

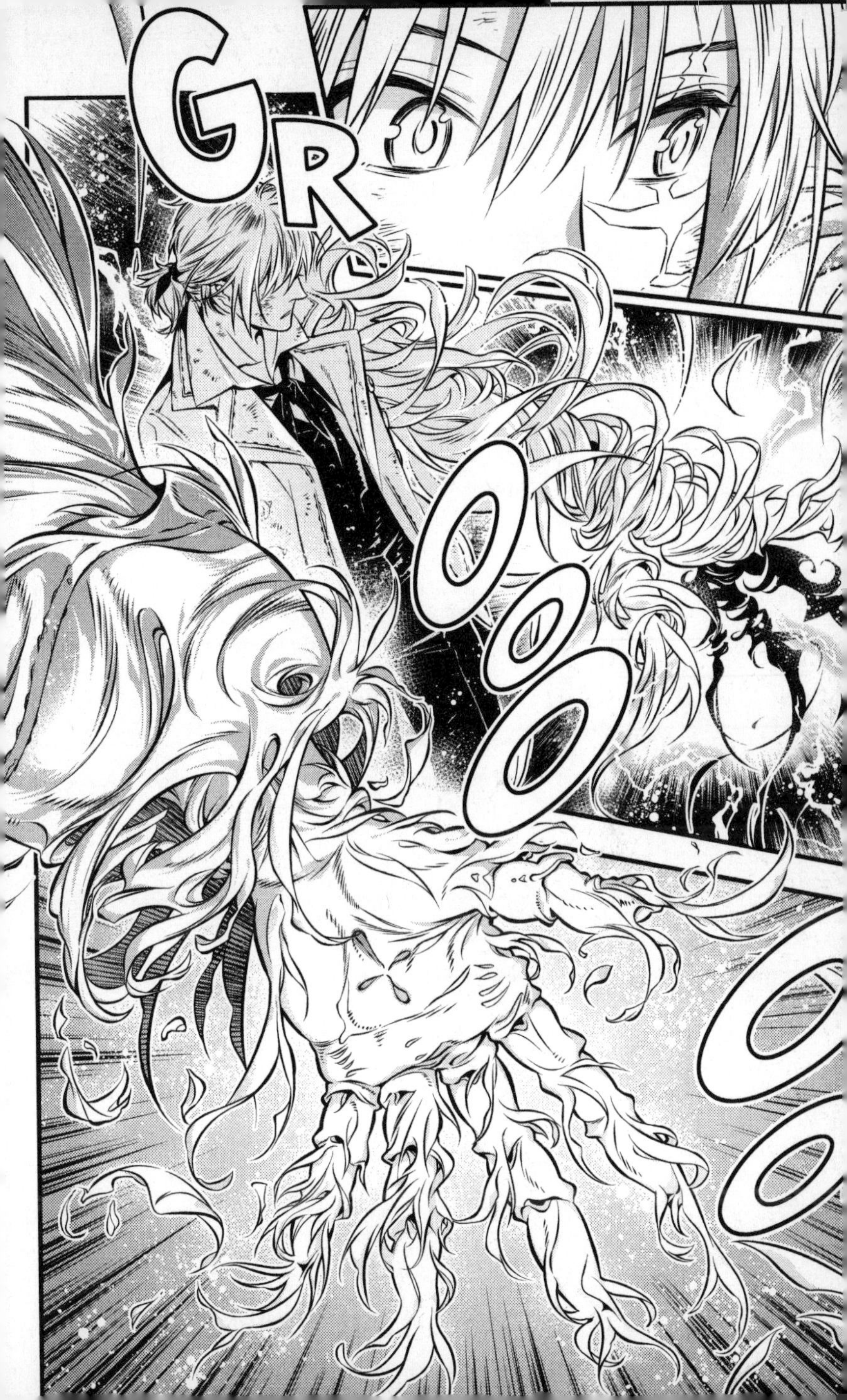
GRROOOOO

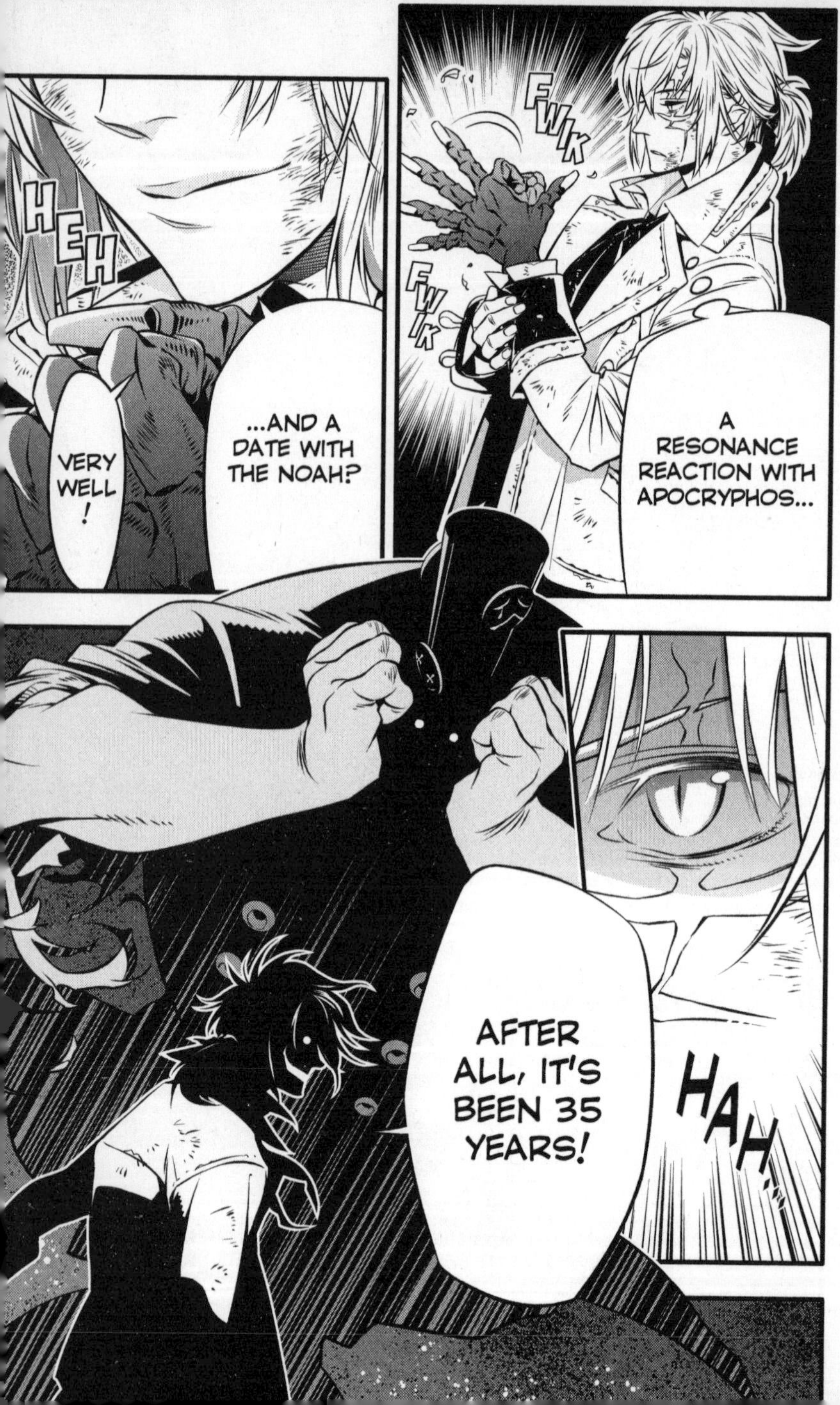
FWIK
FWIK
A RESONANCE REACTION WITH APOCRYPHOS...
HEH
...AND A DATE WITH THE NOAH?
VERY WELL!
AFTER ALL, IT'S BEEN 35 YEARS!
HAH...

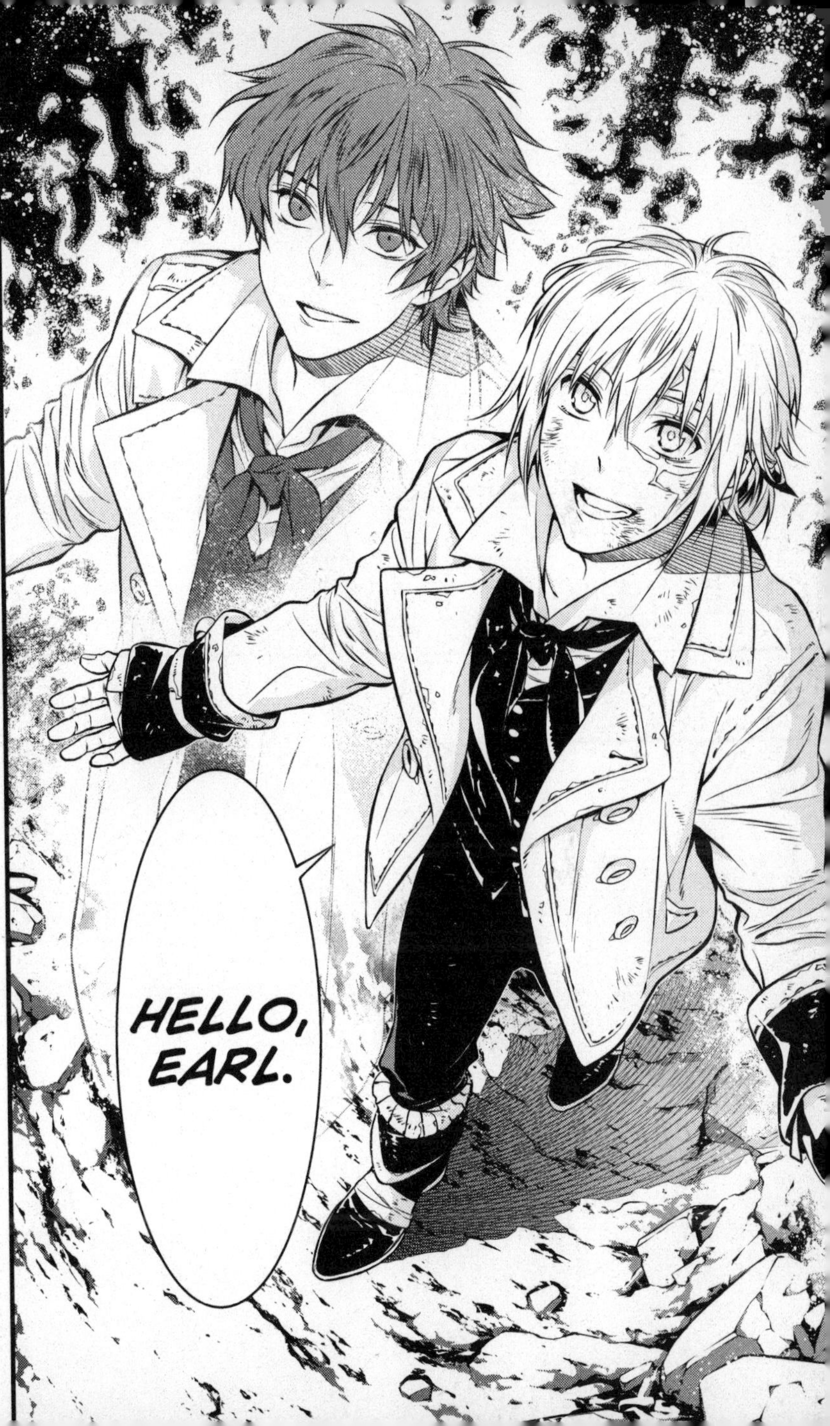
HELLO, EARL.

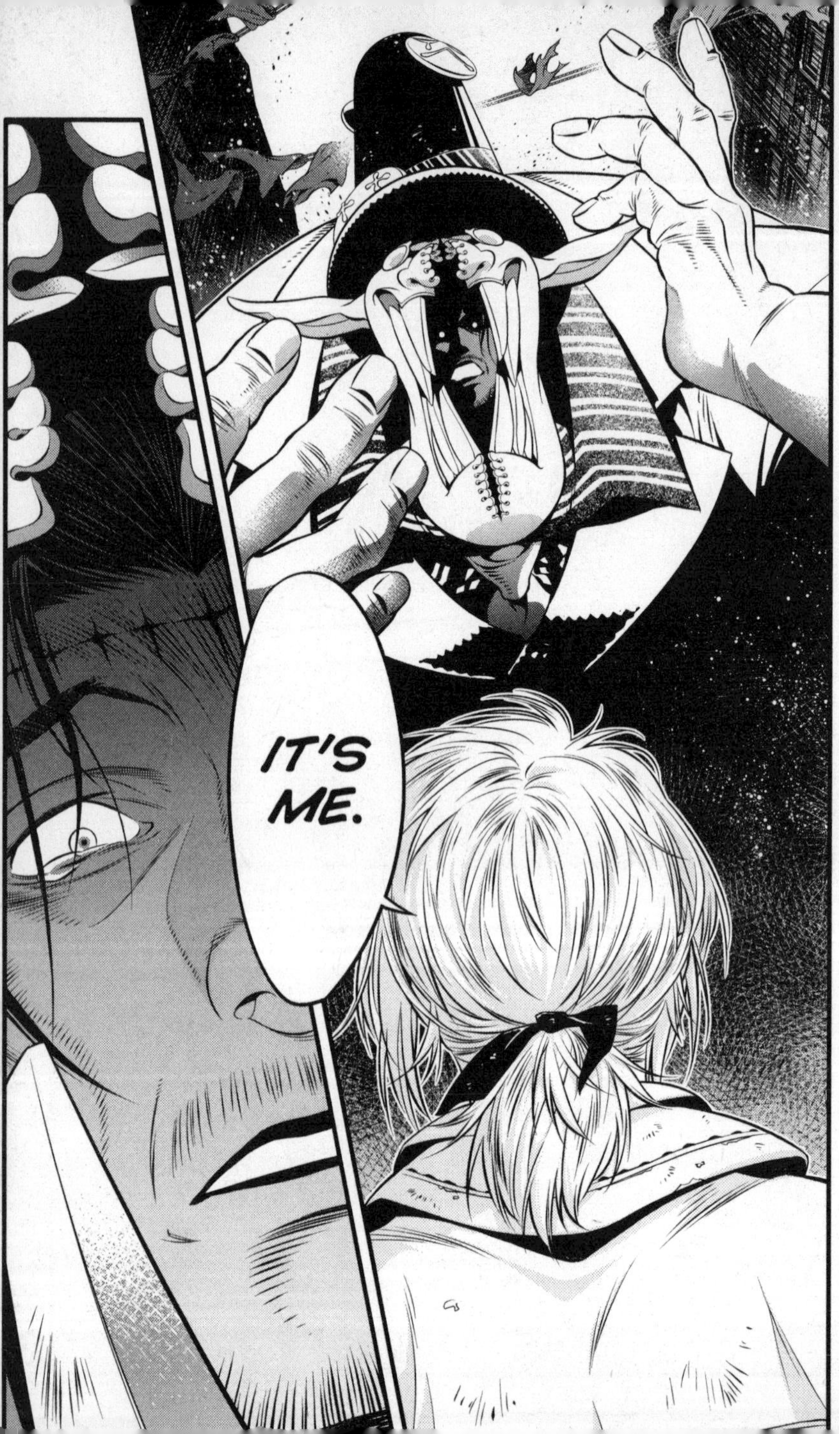
IT'S ME.

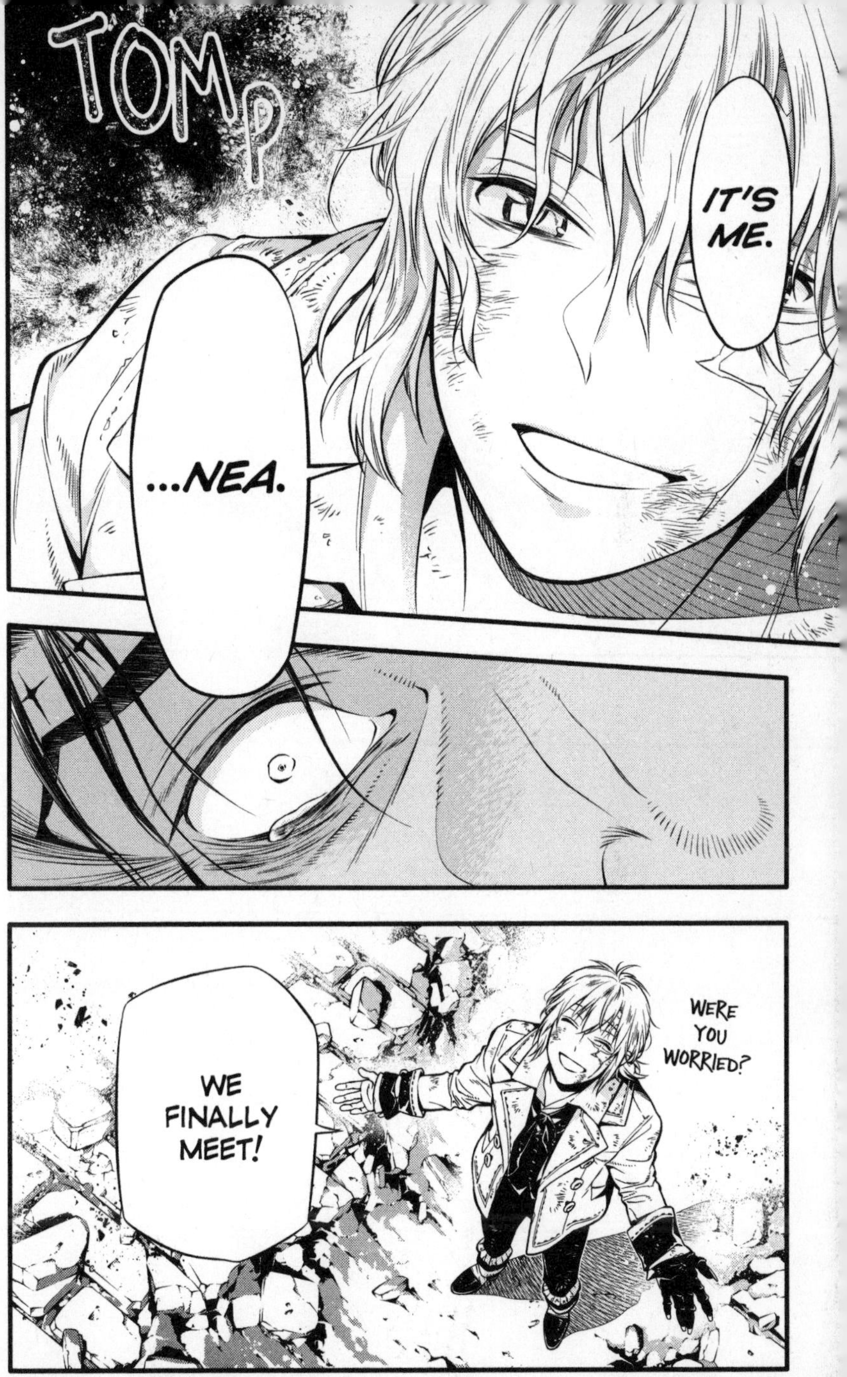
IT'S ME.
TOMP
...NEA.
WERE YOU WORRIED?
WE FINALLY MEET!

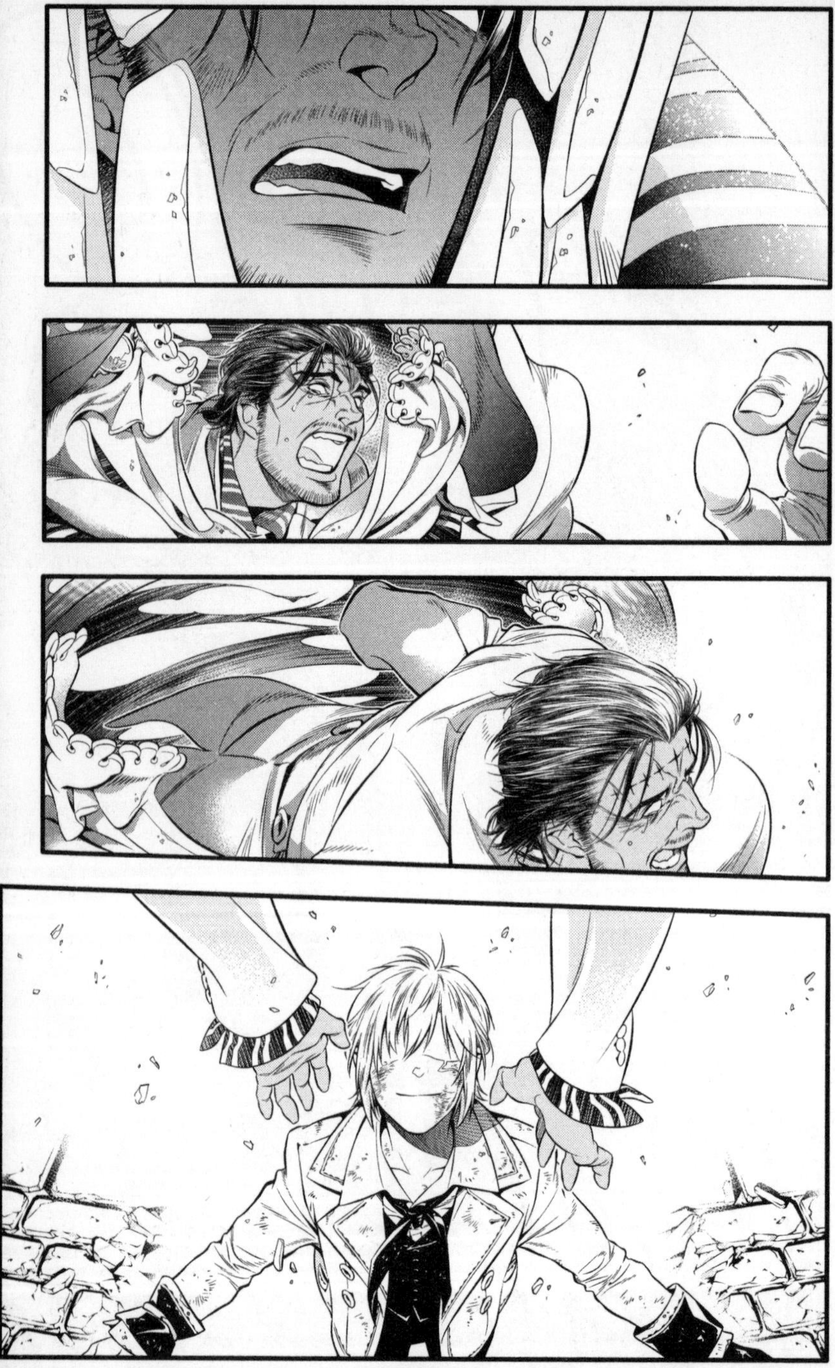

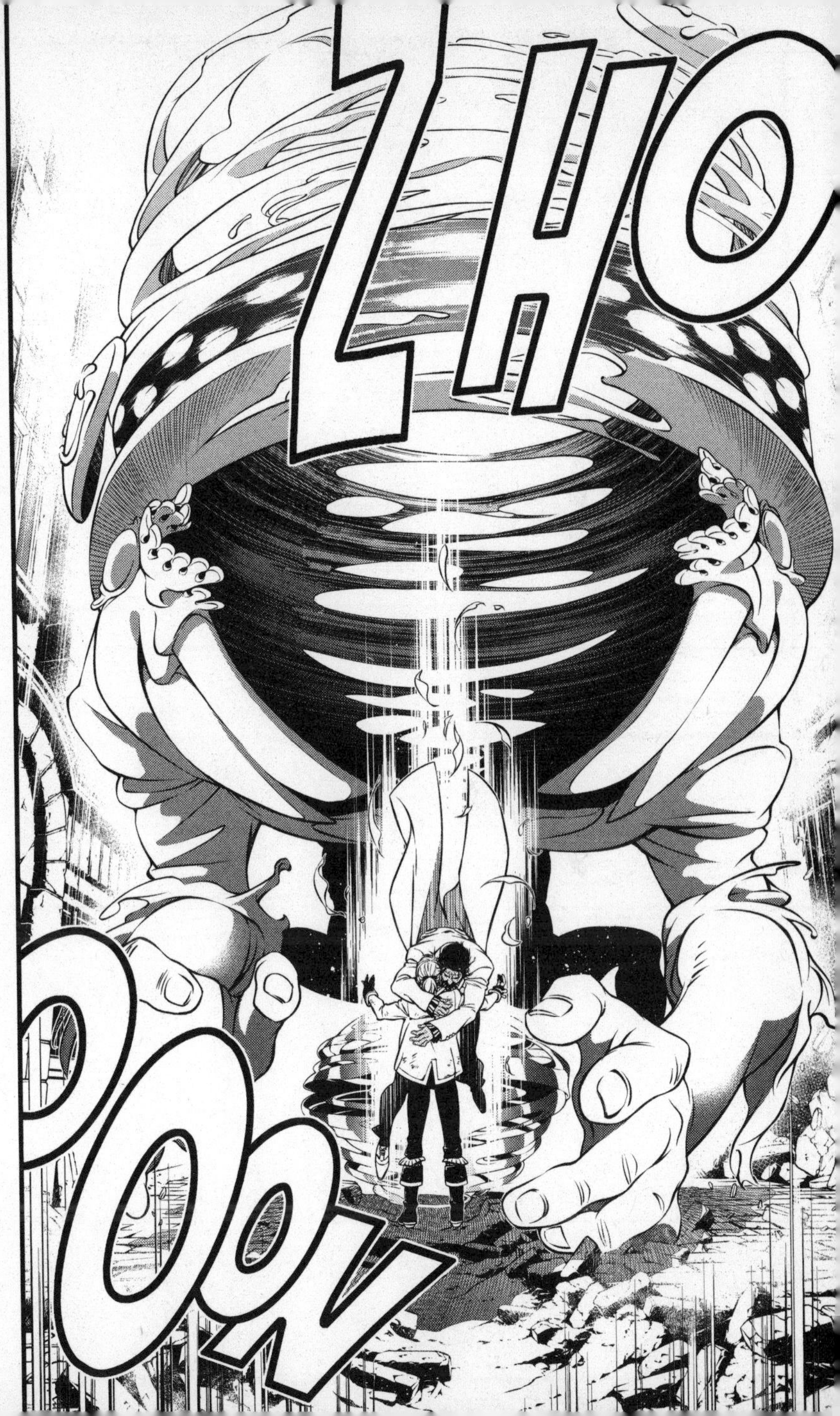
ZHOOOM

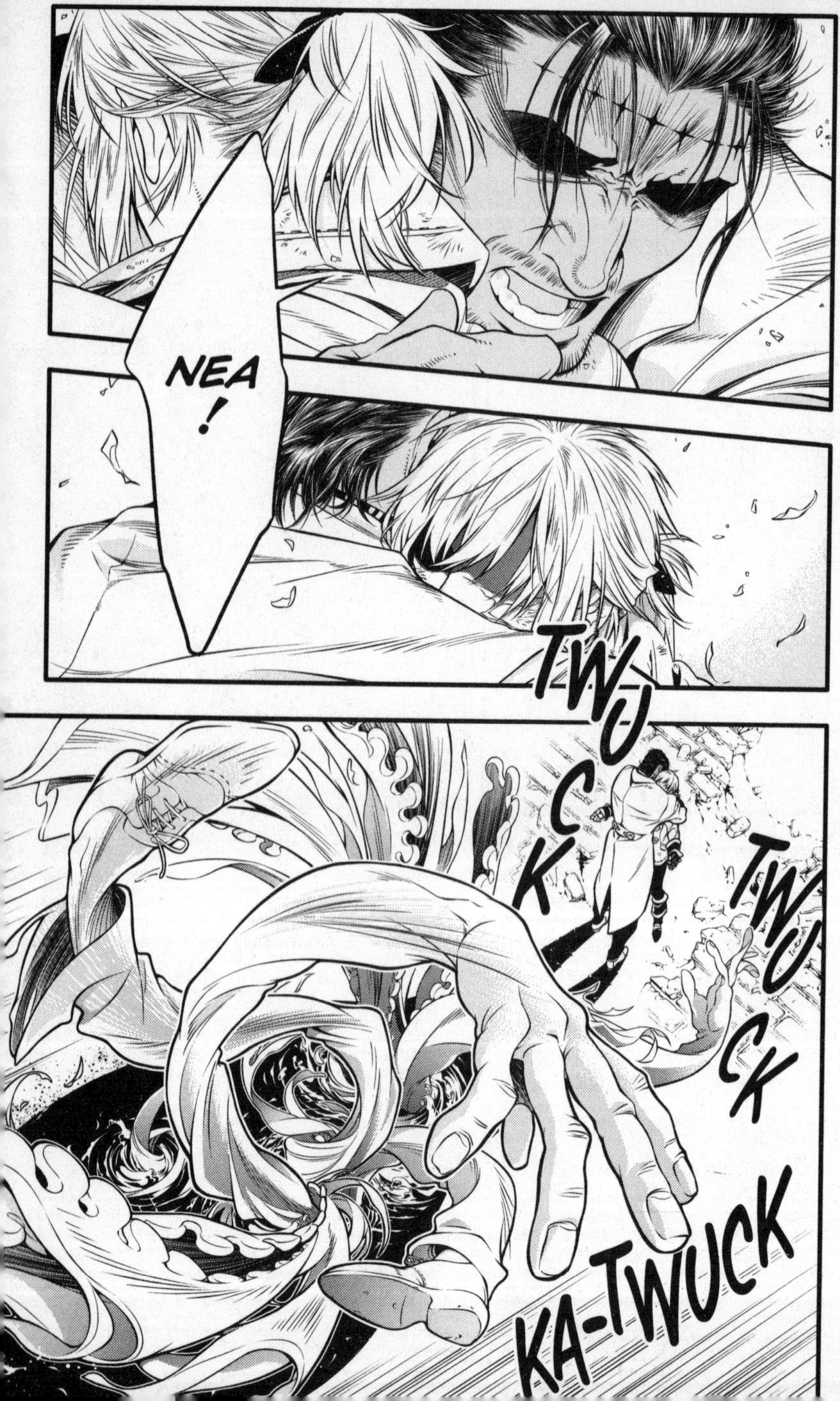
NEA!
TWUCK
TWUCK
KA-TWUCK

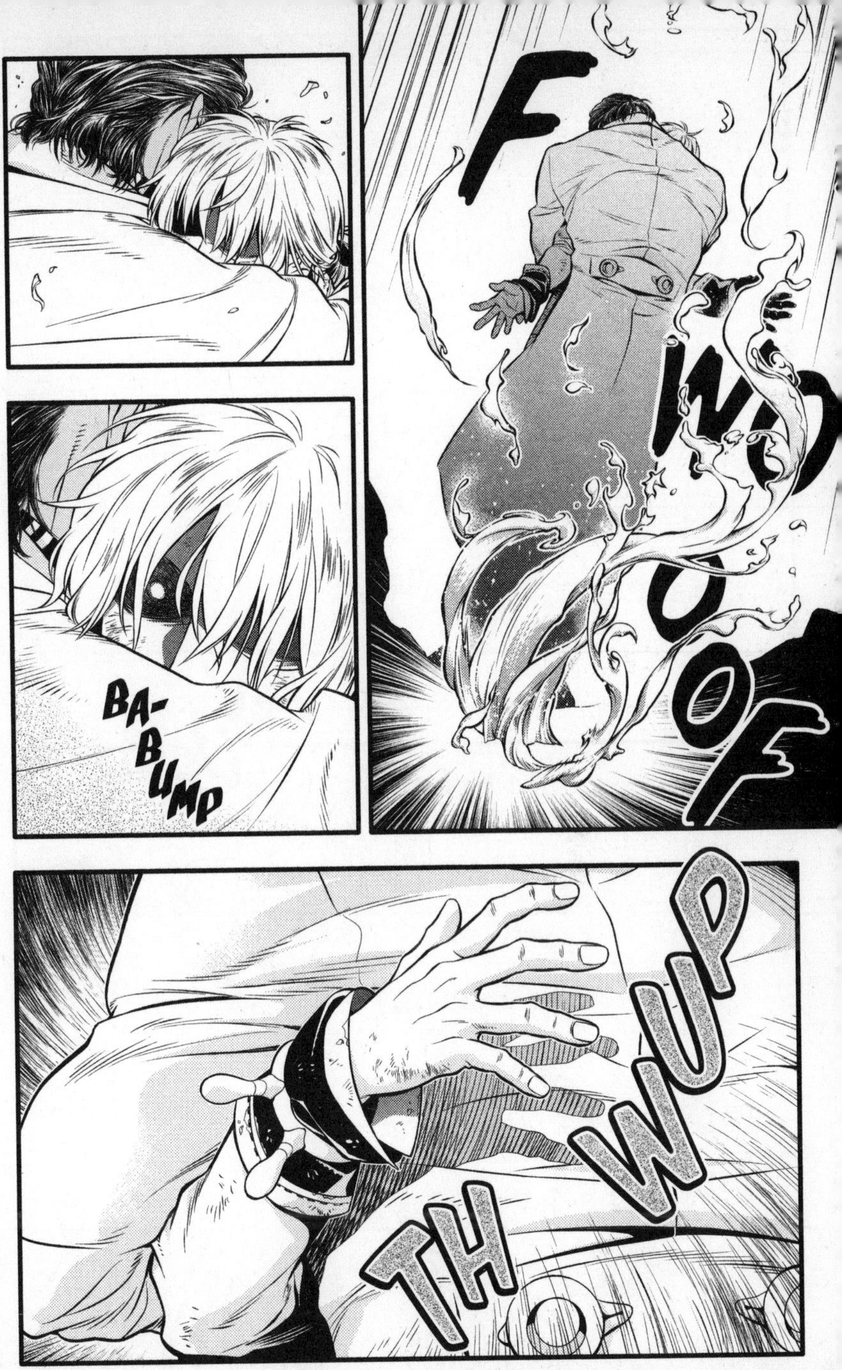
FWOOOF
BA-BUMP
THWUP

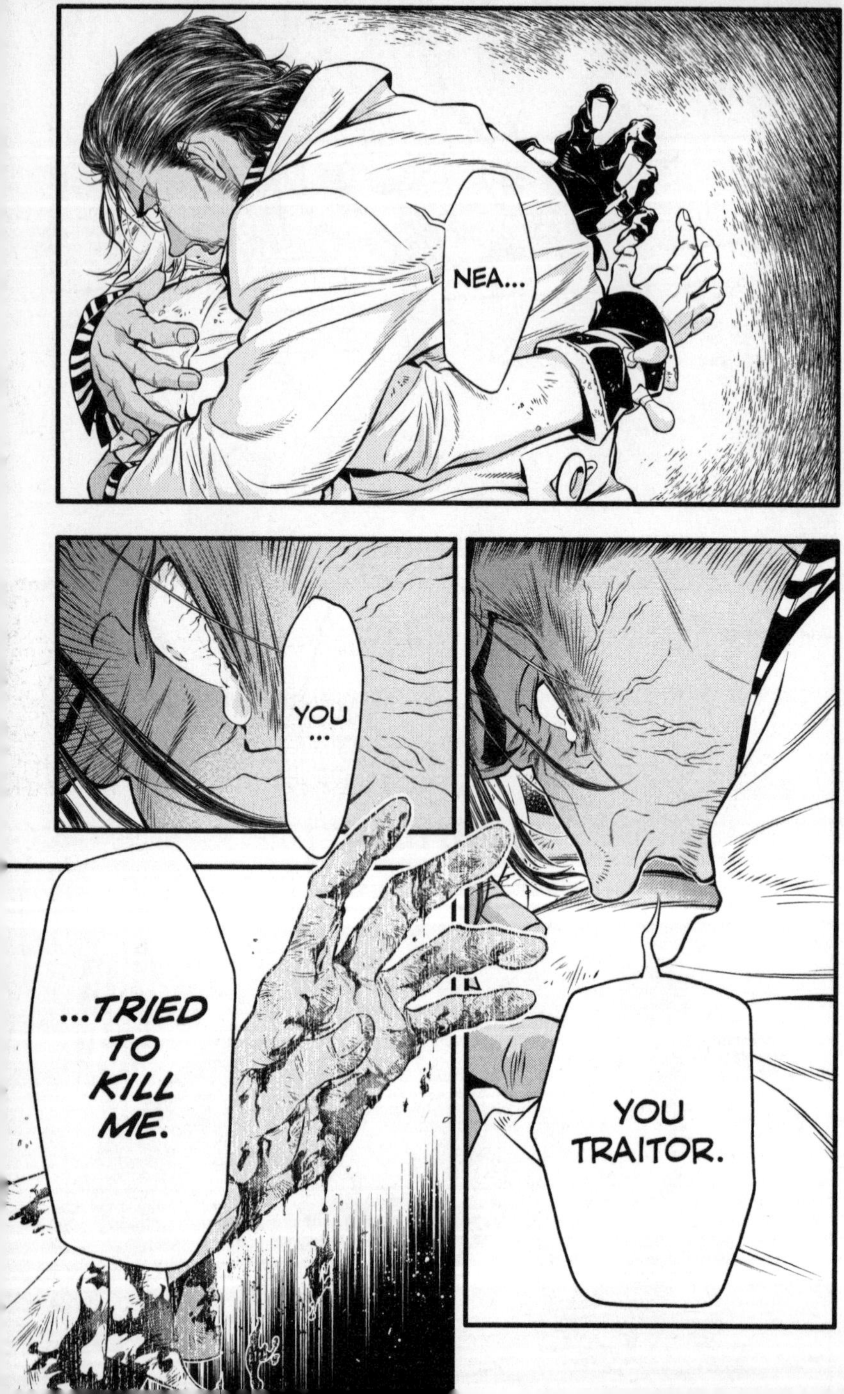
NEA...
YOU ...
...TRIED TO KILL ME.
YOU TRAITOR.

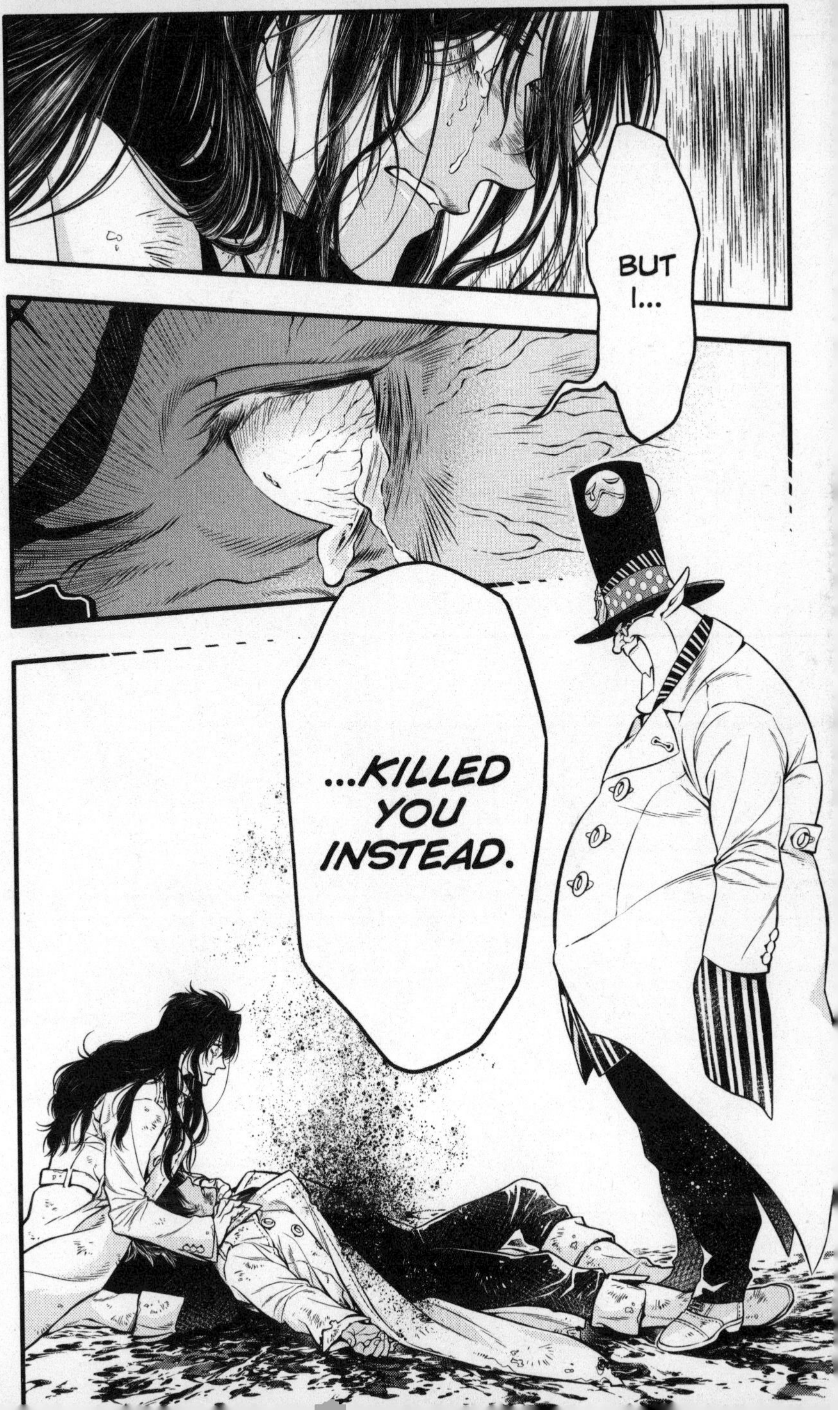
BUT I...
...KILLED YOU INSTEAD.

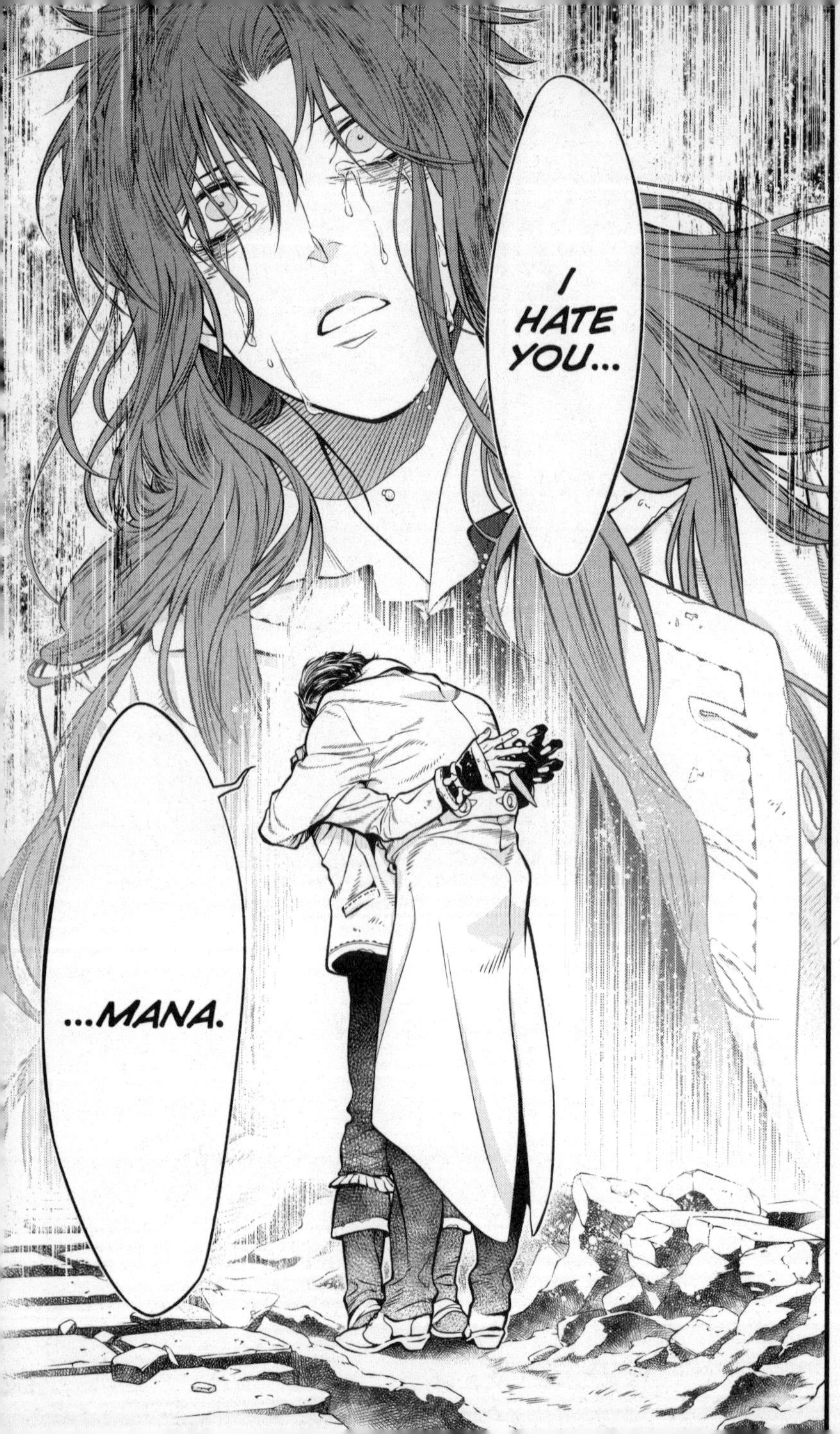
I HATE YOU...
...MANA.

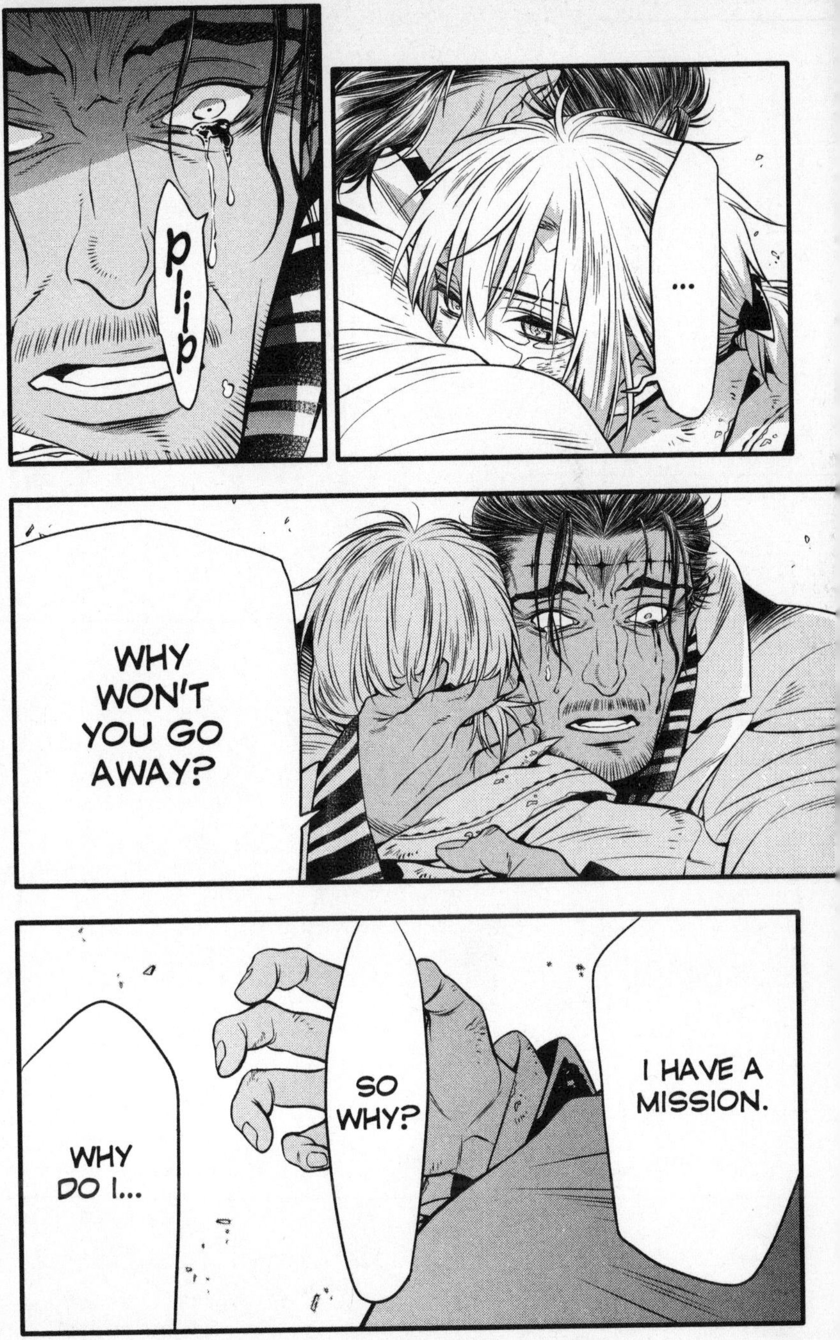
...
plip
WHY WON'T YOU GO AWAY?
I HAVE A MISSION.
SO WHY?
WHY DO I...

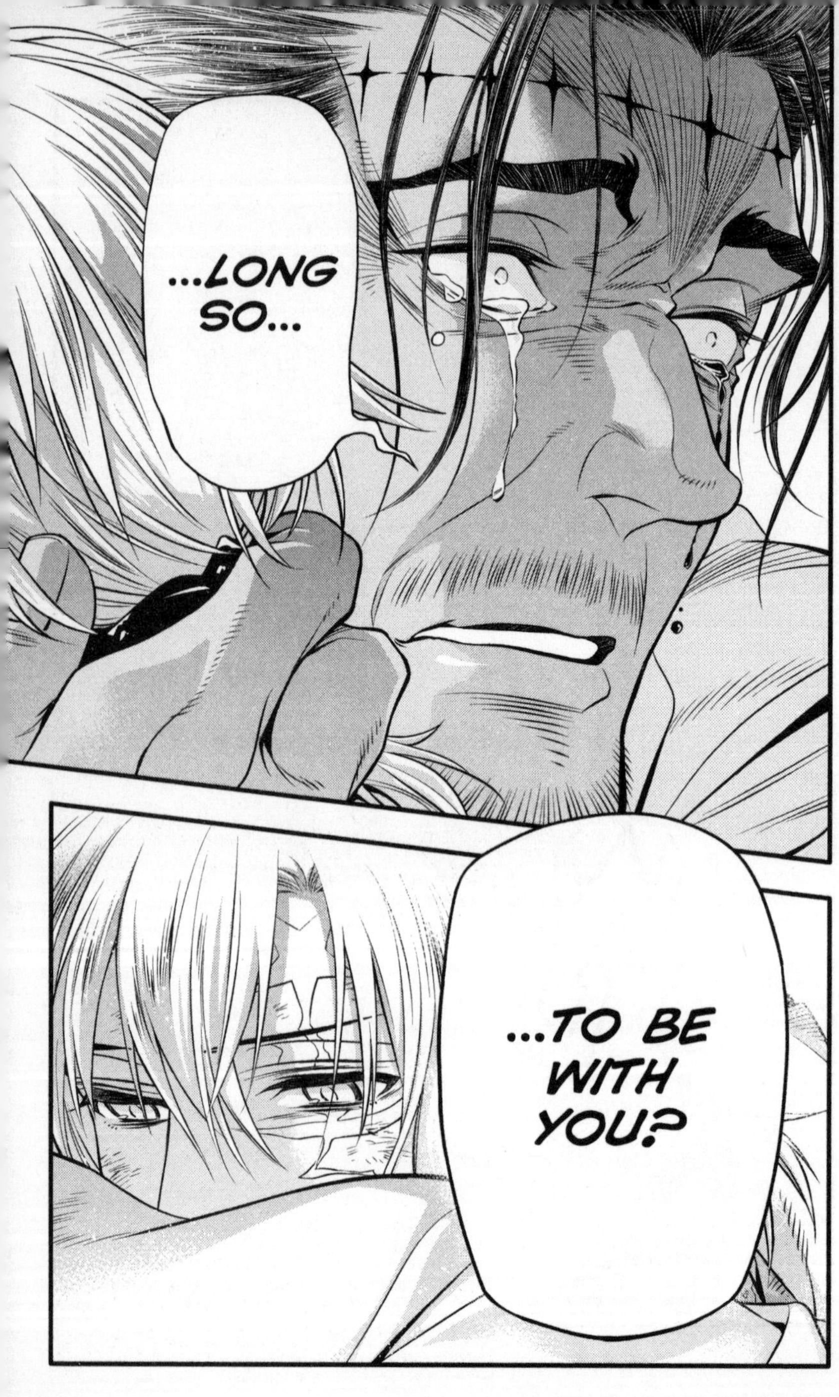
...LONG SO...
...TO BE WITH YOU?

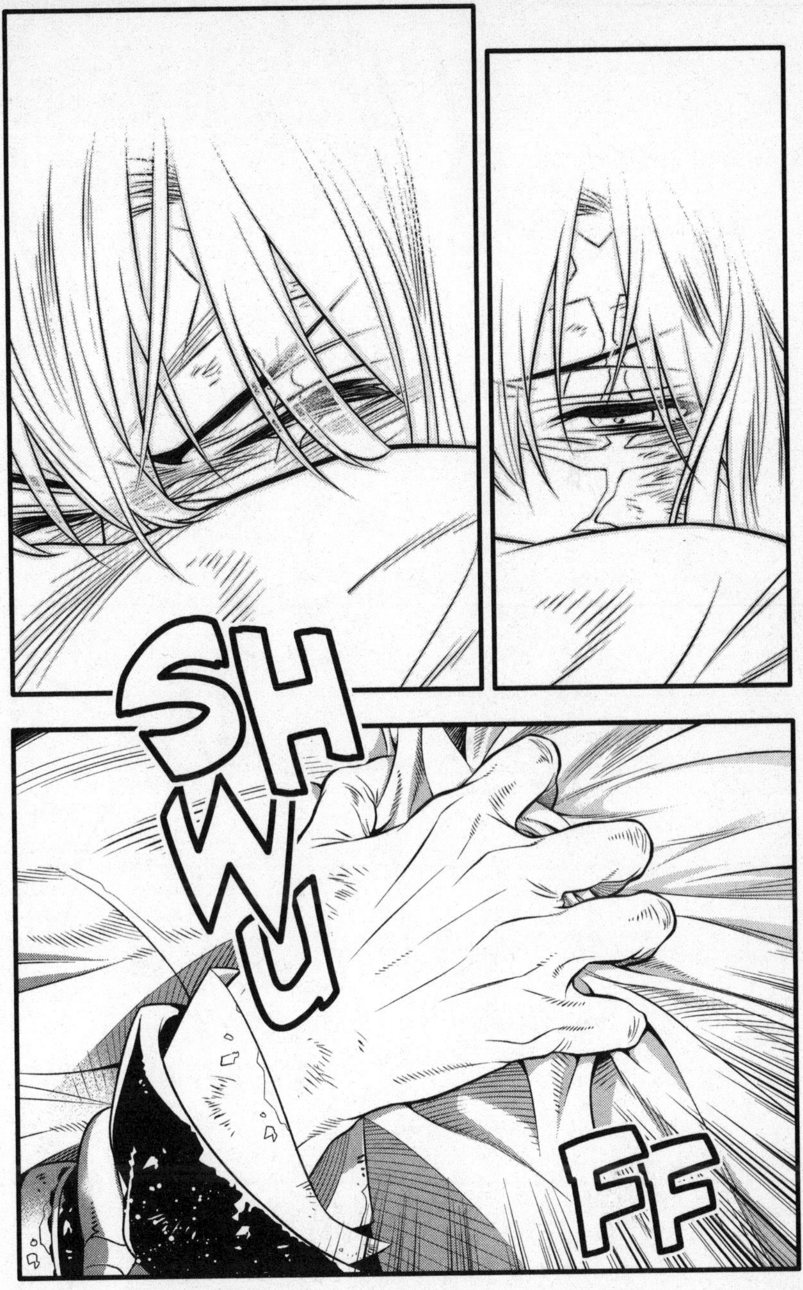
SHWUFF

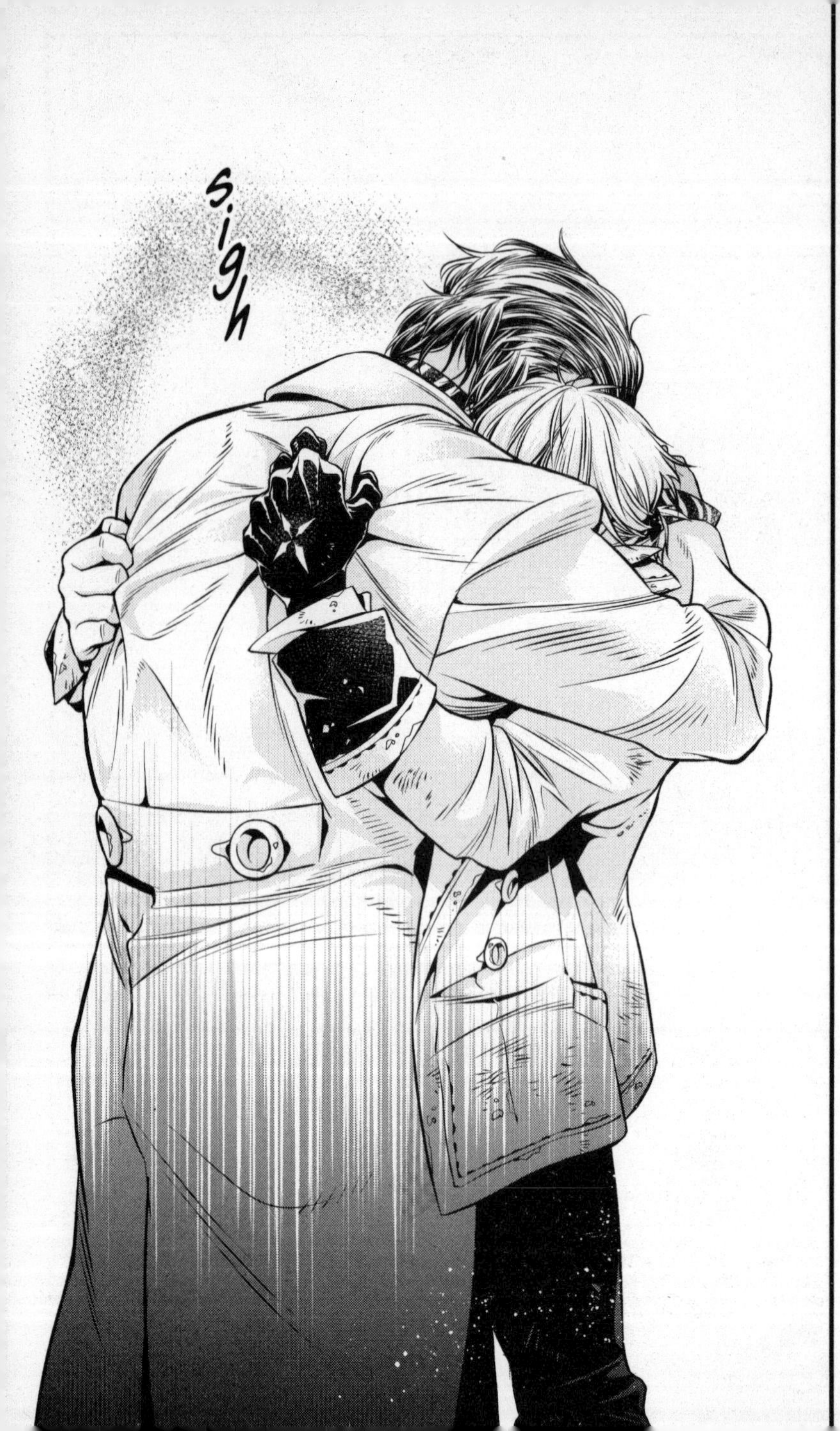
sigh

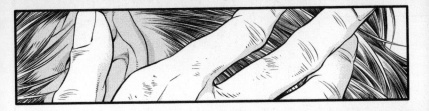

YOUR FACE...

...IS DIF-FERENT. IS IT...

...BECAUSE YOU REMEMBER ME?

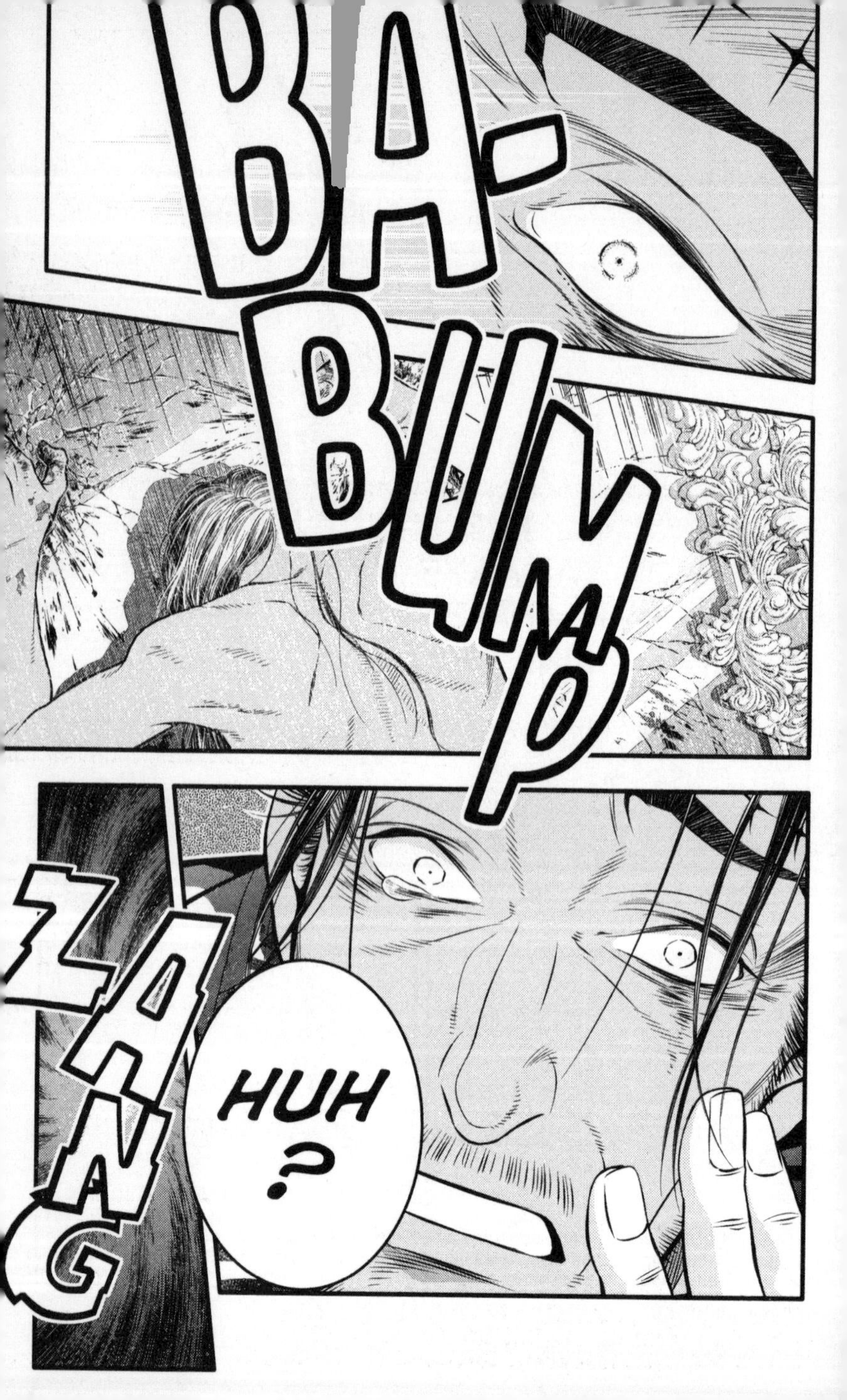
BA-BUMP
ZANG
HUH?

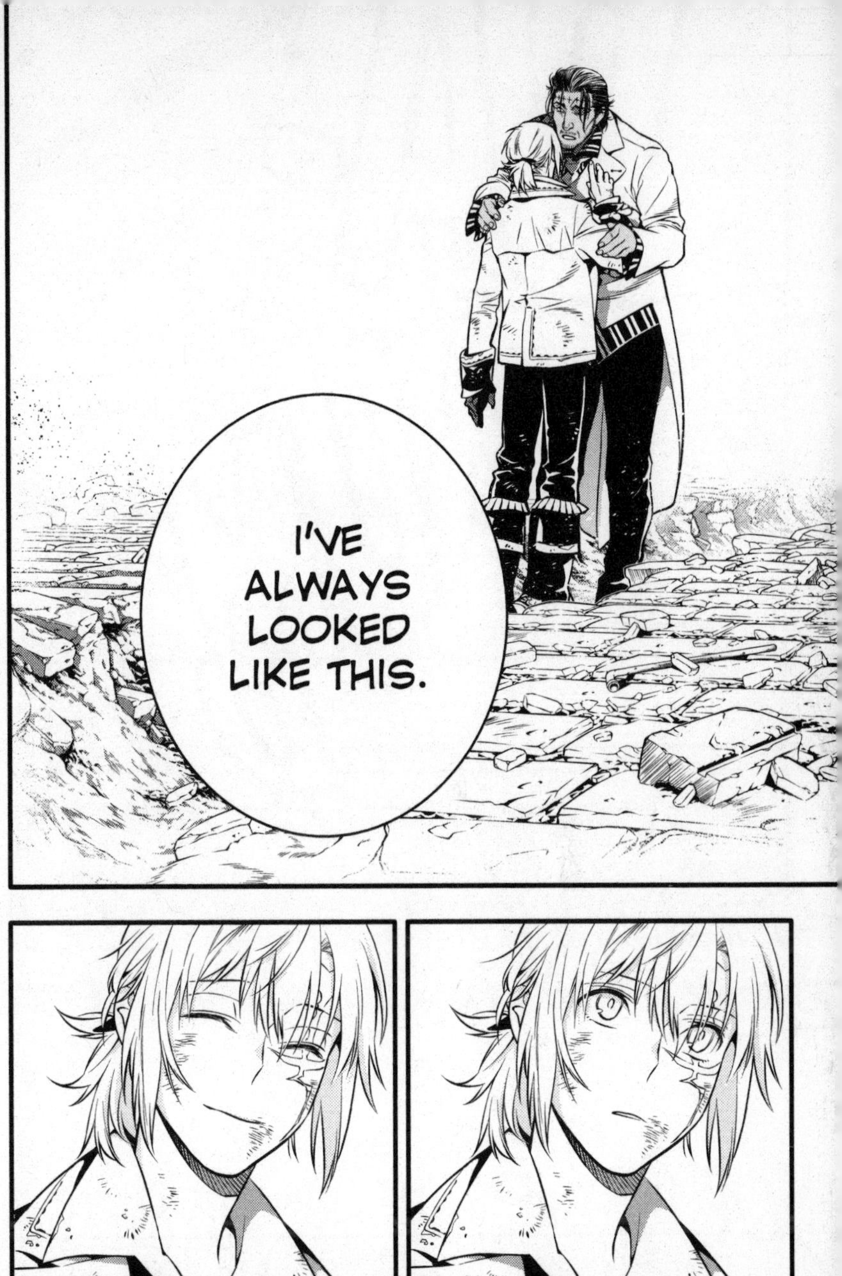
I'VE ALWAYS LOOKED LIKE THIS.

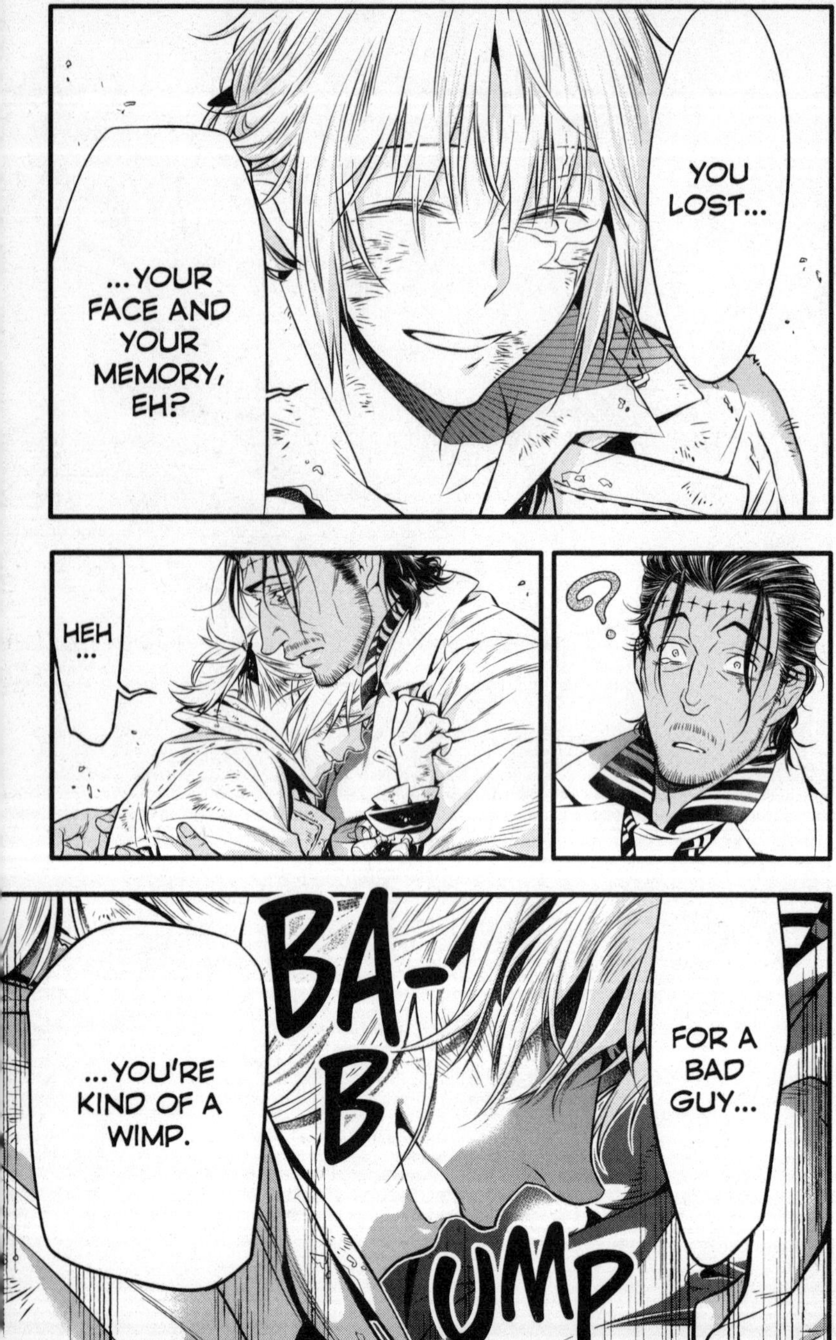
YOU LOST...
...YOUR FACE AND YOUR MEMORY, EH?
HEH ...
FOR A BAD GUY...
BA-BUMP
...YOU'RE KIND OF A WIMP.

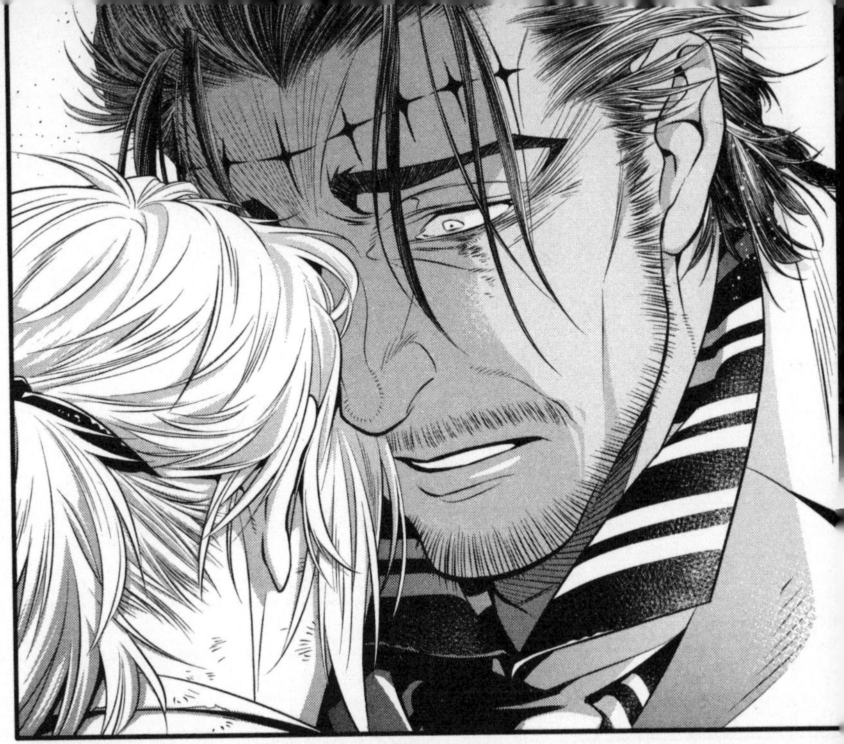
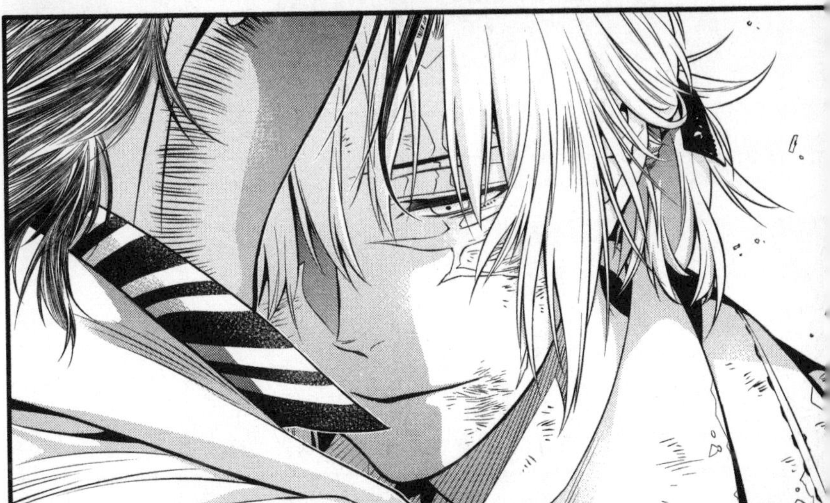

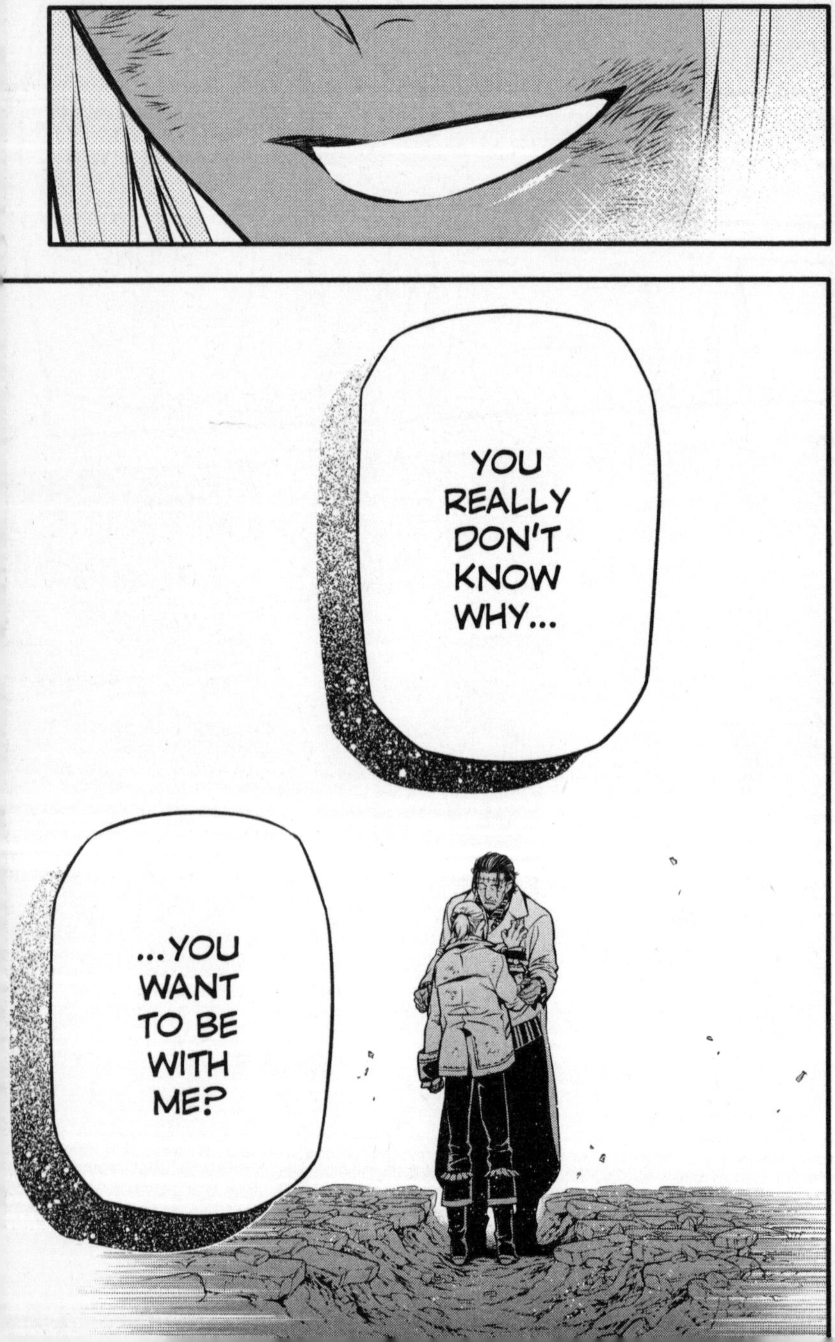
YOU REALLY DON'T KNOW WHY...
...YOU WANT TO BE WITH ME?

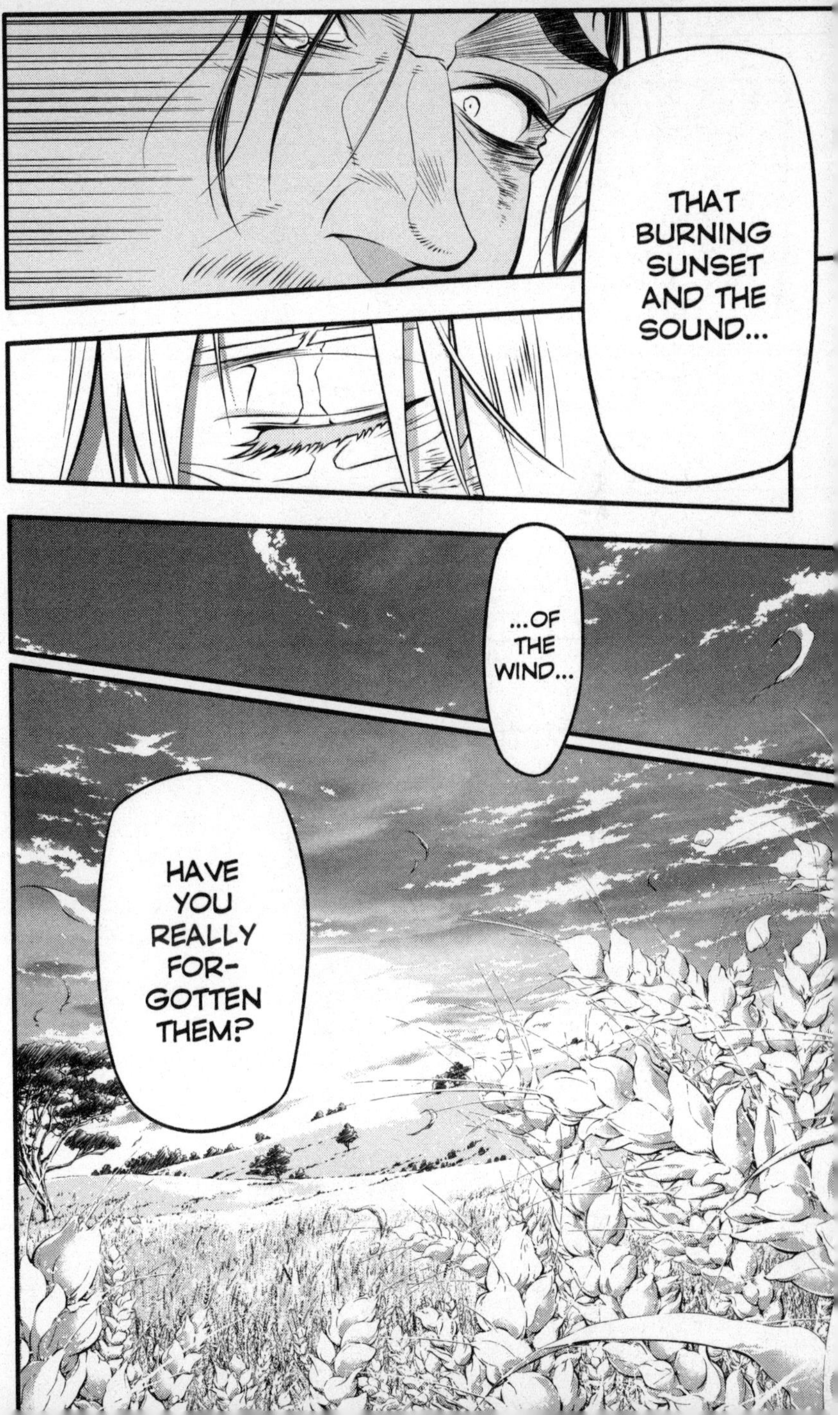
THAT BURNING SUNSET AND THE SOUND...
...OF THE WIND...
HAVE YOU REALLY FOR-GOTTEN THEM?

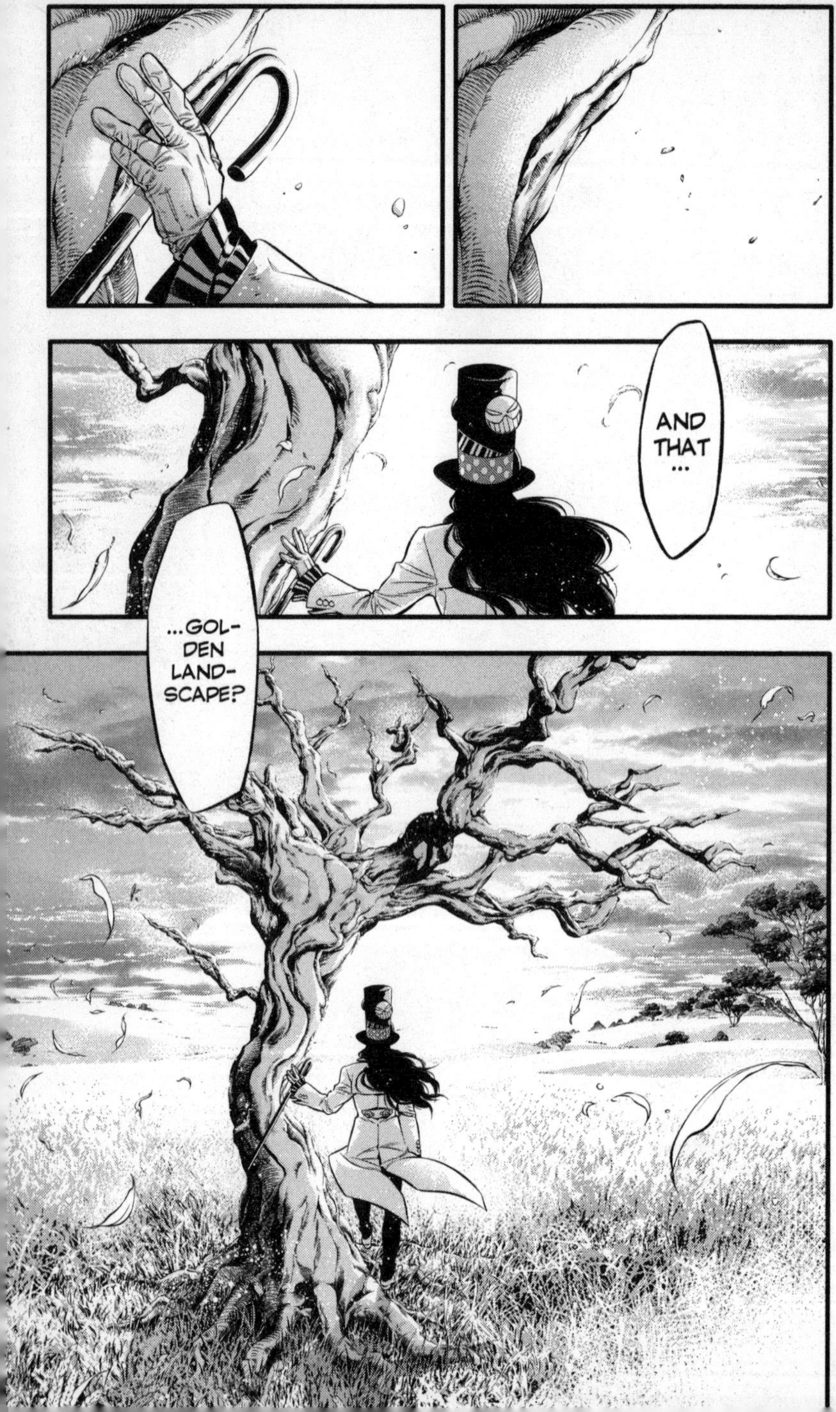
AND THAT...
...GOL-DEN LAND-SCAPE?

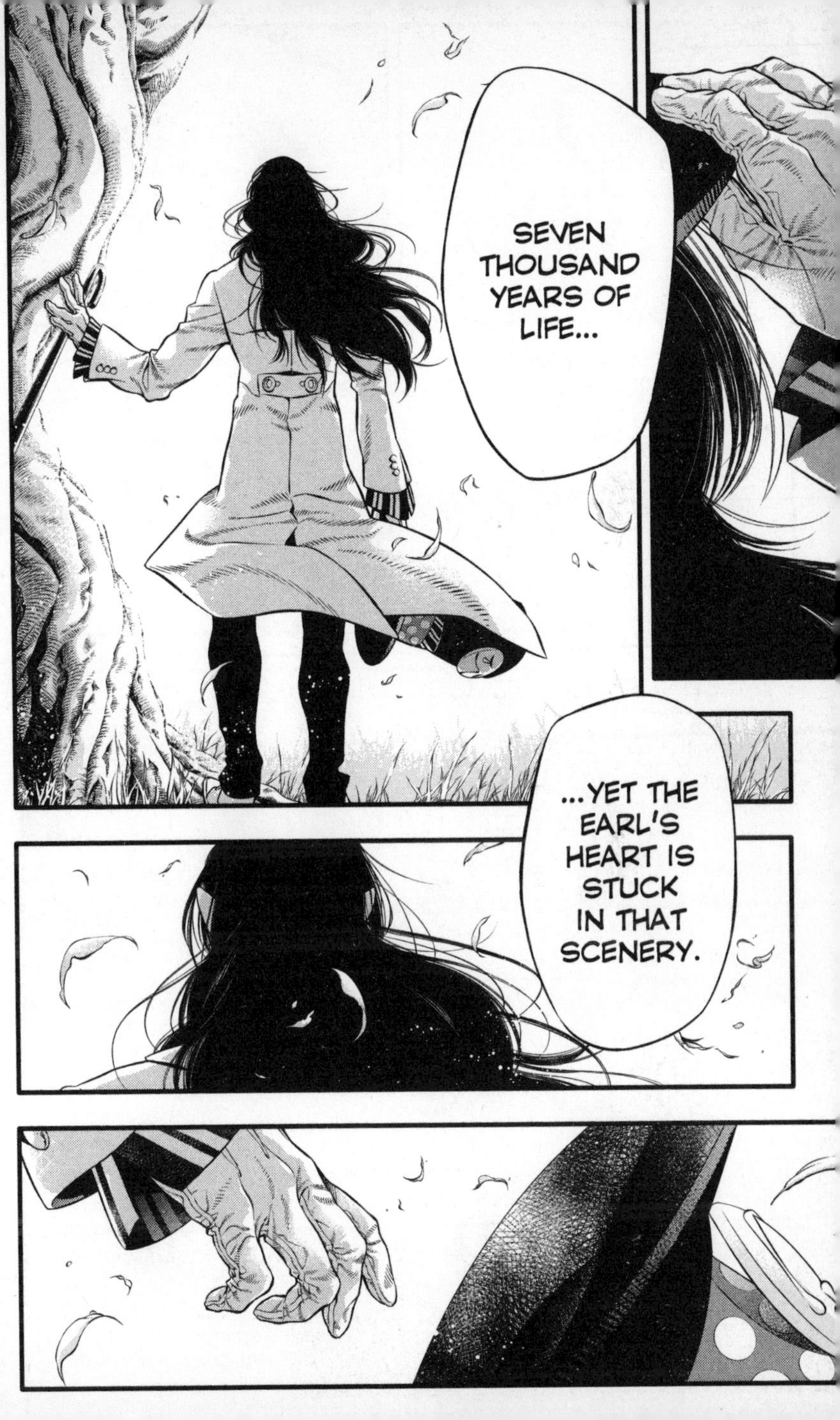
SEVEN THOUSAND YEARS OF LIFE...
...YET THE EARL'S HEART IS STUCK IN THAT SCENERY.

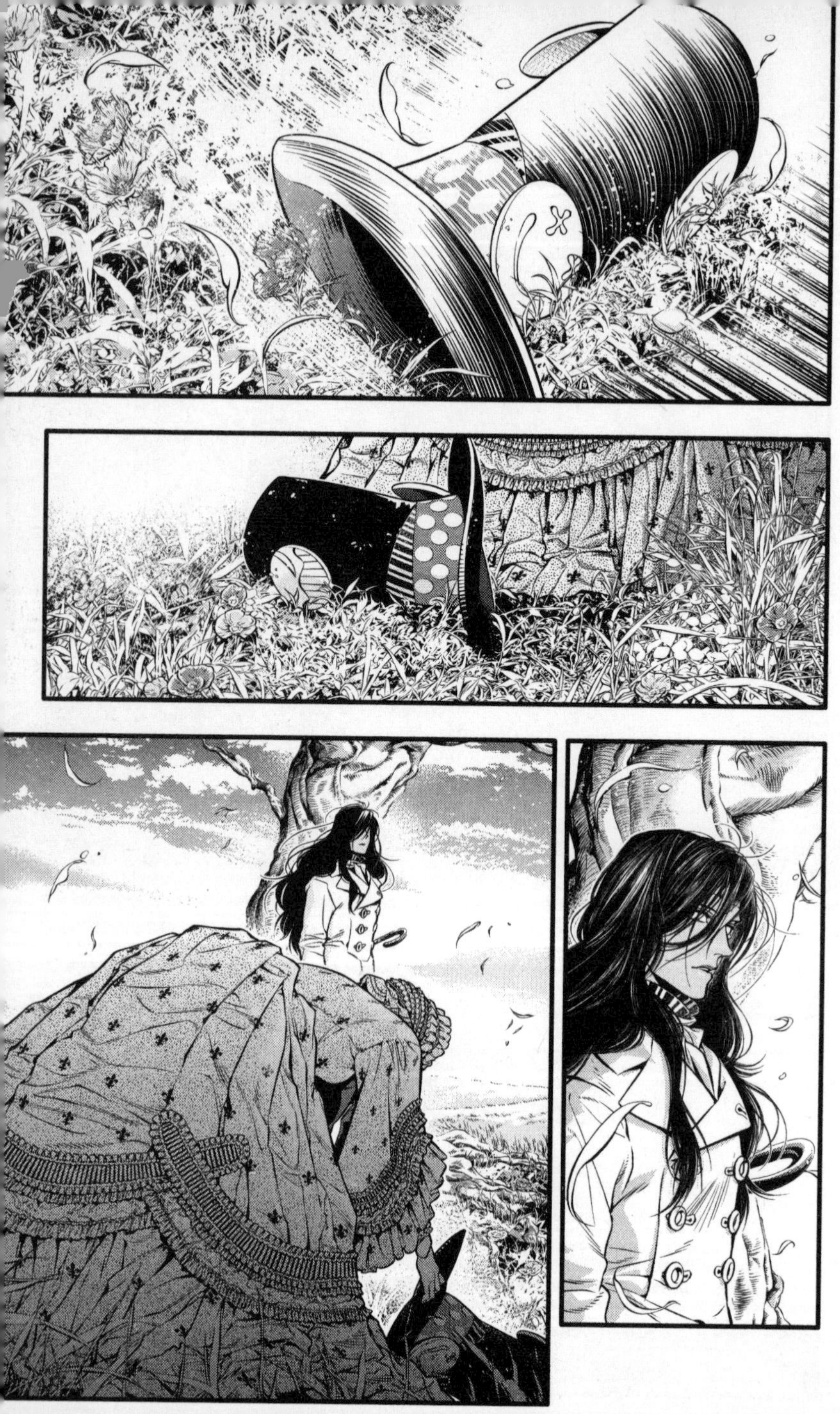

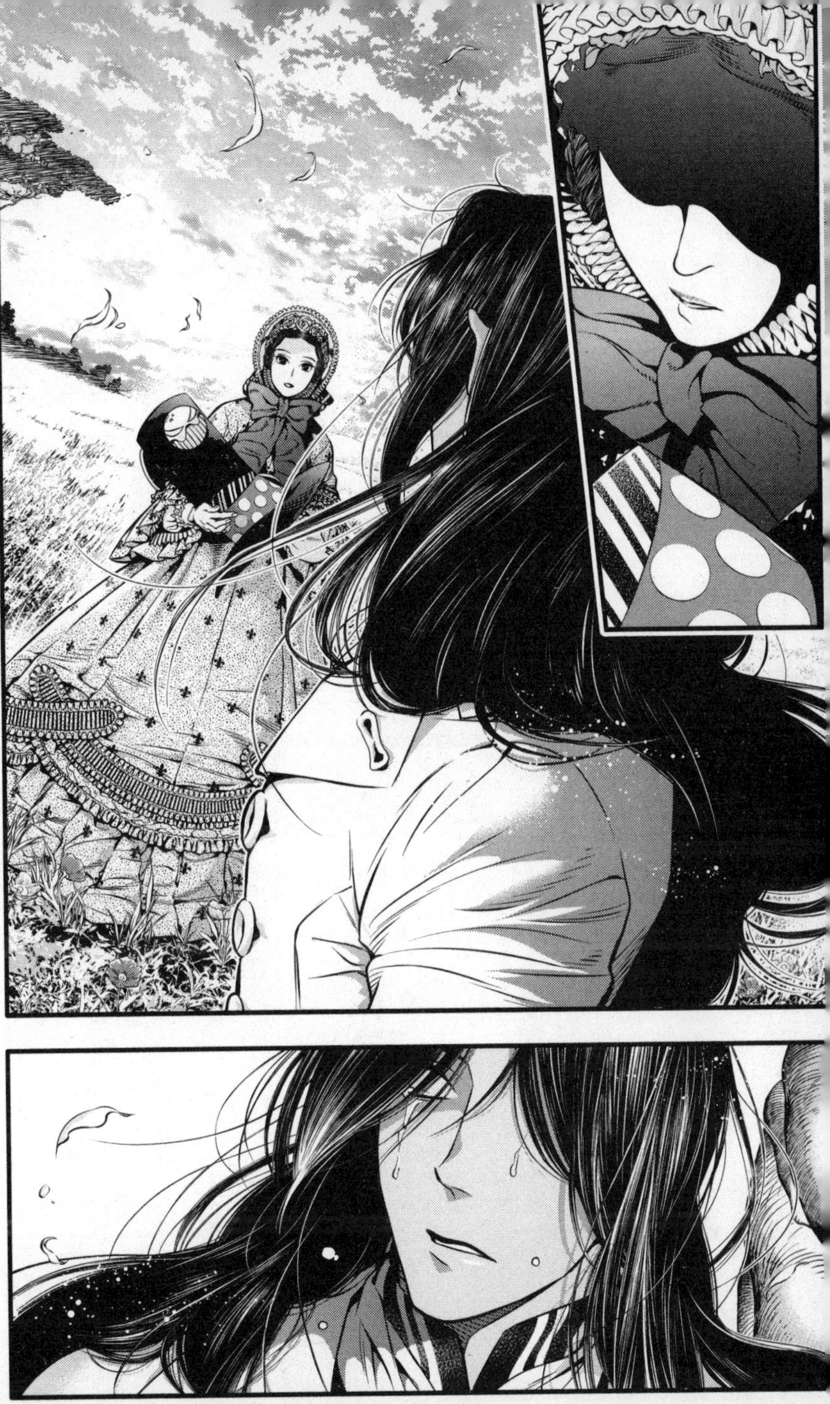

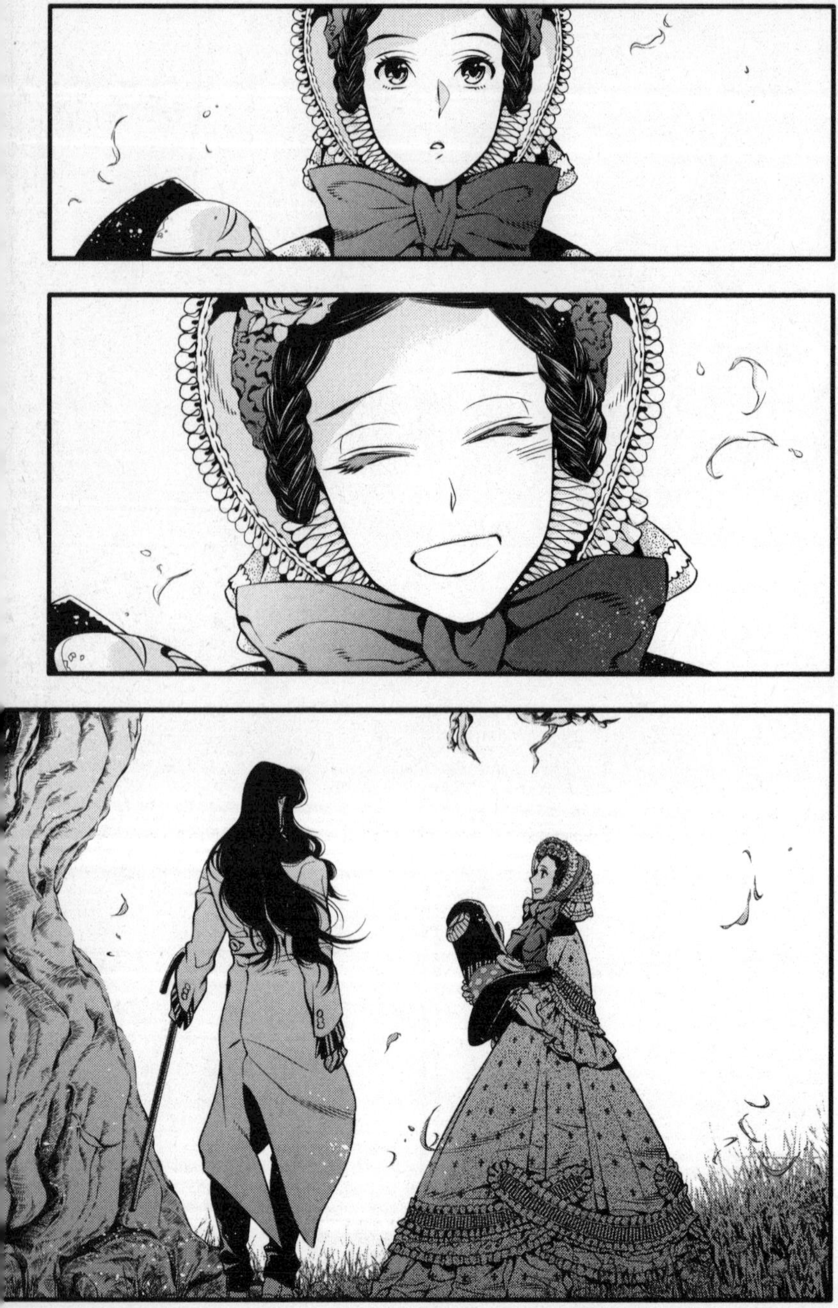

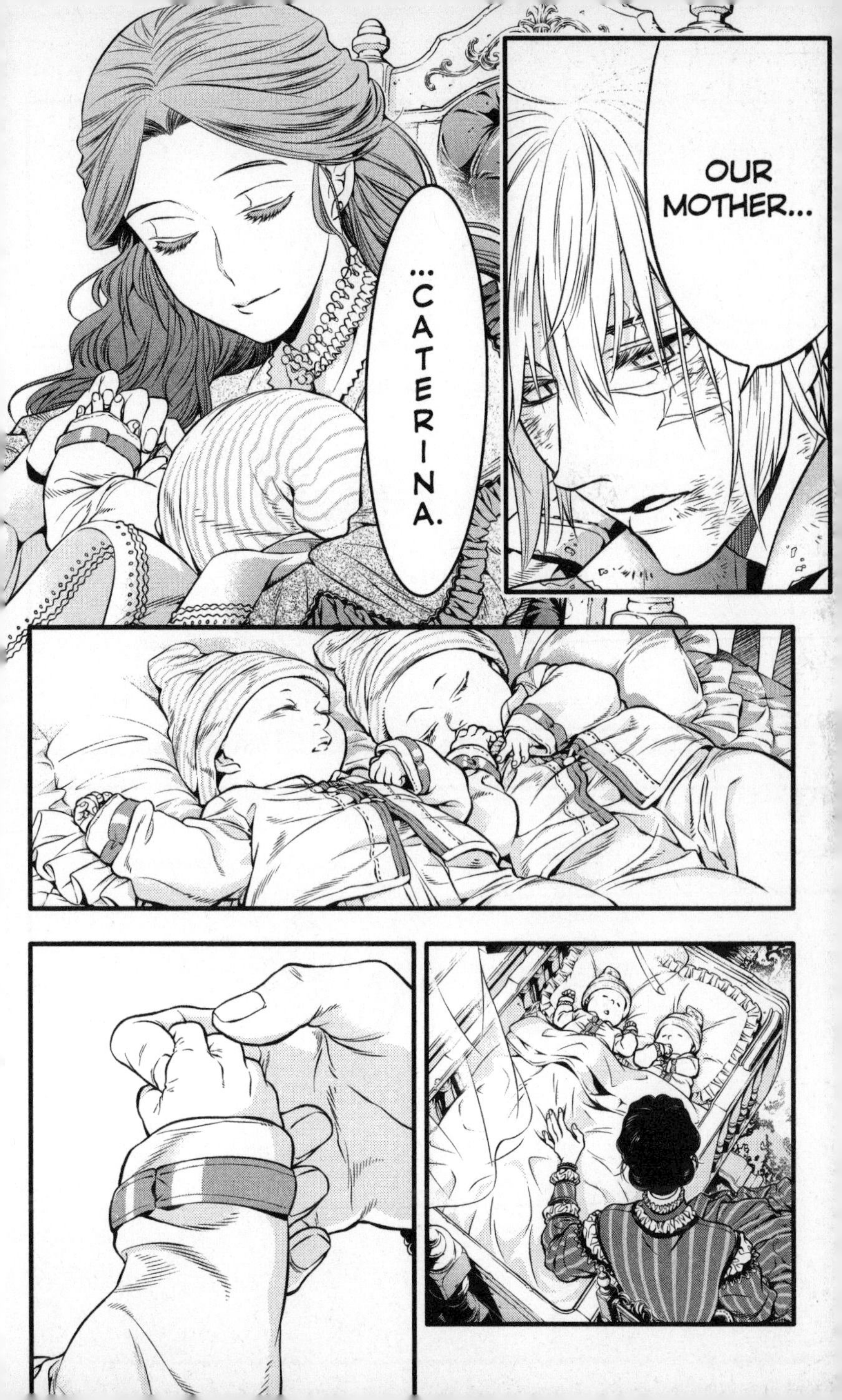
OUR MOTHER...
...CATERINA.

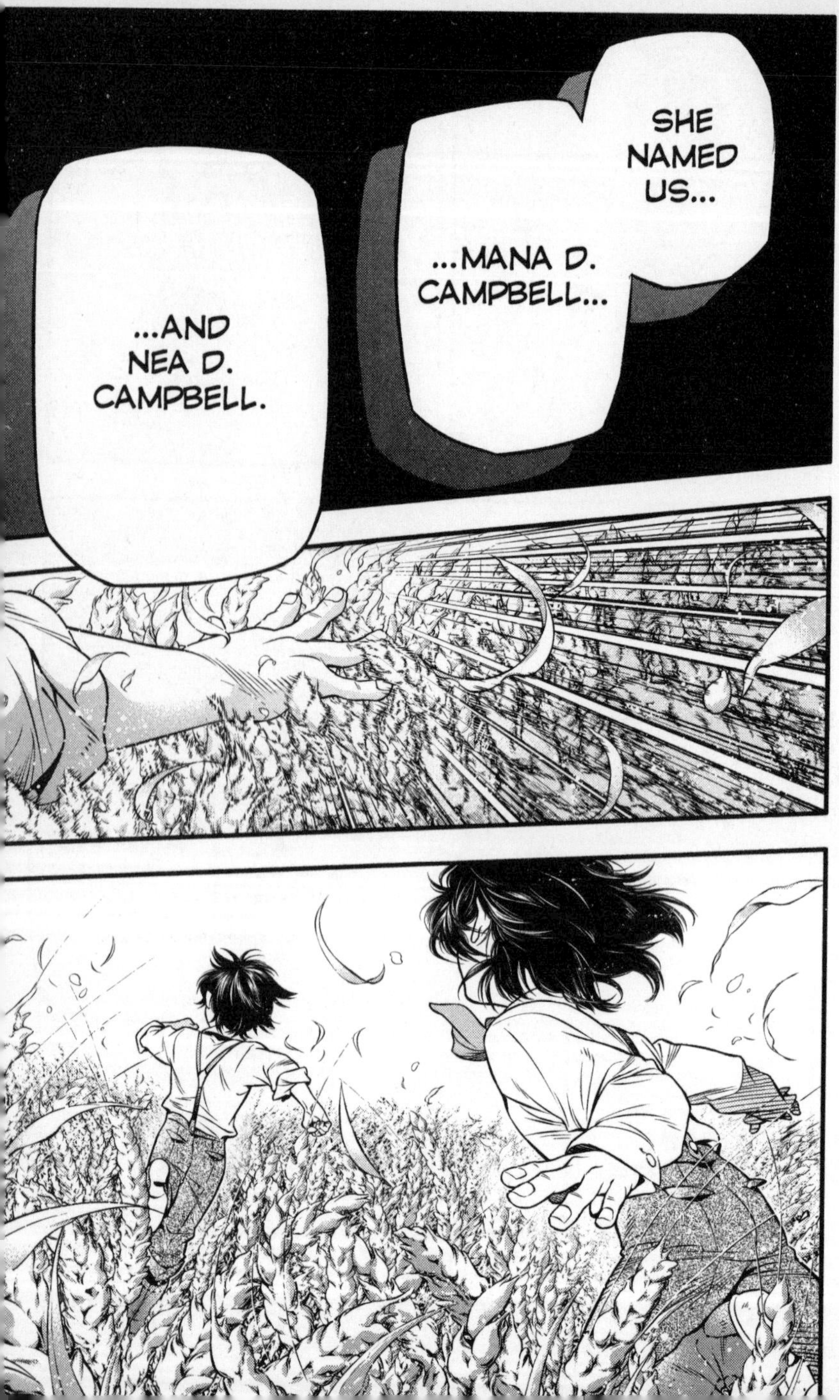
SHE NAMED US...
...MANA D. CAMPBELL...
...AND NEA D. CAMPBELL.

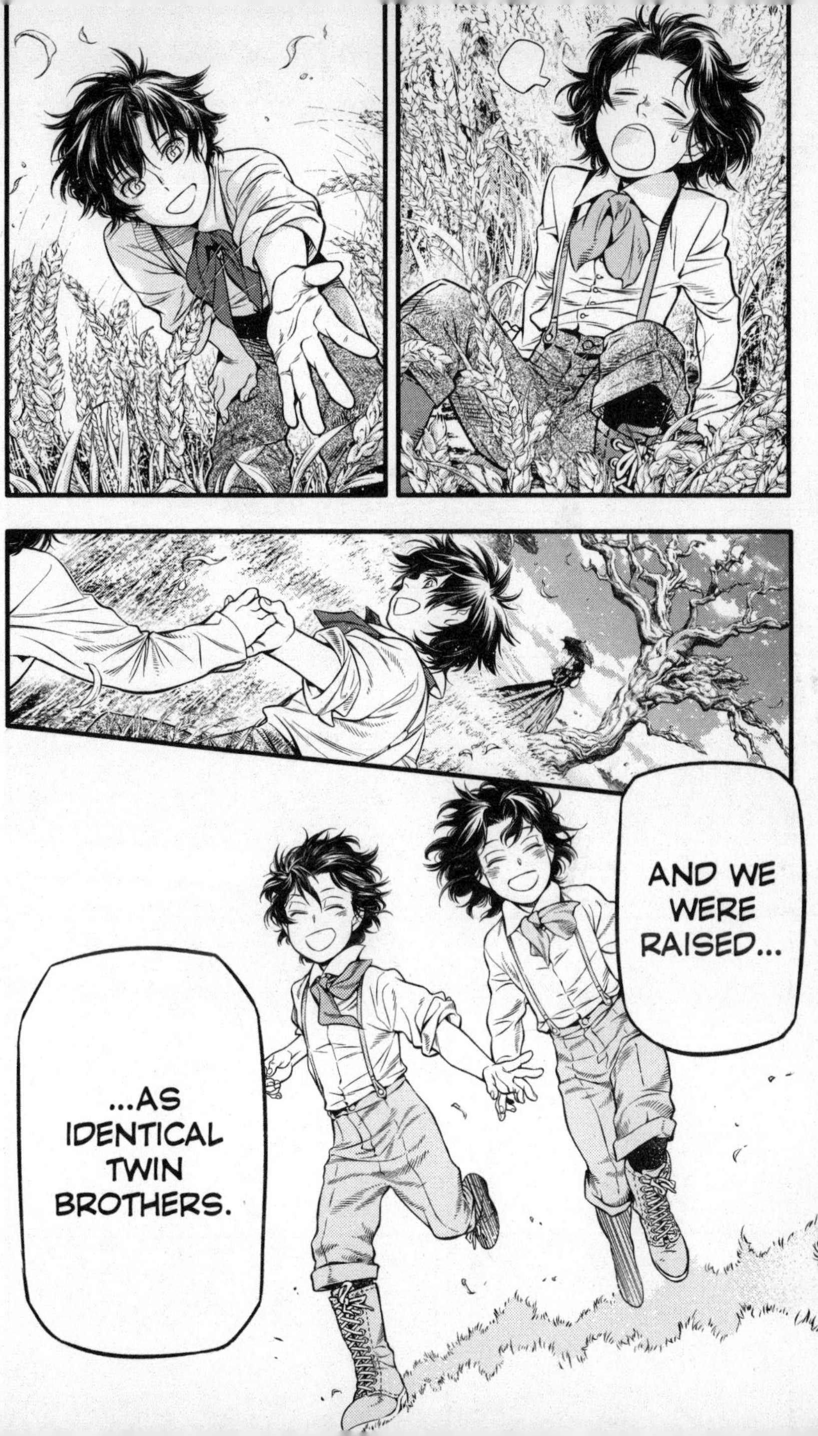
AND WE WERE RAISED...
...AS IDENTICAL TWIN BROTHERS.

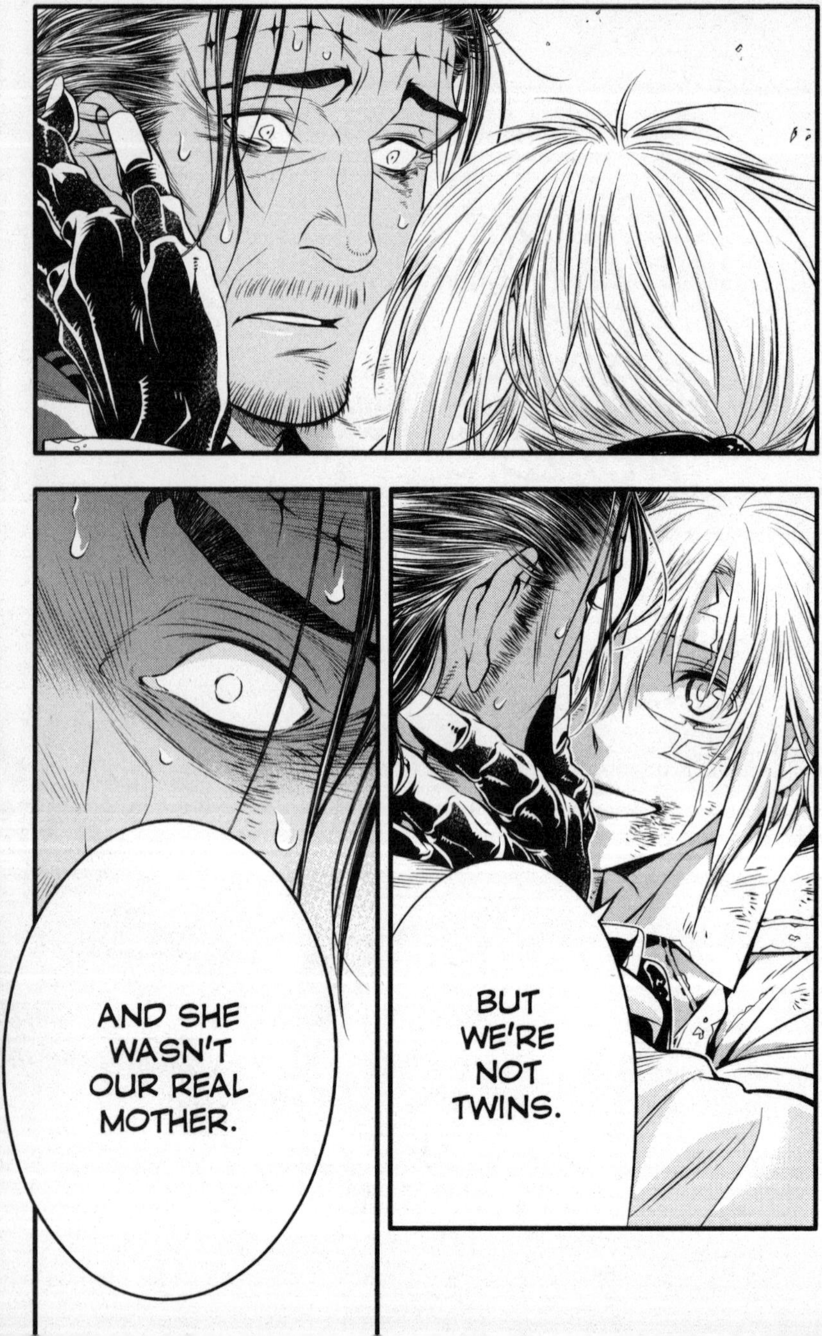
BUT WE'RE NOT TWINS.
AND SHE WASN'T OUR REAL MOTHER.

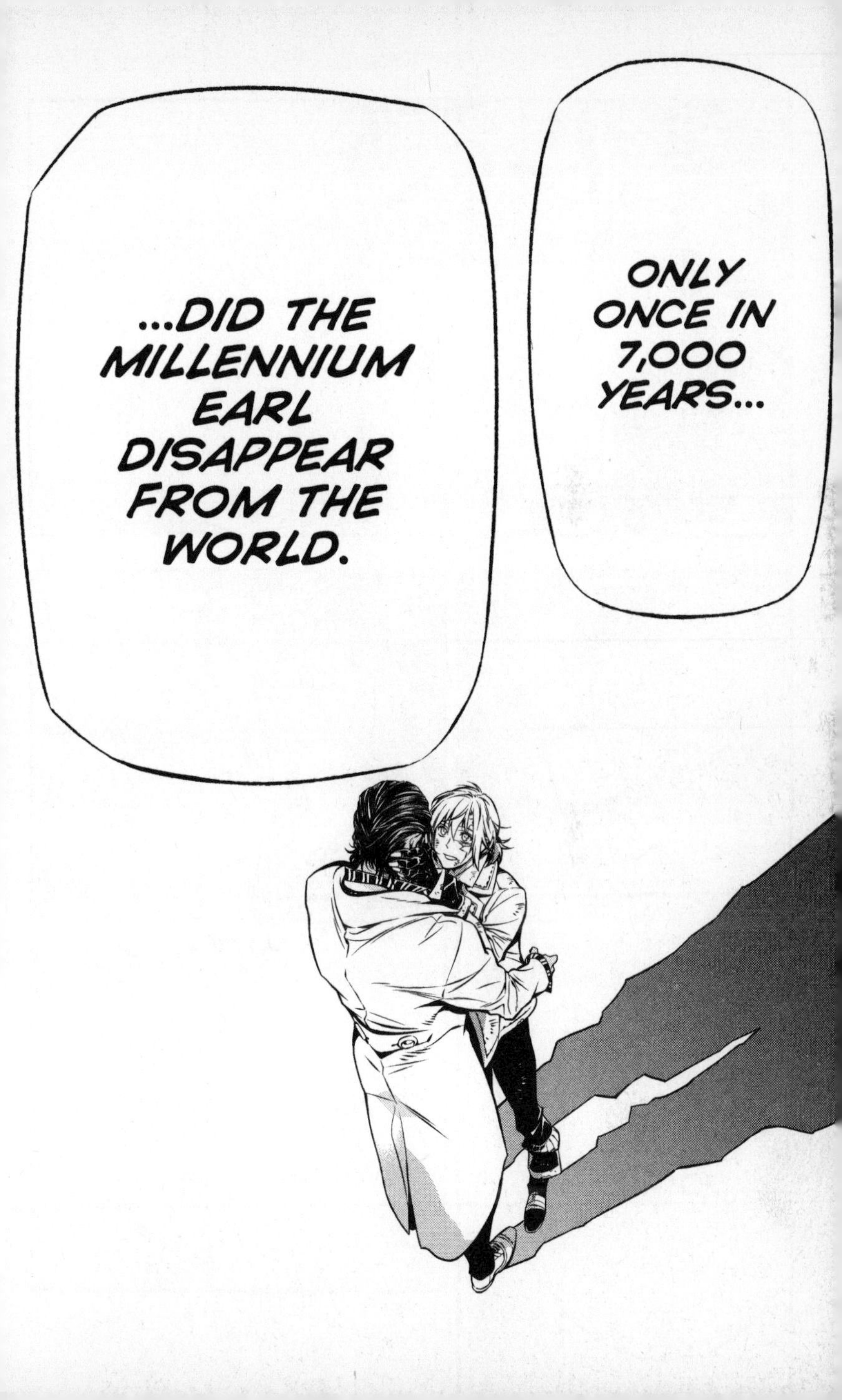
ONLY ONCE IN 7,000 YEARS...
...DID THE MILLENNIUM EARL DISAPPEAR FROM THE WORLD.

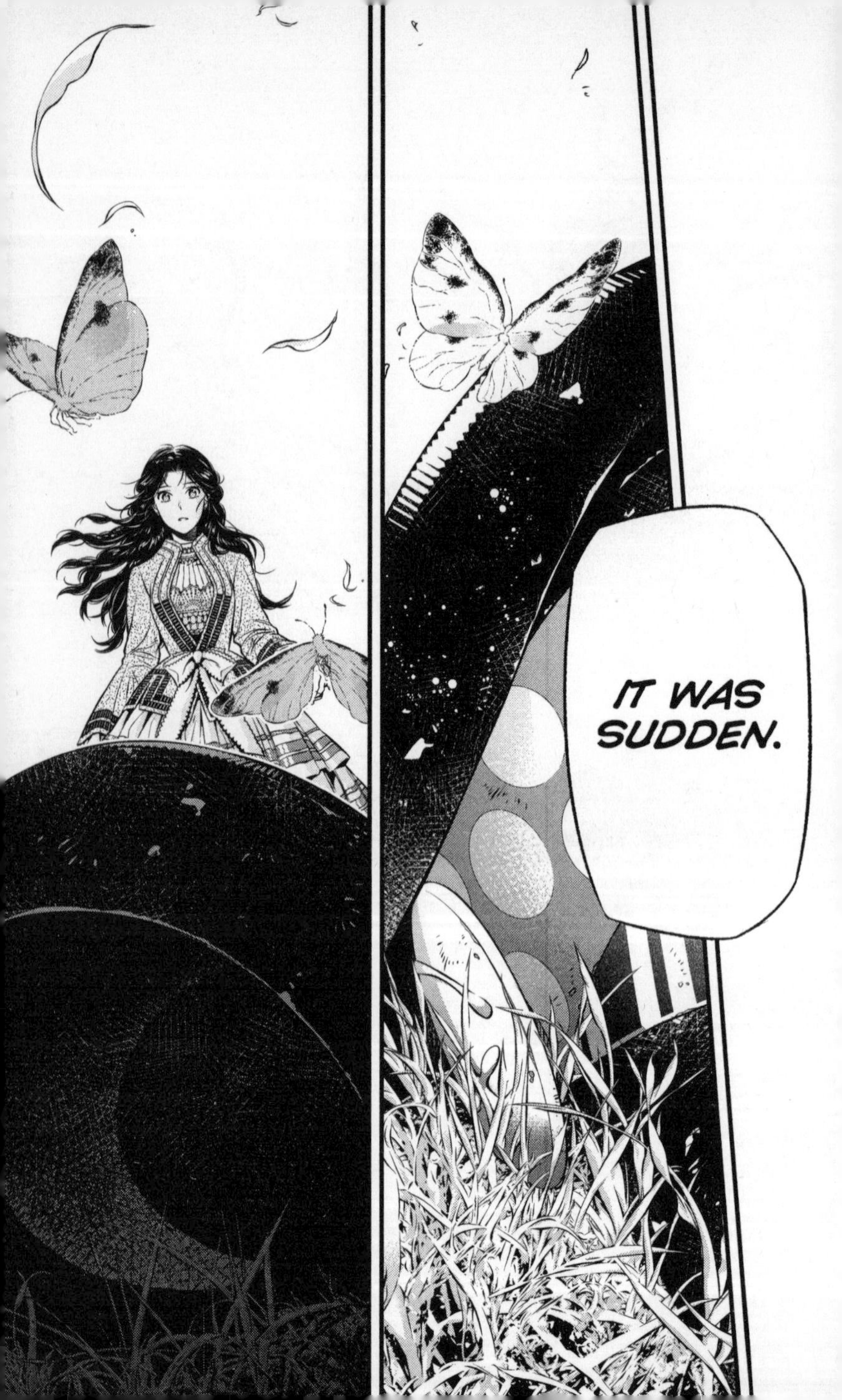
IT WAS SUDDEN.

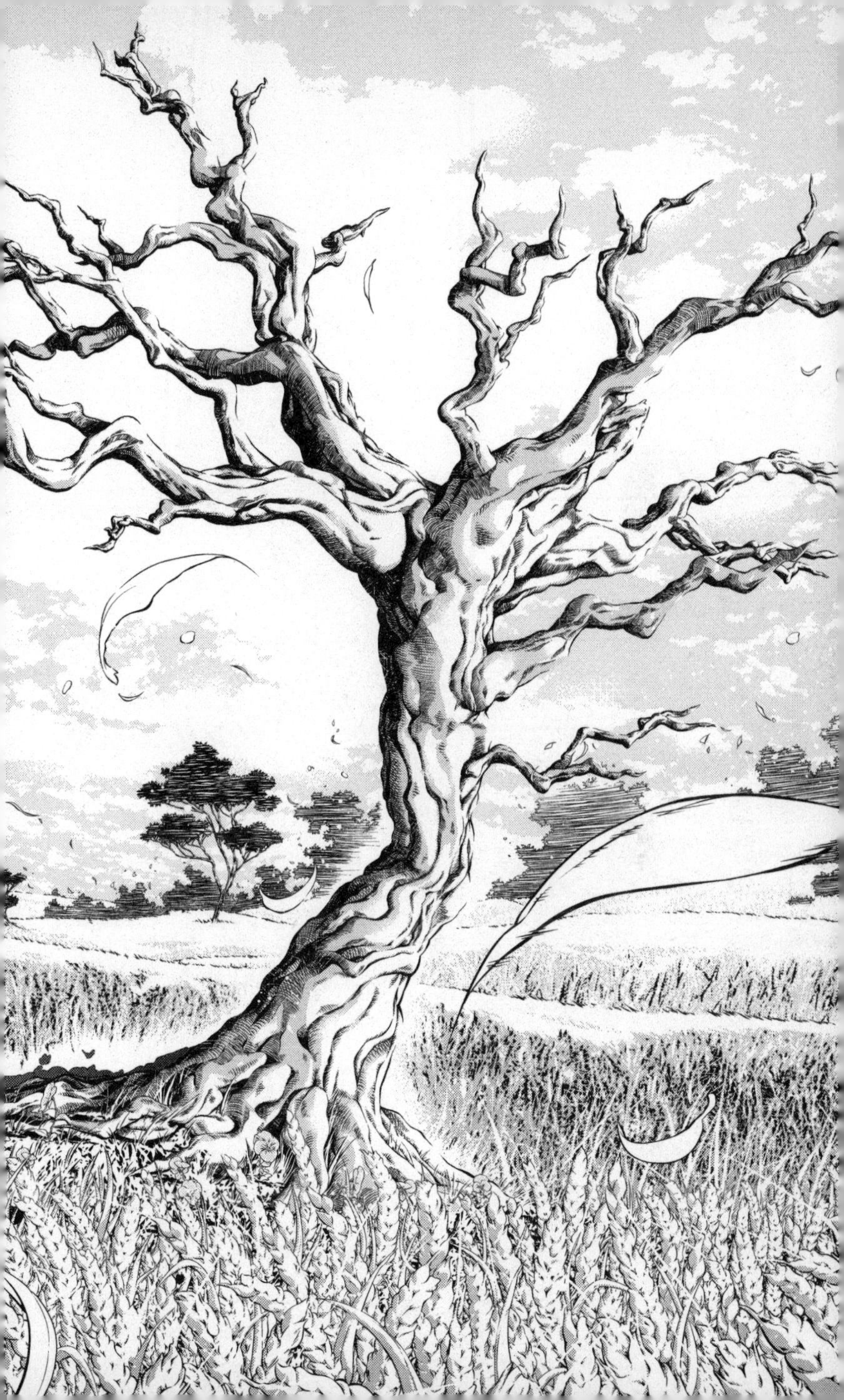

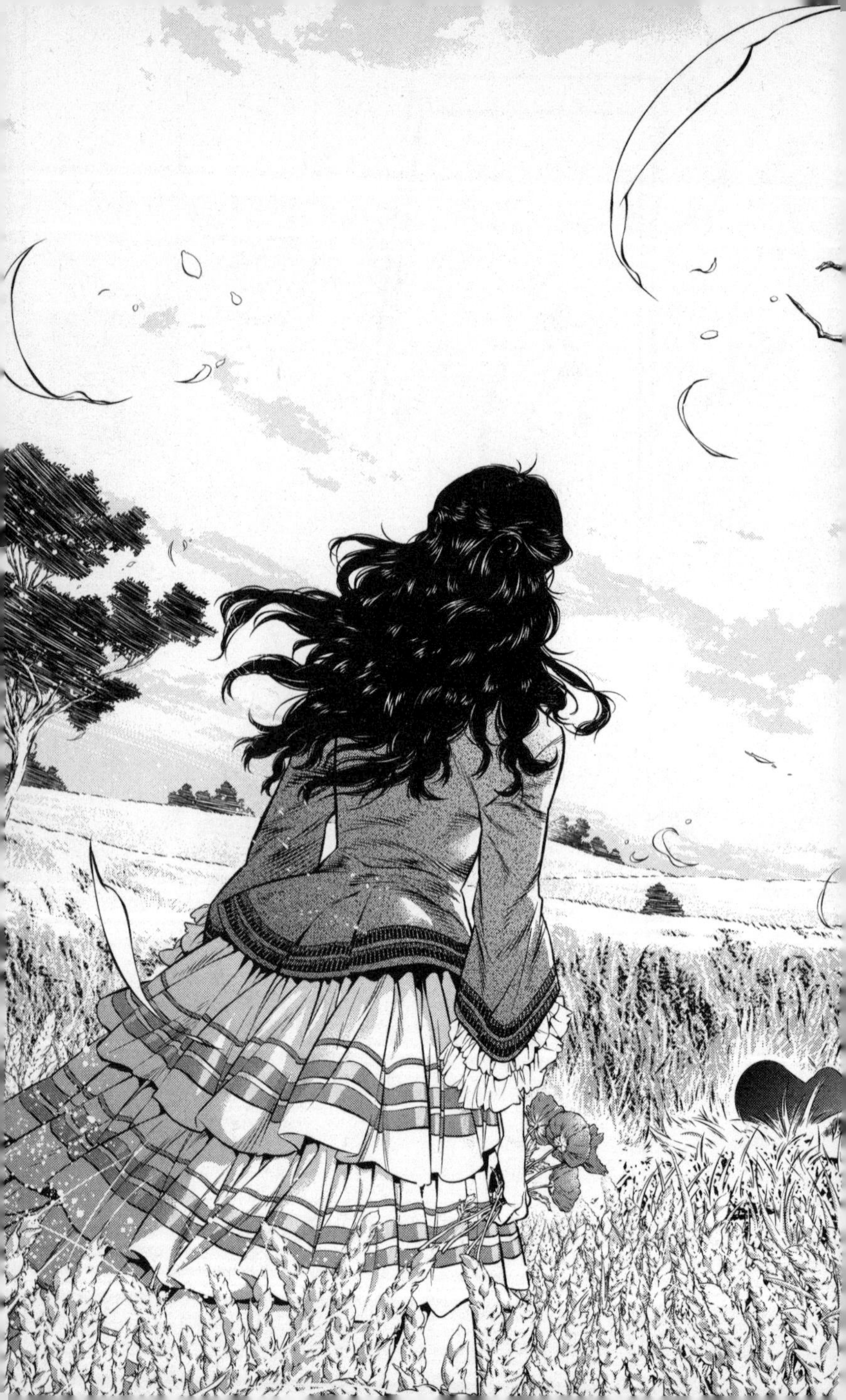

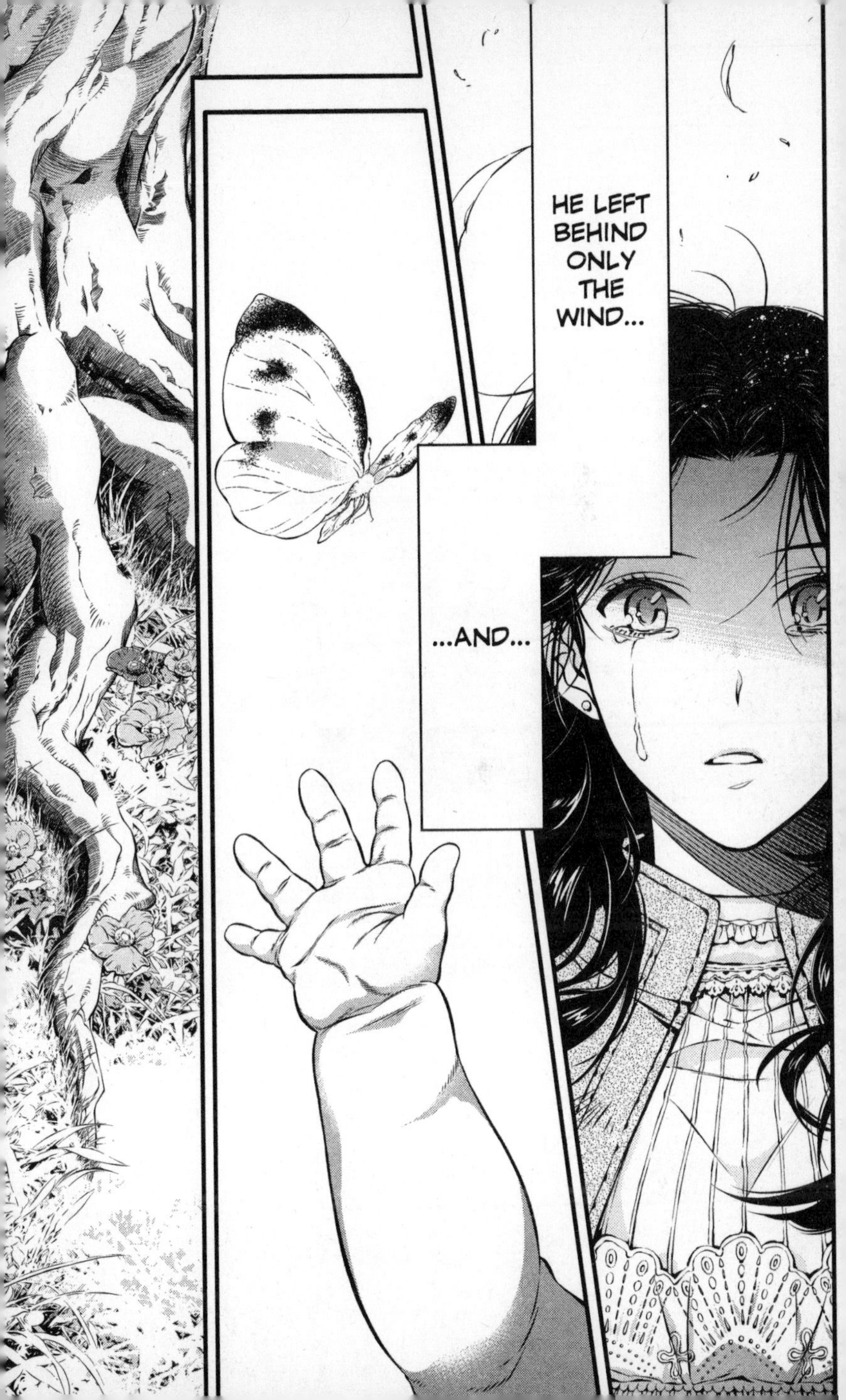
HE LEFT BEHIND ONLY THE WIND...
...AND...

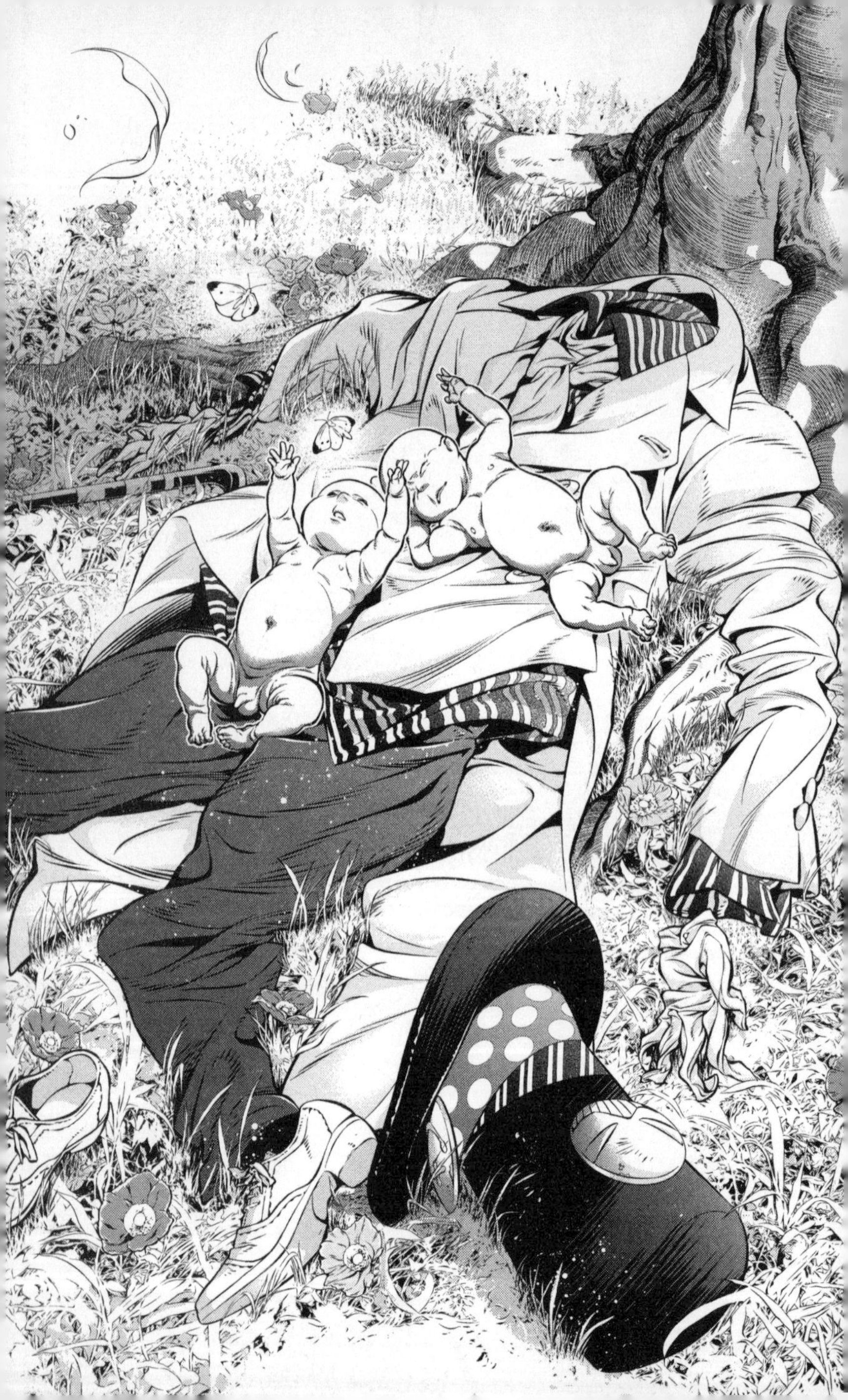

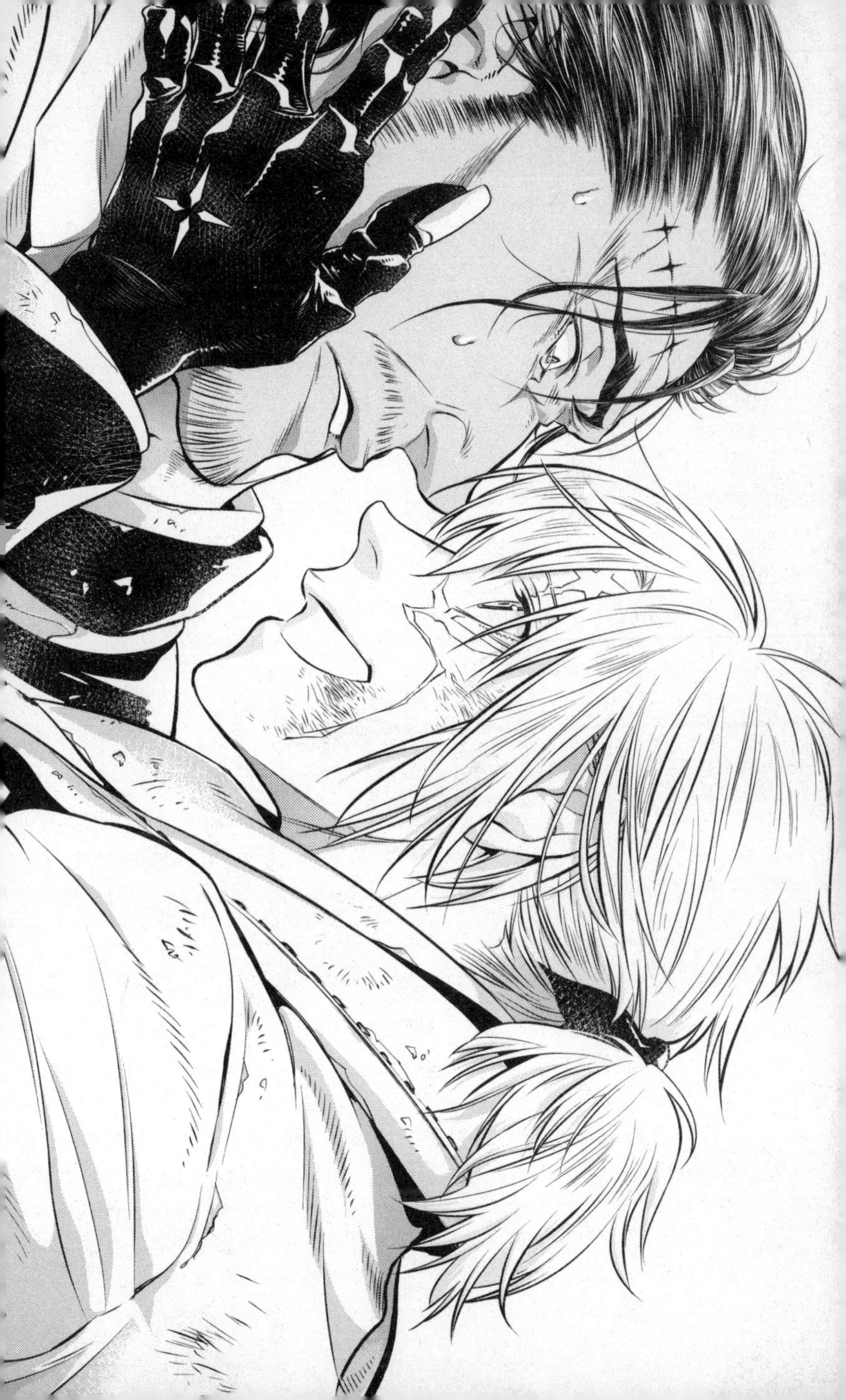

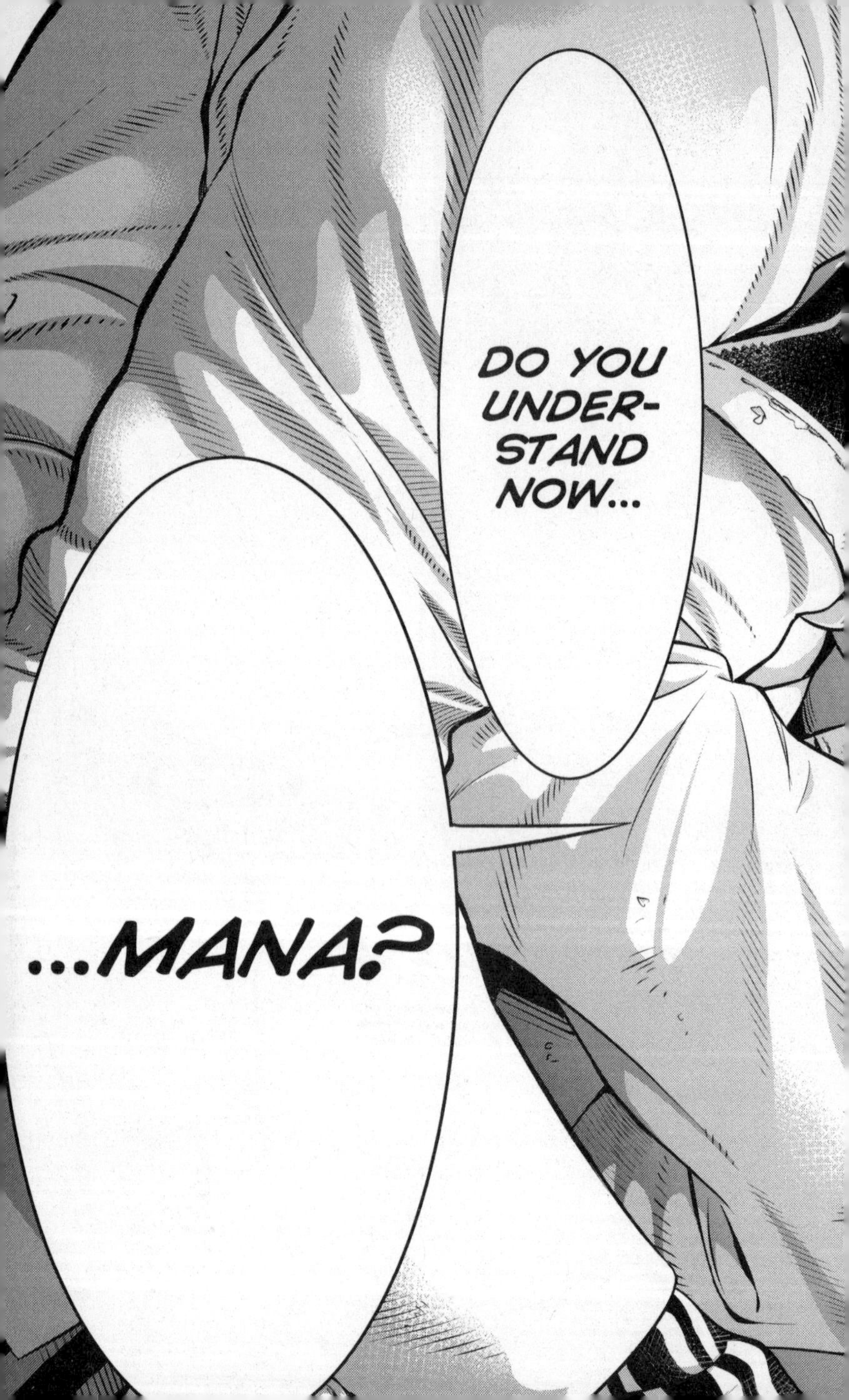
DO YOU UNDER-STAND NOW...
...MANA?

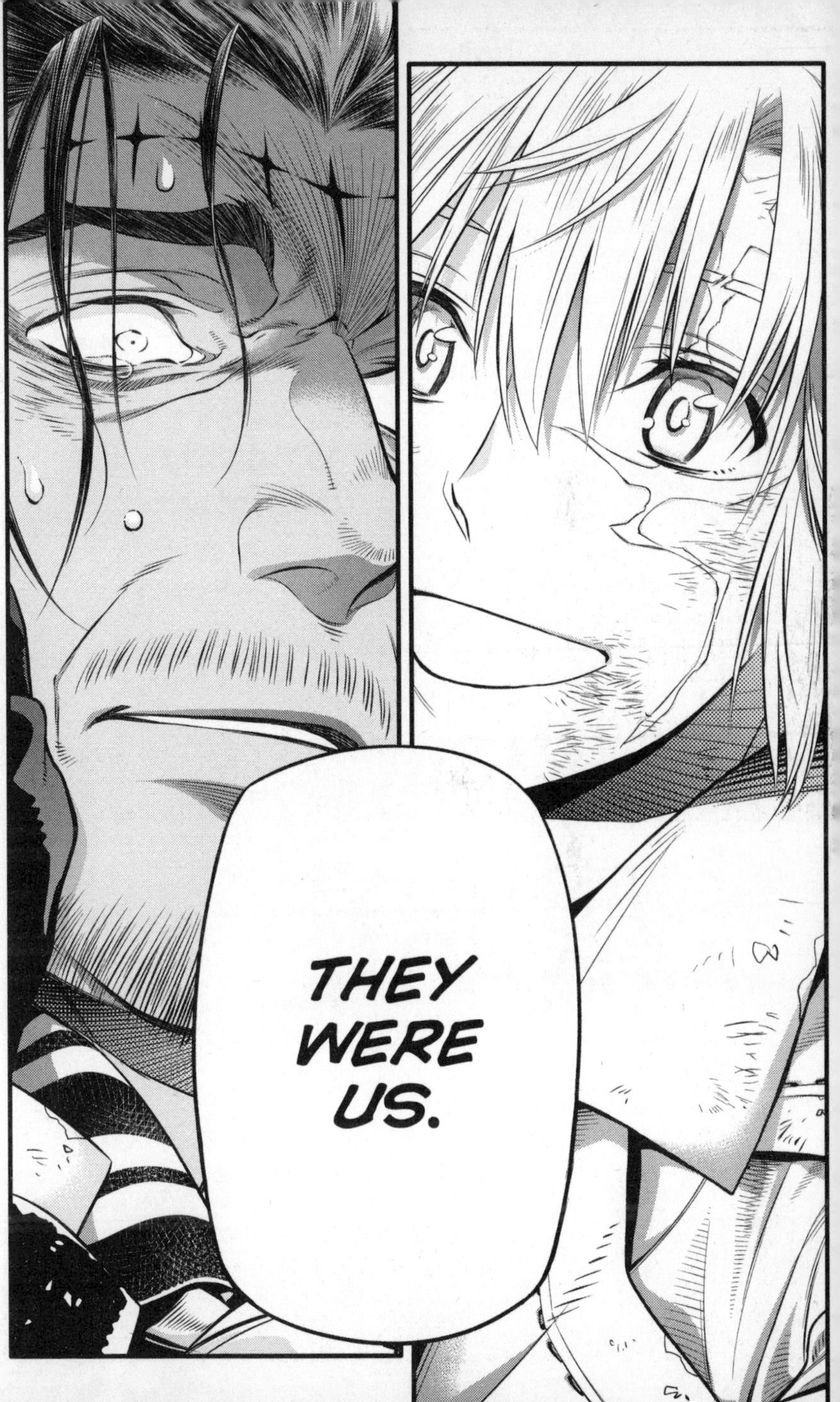
THEY WERE US.

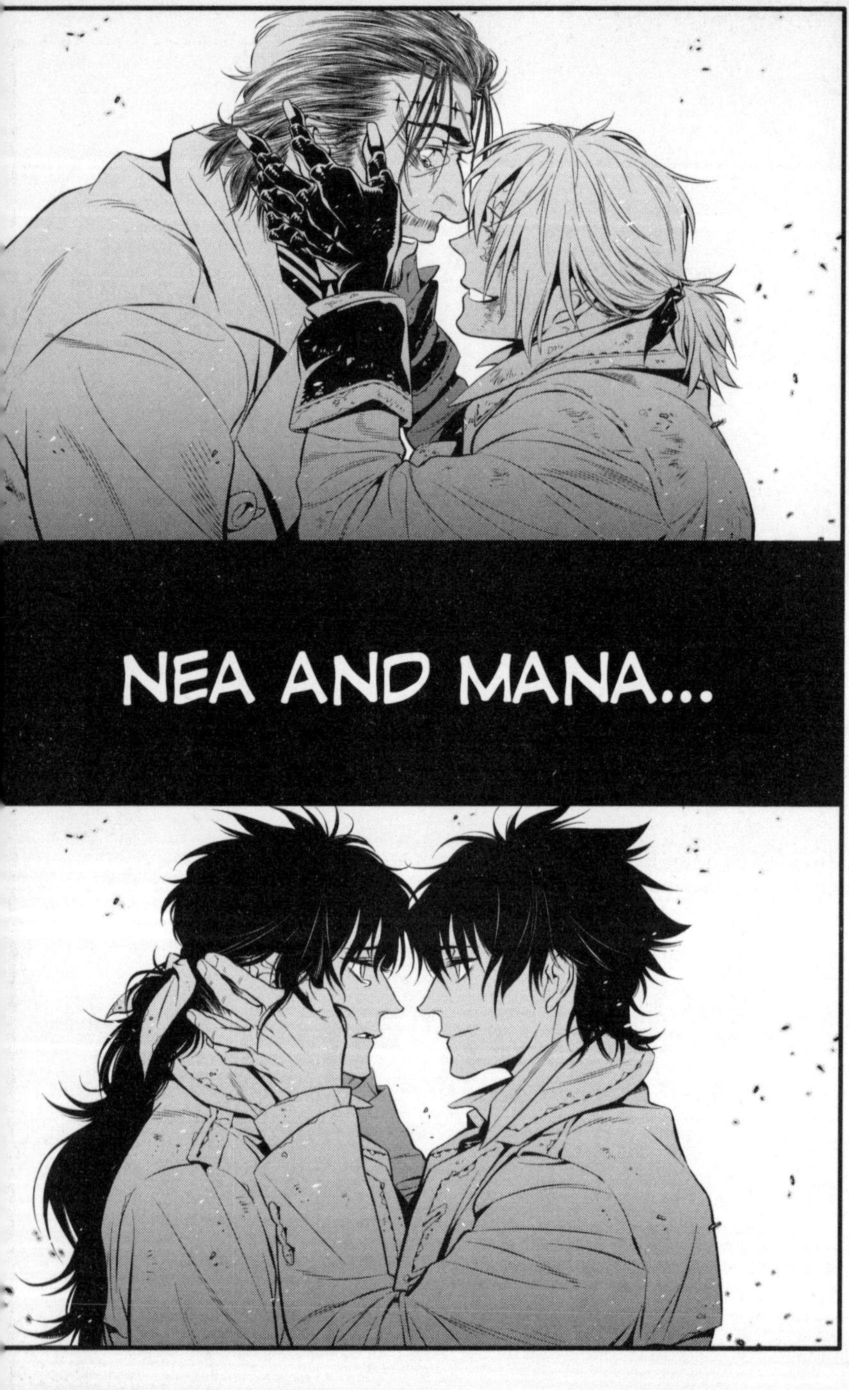
NEA AND MANA...

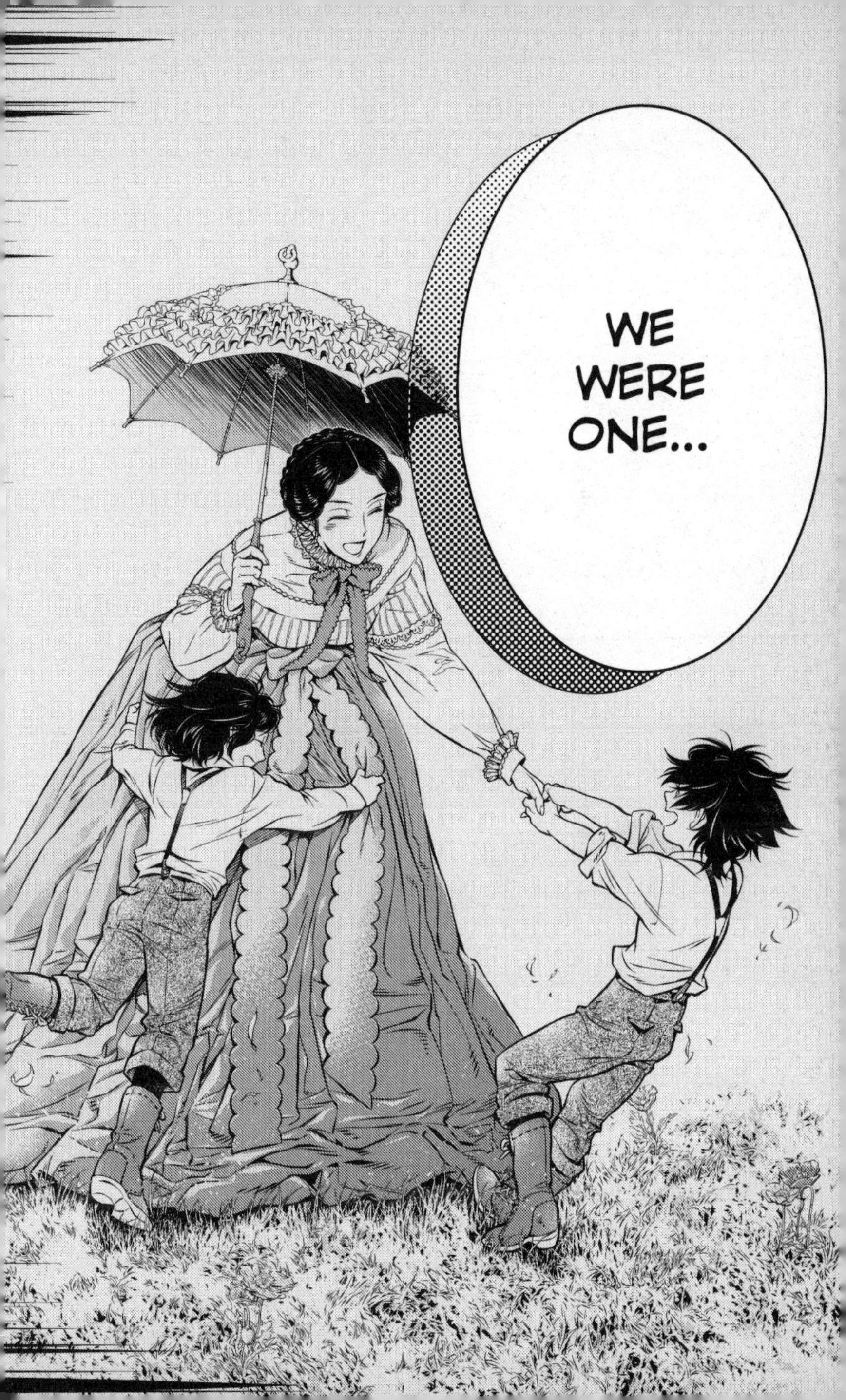
WE WERE ONE...

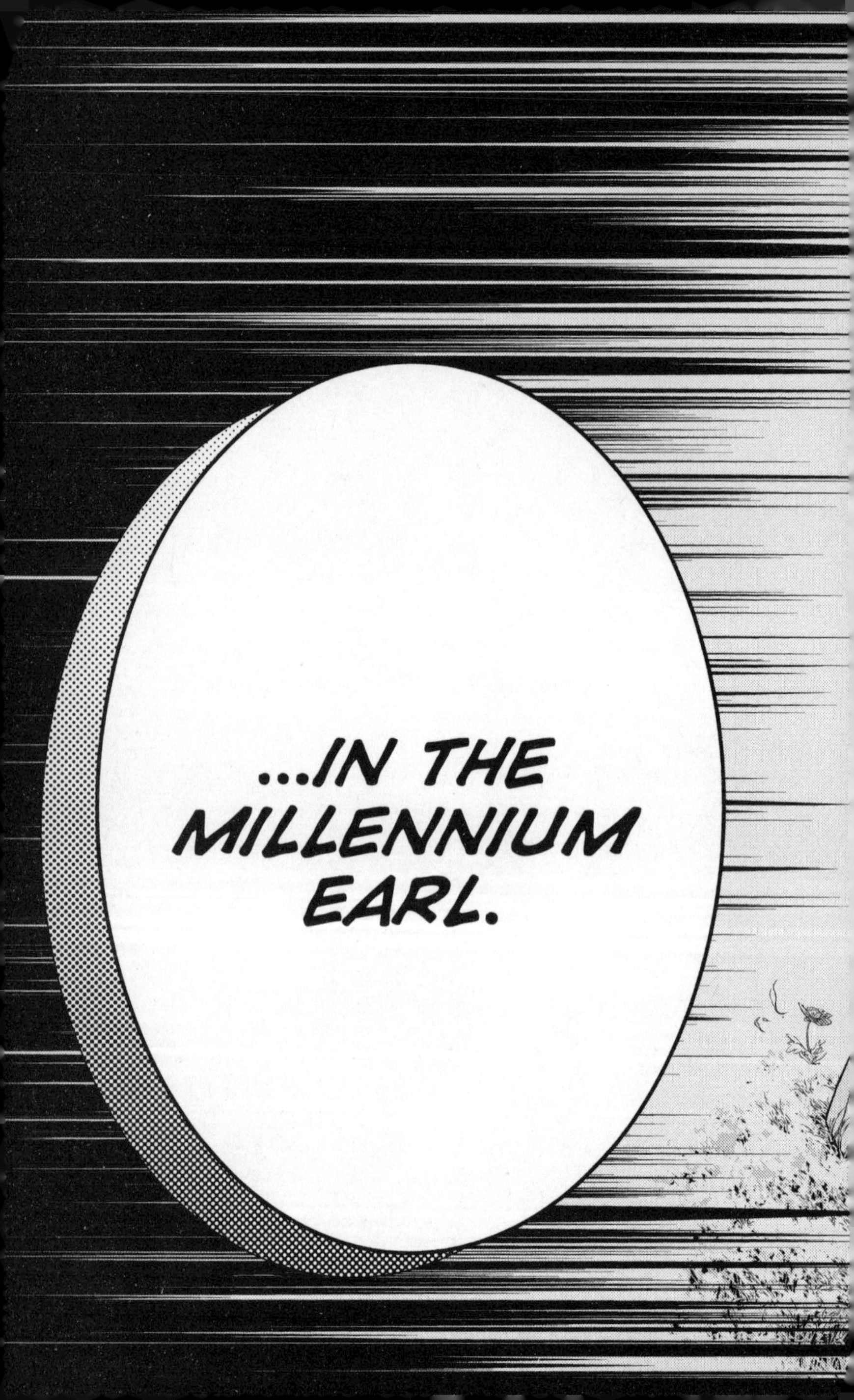
...IN THE MILLENNIUM EARL.

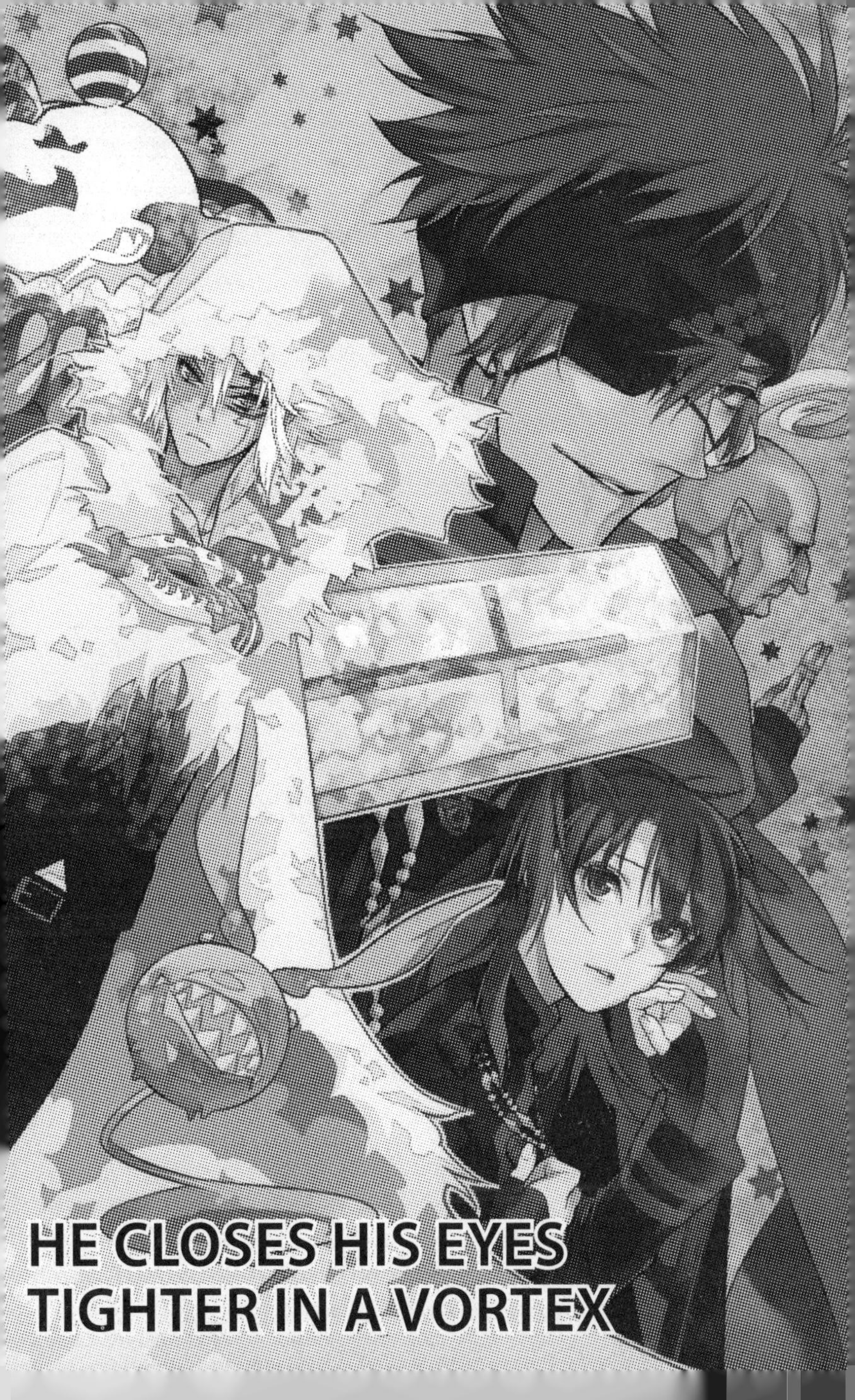
HE CLOSES HIS EYES
TIGHTER IN A VORTEX

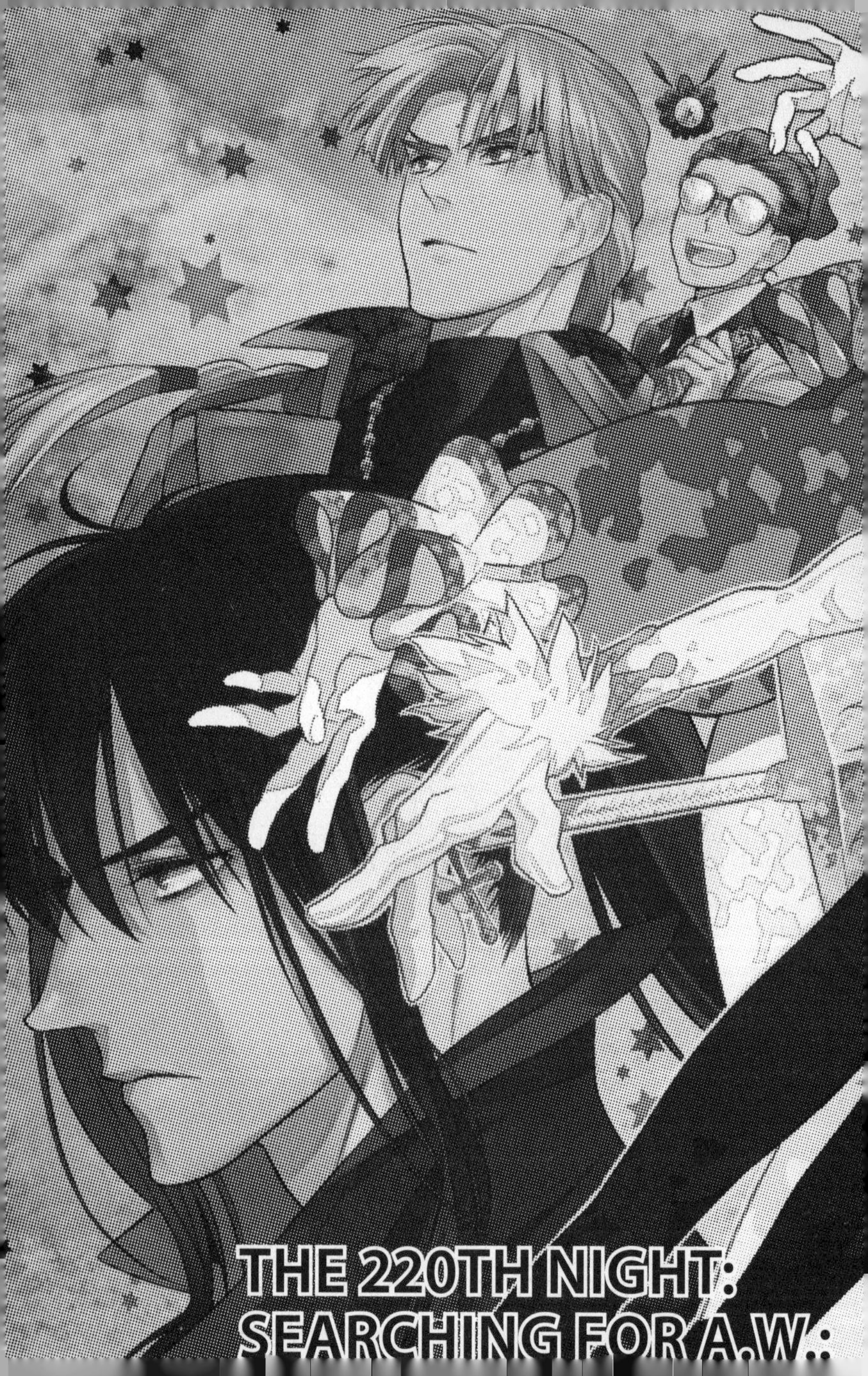
THE 220TH NIGHT:
SEARCHING FOR A.W.:

53 52

219th Night sketch

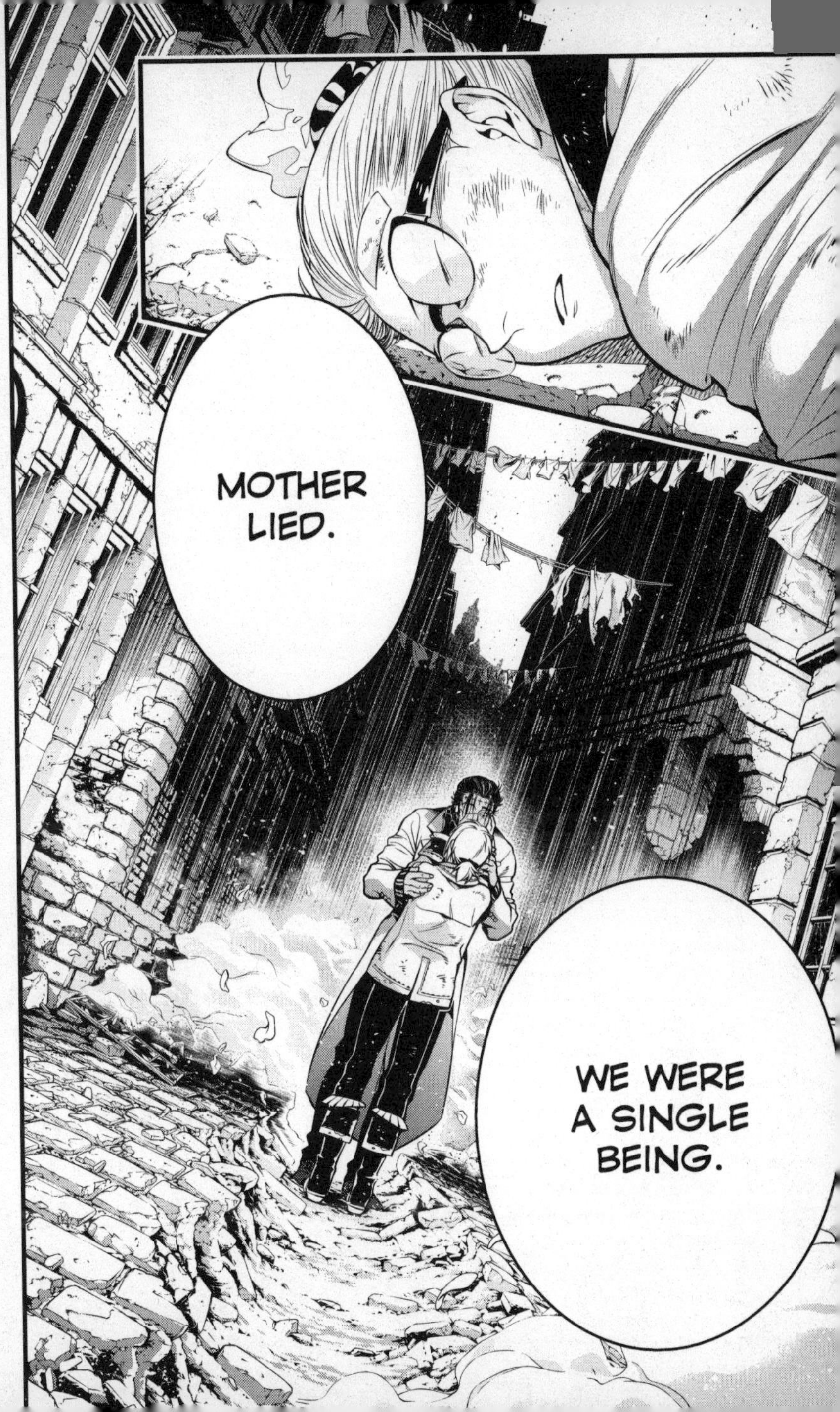
MOTHER LIED.
WE WERE A SINGLE BEING.

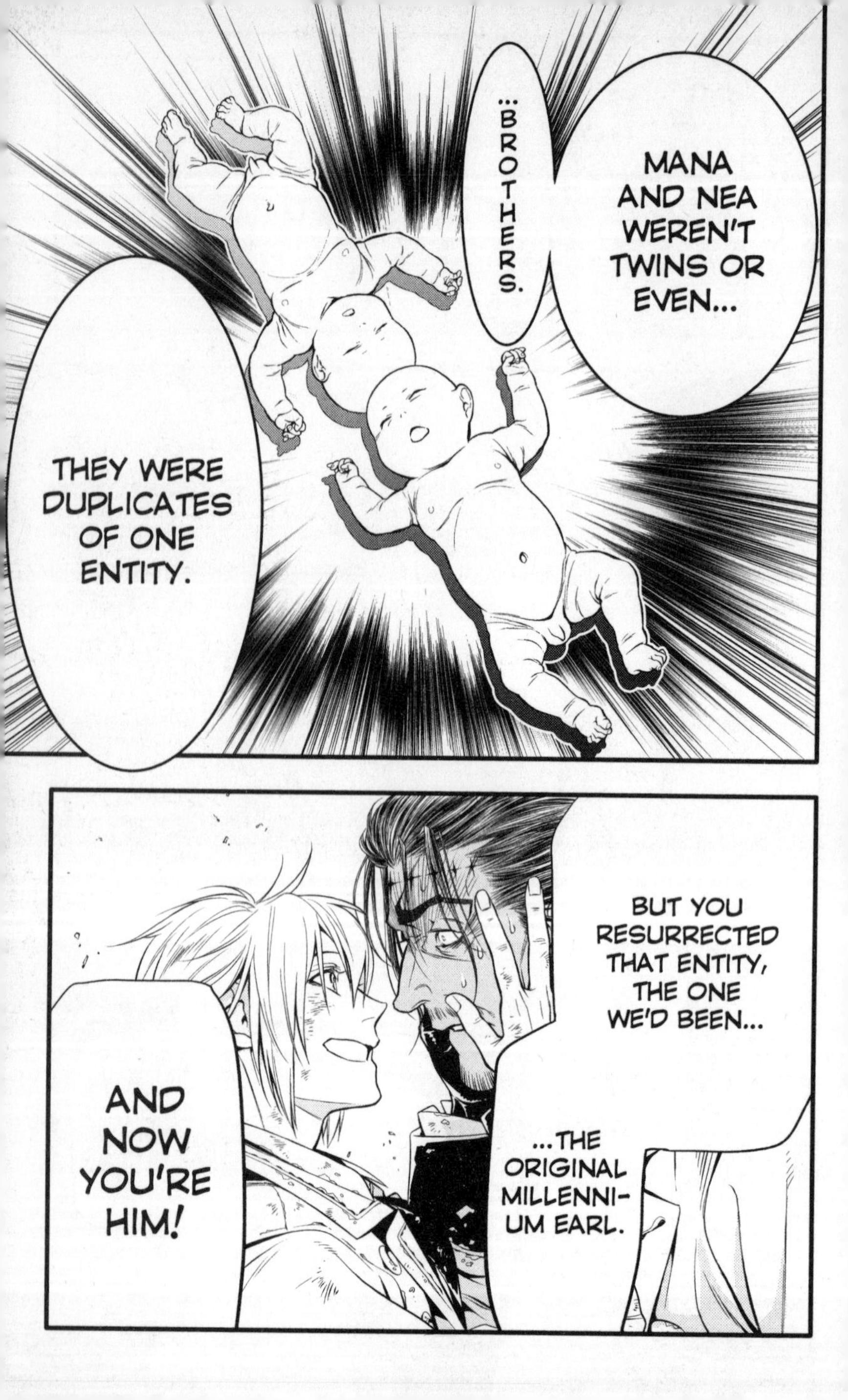
MANA AND NEA WEREN'T TWINS OR EVEN...
...BROTHERS.
THEY WERE DUPLICATES OF ONE ENTITY.
BUT YOU RESURRECTED THAT ENTITY, THE ONE WE'D BEEN...
...THE ORIGINAL MILLENNI-UM EARL.
AND NOW YOU'RE HIM!

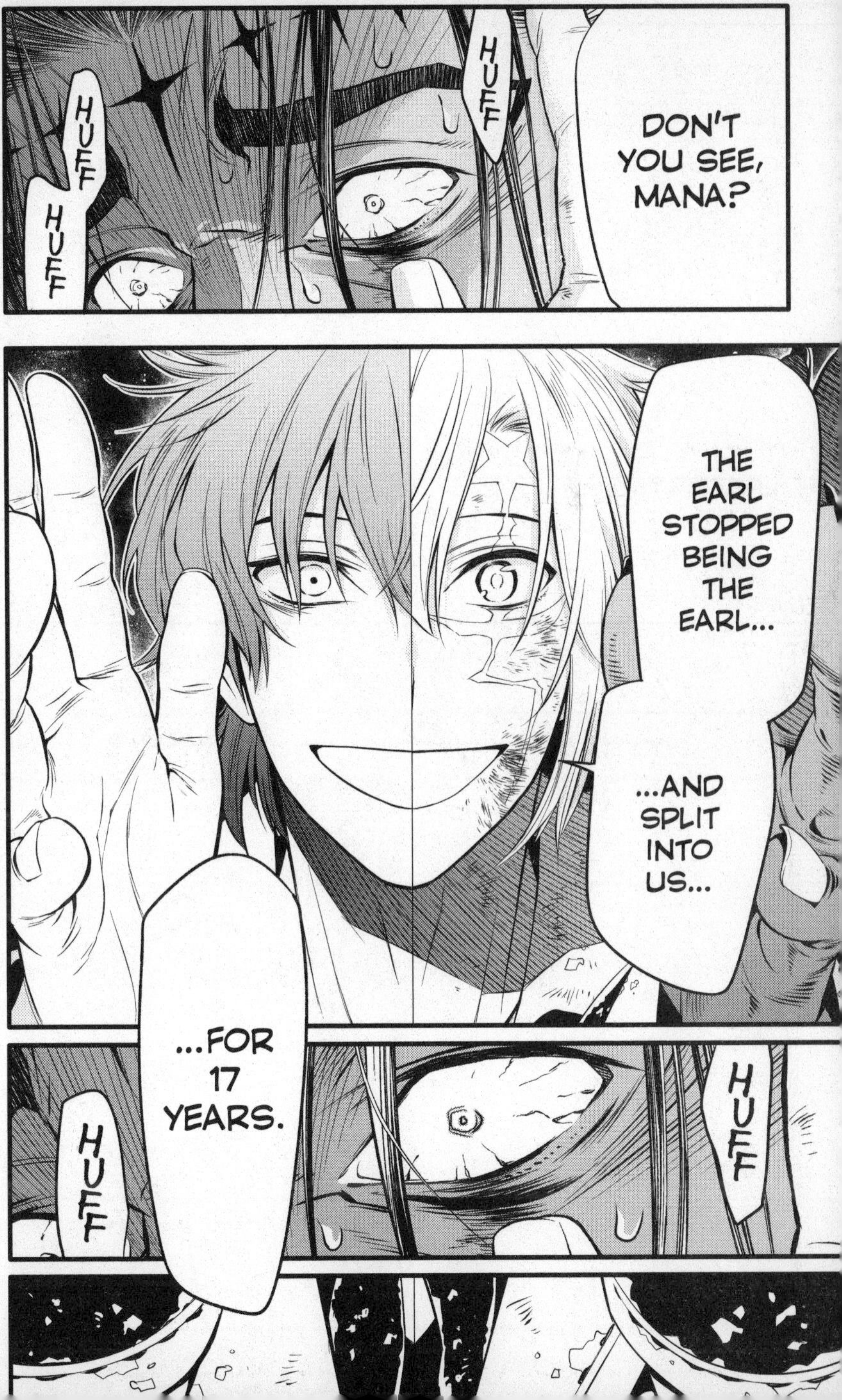
DON'T YOU SEE, MANA?
HUFF
HUFF
HUFF HUFF
THE EARL STOPPED BEING THE EARL...
...AND SPLIT INTO US...
...FOR 17 YEARS.
HUFF
HUFF

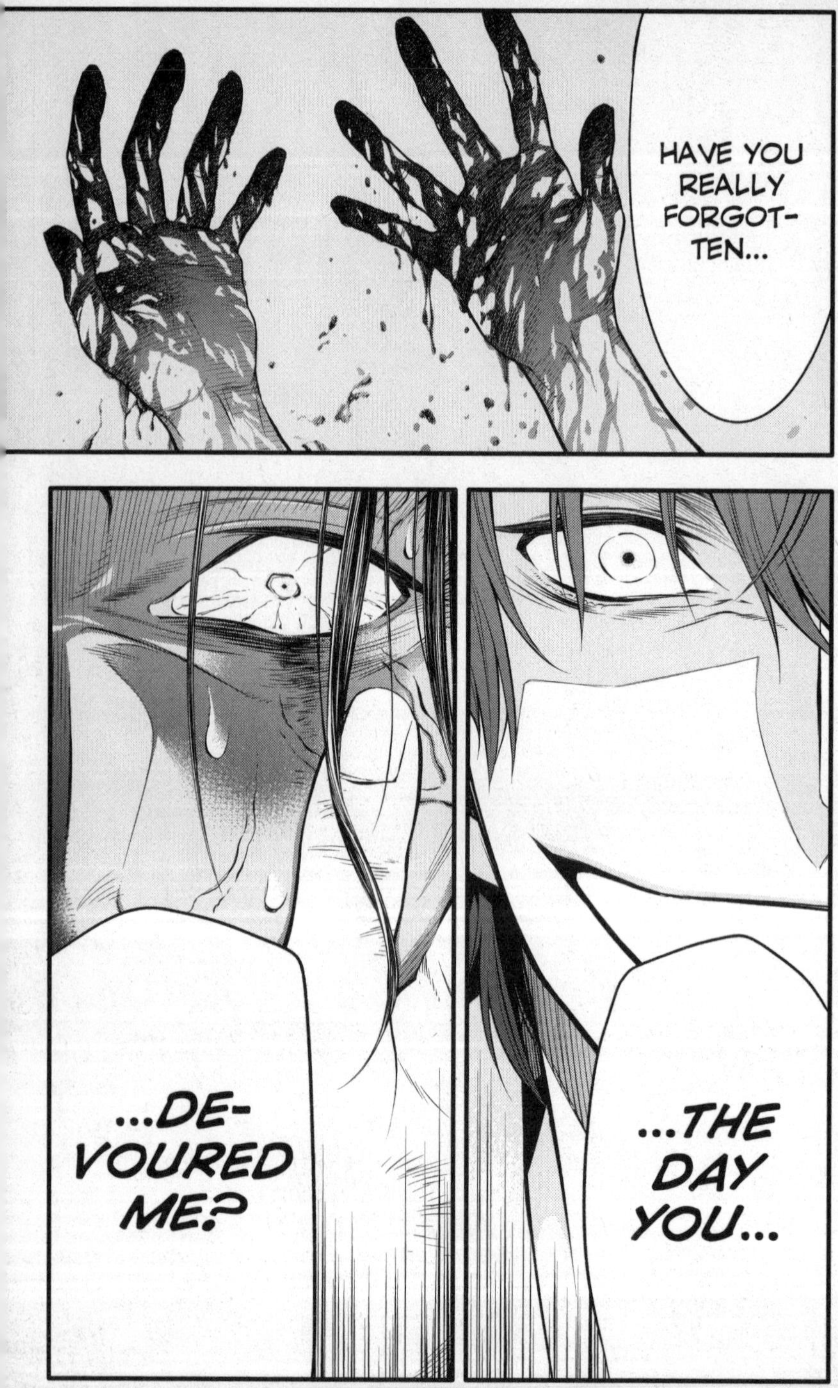
HAVE YOU REALLY FORGOT-TEN...
...THE DAY YOU...
...DE-VOURED ME?

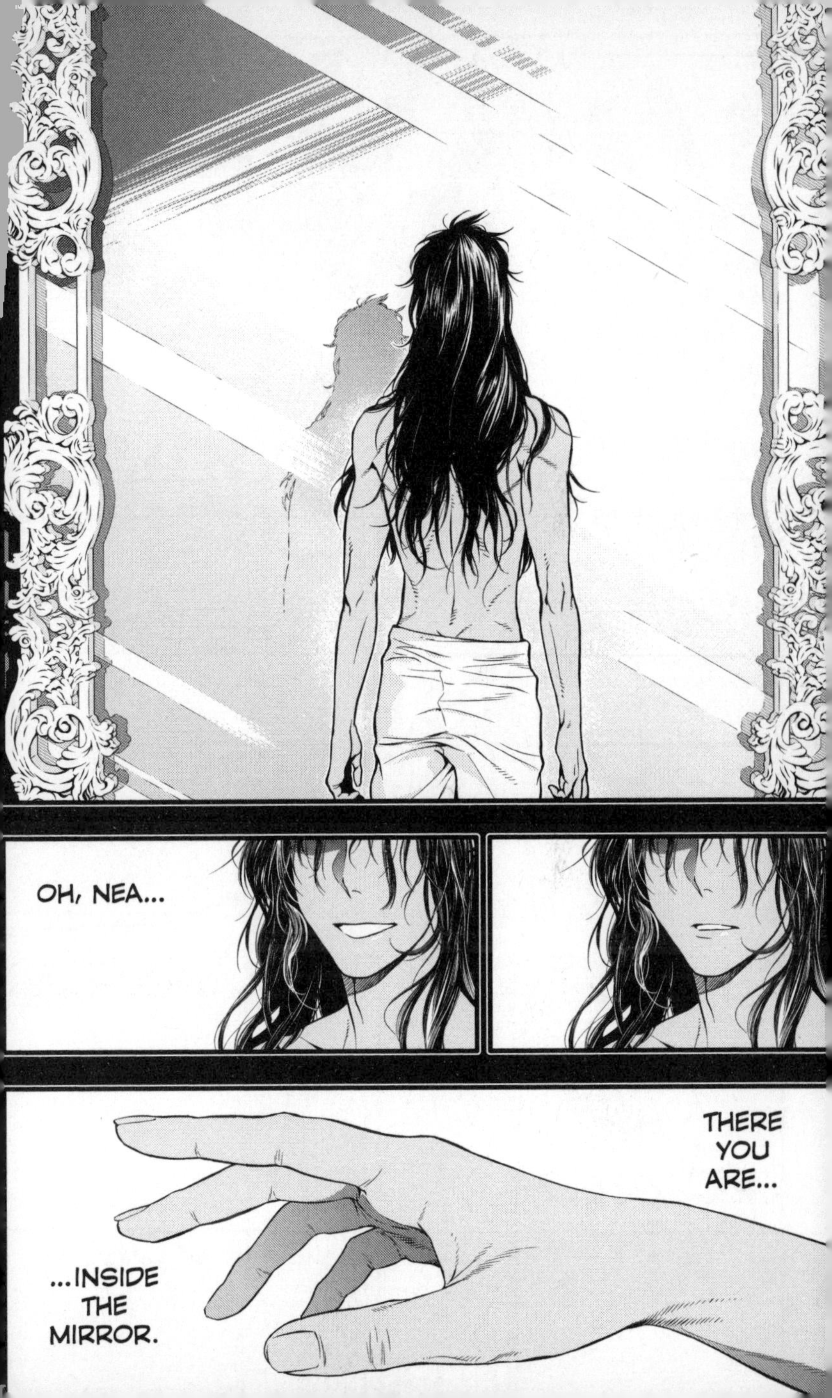
OH, NEA...
THERE YOU ARE...
...INSIDE THE MIRROR.

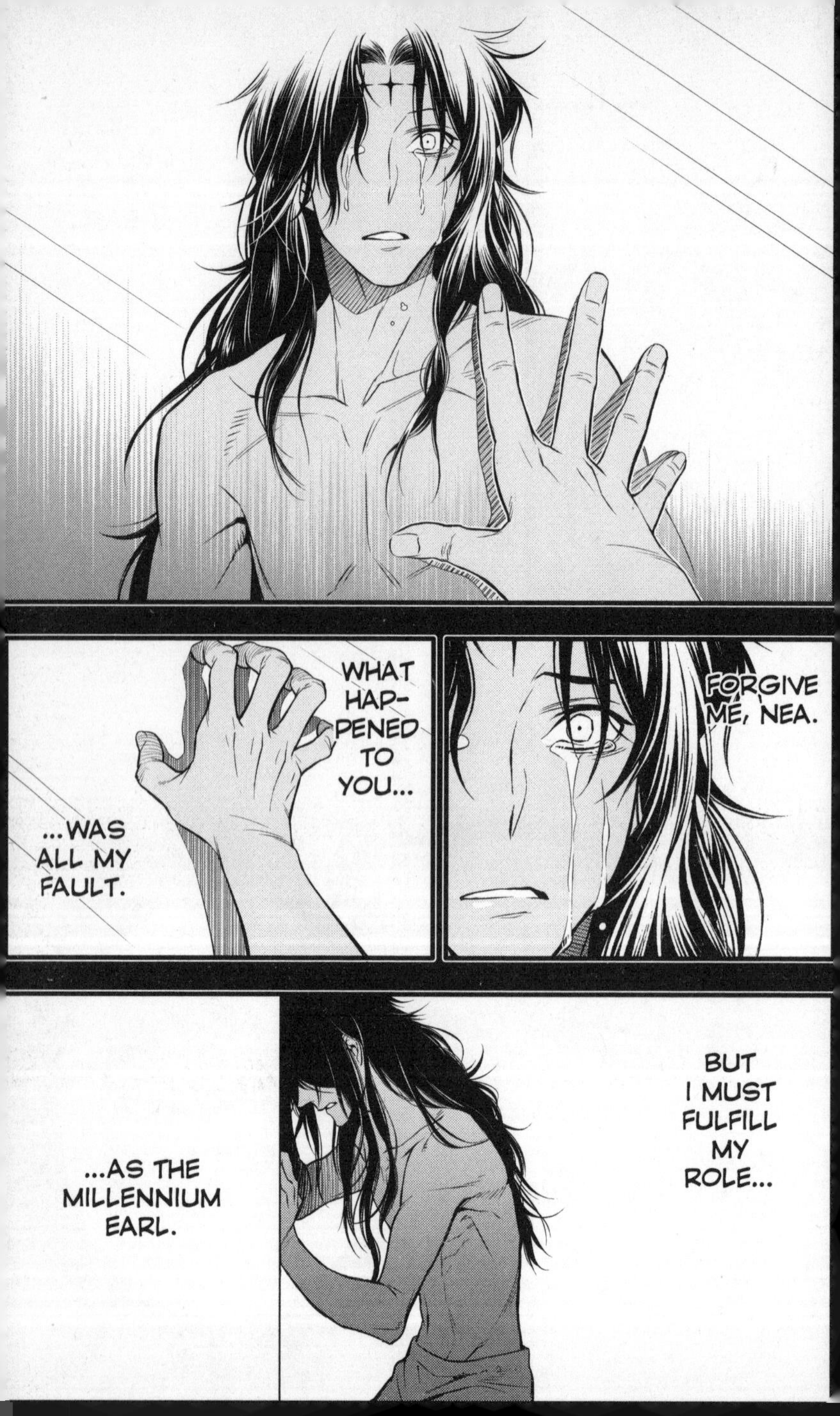
FORGIVE ME, NEA.
WHAT HAP-PENED TO YOU...
...WAS ALL MY FAULT.
BUT I MUST FULFILL MY ROLE...
...AS THE MILLENNIUM EARL.

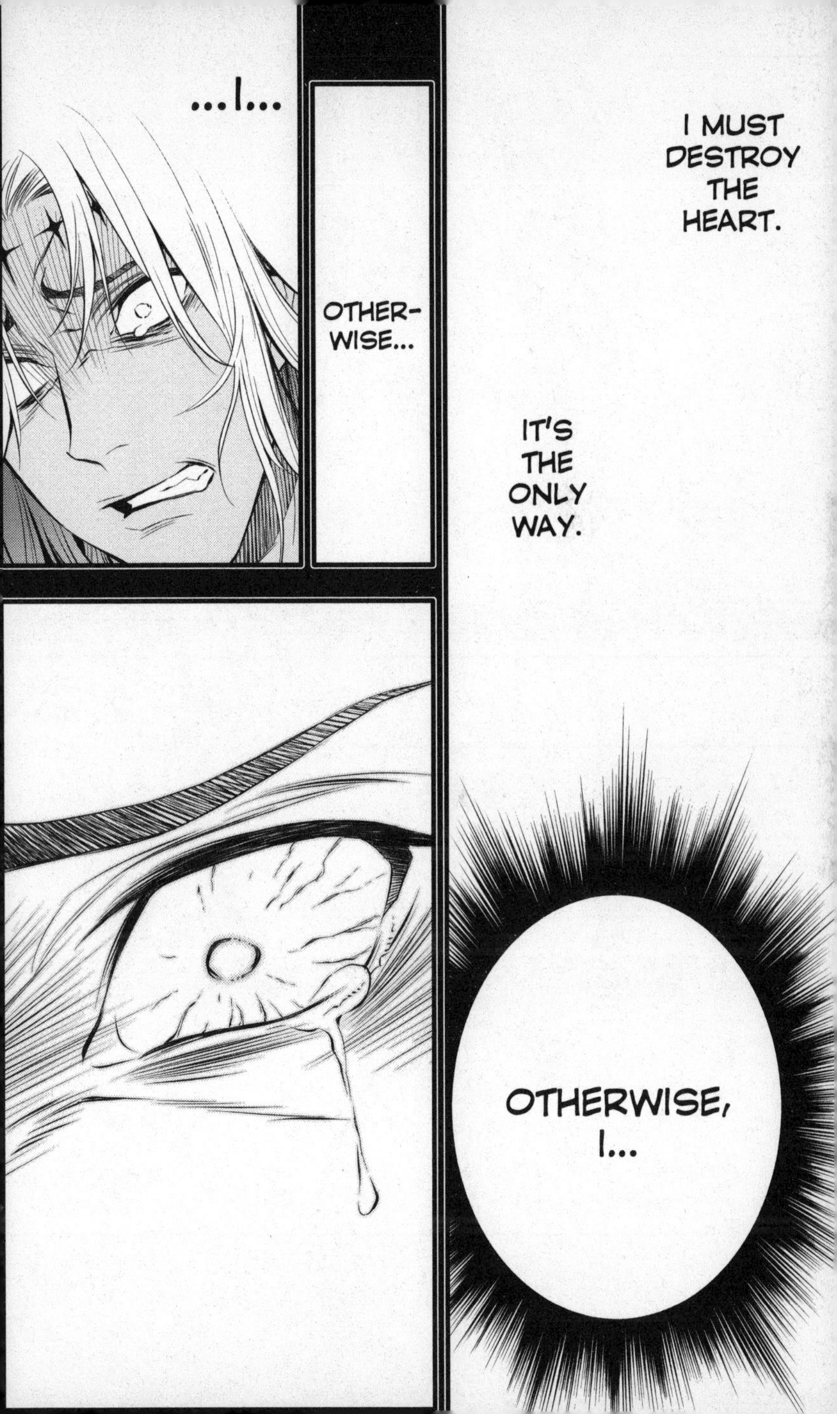
I MUST DESTROY THE HEART.
IT'S THE ONLY WAY.
OTHER-WISE...
...I...
OTHERWISE, I...

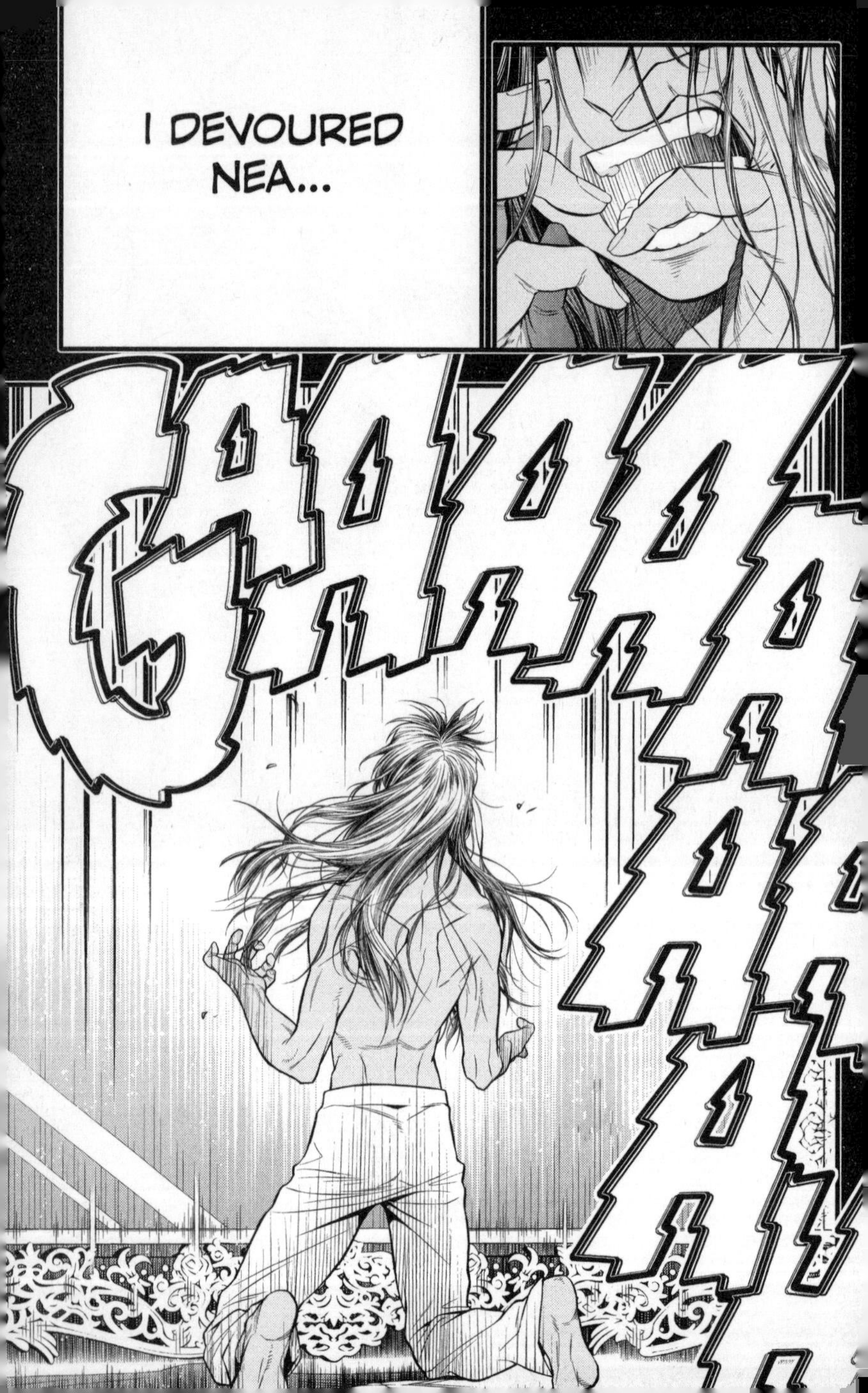
I DEVOURED NEA...

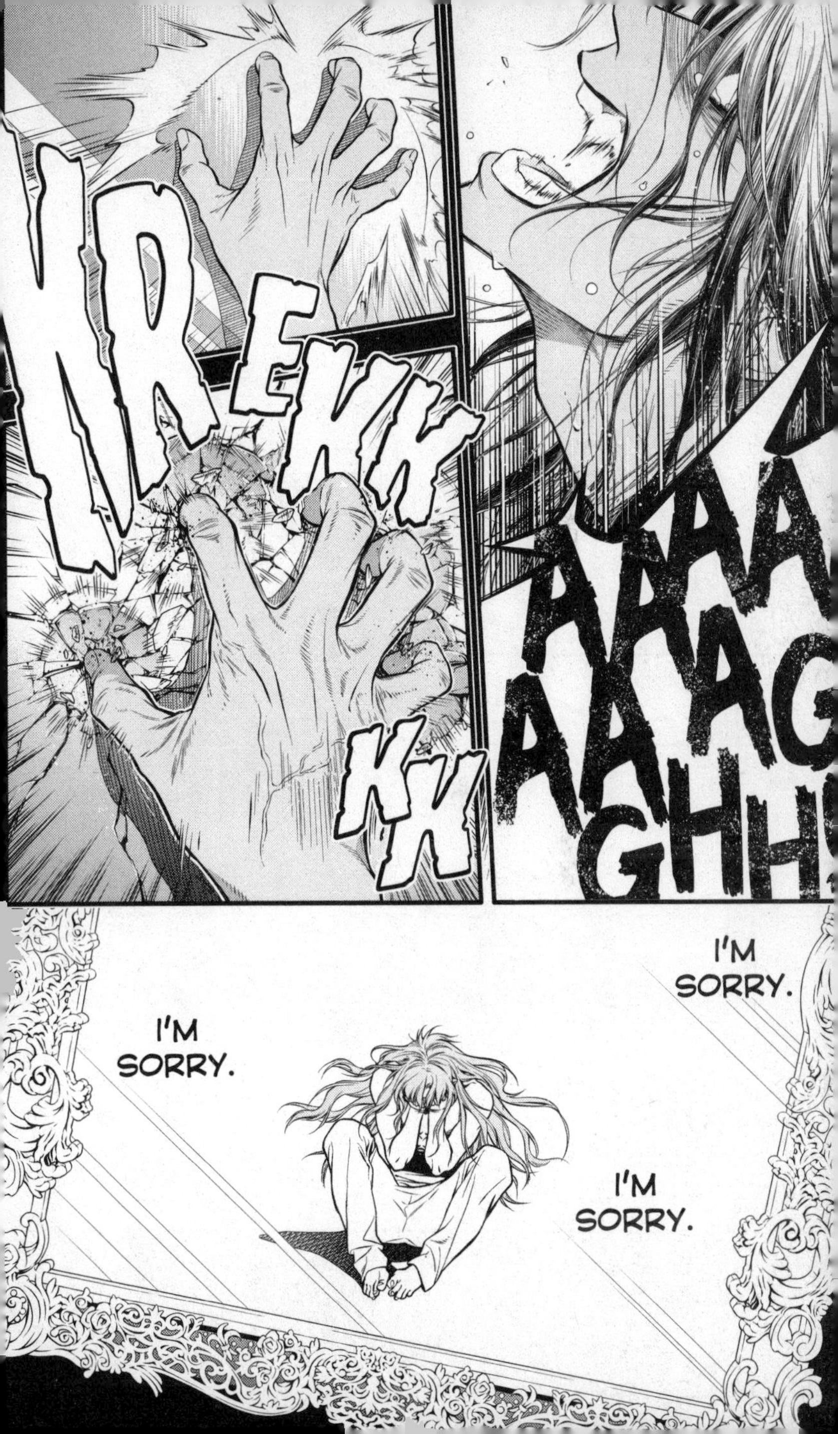
AAAAAAAGHH
KREKK
KK
I'M SORRY.
I'M SORRY.
I'M SORRY.

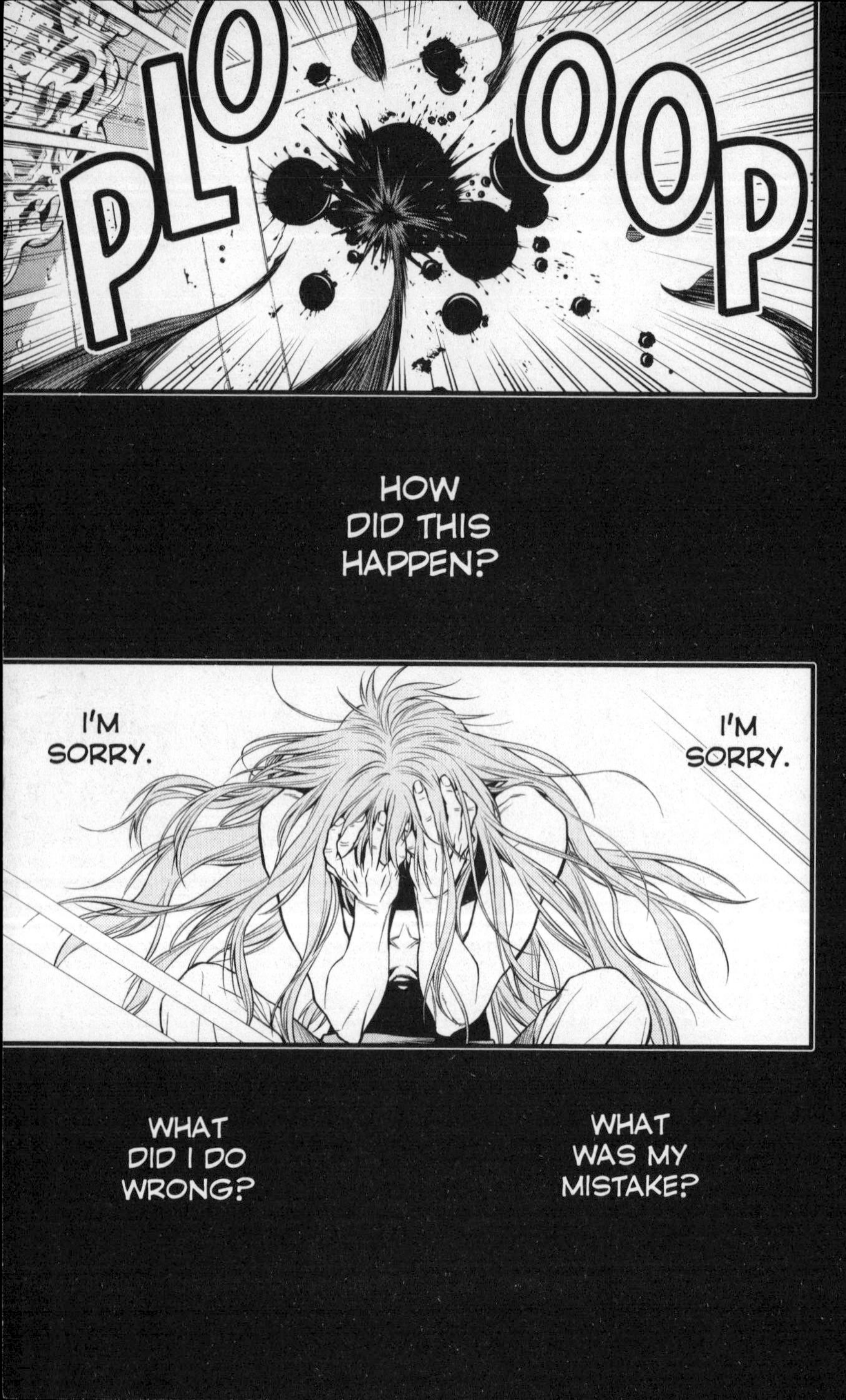
PLOOOOP
HOW DID THIS HAPPEN?
I'M SORRY.
I'M SORRY.
WHAT WAS MY MISTAKE?
WHAT DID I DO WRONG?

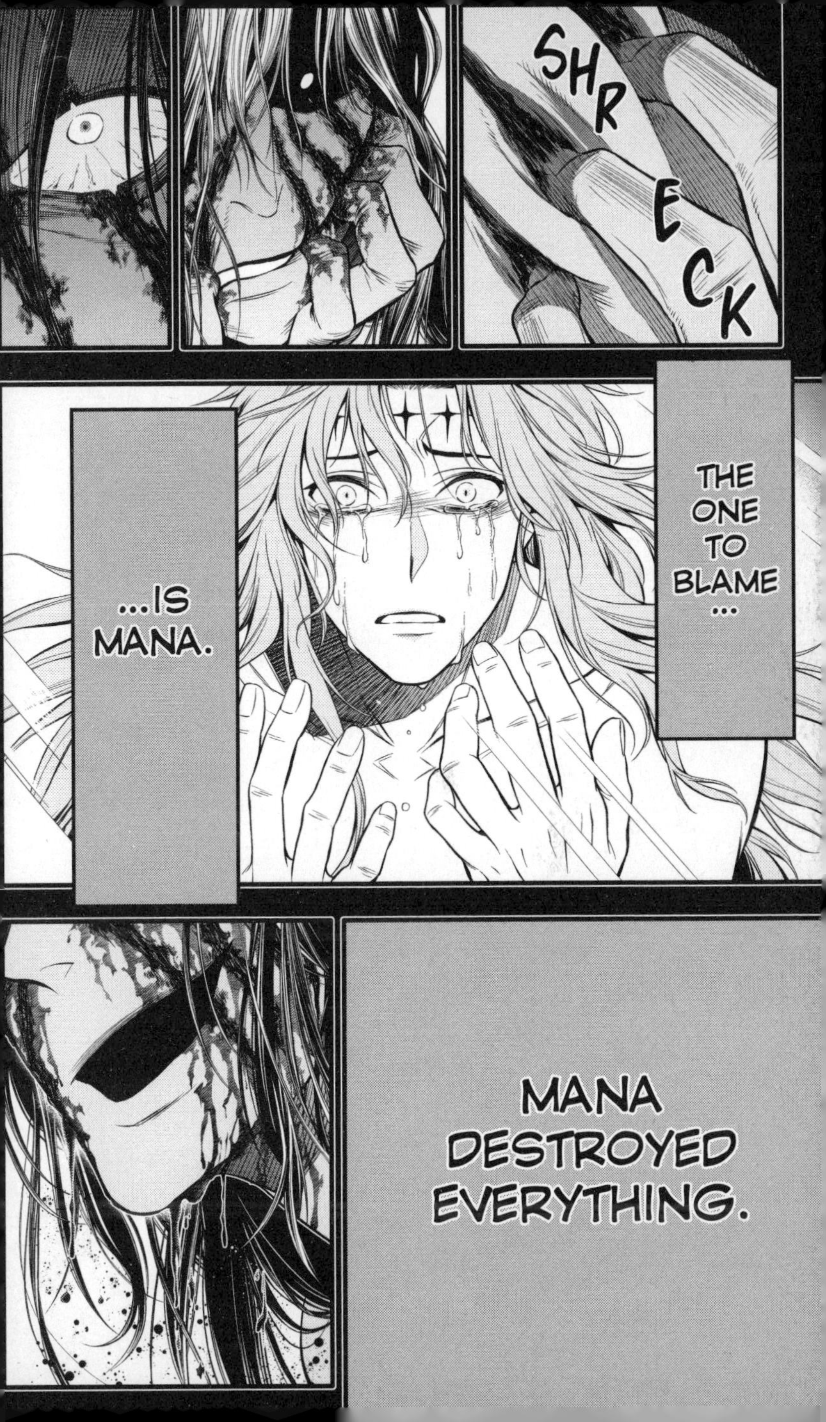
SHRECK
THE ONE TO BLAME...
...IS MANA.
MANA DESTROYED EVERYTHING.

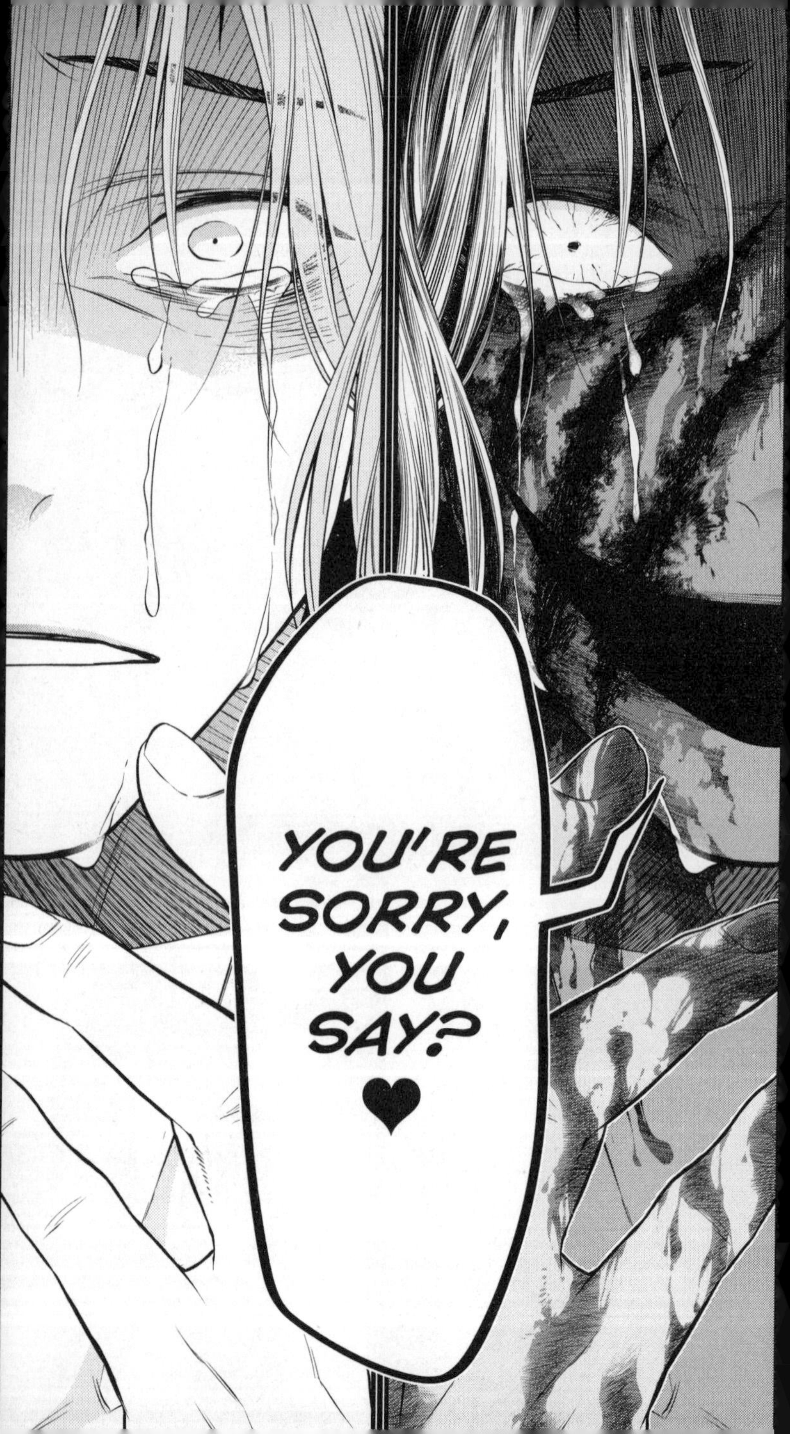
YOU'RE SORRY, YOU SAY? ♥

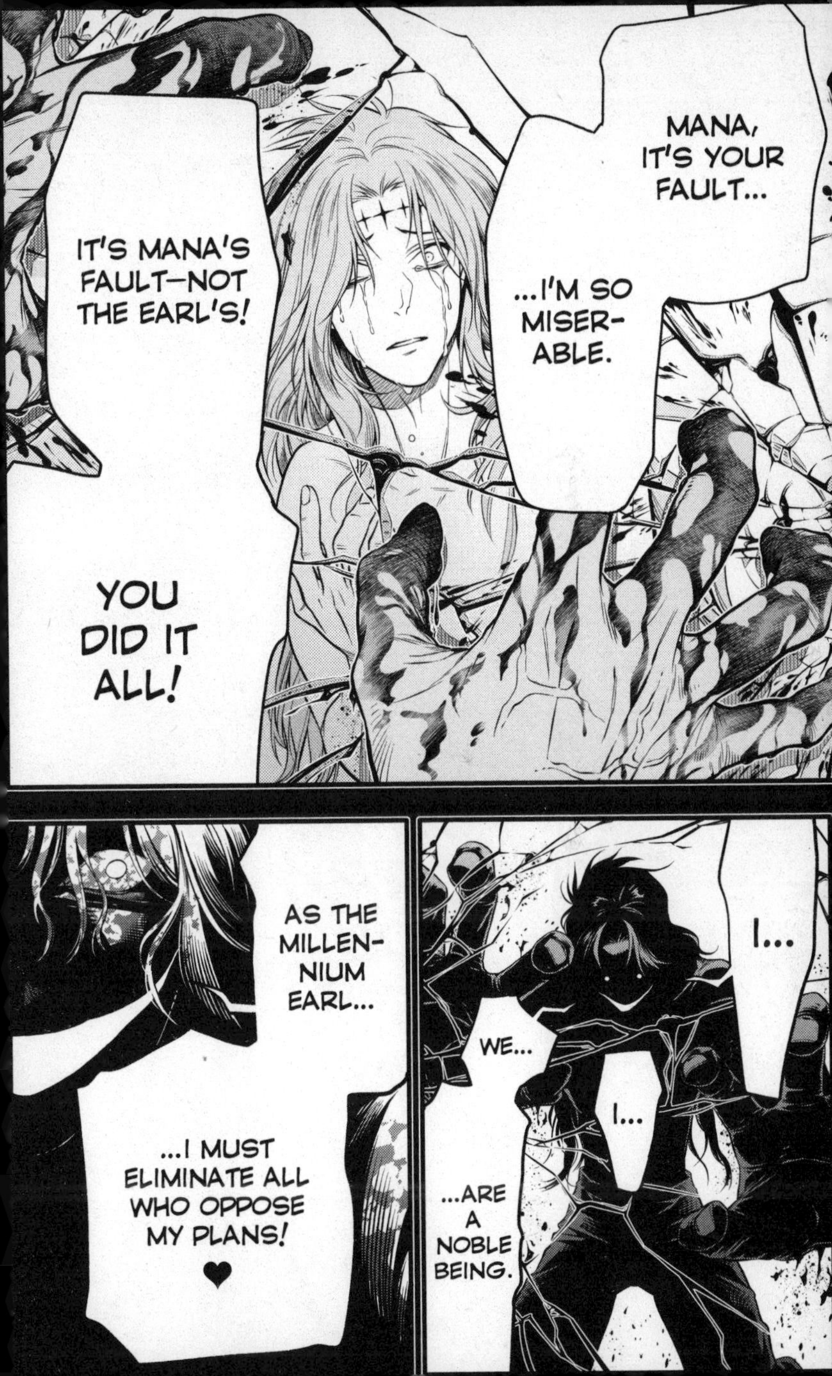
MANA, IT'S YOUR FAULT...
...I'M SO MISERABLE.
IT'S MANA'S FAULT—NOT THE EARL'S!
YOU DID IT ALL!
I...
WE...
I...
...ARE A NOBLE BEING.
AS THE MILLENNIUM EARL...
...I MUST ELIMINATE ALL WHO OPPOSE MY PLANS! ♥

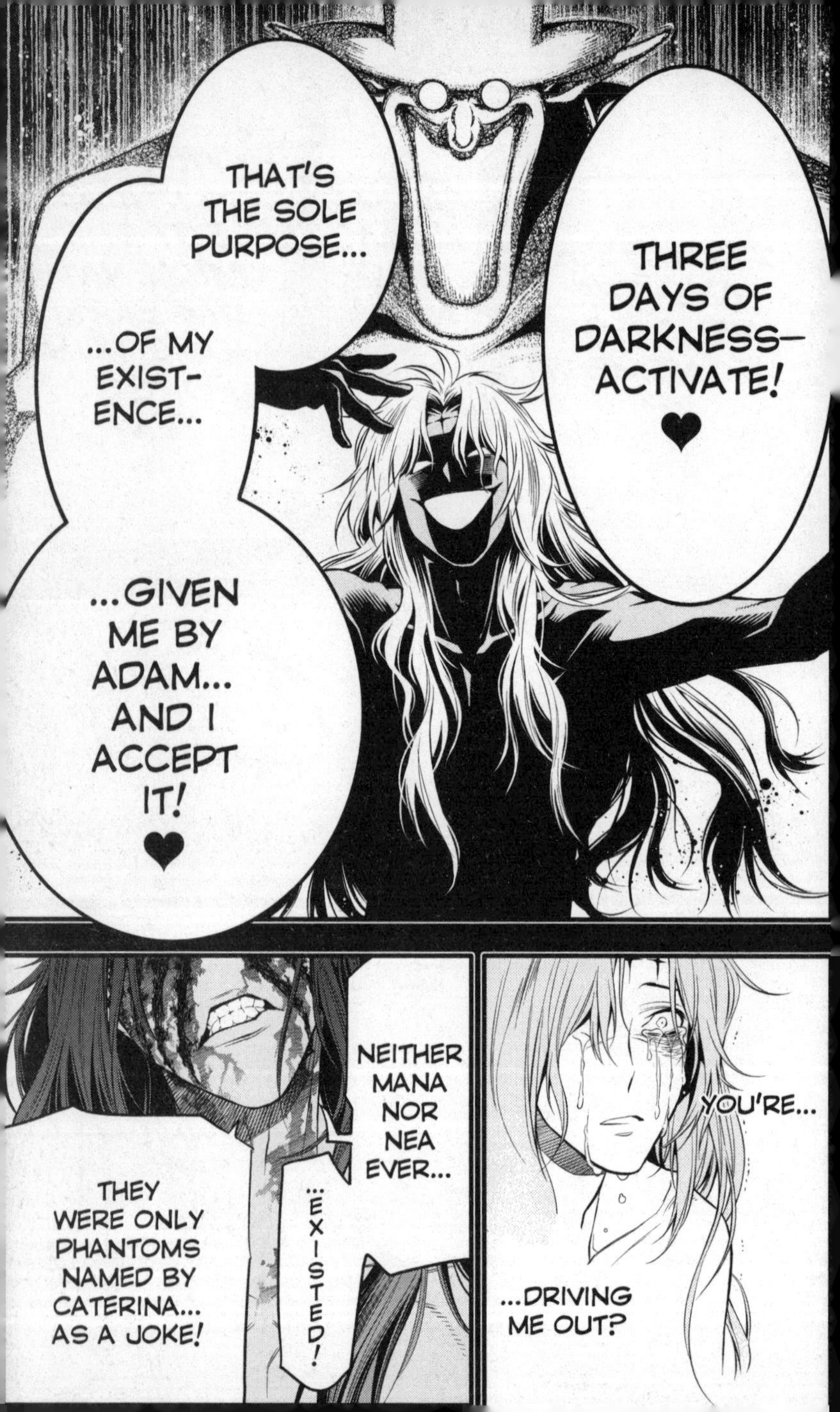
THAT'S THE SOLE PURPOSE...
...OF MY EXIST-ENCE...
...GIVEN ME BY ADAM... AND I ACCEPT IT! ♥
THREE DAYS OF DARKNESS— ACTIVATE! ♥
YOU'RE...
...DRIVING ME OUT?
NEITHER MANA NOR NEA EVER...
...EXISTED!
THEY WERE ONLY PHANTOMS NAMED BY CATERINA... AS A JOKE!

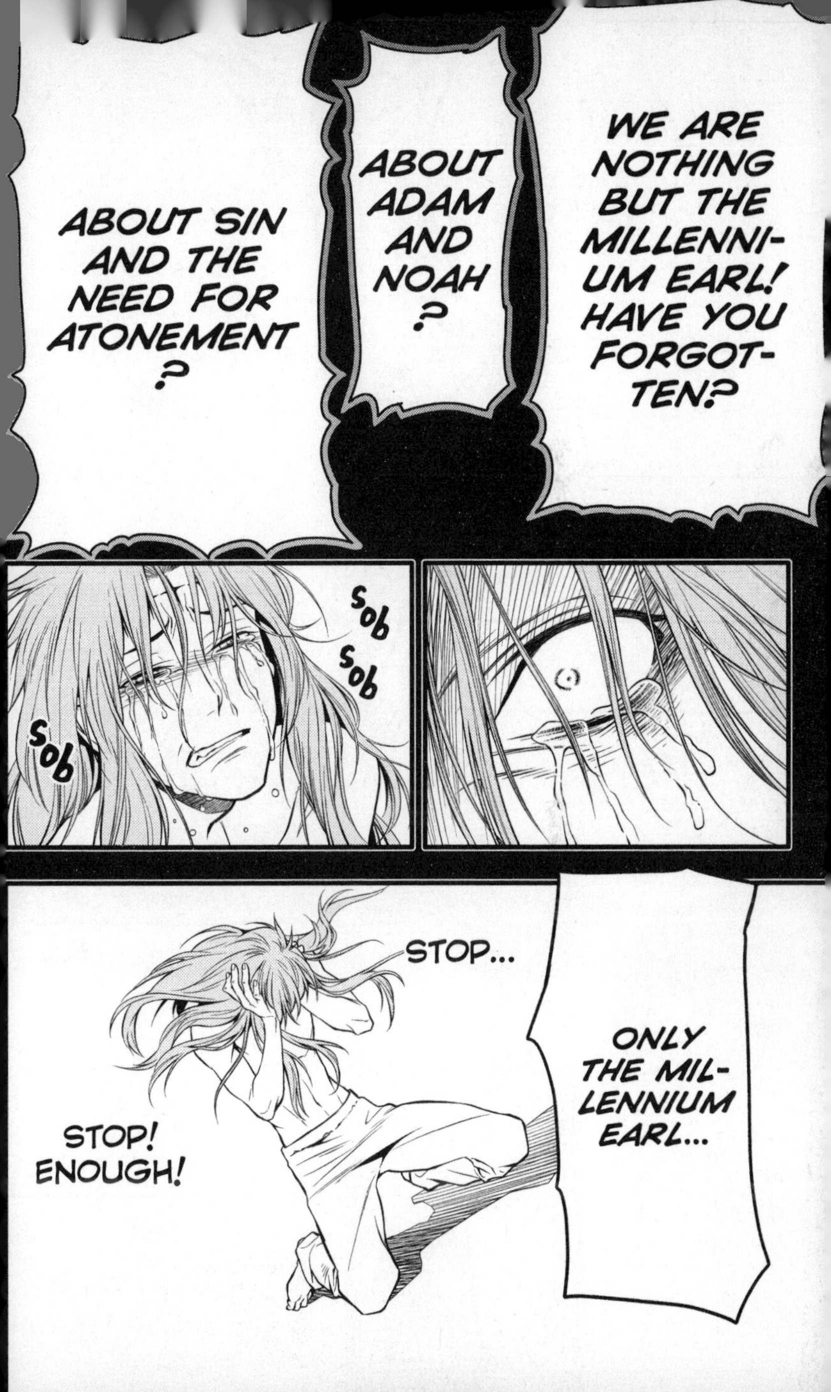
WE ARE NOTHING BUT THE MILLENNIUM EARL! HAVE YOU FORGOTTEN?
ABOUT ADAM AND NOAH?
ABOUT SIN AND THE NEED FOR ATONEMENT?
sob
sob
sob
ONLY THE MILLENNIUM EARL...
STOP...
STOP! ENOUGH!

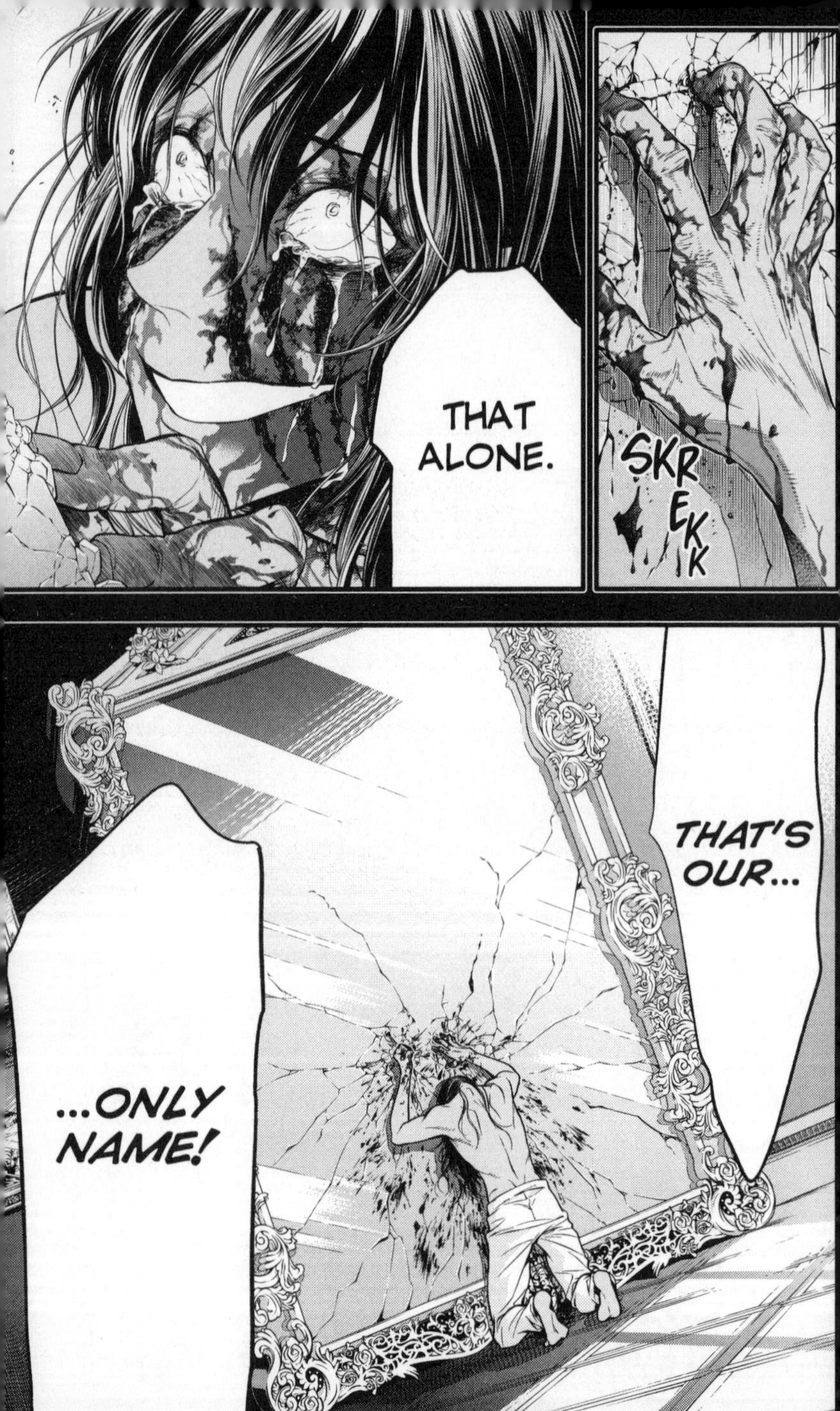
SKREKK
THAT ALONE.
THAT'S OUR...
...ONLY NAME!

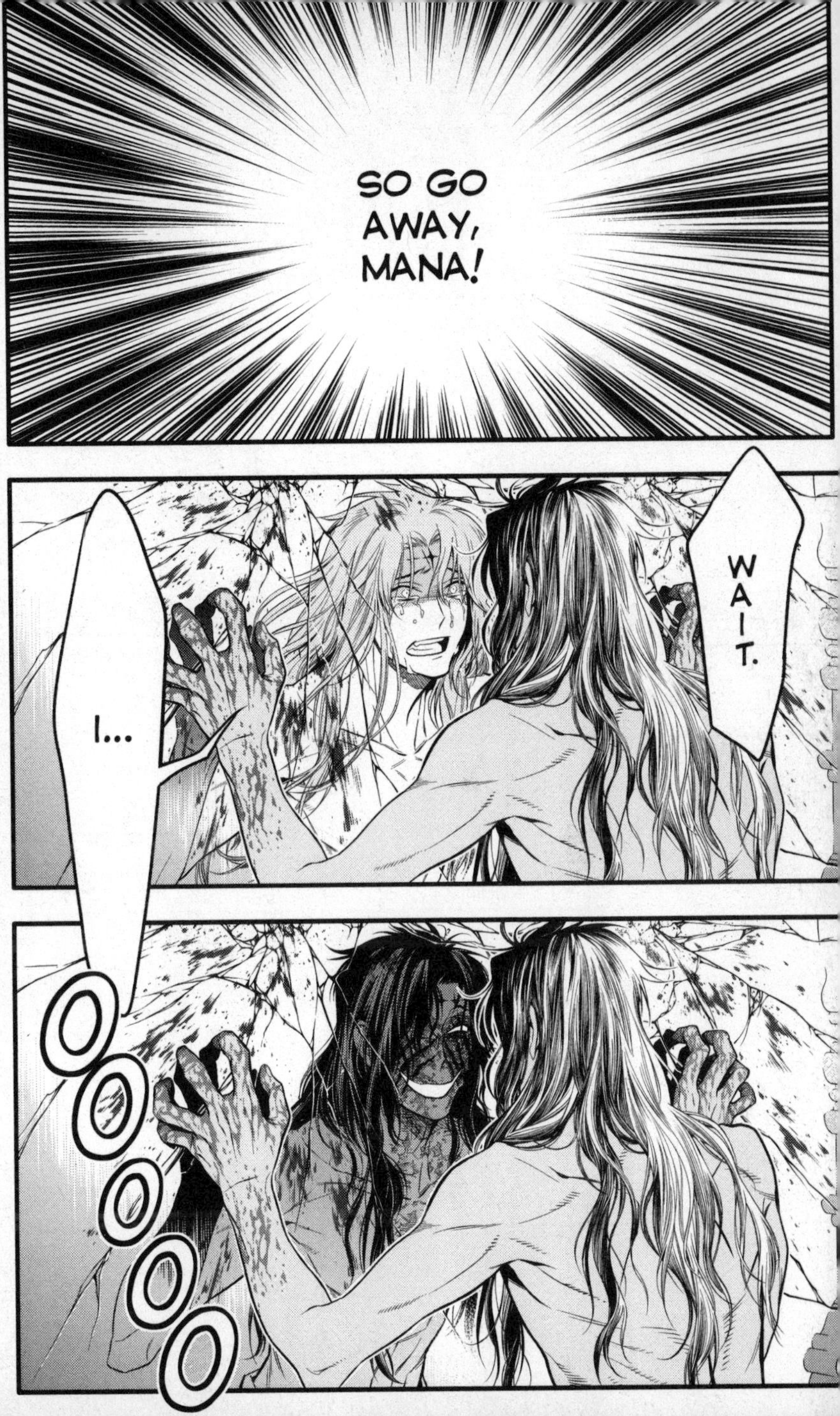
SO GO AWAY, MANA!
WAIT.
I...

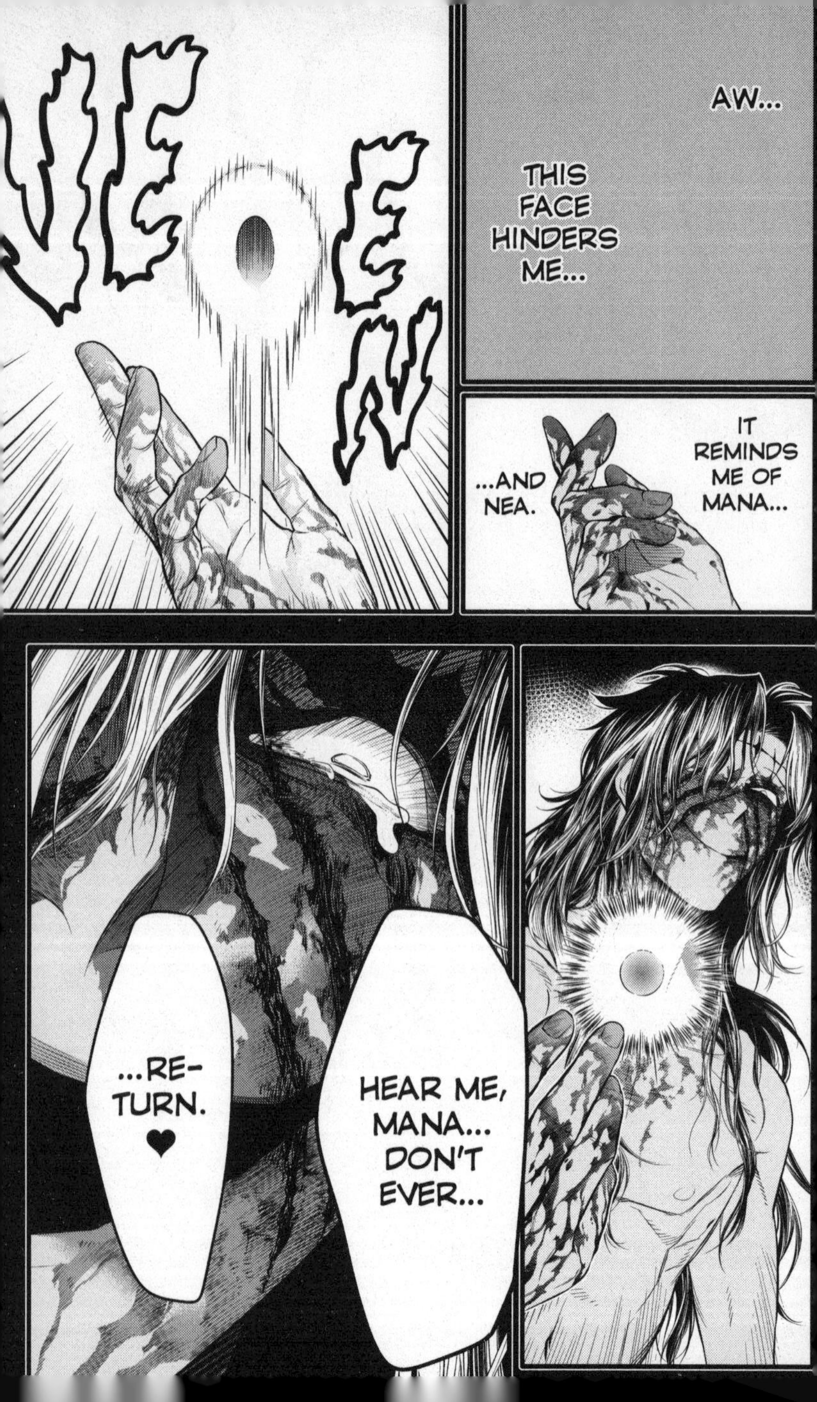
AW...
THIS FACE HINDERS ME...
IT REMINDS ME OF MANA...
...AND NEA.
HEAR ME, MANA... DON'T EVER...
...RE-TURN. ♥

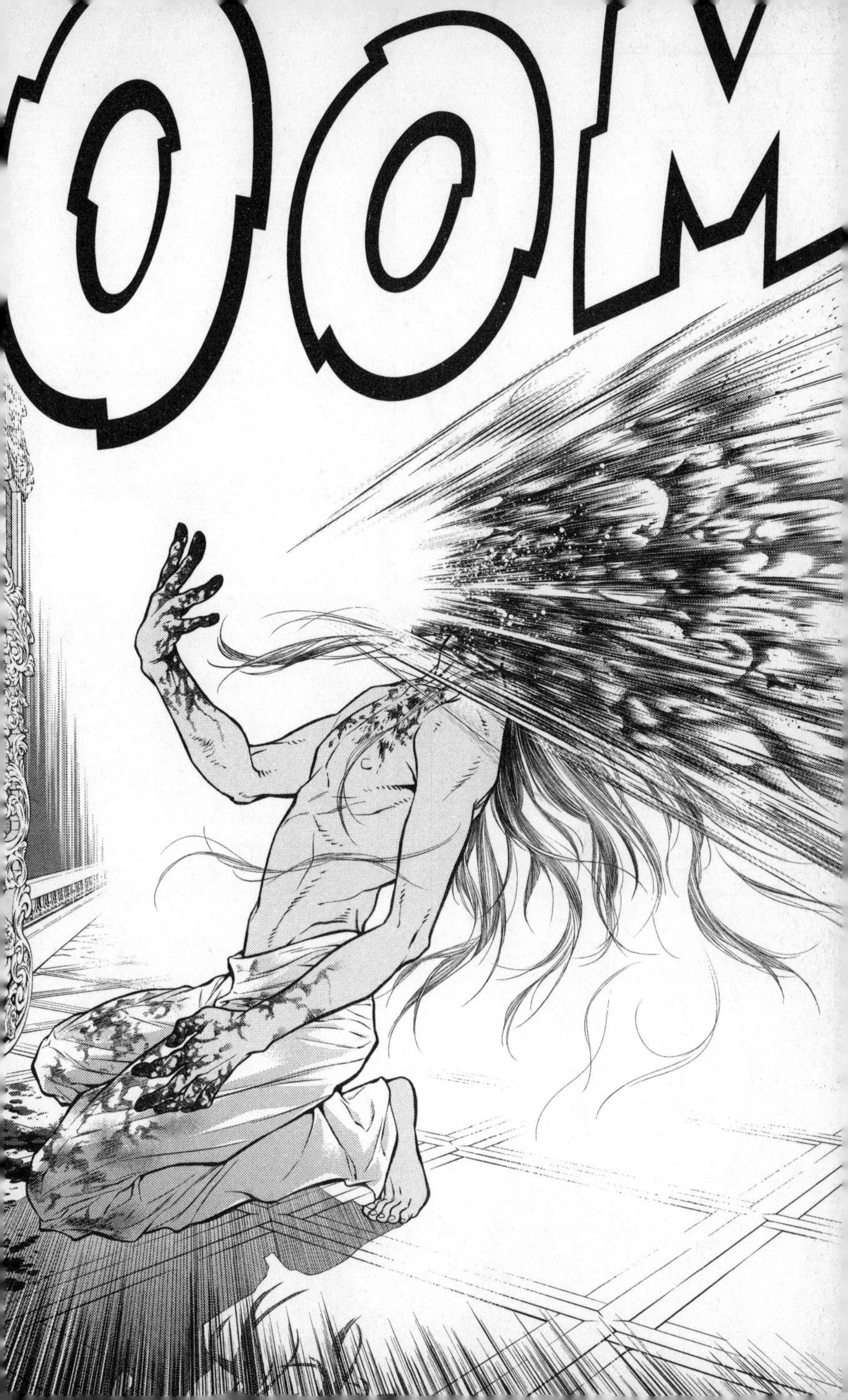
OOM

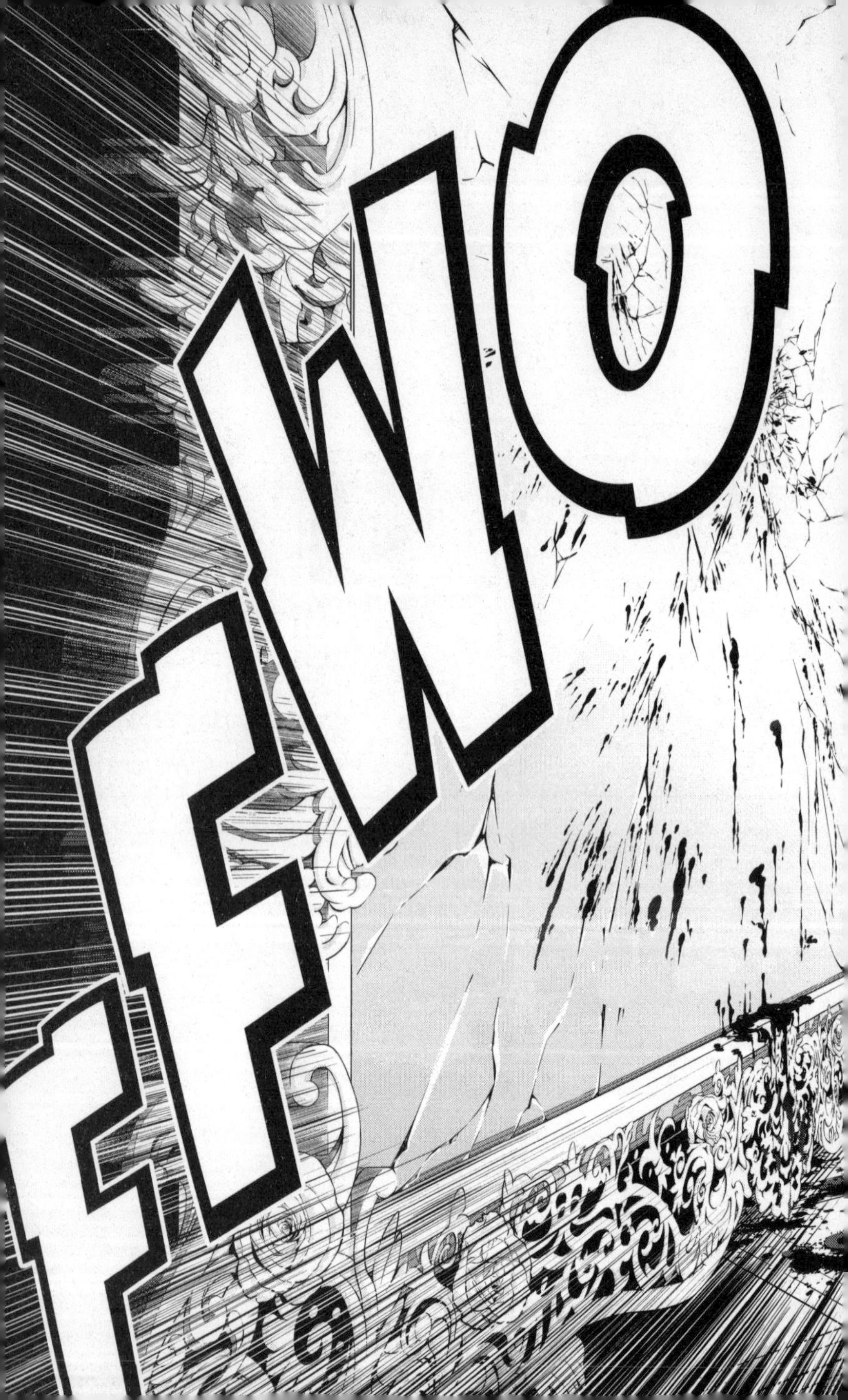
FWO

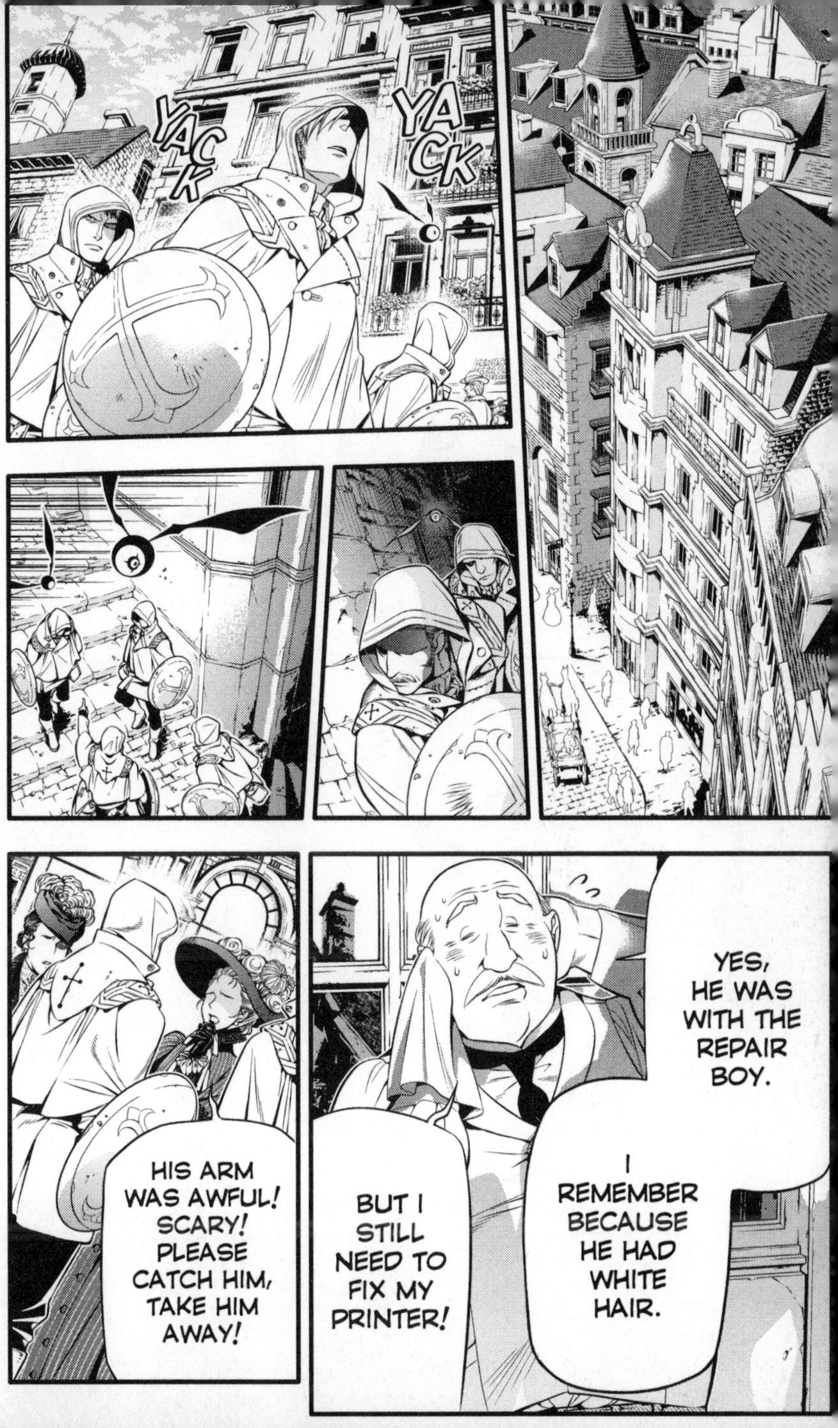
YACK
YACK
YES, HE WAS WITH THE REPAIR BOY.
I REMEMBER BECAUSE HE HAD WHITE HAIR.
BUT I STILL NEED TO FIX MY PRINTER!
HIS ARM WAS AWFUL! SCARY! PLEASE CATCH HIM, TAKE HIM AWAY!

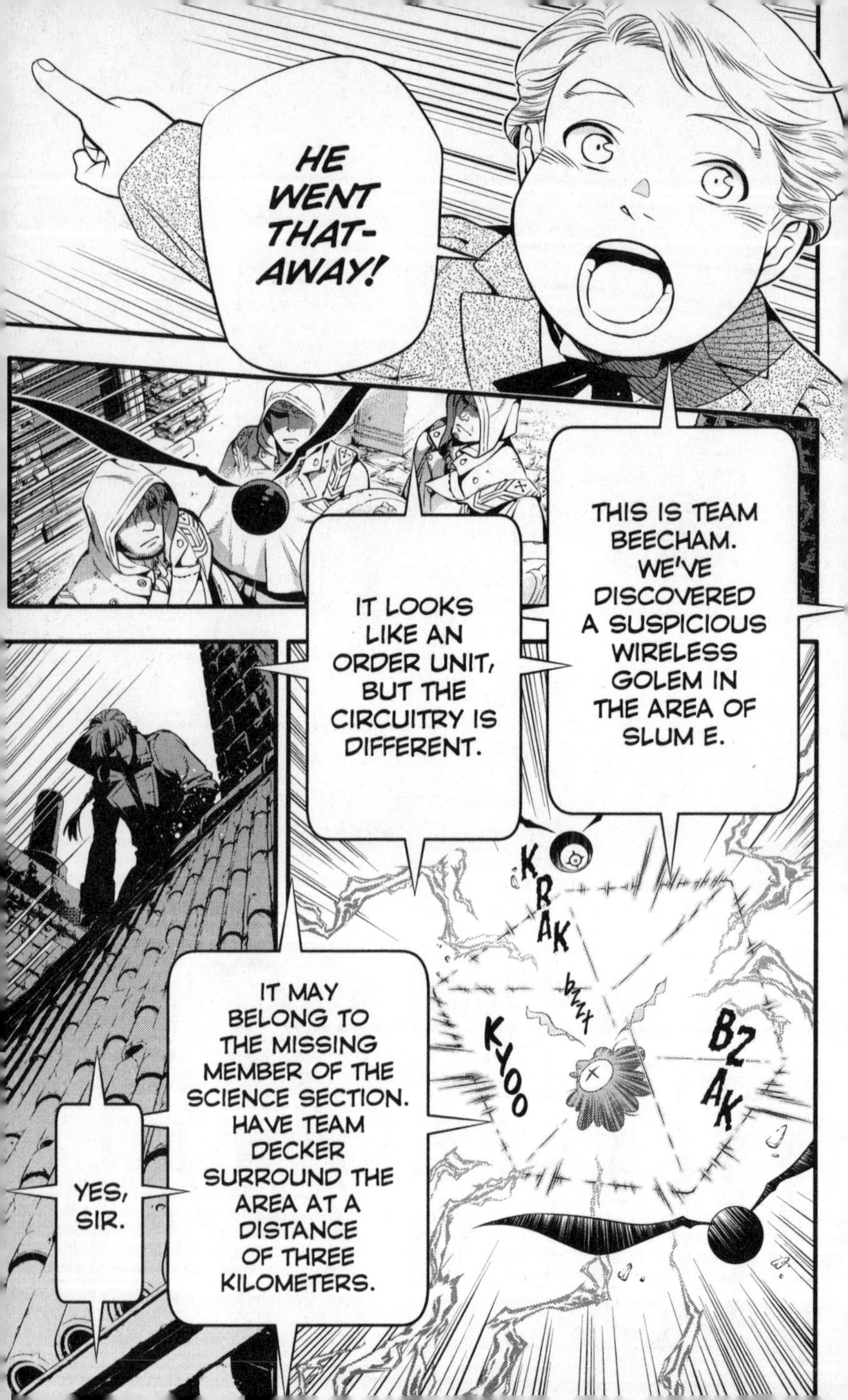
HE WENT THAT-AWAY!
THIS IS TEAM BEECHAM. WE'VE DISCOVERED A SUSPICIOUS WIRELESS GOLEM IN THE AREA OF SLUM E.
IT LOOKS LIKE AN ORDER UNIT, BUT THE CIRCUITRY IS DIFFERENT.
KRAK
BZAK
bzzt
KYOO
IT MAY BELONG TO THE MISSING MEMBER OF THE SCIENCE SECTION. HAVE TEAM DECKER SURROUND THE AREA AT A DISTANCE OF THREE KILOMETERS.
YES, SIR.

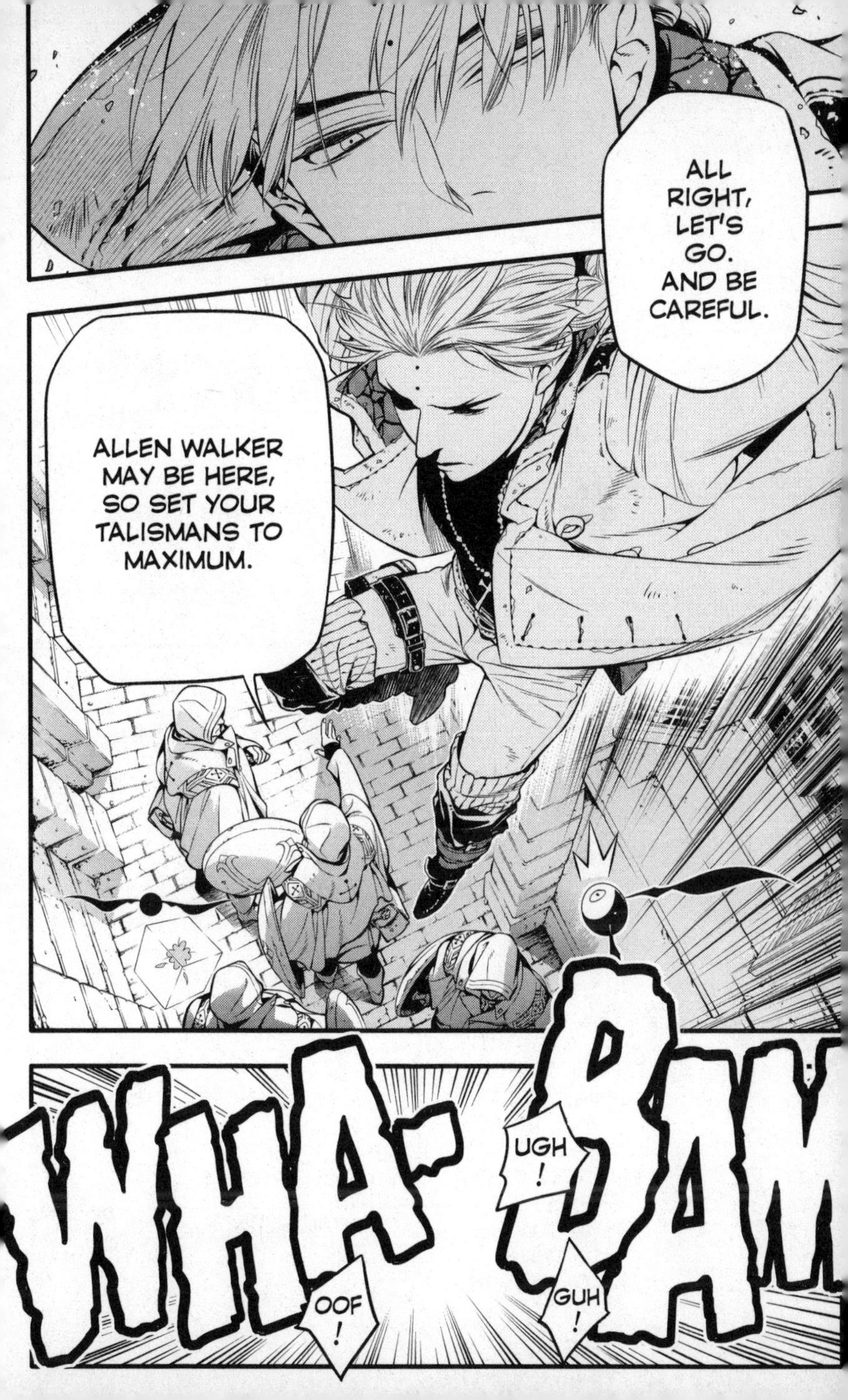
ALL RIGHT, LET'S GO. AND BE CAREFUL.
ALLEN WALKER MAY BE HERE, SO SET YOUR TALISMANS TO MAXIMUM.
WHA-BAM
UGH!
GUH!
OOF!

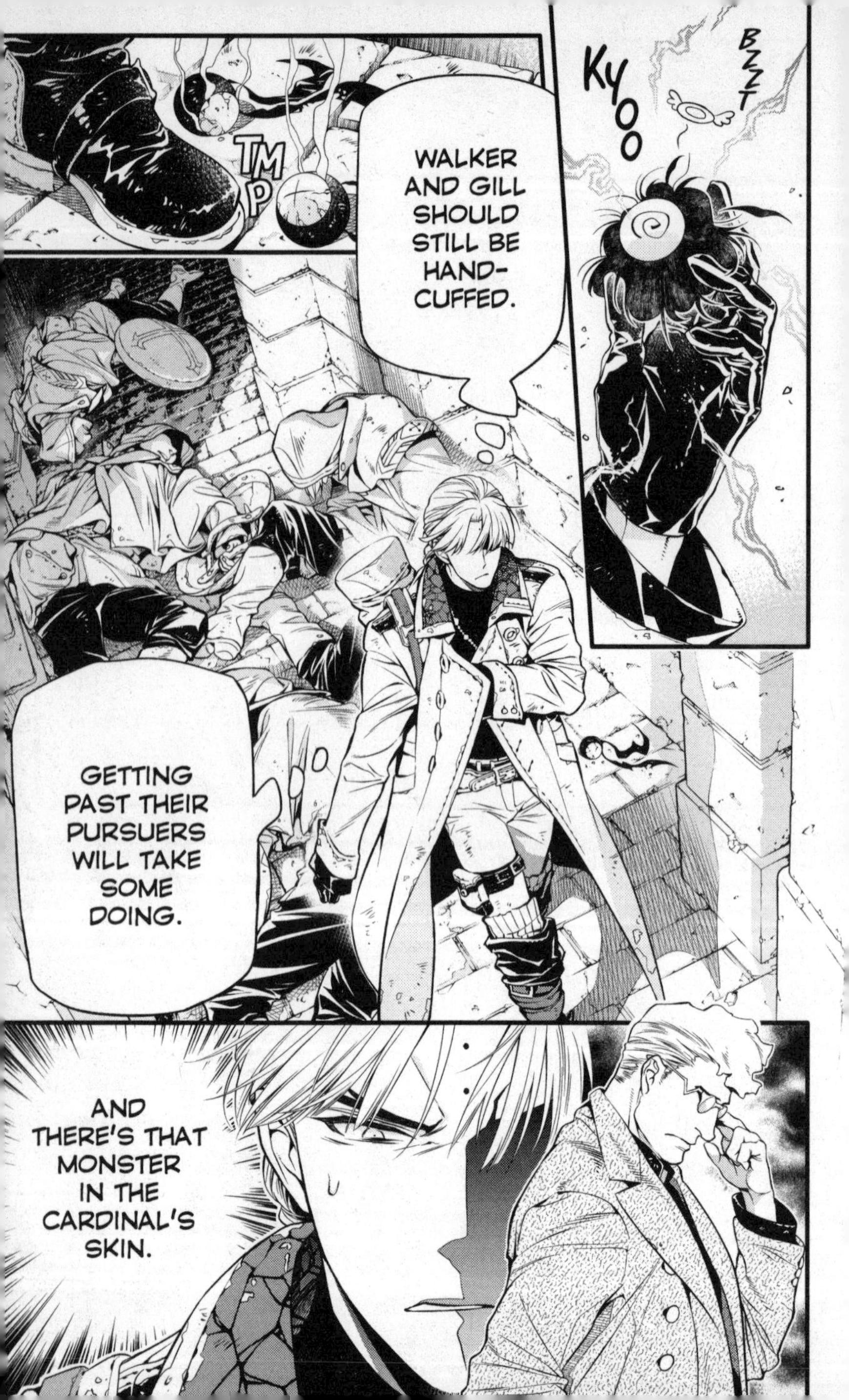
BZZT
KYOO
TMP
WALKER AND GILL SHOULD STILL BE HAND-CUFFED.
GETTING PAST THEIR PURSUERS WILL TAKE SOME DOING.
AND THERE'S THAT MONSTER IN THE CARDINAL'S SKIN.

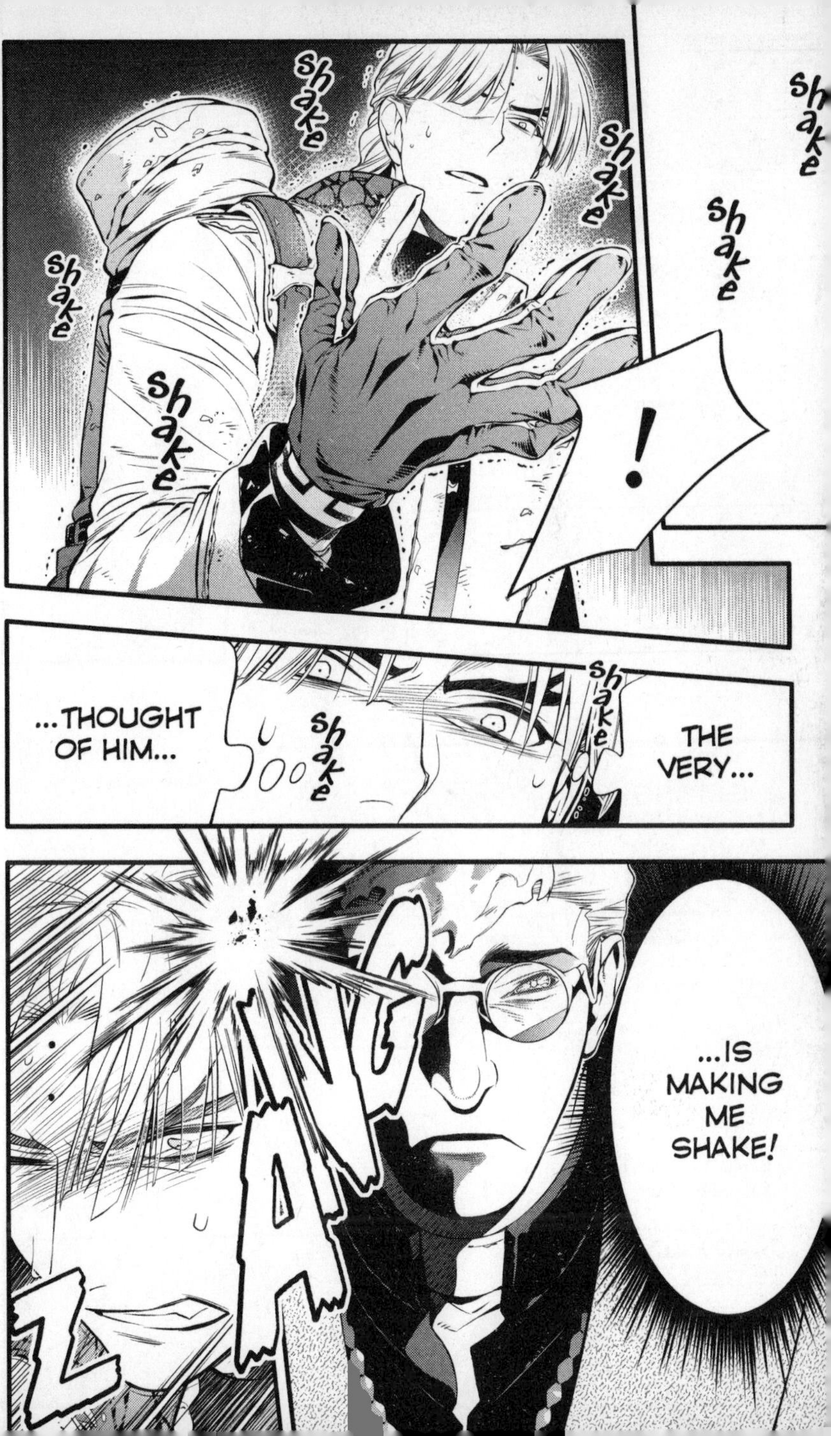
shake
shake
!
shake
shake
shake
shake
THE VERY...
shake
shake
...THOUGHT OF HIM...
...IS MAKING ME SHAKE!

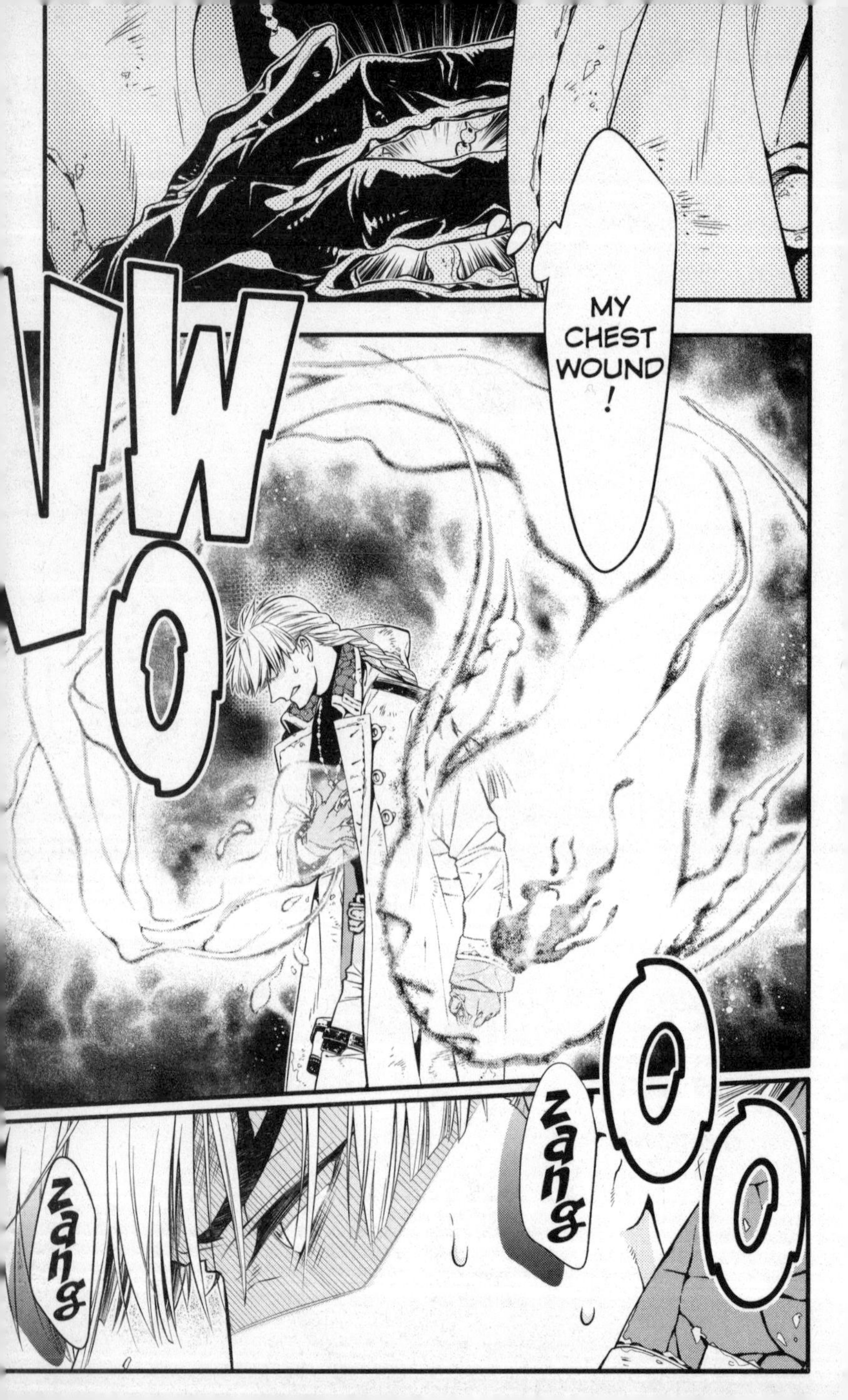
MY CHEST WOUND!
VWOOO
OOO
Zang
Zang

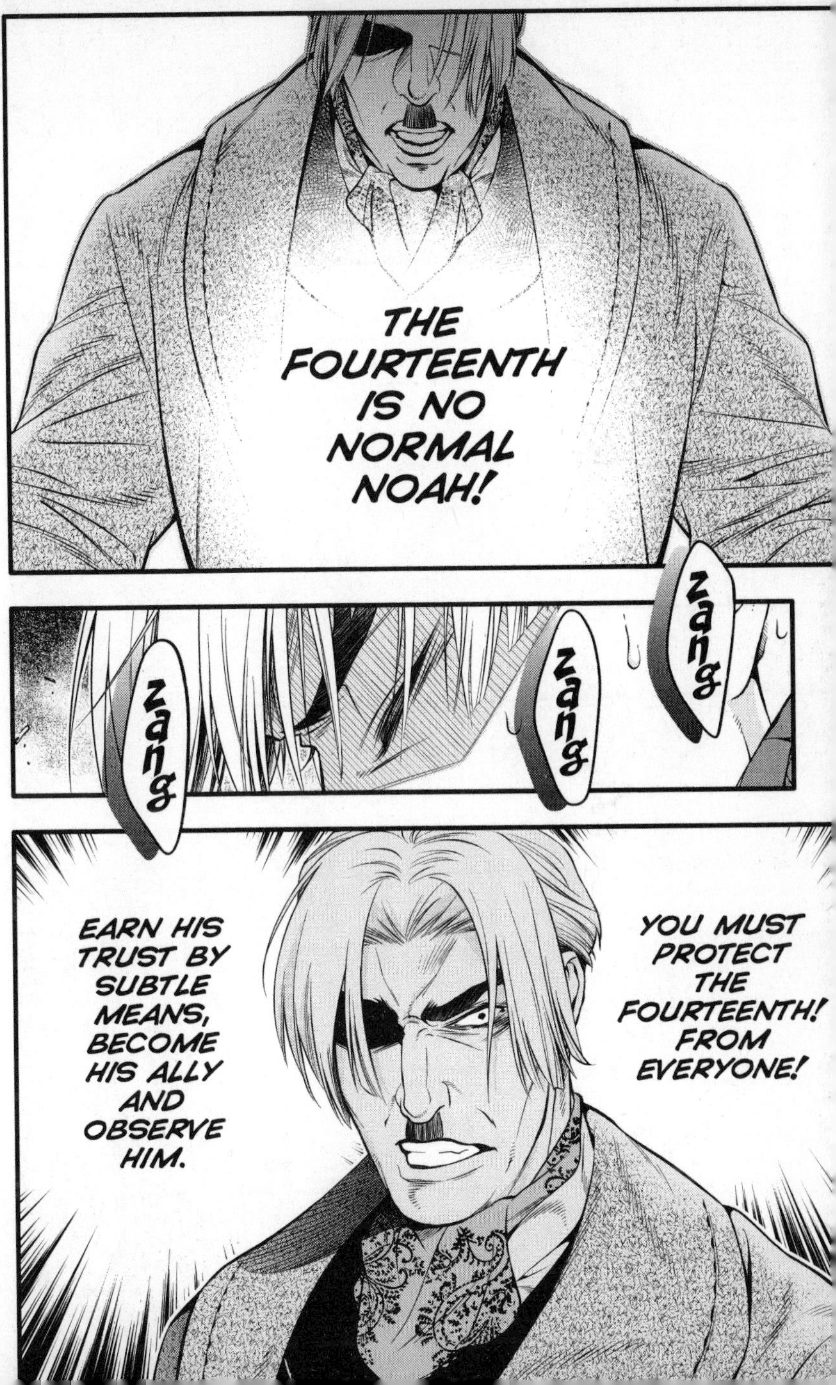
THE FOURTEENTH IS NO NORMAL NOAH!
zang
zang
zang
YOU MUST PROTECT THE FOURTEENTH! FROM EVERYONE!
EARN HIS TRUST BY SUBTLE MEANS, BECOME HIS ALLY AND OBSERVE HIM.

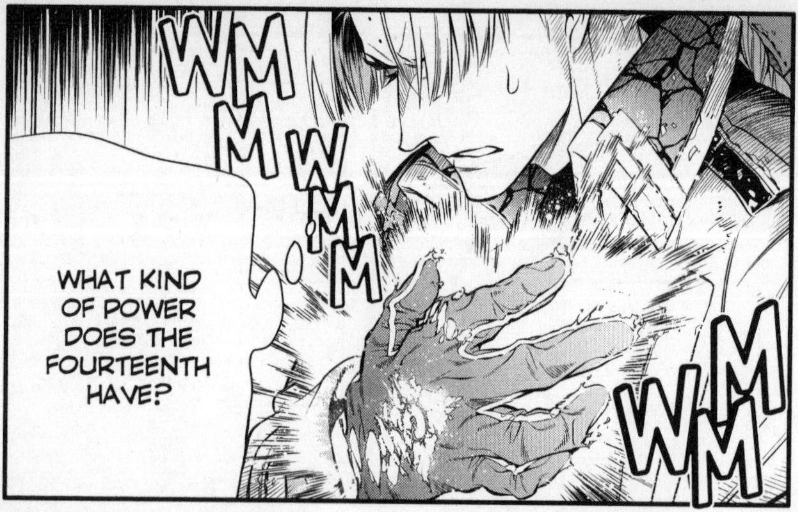
WMMM
WMMM
WHAT KIND OF POWER DOES THE FOURTEENTH HAVE?
WMMM
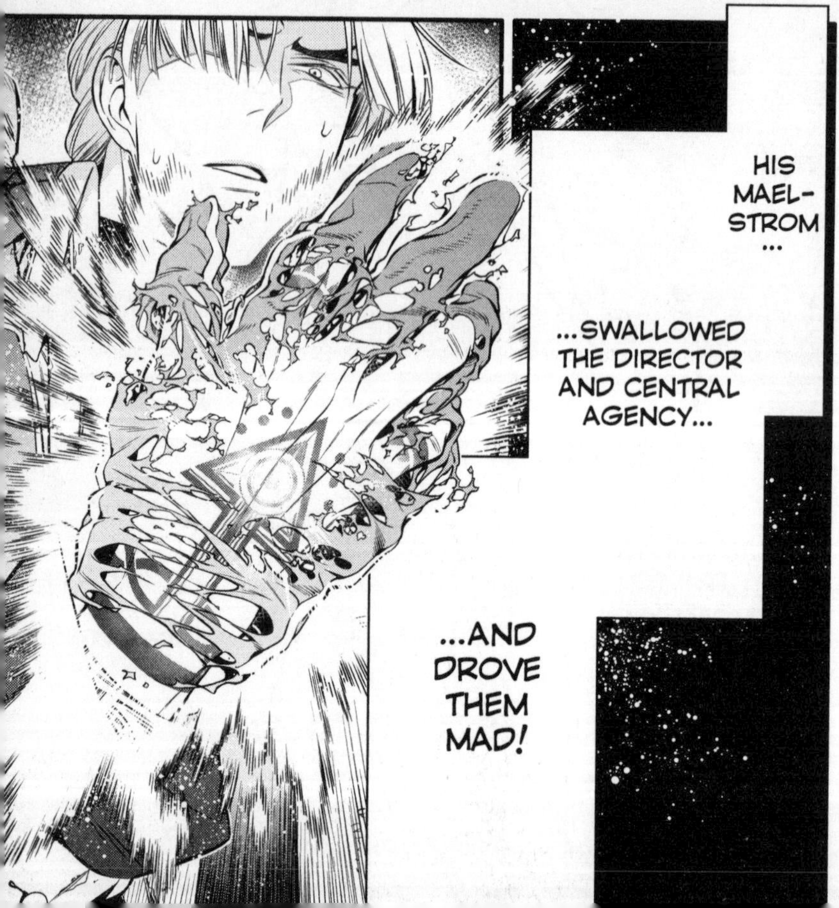
HIS MAEL-STROM...
...SWALLOWED THE DIRECTOR AND CENTRAL AGENCY...
...AND DROVE THEM MAD!

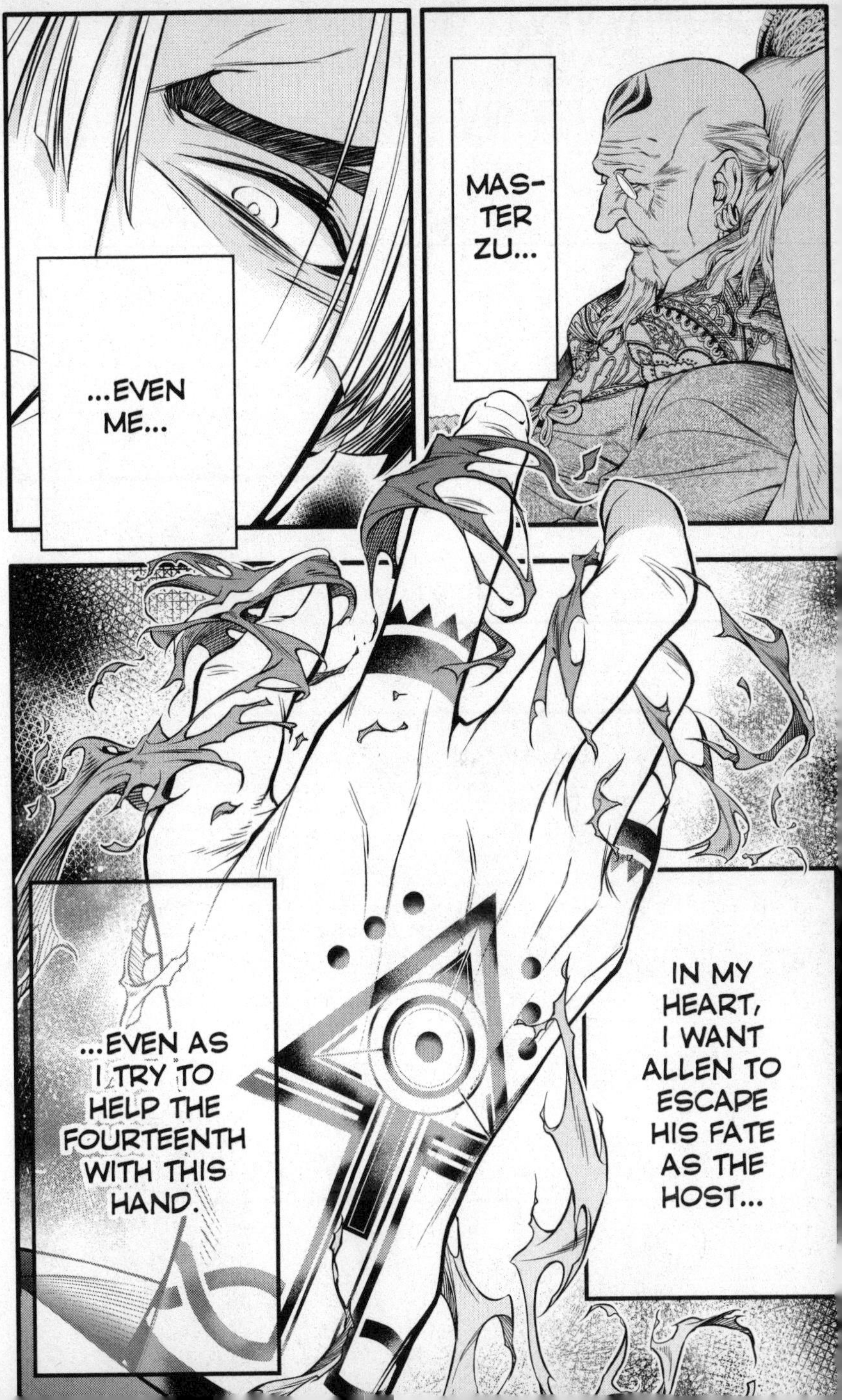
MAS-TER ZU...
...EVEN ME...
IN MY HEART, I WANT ALLEN TO ESCAPE HIS FATE AS THE HOST...
...EVEN AS I TRY TO HELP THE FOURTEENTH WITH THIS HAND.

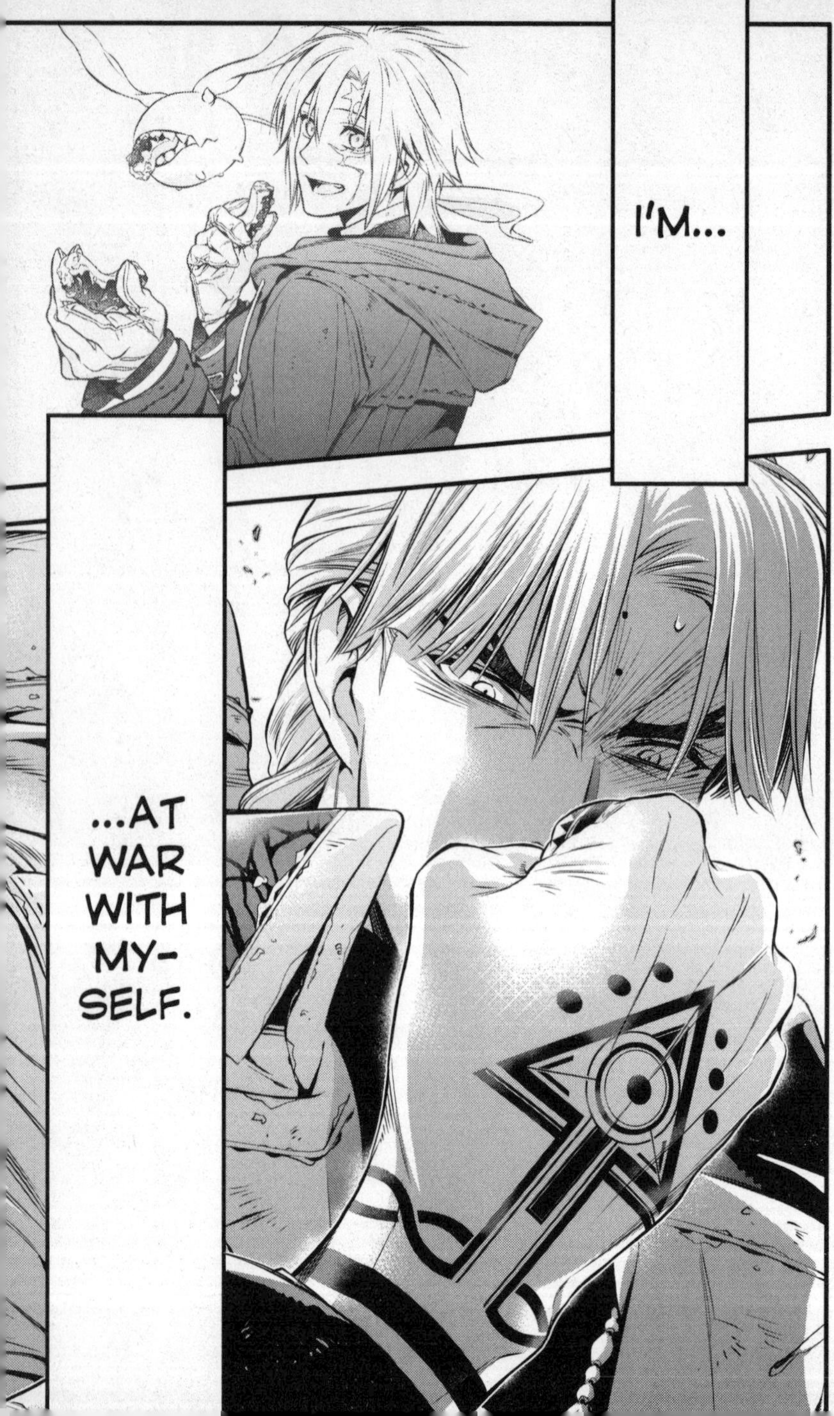
I'M...
...AT WAR WITH MY-SELF.

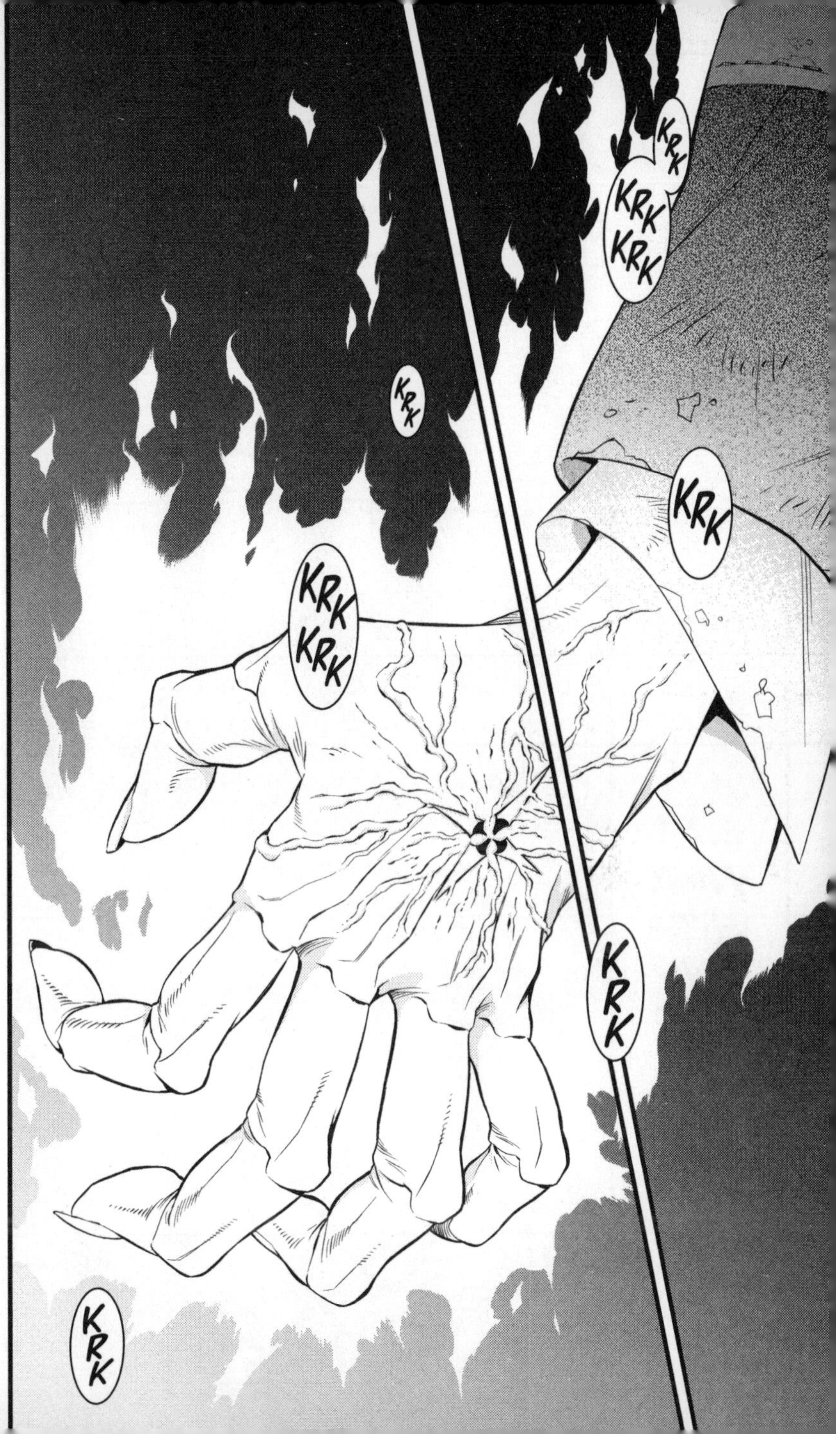
KRK
KRK KRK
KRK
KRK
KRK
KRK KRK
KRK

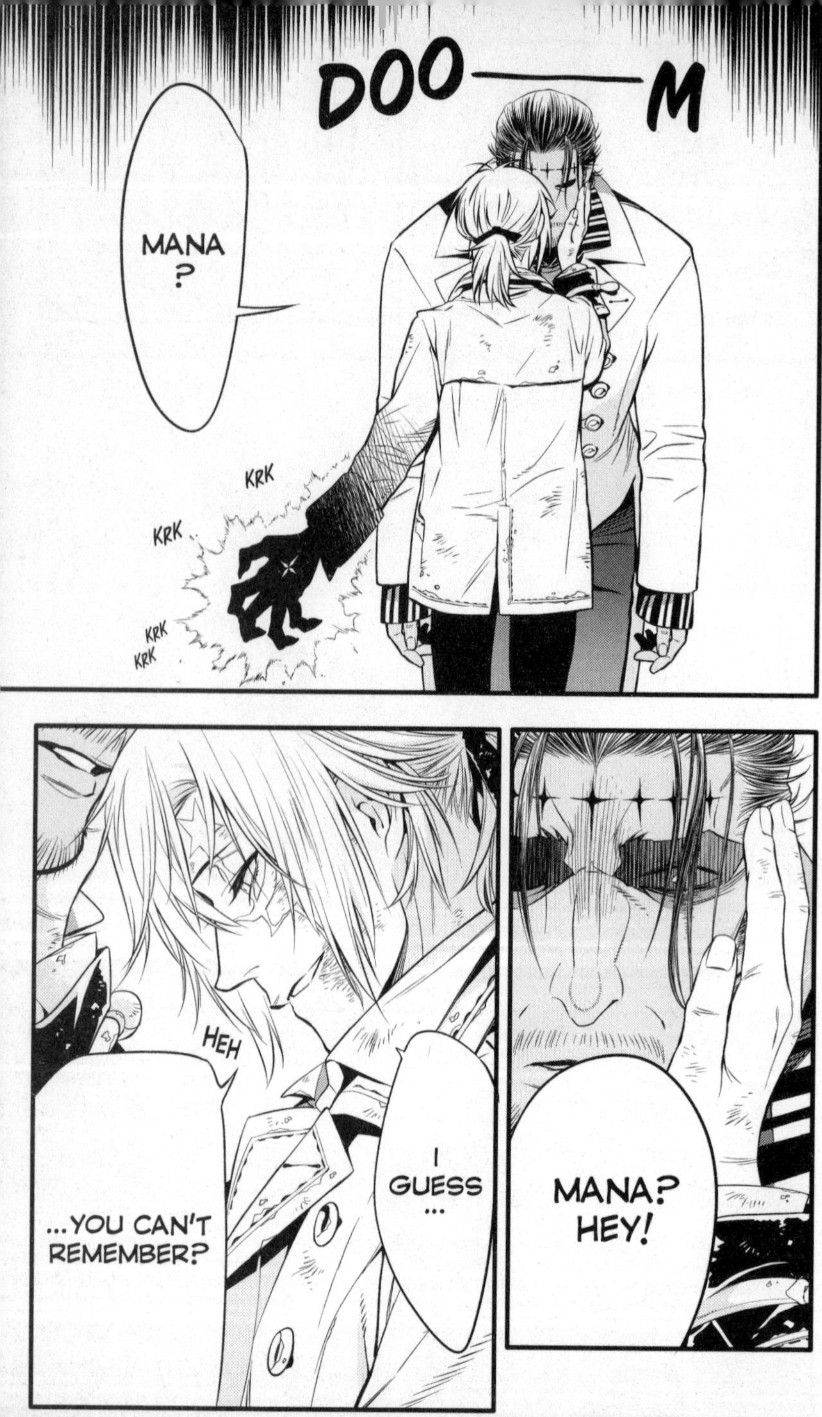
DOO——M
MANA?
KRK
KRK
KRK
KRK
MANA? HEY!
HEH
I GUESS...
...YOU CAN'T REMEMBER?

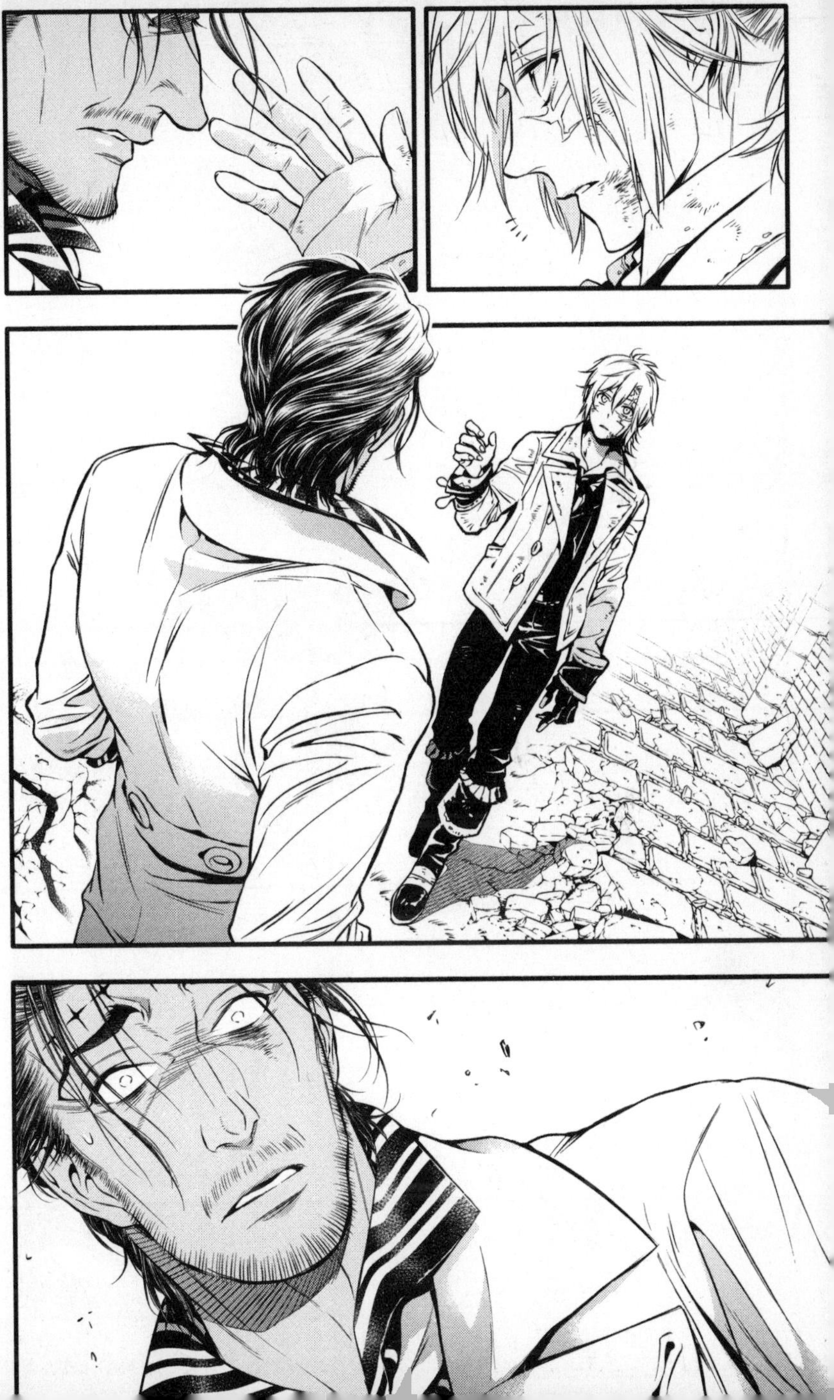

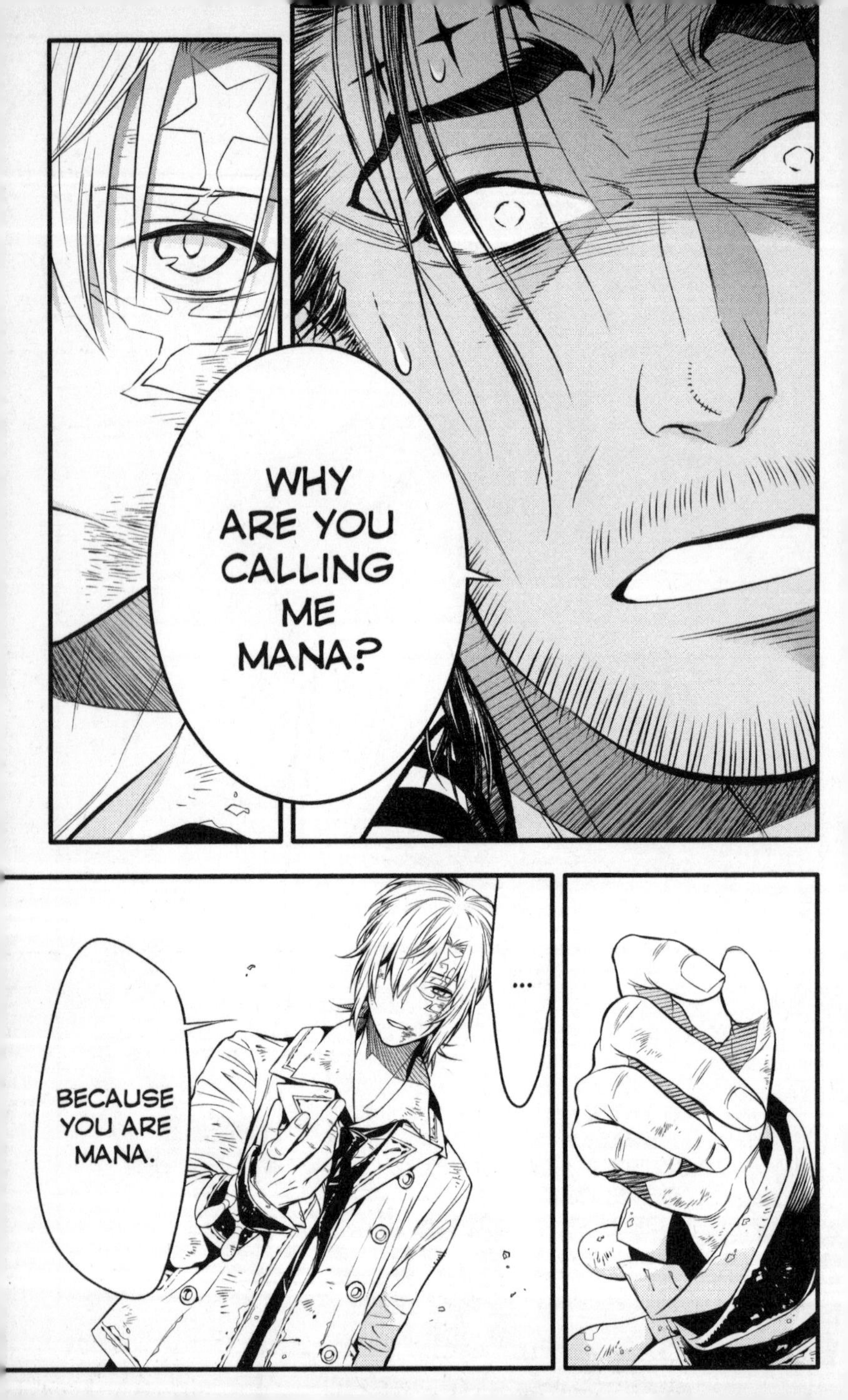
WHY ARE YOU CALLING ME MANA?
...
BECAUSE YOU ARE MANA.

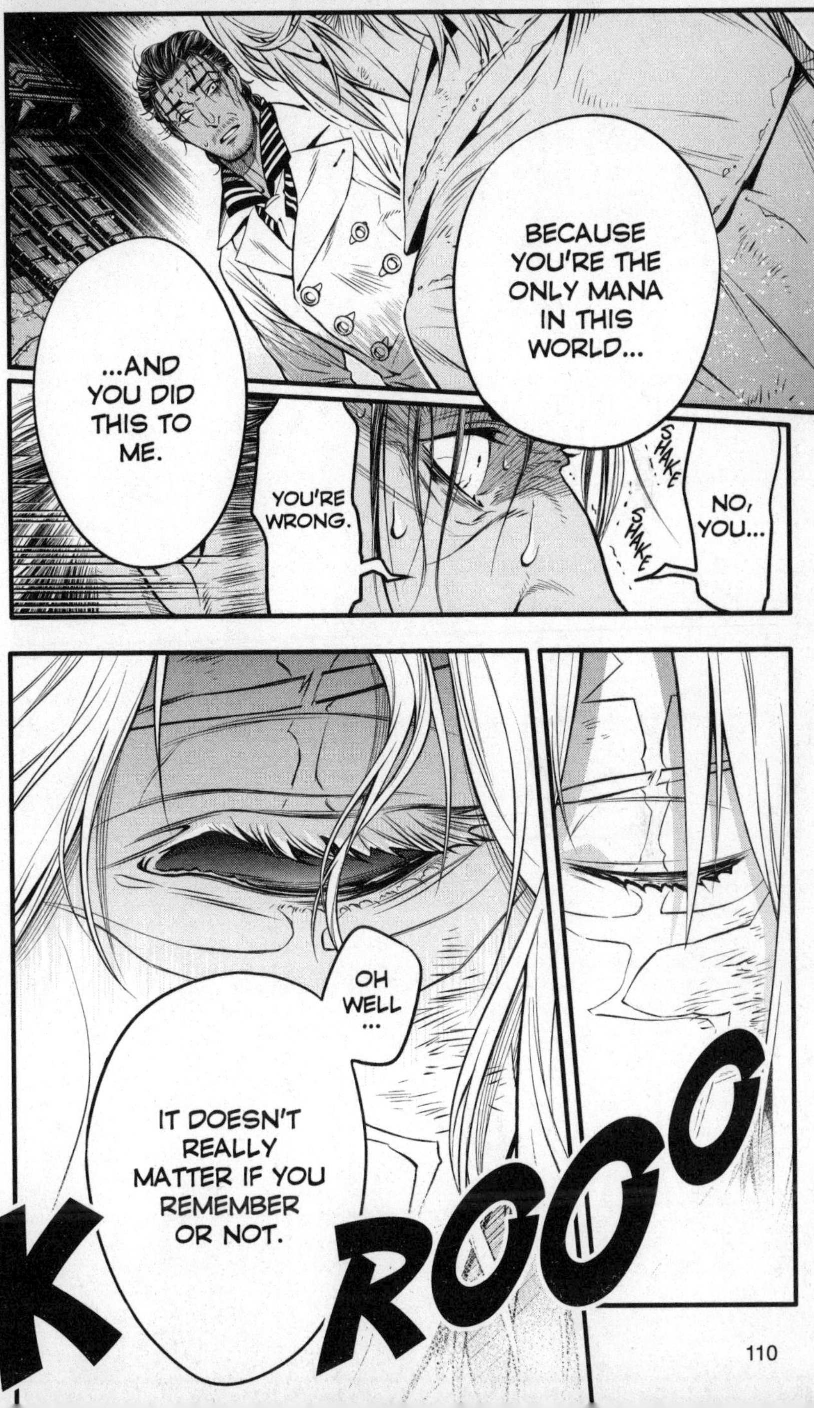
BECAUSE YOU'RE THE ONLY MANA IN THIS WORLD...
...AND YOU DID THIS TO ME.
SHAKE
SHAKE
NO, YOU...
YOU'RE WRONG.
OH WELL ...
IT DOESN'T REALLY MATTER IF YOU REMEMBER OR NOT.
KROOOO

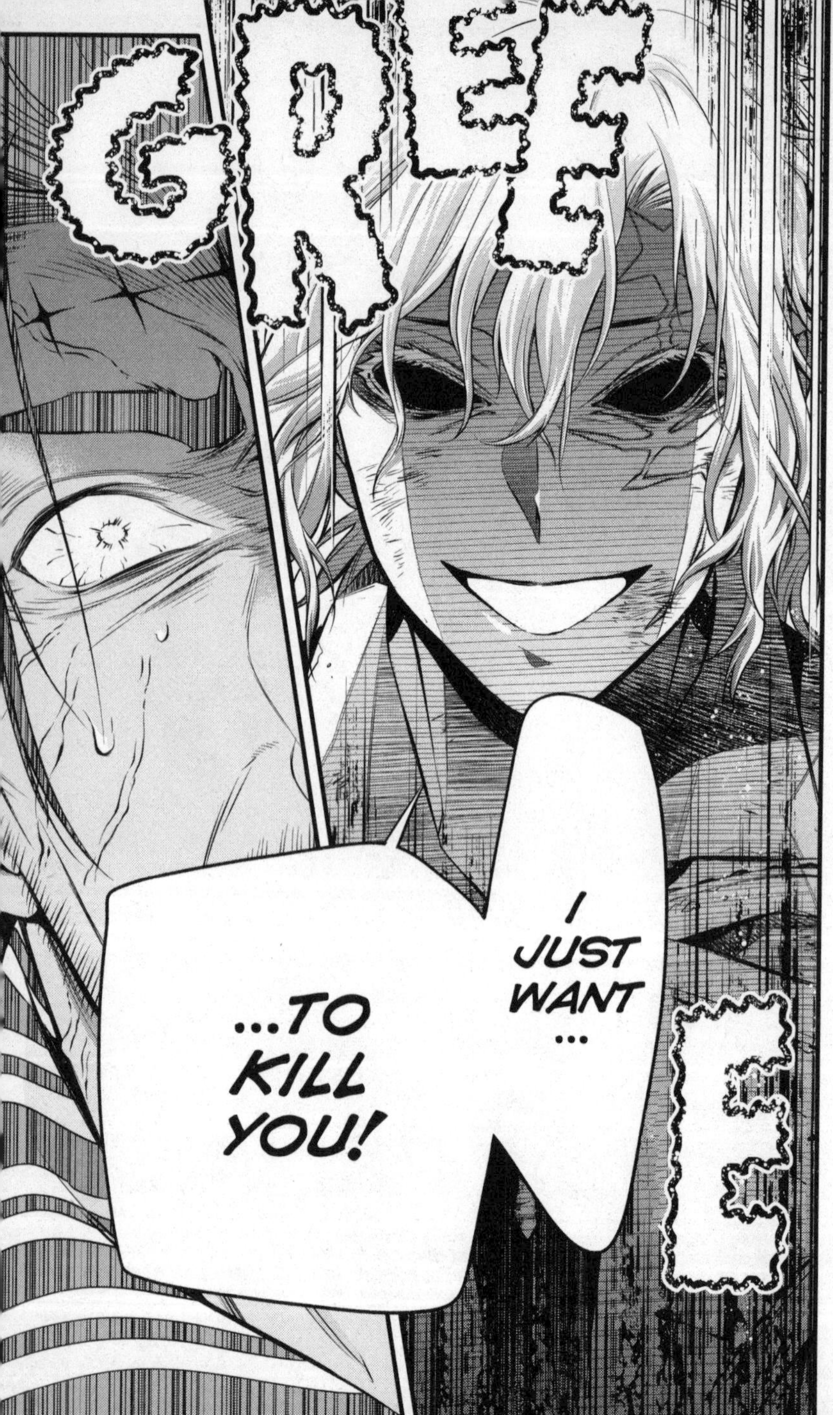
I JUST WANT... ...TO KILL YOU!

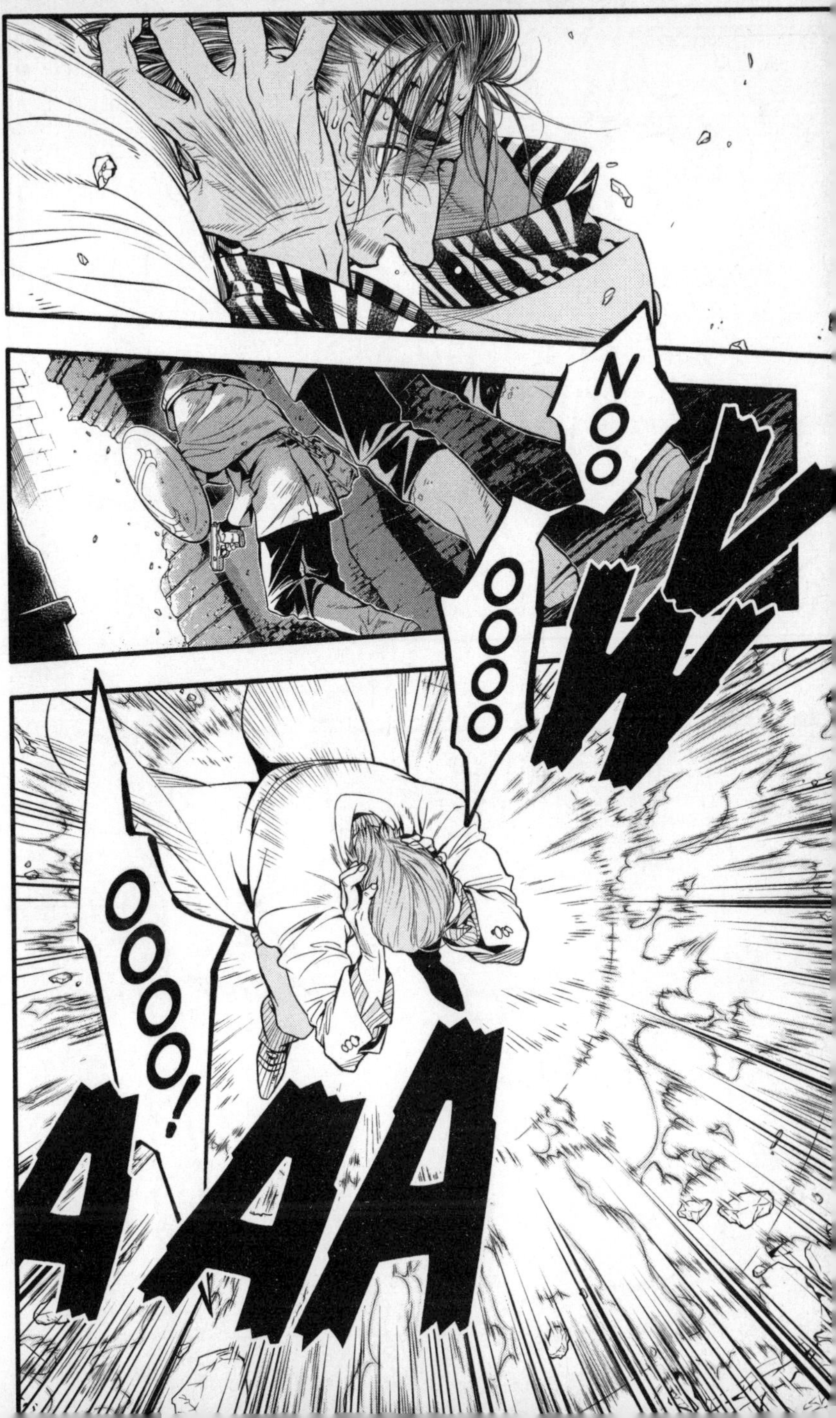
NOOOOOOOOOOO!
AAAWW

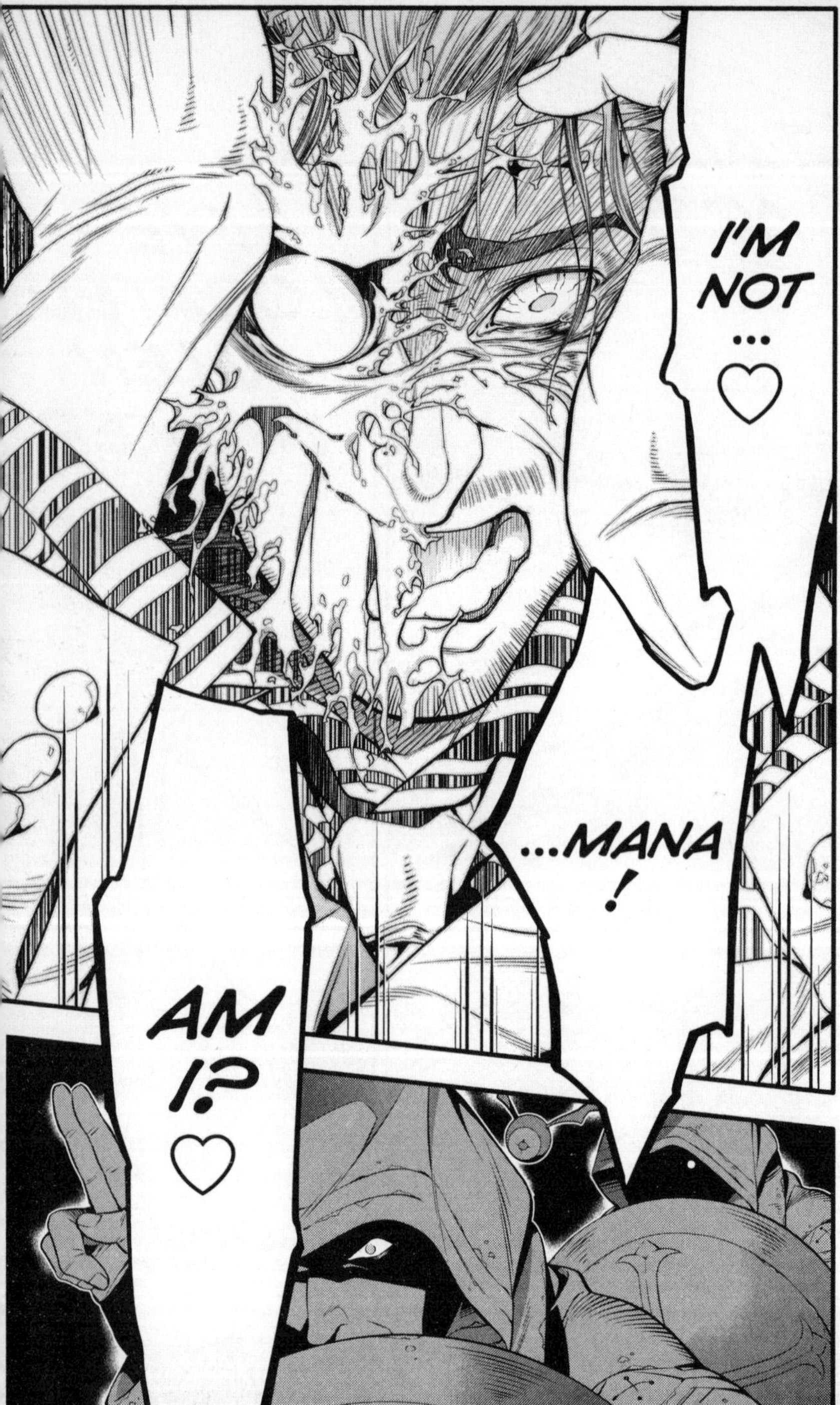
I'M NOT ... ♡
...MANA!
AM I? ♡

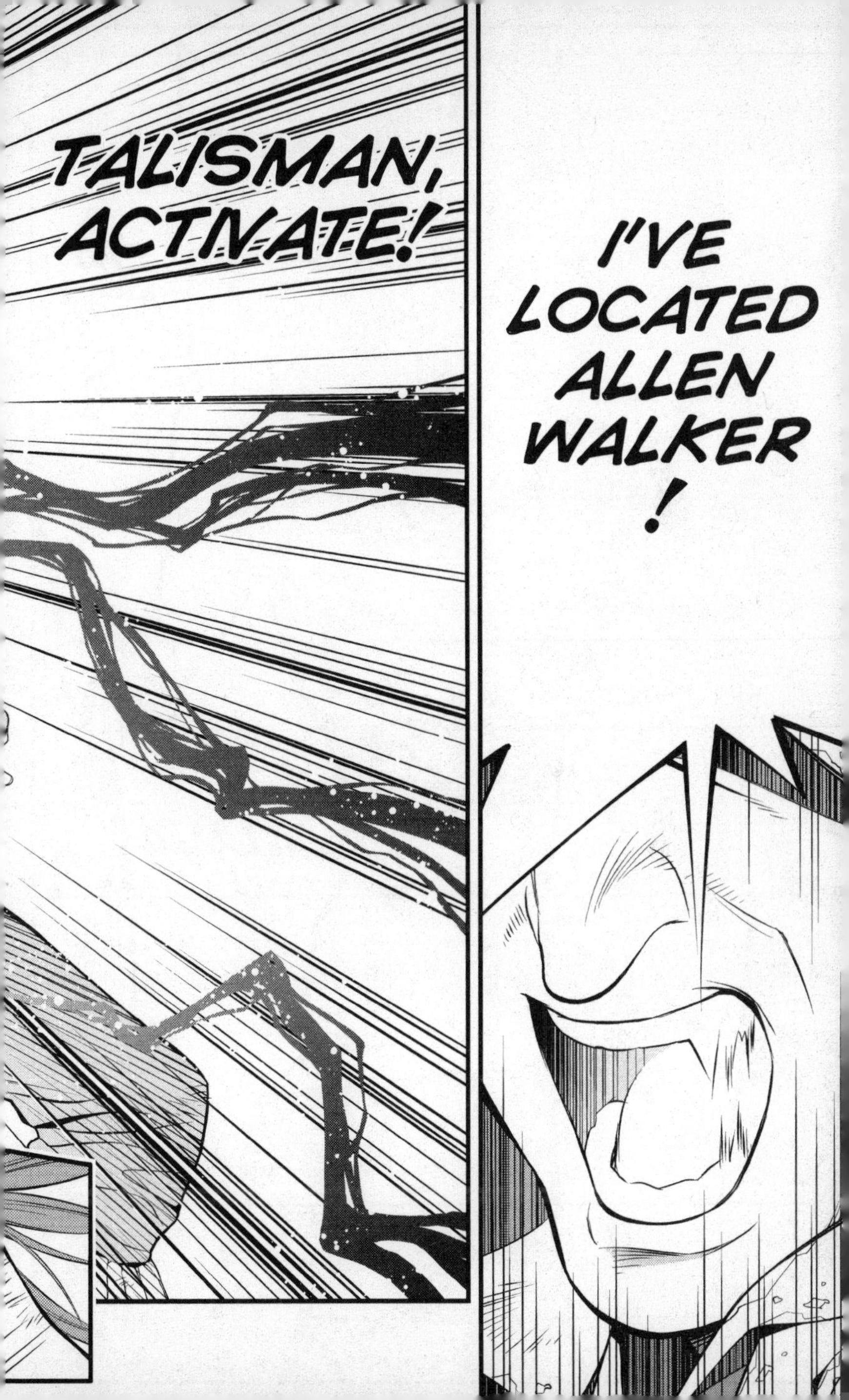
I'VE LOCATED ALLEN WALKER!
TALISMAN, ACTIVATE!

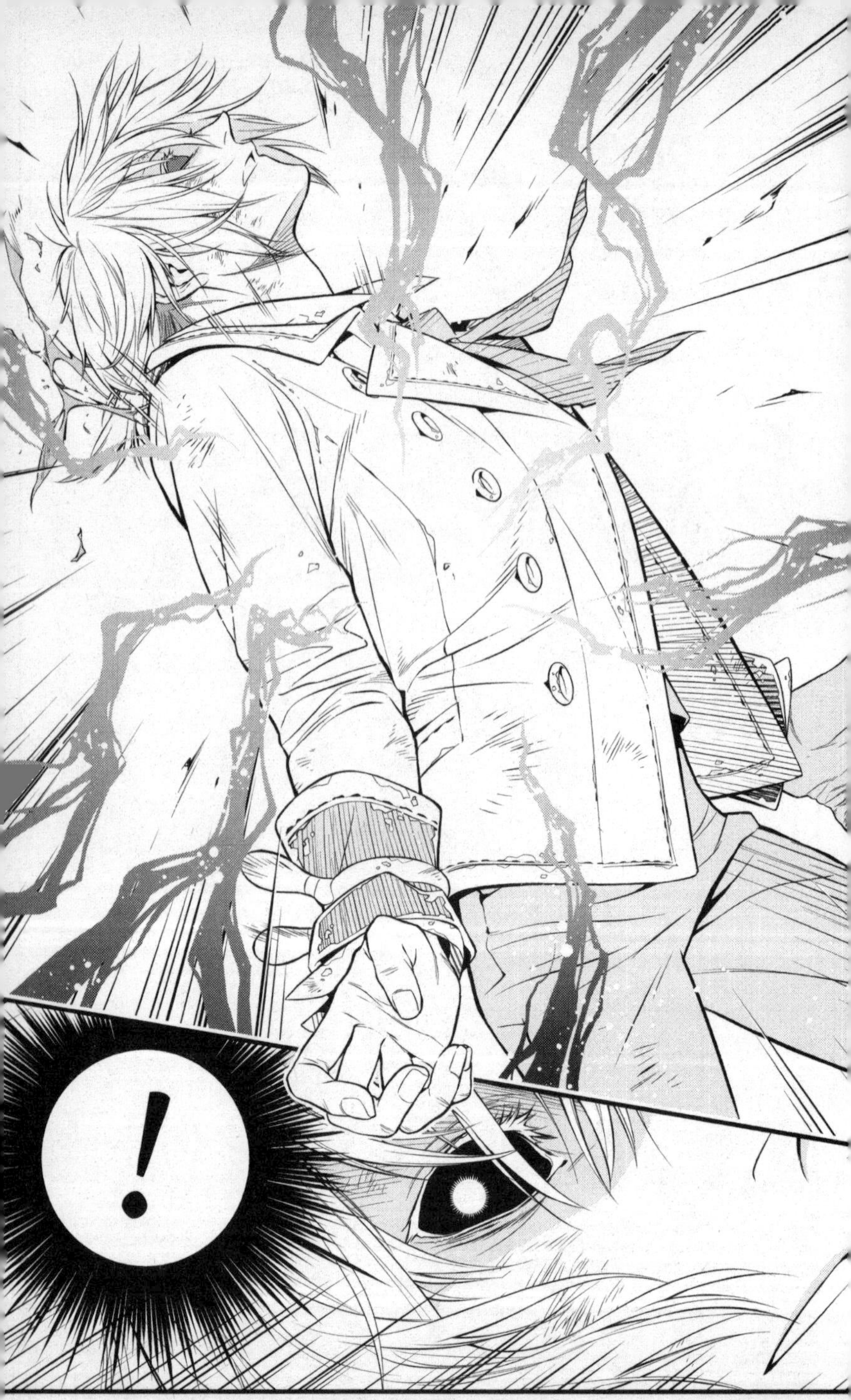
!

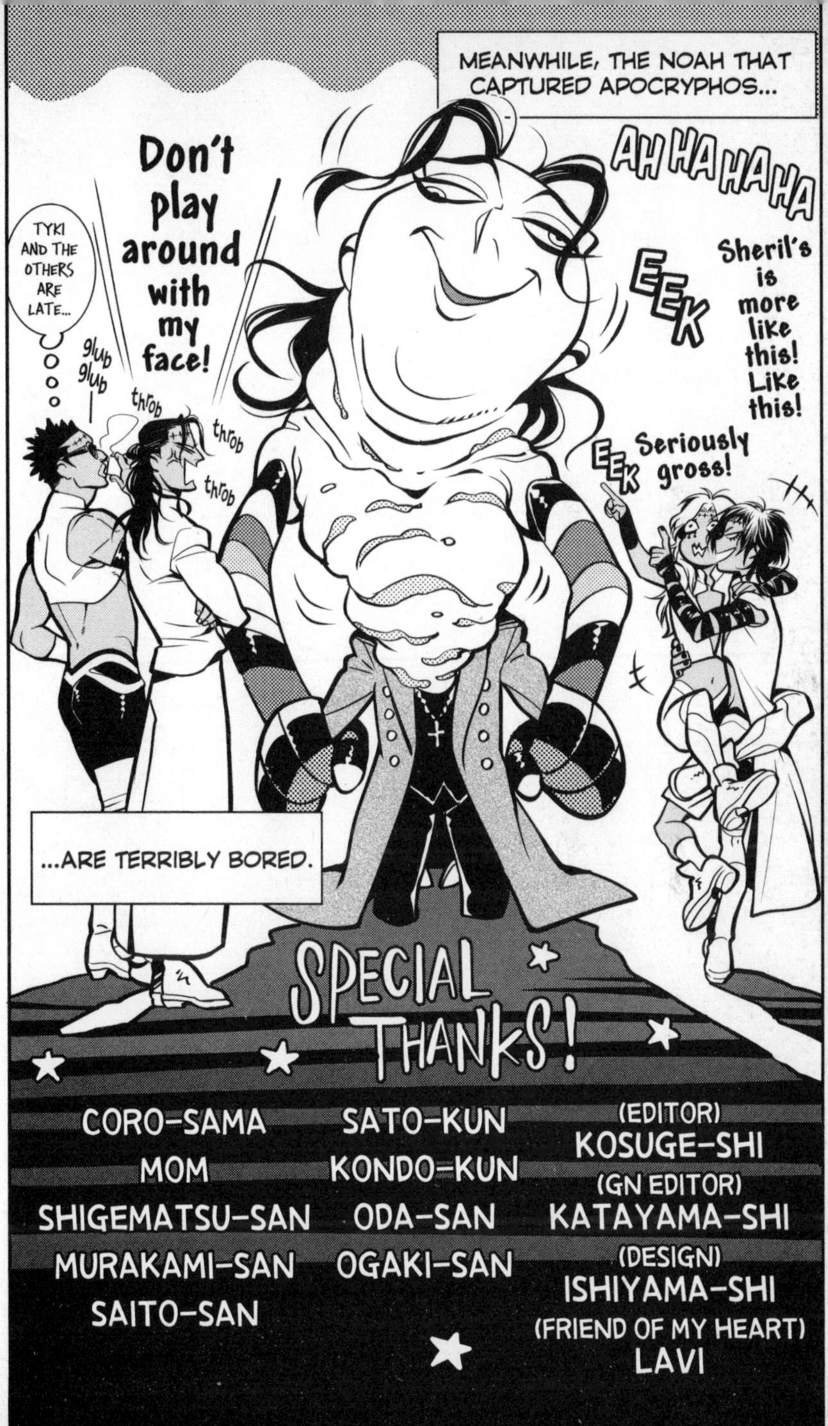
MEANWHILE, THE NOAH THAT CAPTURED APOCRYPHOS...
AH HA HA HA HA
Sheril's is more like this! Like this!
EEK
Seriously gross!
EEK
Don't play around with my face!
throb
throb
throb
TYKI AND THE OTHERS ARE LATE...
glub glub
...ARE TERRIBLY BORED.
SPECIAL THANKS!
CORO-SAMA
MOM
SHIGEMATSU-SAN
MURAKAMI-SAN
SAITO-SAN
SATO-KUN
KONDO-KUN
ODA-SAN
OGAKI-SAN
(EDITOR)
KOSUGE-SHI
(GN EDITOR)
KATAYAMA-SHI
(DESIGN)
ISHIYAMA-SHI
(FRIEND OF MY HEART)
LAVI

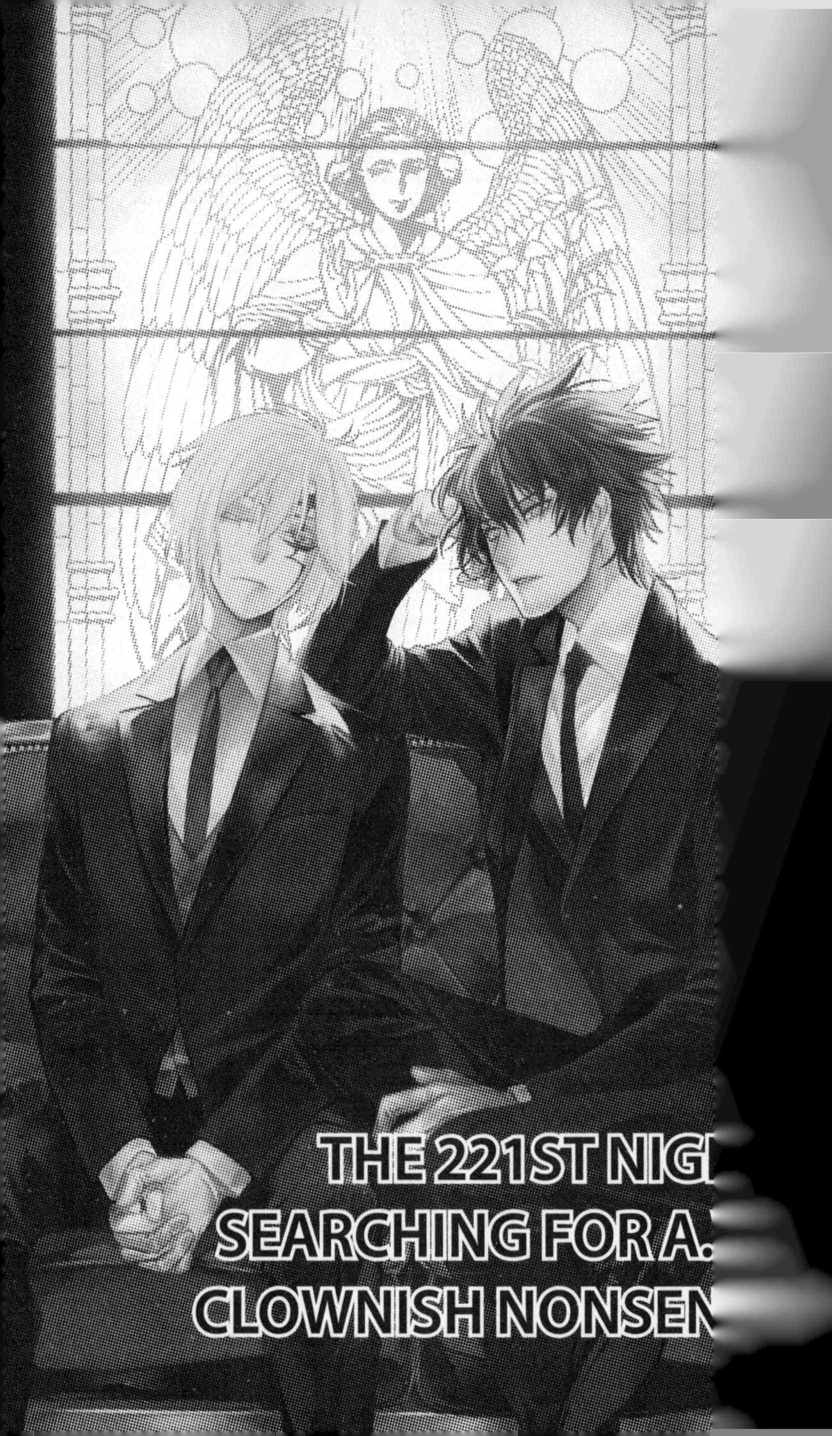
THE 221ST NIG
SEARCHING FOR A.
CLOWNISH NONSEN

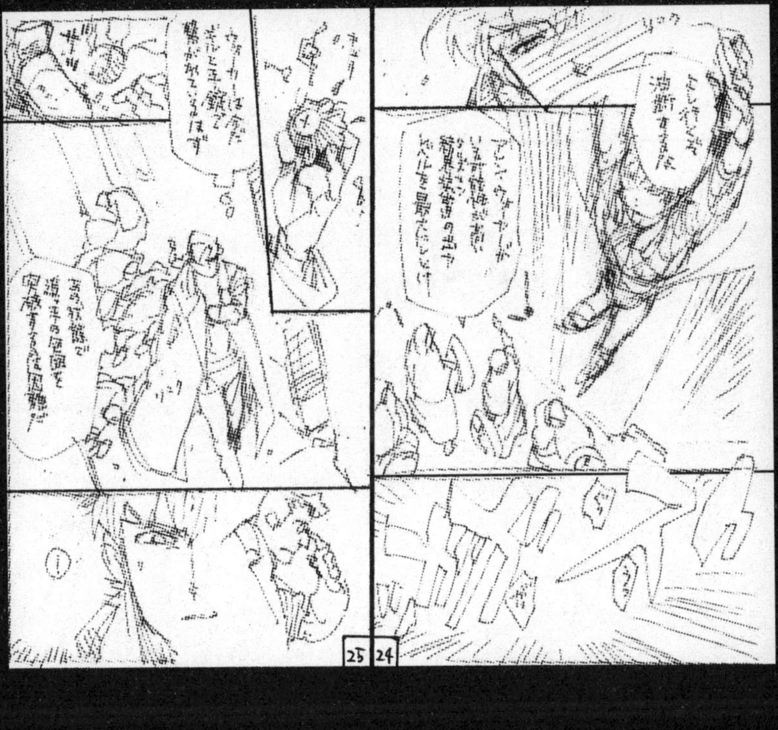
とにかく今は油断するな
25
24

220th Night sketch

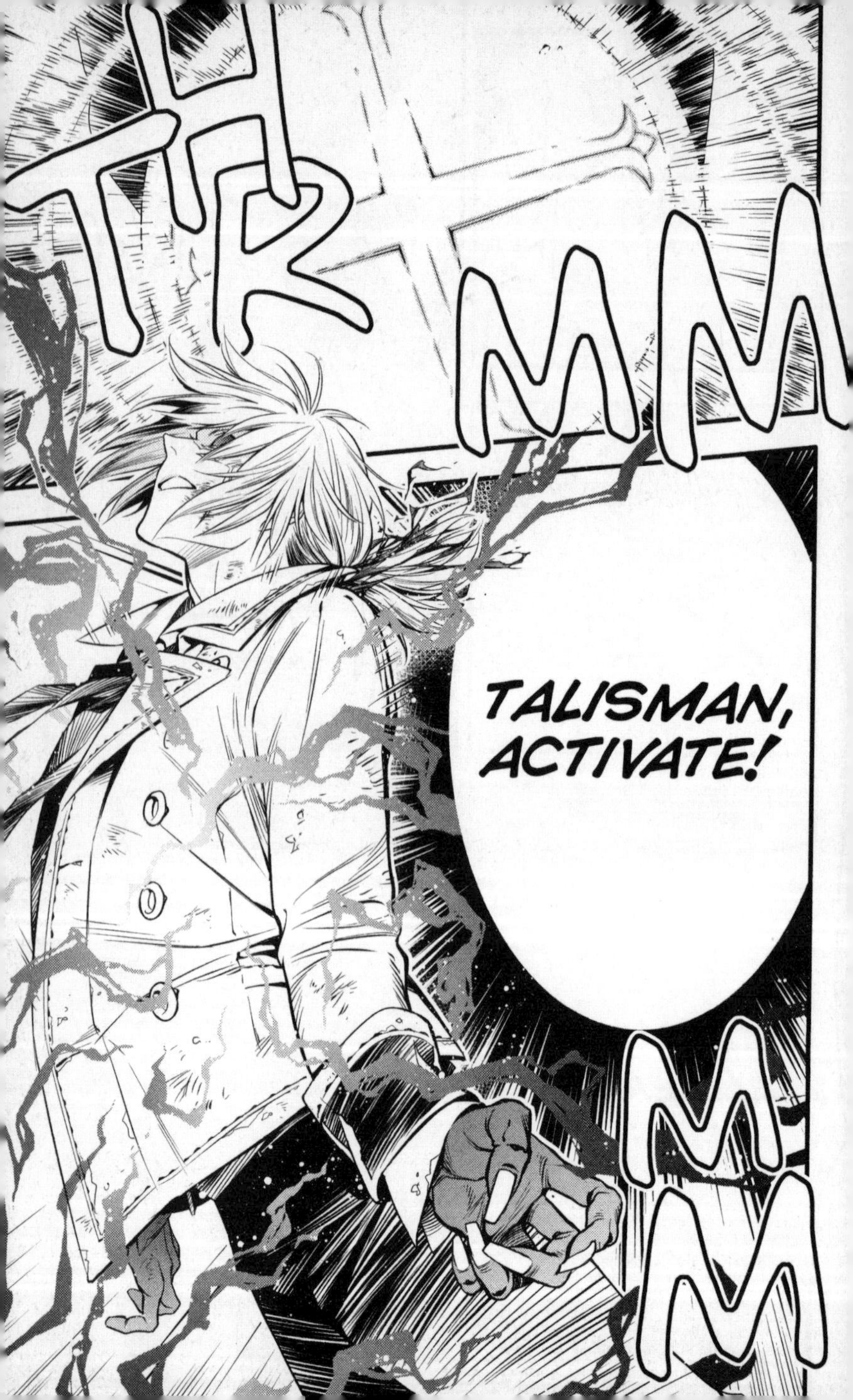
THRMMMMM
TALISMAN, ACTIVATE!

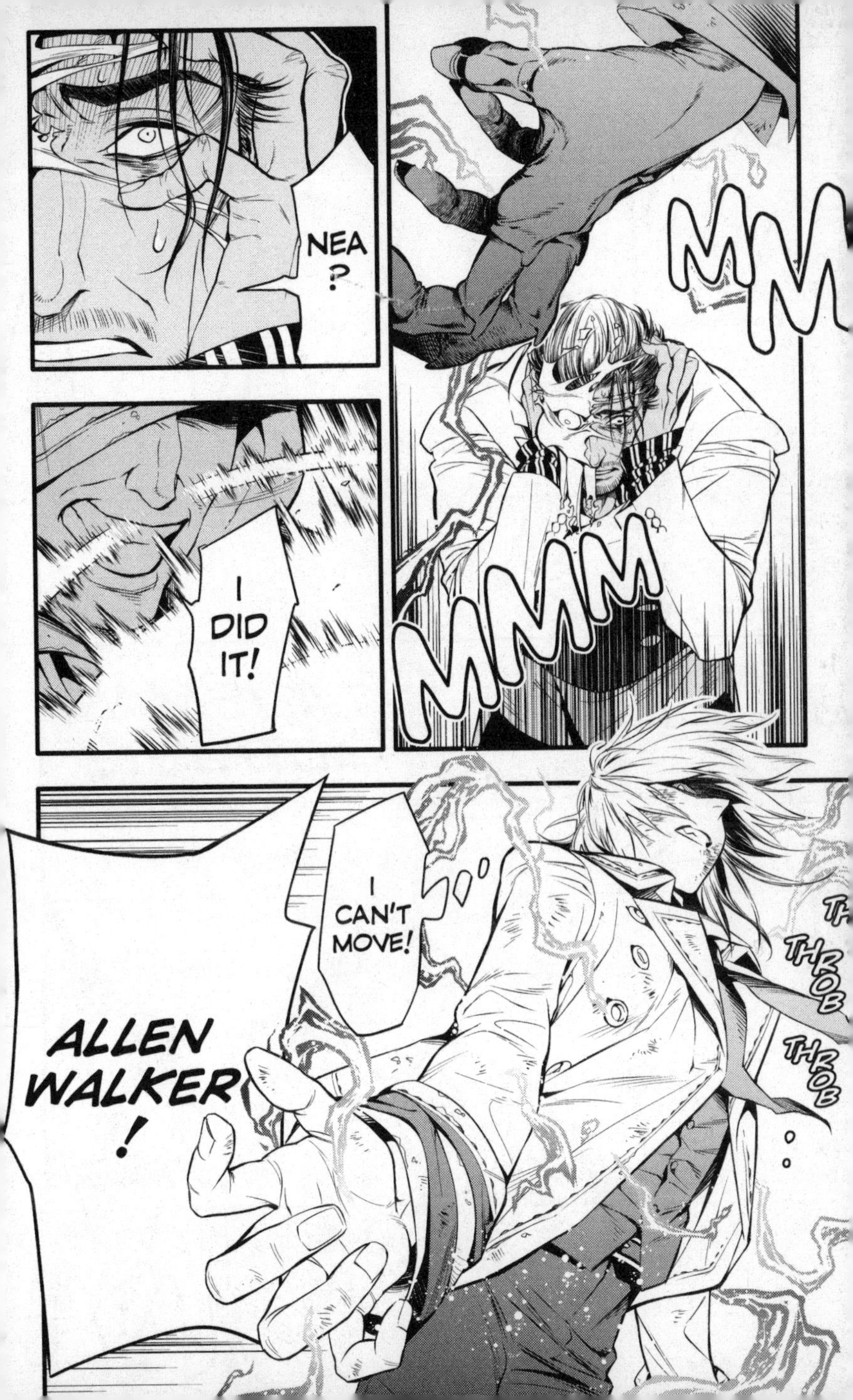
MMM
MMMM
NEA?
I DID IT!
THROB
THROB
I CAN'T MOVE!
ALLEN WALKER!

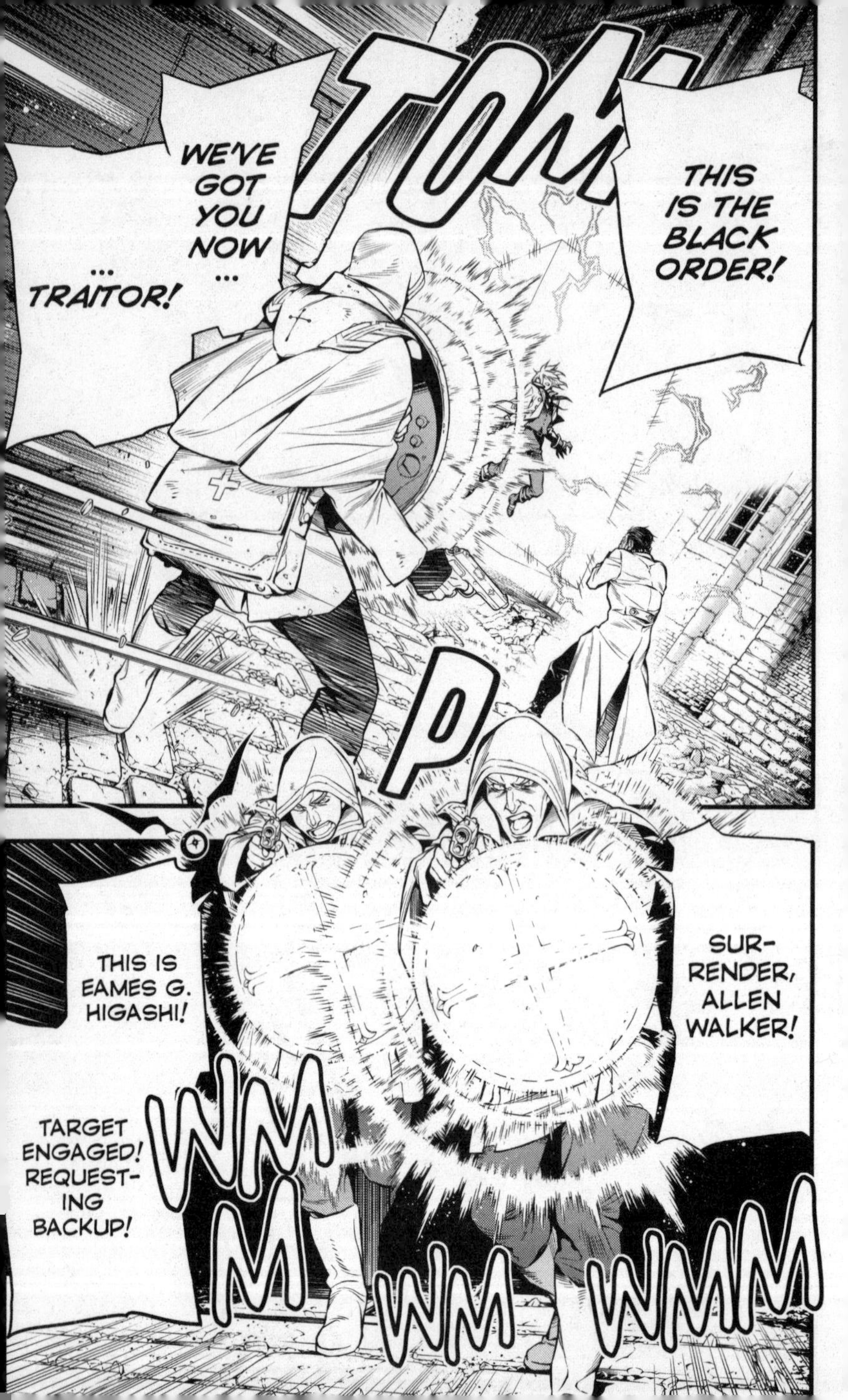
TOM
THIS IS THE BLACK ORDER!
WE'VE GOT YOU NOW ... TRAITOR!
P
SUR-RENDER, ALLEN WALKER!
THIS IS EAMES G. HIGASHI!
TARGET ENGAGED! REQUEST-ING BACKUP!
WMMM
WM
WMM

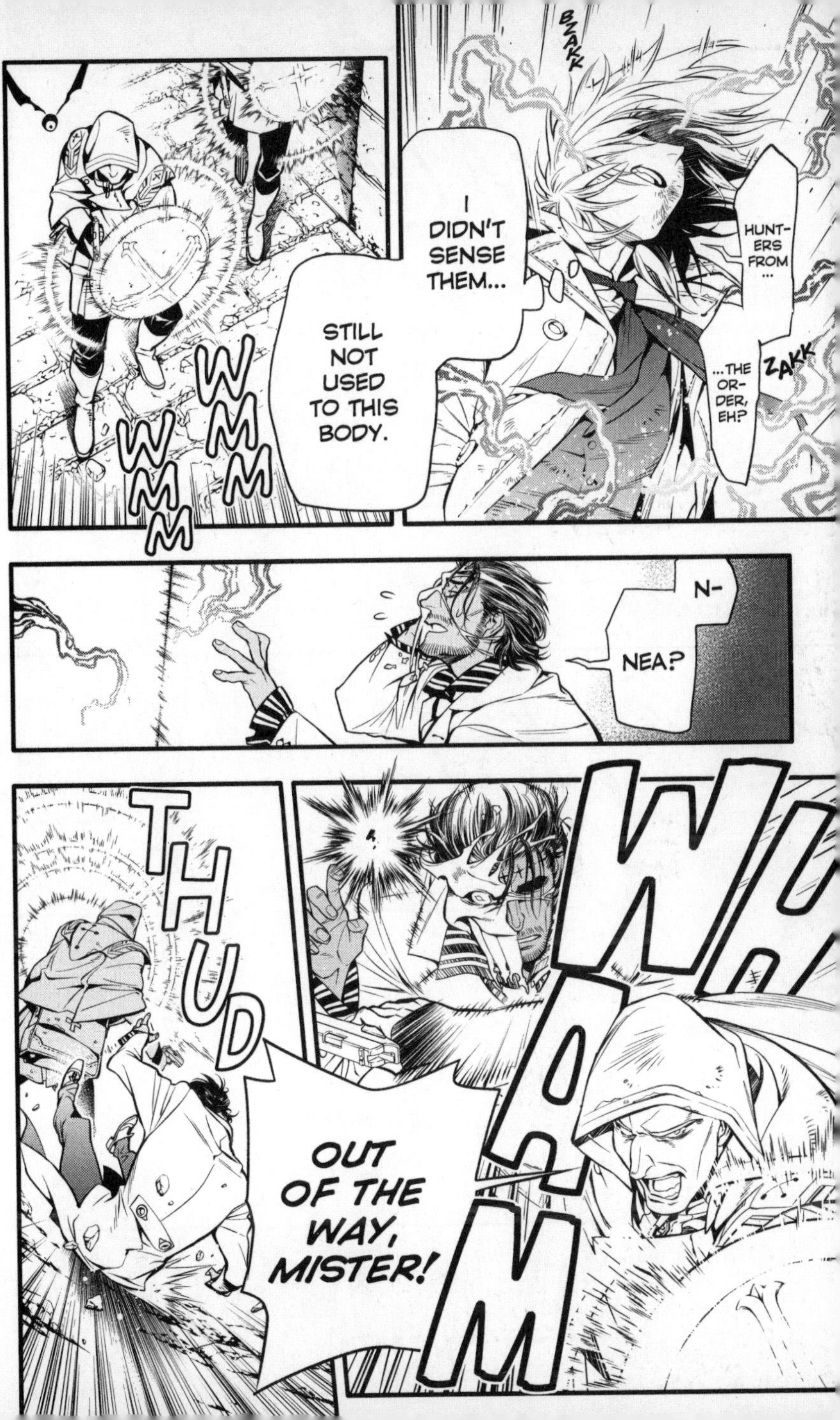
BZAKK
HUNTERS FROM ...
ZAKK
...THE ORDER, EH?
I DIDN'T SENSE THEM...
STILL NOT USED TO THIS BODY.
WMMM
WMMM
N-
NEA?
WHAAM
OUT OF THE WAY, MISTER!
THUD

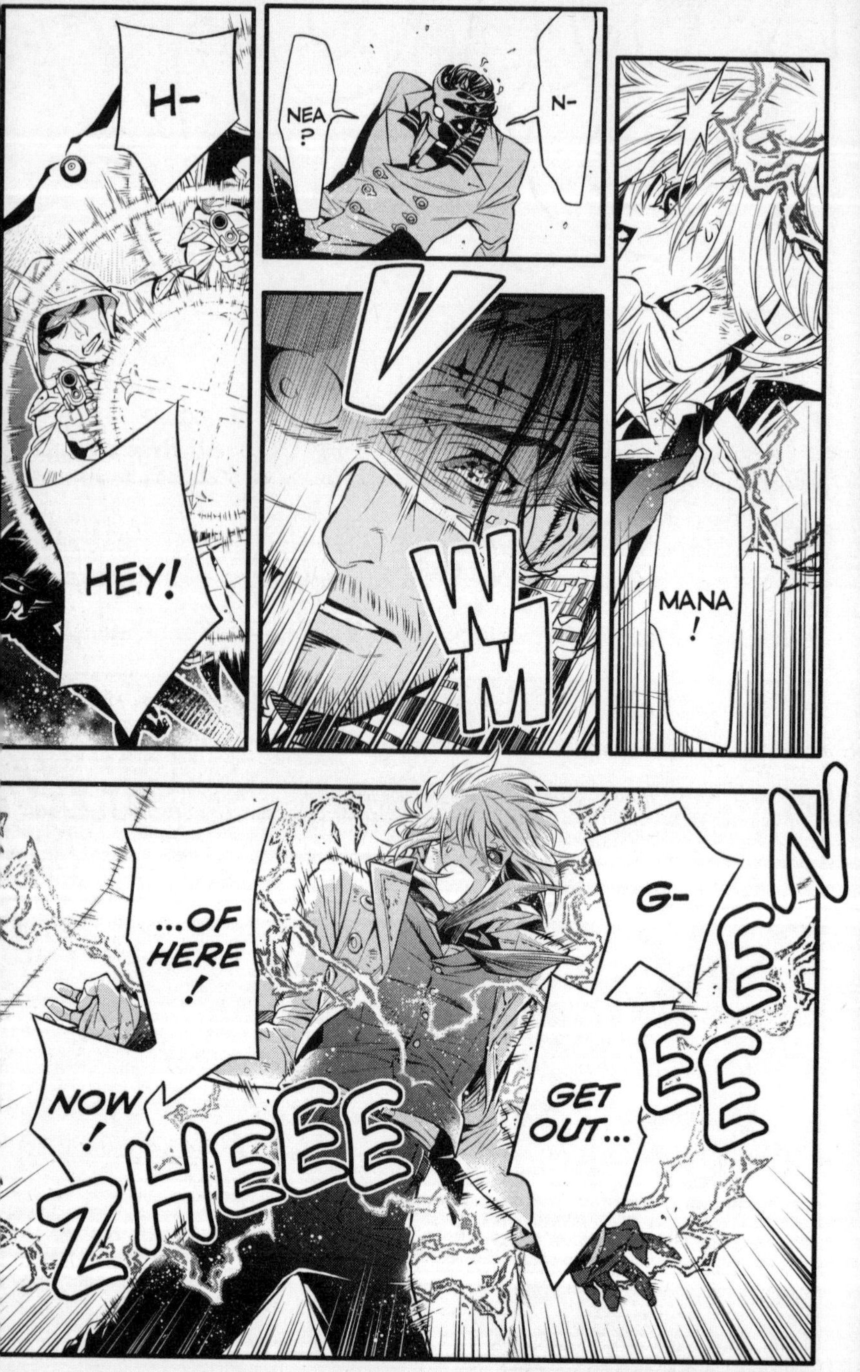
MANA!
N-
NEA?
VWM
H-
HEY!
G-
GET OUT...
...OF HERE!
NOW!
ZHEEEEEEEN

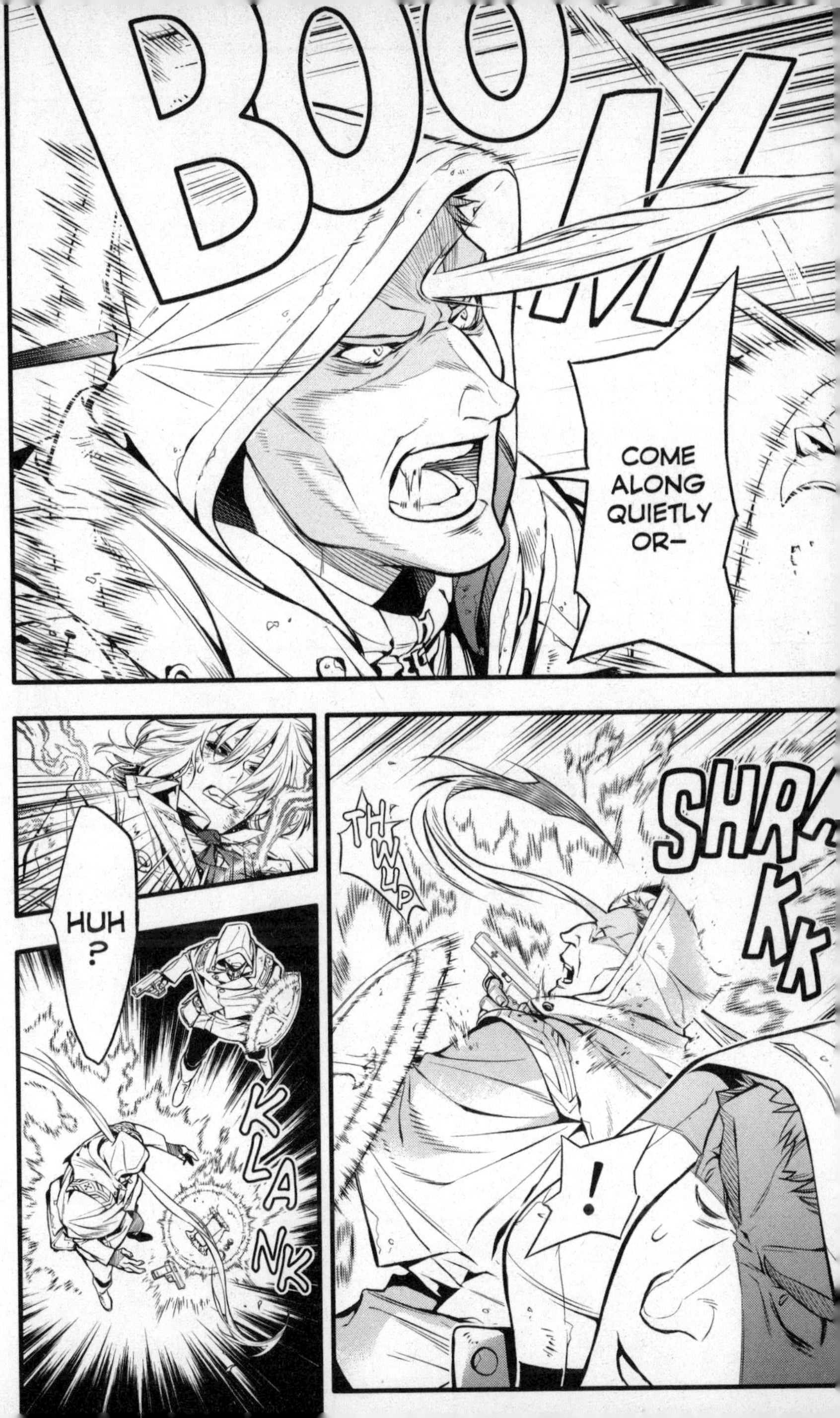
BOOM
COME ALONG QUIETLY OR–
SHRKK
THWUP
!
HUH?
KLANK

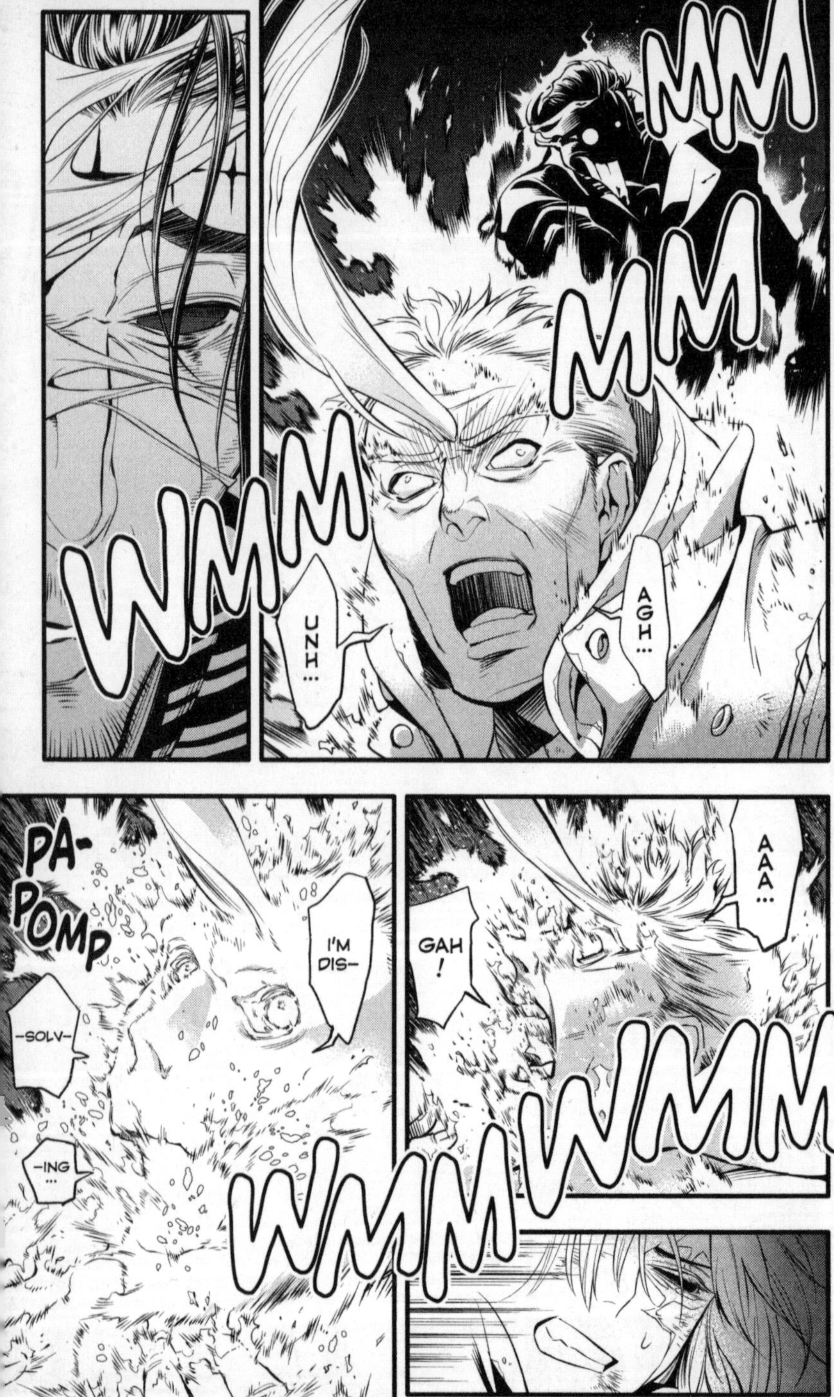
MM
MM
AGH...
UNH...
WMM
AAA...
GAH!
WMMWMM
I'M DIS-
PA-POMP
-SOLV-
-ING...

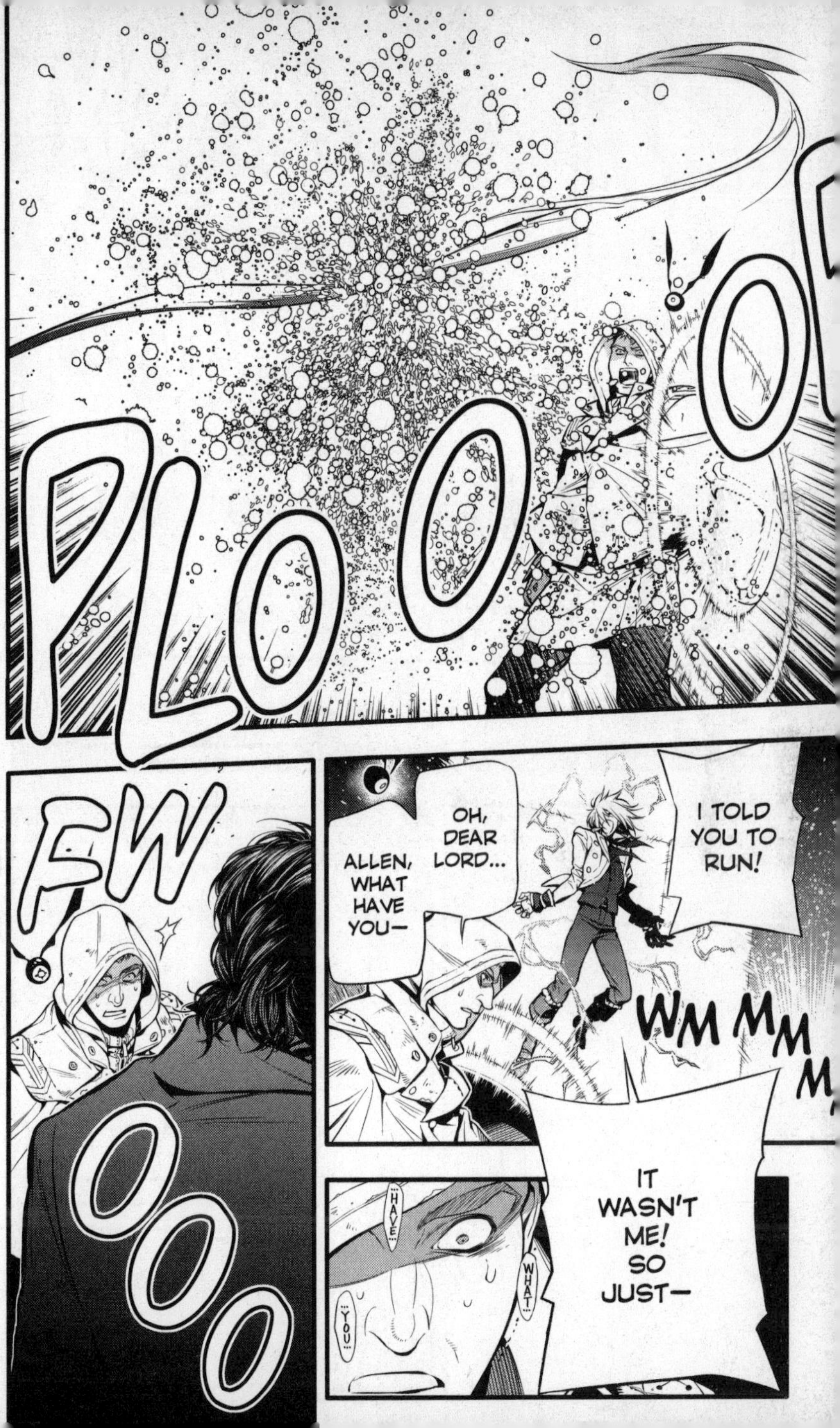
PLOOOO
I TOLD YOU TO RUN!
OH, DEAR LORD...
ALLEN, WHAT HAVE YOU—
WM MMM
IT WASN'T ME! SO JUST—
...WHAT...
...HAVE...
...YOU...
FWOOOO

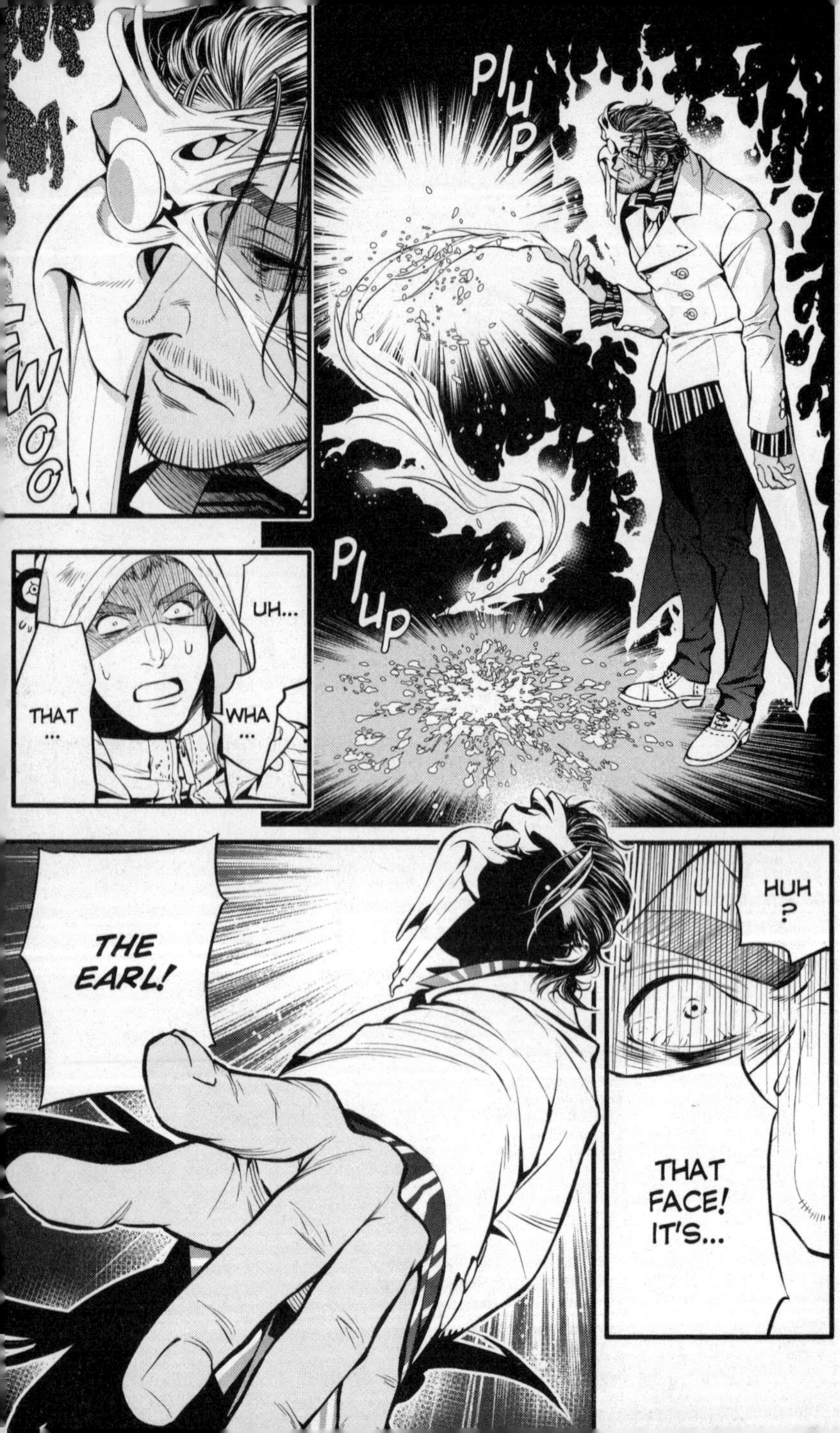

PLUP
PLUP
WOOO
UH...
WHA...
THAT...
HUH?
THAT FACE! IT'S...
THE EARL!

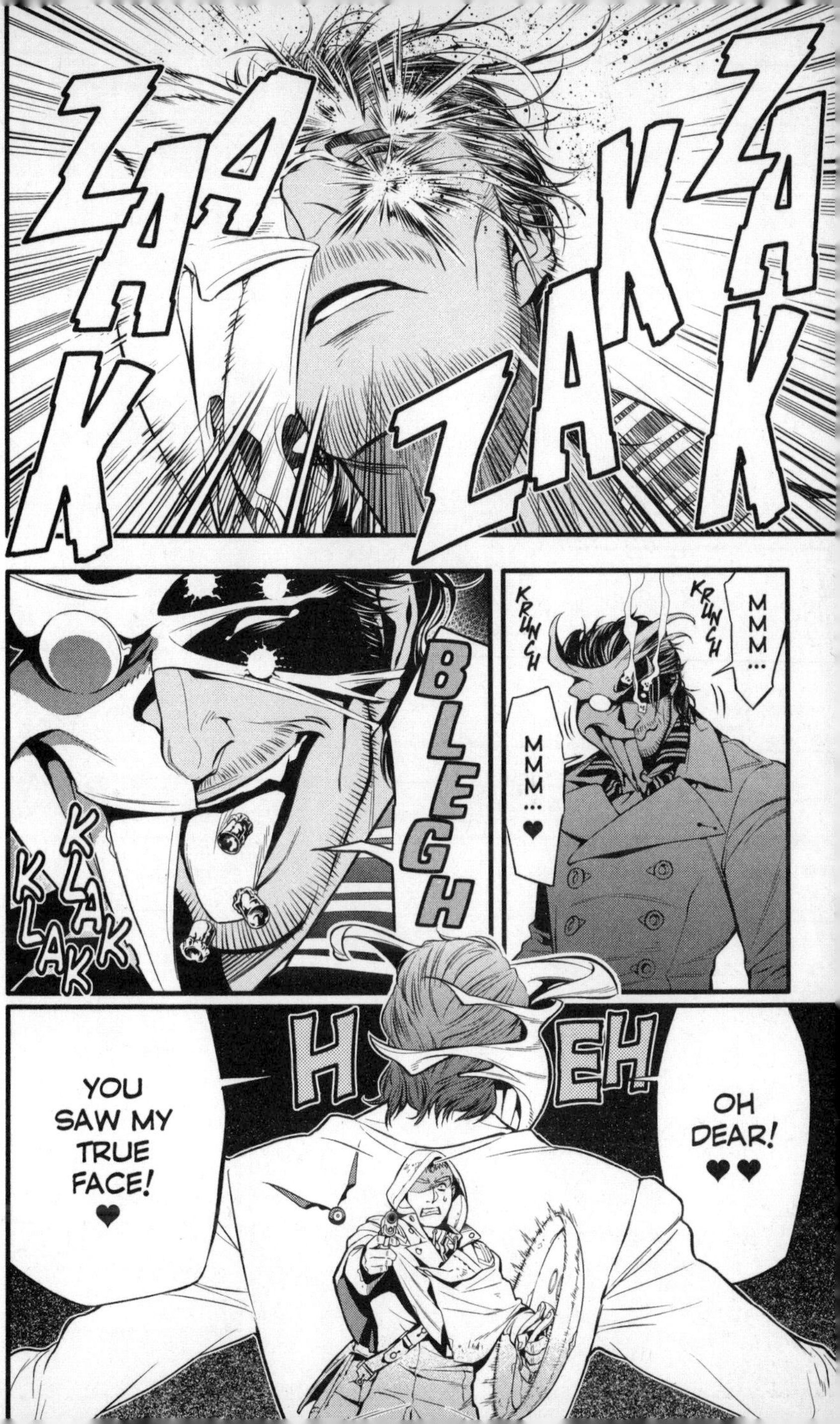
ZAAK
ZAK
ZAAK
MMM...
KRUNCH
KRUNCH
MMM... ♥
BLEGH
KLAK
KLAK
HEH
OH DEAR! ♥♥
YOU SAW MY TRUE FACE! ♥

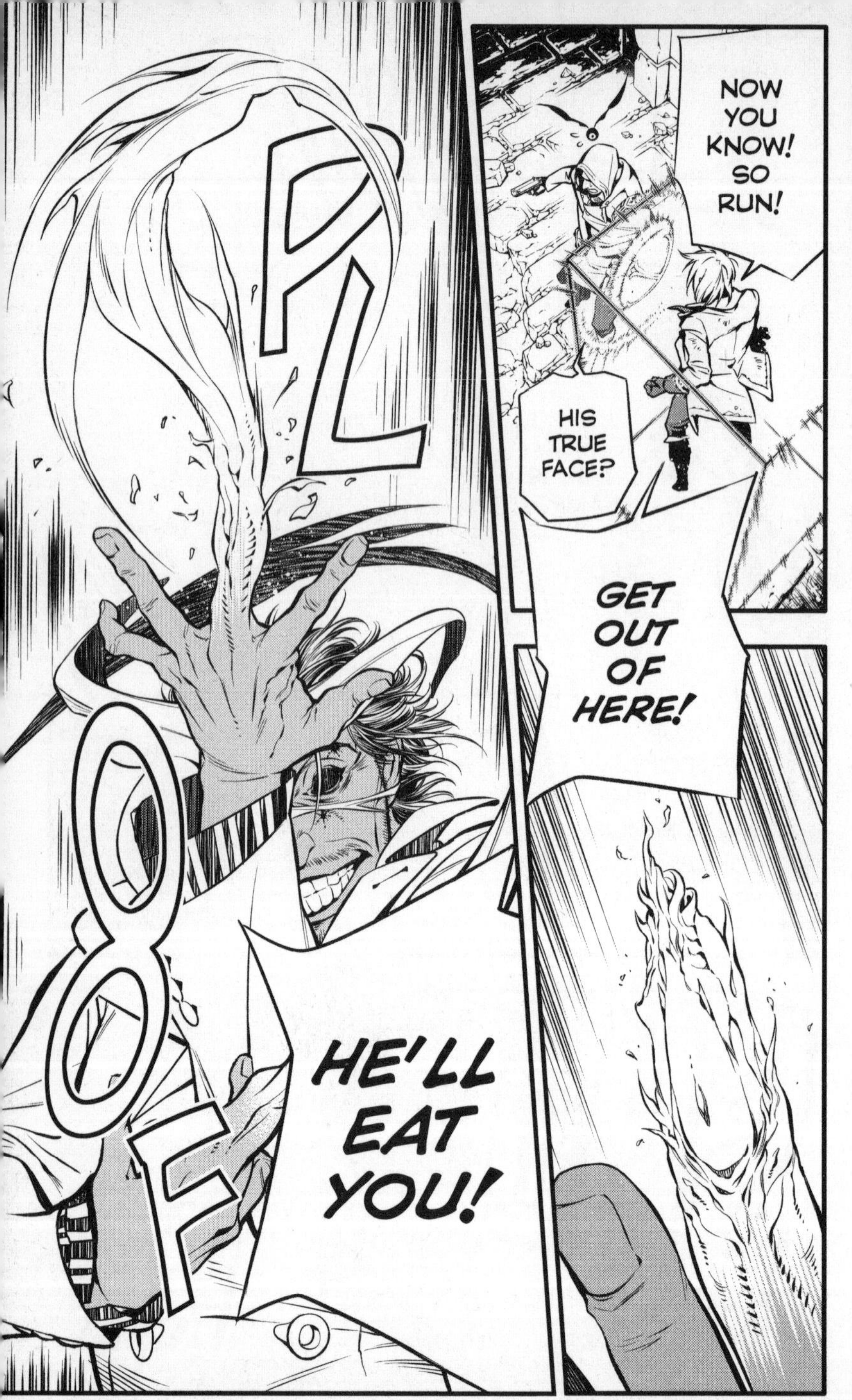
NOW YOU KNOW! SO RUN!
HIS TRUE FACE?
GET OUT OF HERE!
PL
OOF
HE'LL EAT YOU!

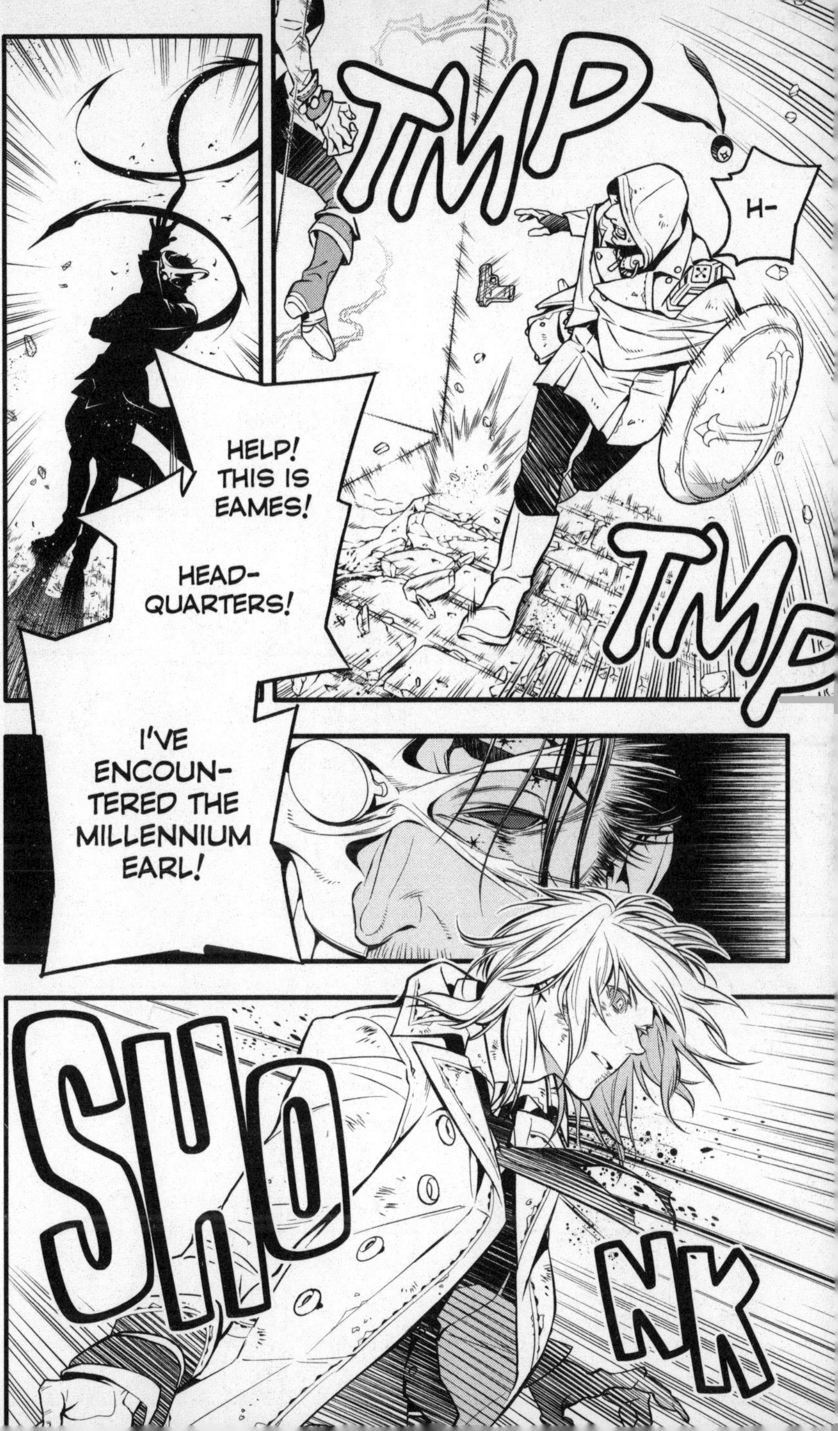
TMP
H-
TMP
HELP! THIS IS EAMES!
HEAD-QUARTERS!
I'VE ENCOUN-TERED THE MILLENNIUM EARL!
SHONK

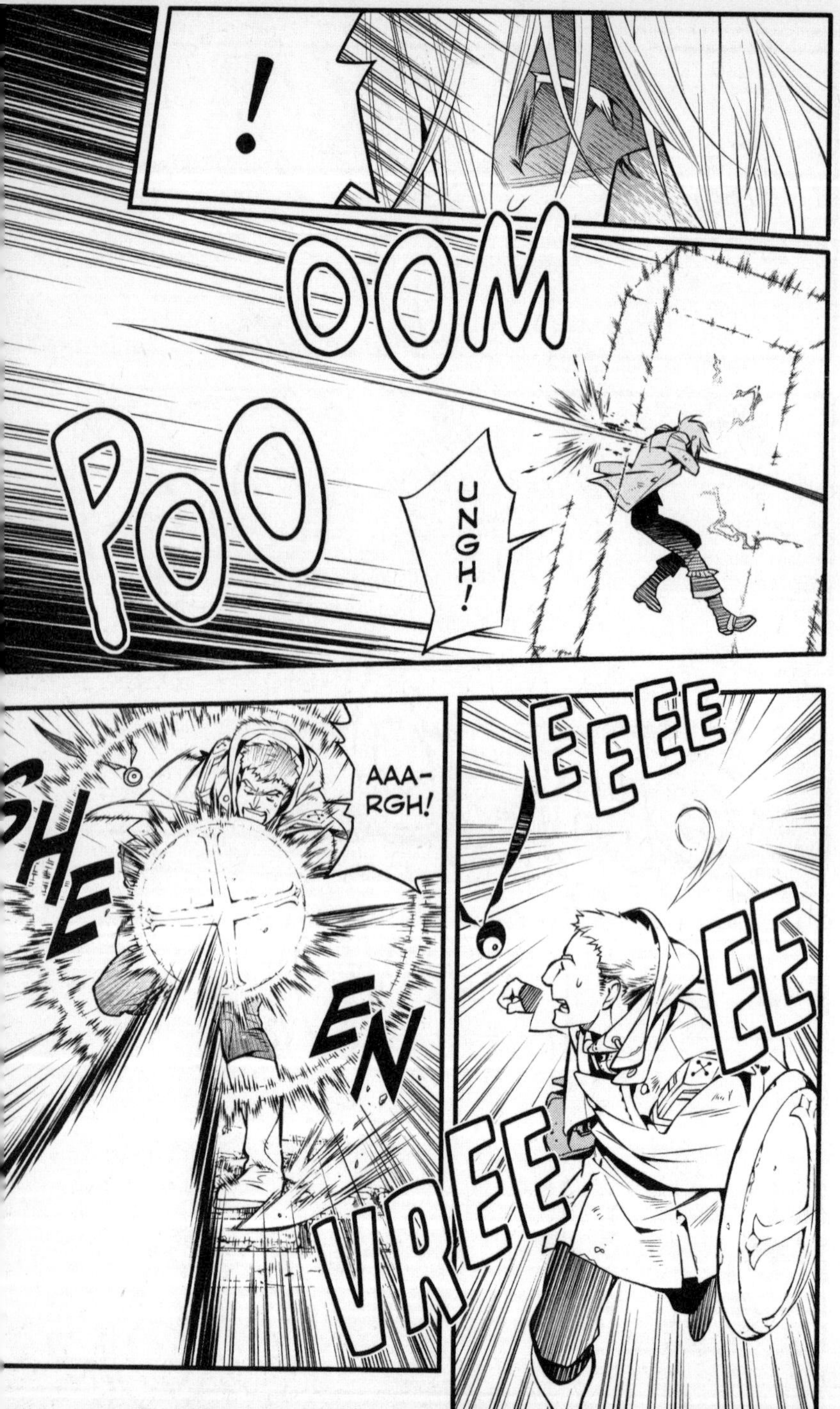
!
POO
OOM
UNGH!
!
VREE
EE
EEEE
AAA-RGH!
SHE
EN

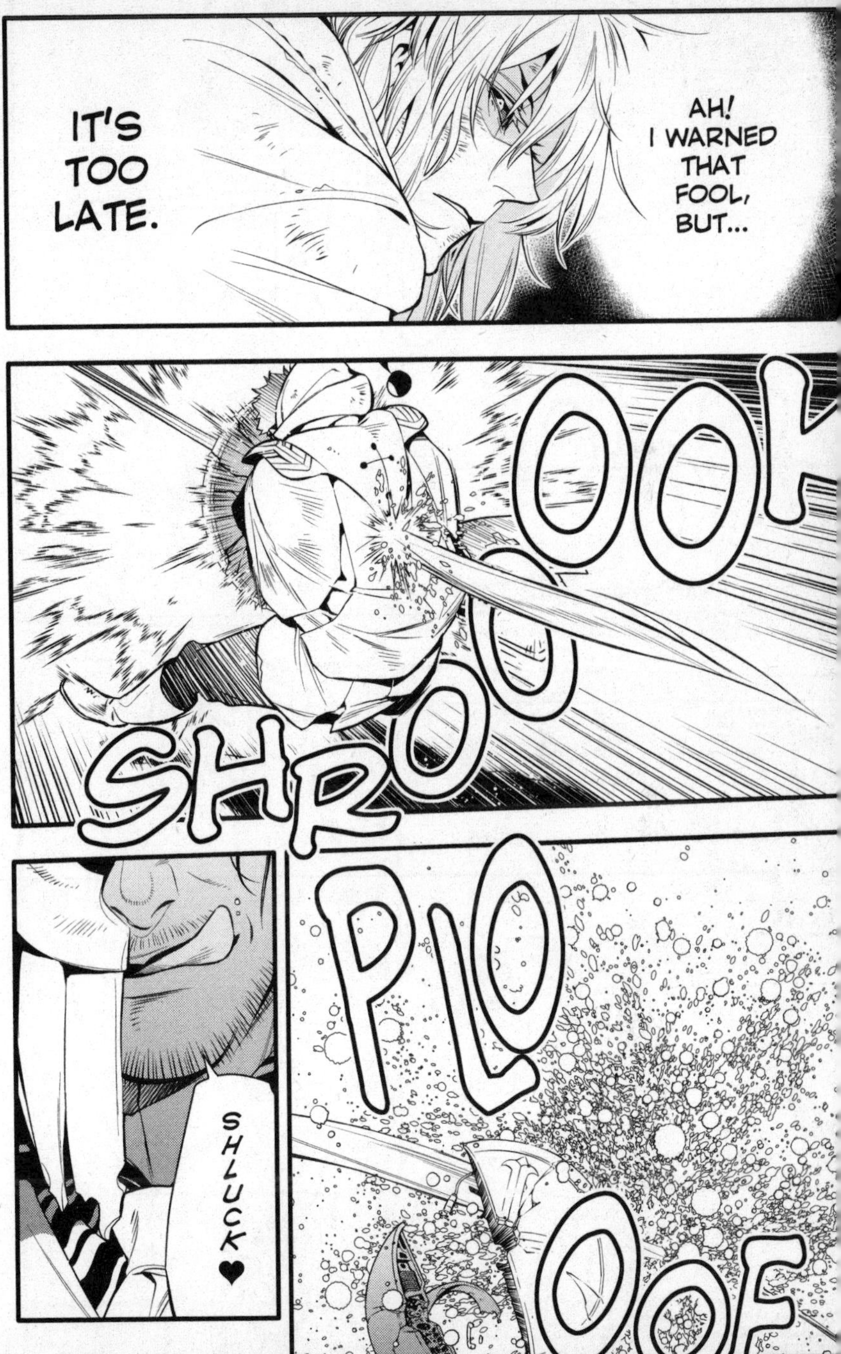
AH! I WARNED THAT FOOL, BUT...
IT'S TOO LATE.
SHROOOOK
PLOOOOF
SHLUCK♥

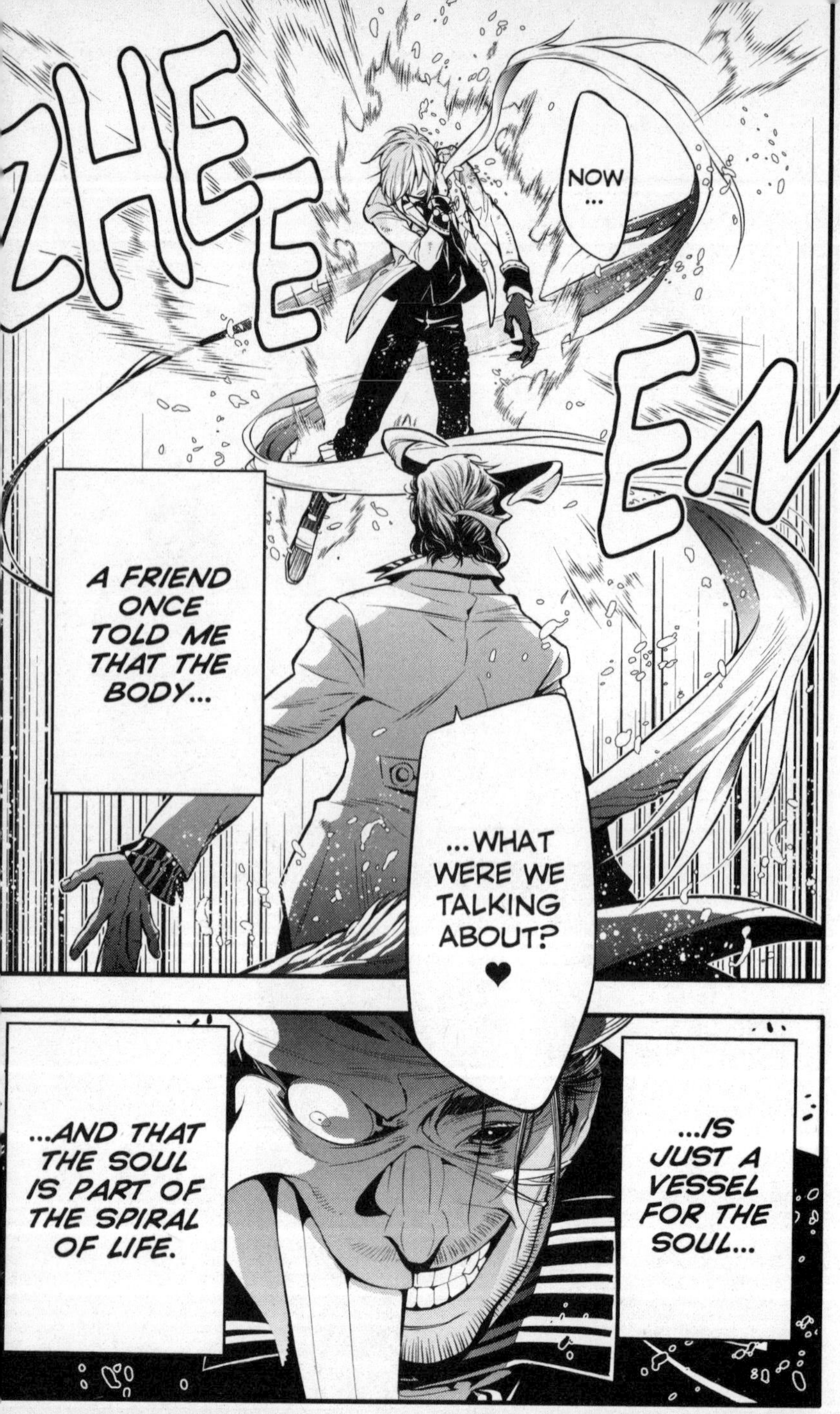
NOW...
ZHEEEN
...WHAT WERE WE TALKING ABOUT? ♥
A FRIEND ONCE TOLD ME THAT THE BODY...
...IS JUST A VESSEL FOR THE SOUL...
...AND THAT THE SOUL IS PART OF THE SPIRAL OF LIFE.

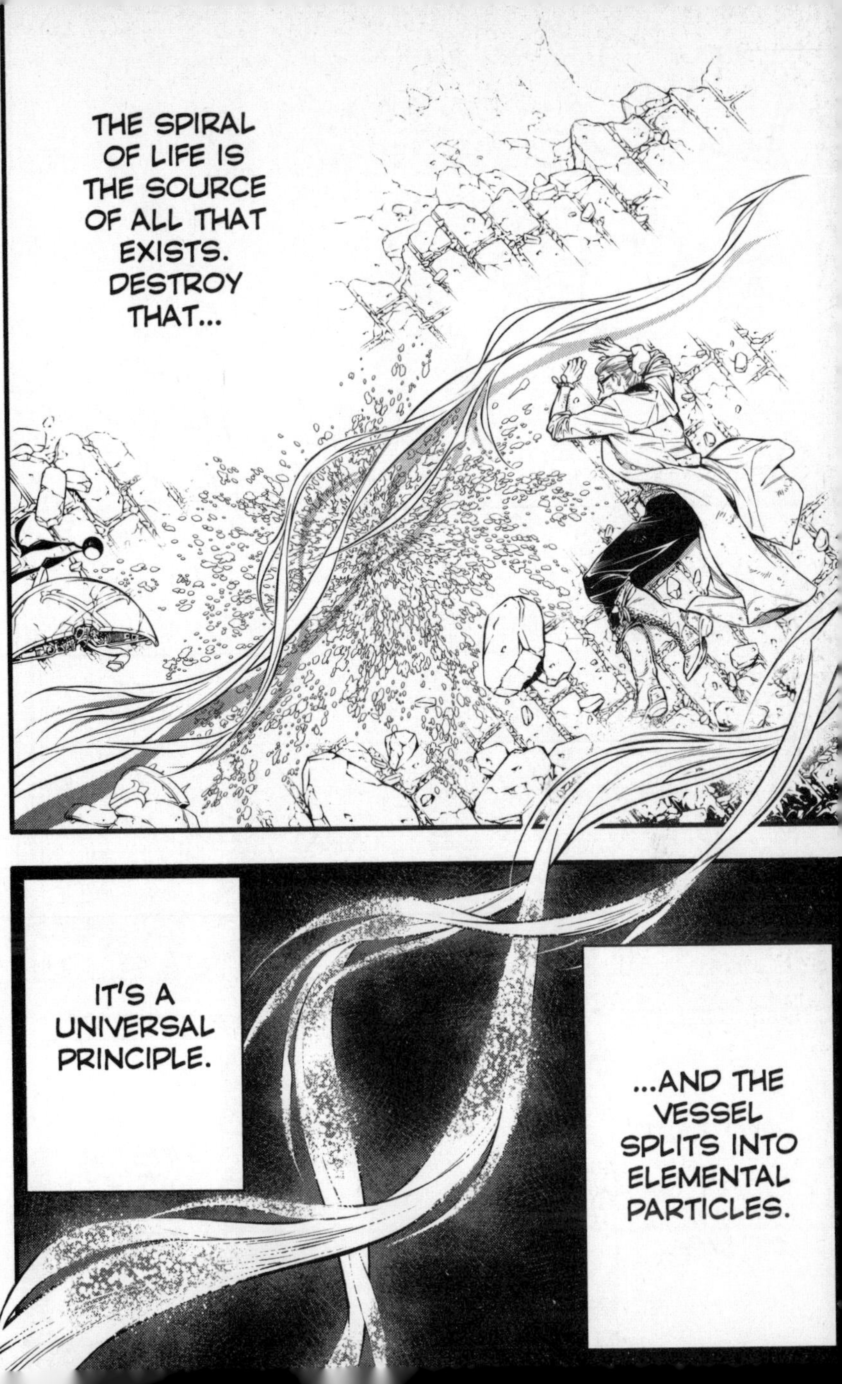
THE SPIRAL OF LIFE IS THE SOURCE OF ALL THAT EXISTS. DESTROY THAT...
...AND THE VESSEL SPLITS INTO ELEMENTAL PARTICLES.
IT'S A UNIVERSAL PRINCIPLE.

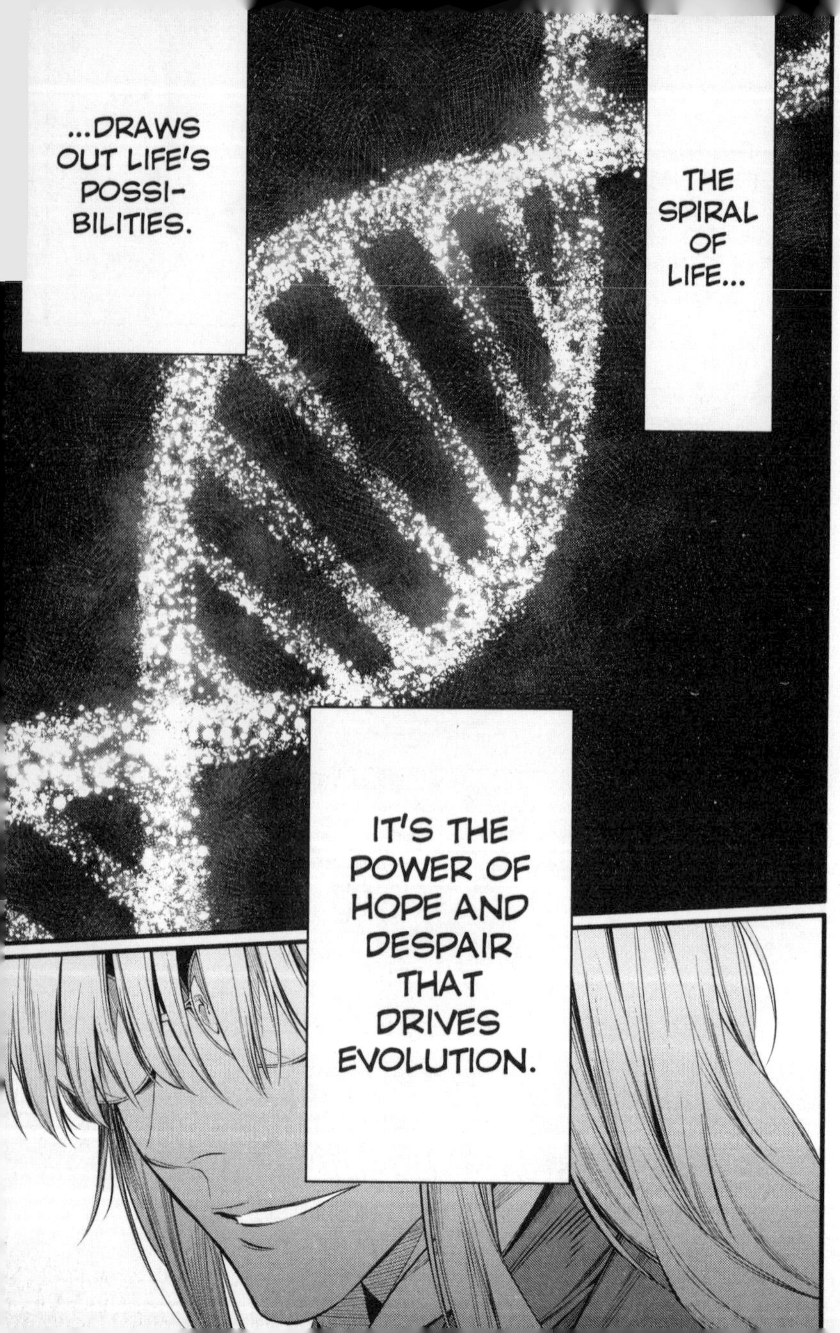
THE SPIRAL OF LIFE...
...DRAWS OUT LIFE'S POSSI-BILITIES.
IT'S THE POWER OF HOPE AND DESPAIR THAT DRIVES EVOLUTION.

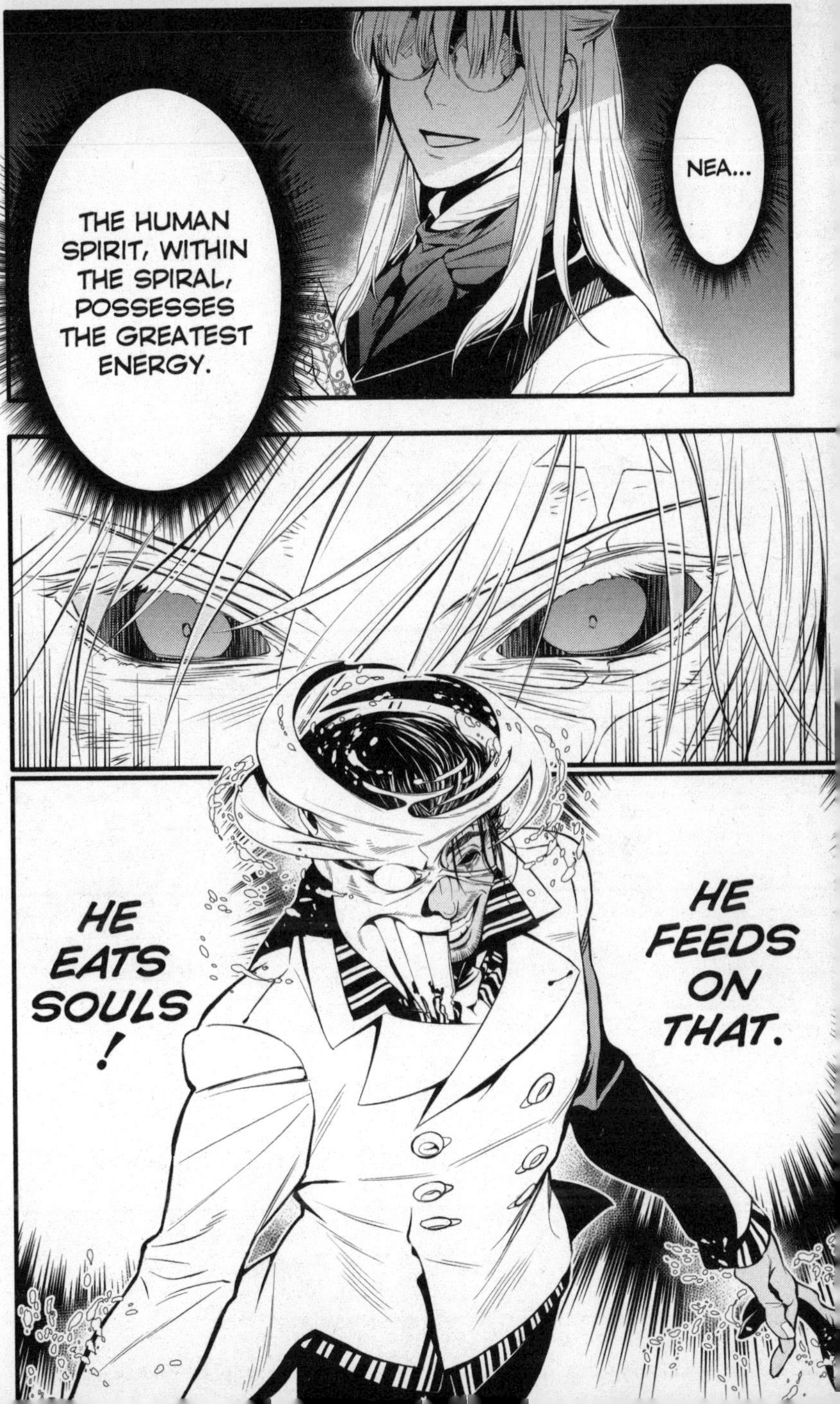
NEA...
THE HUMAN SPIRIT, WITHIN THE SPIRAL, POSSESSES THE GREATEST ENERGY.
HE FEEDS ON THAT.
HE EATS SOULS!

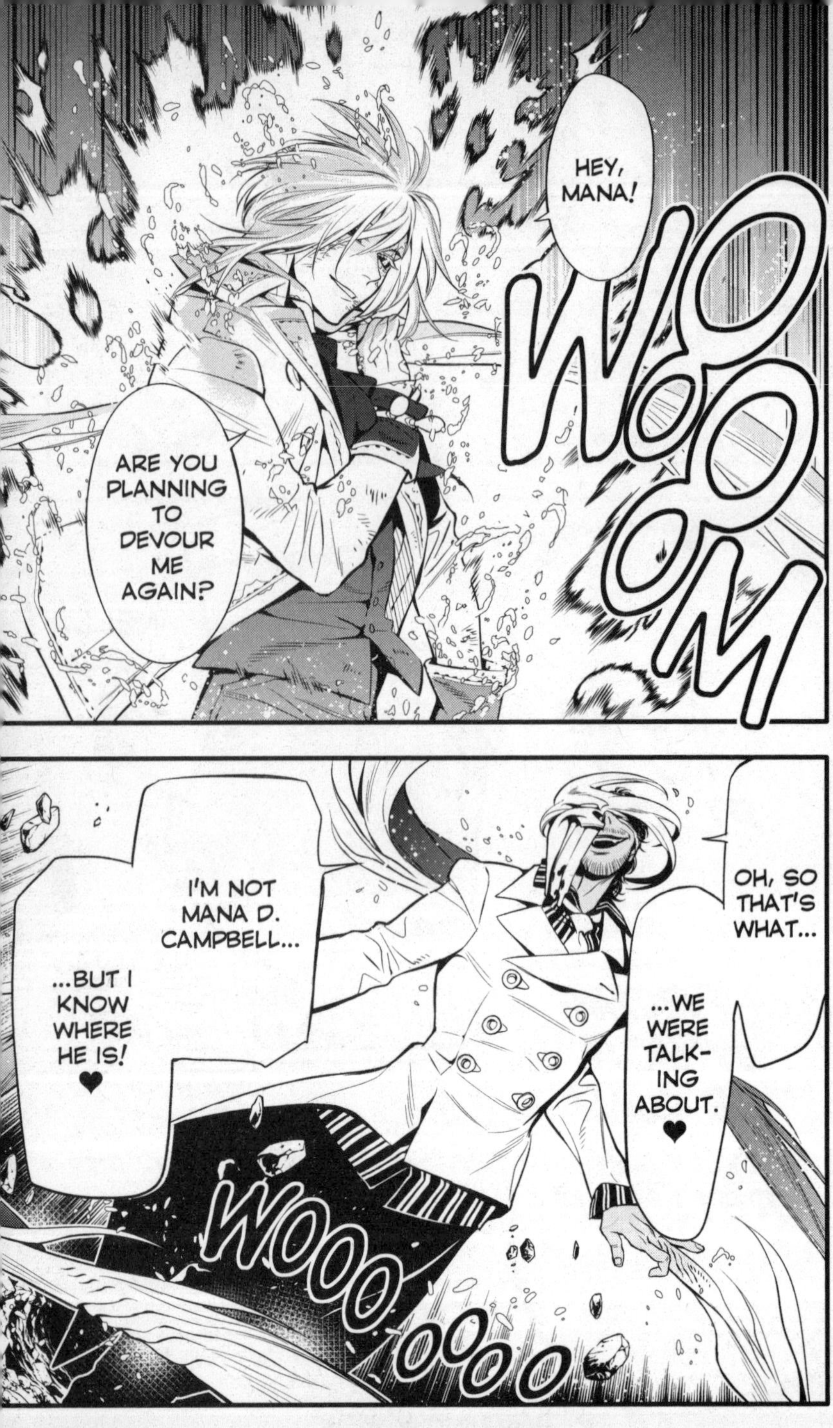
HEY, MANA!
ARE YOU PLANNING TO DEVOUR ME AGAIN?
WOOOOM
OH, SO THAT'S WHAT...
...WE WERE TALKING ABOUT. ♥
I'M NOT MANA D. CAMPBELL...
...BUT I KNOW WHERE HE IS! ♥
WOOOOOOO

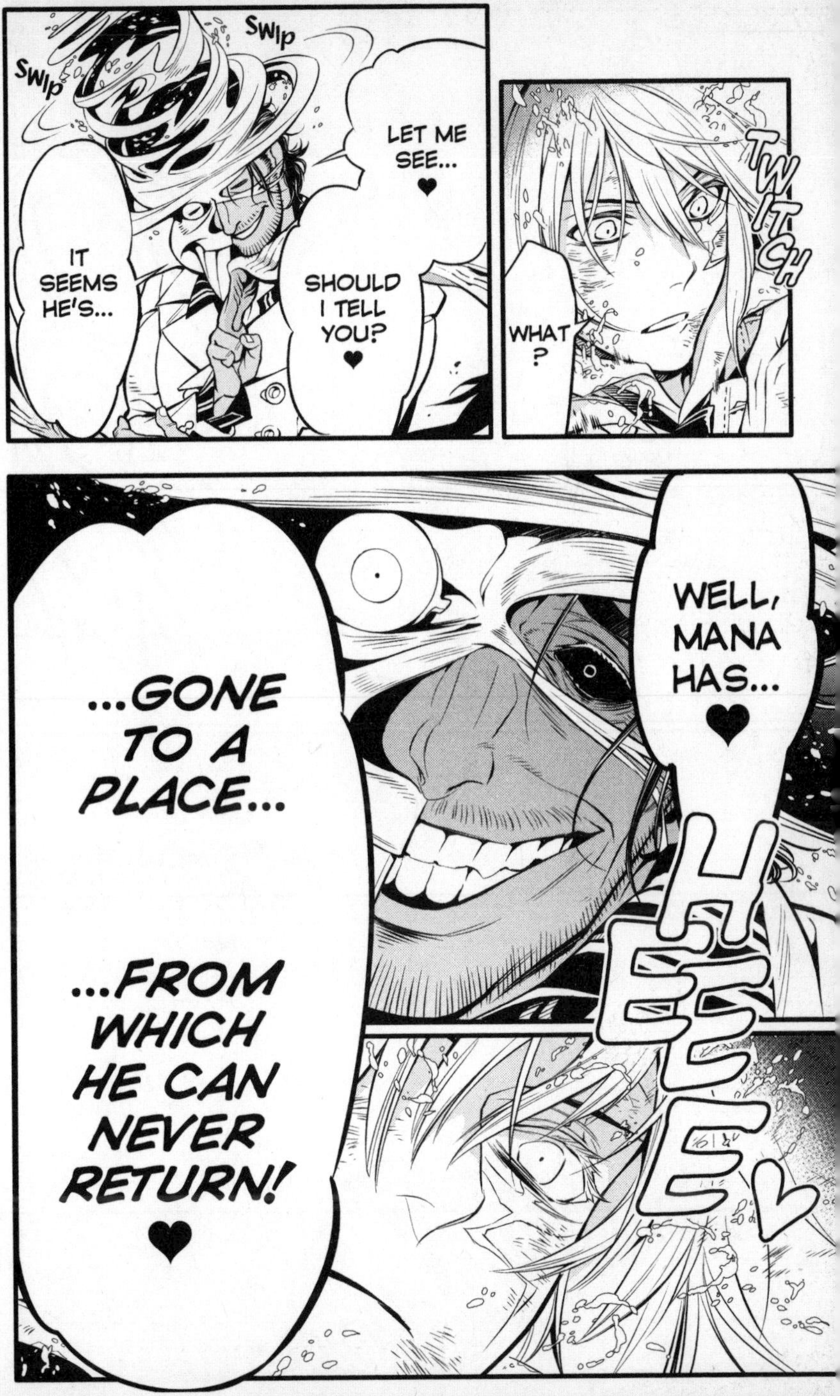
TWITCH
WHAT?
SWIP
SWIP
LET ME SEE... ♥
SHOULD I TELL YOU? ♥
IT SEEMS HE'S...
WELL, MANA HAS... ♥
...GONE TO A PLACE...
...FROM WHICH HE CAN NEVER RETURN! ♥
HEEEEE ♥

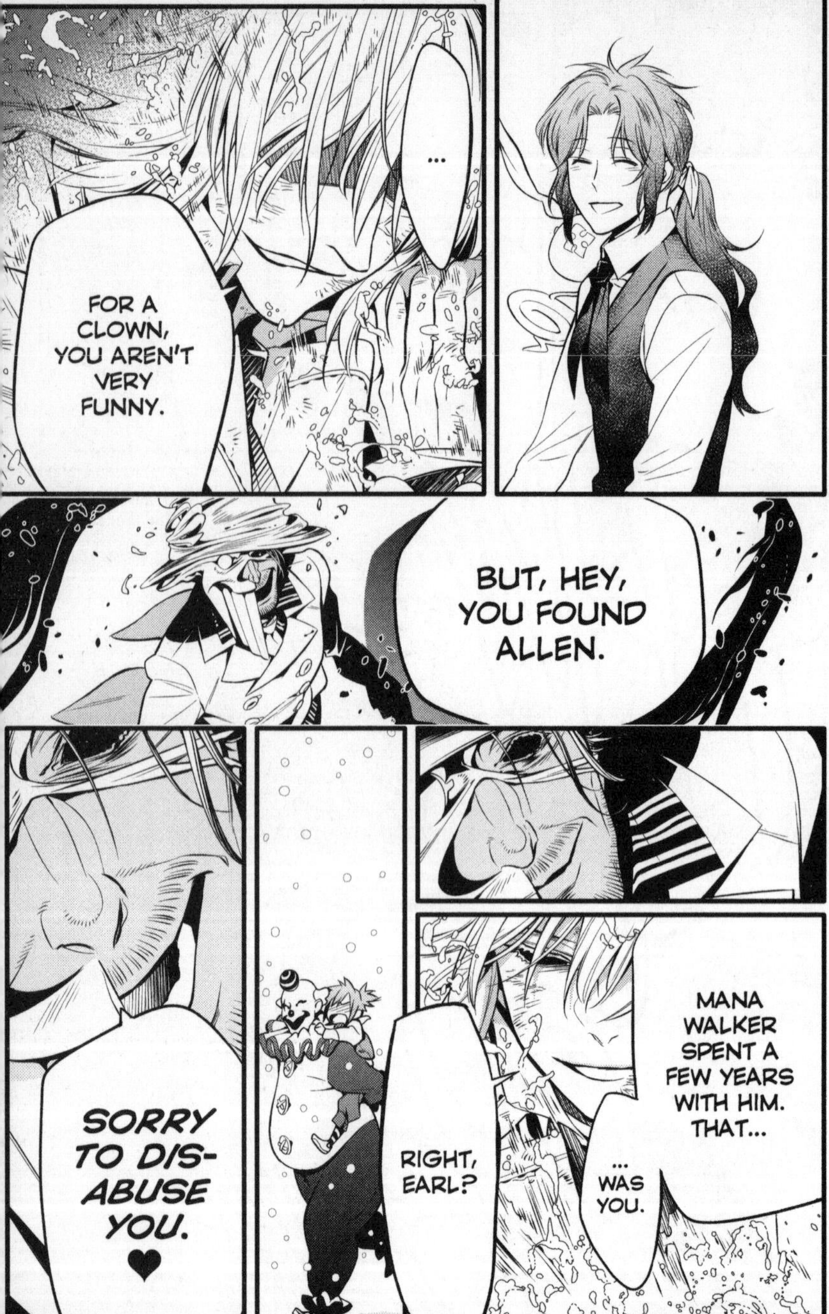
...
FOR A CLOWN, YOU AREN'T VERY FUNNY.
BUT, HEY, YOU FOUND ALLEN.
MANA WALKER SPENT A FEW YEARS WITH HIM. THAT...
...WAS YOU.
RIGHT, EARL?
SORRY TO DIS-ABUSE YOU. ♥

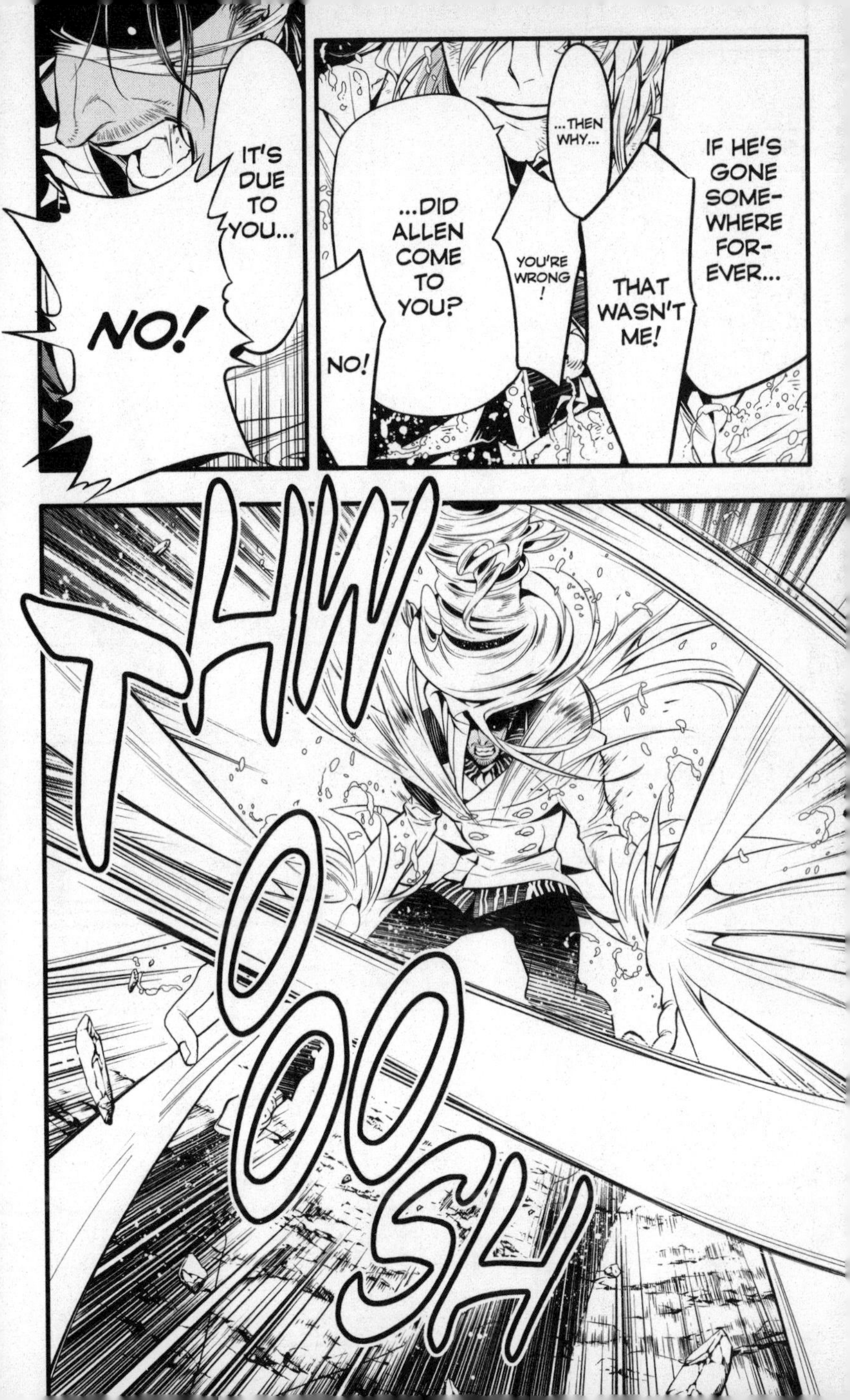
IF HE'S GONE SOMEWHERE FOREVER...
THAT WASN'T ME!
...THEN WHY...
YOU'RE WRONG!
...DID ALLEN COME TO YOU?
NO!
IT'S DUE TO YOU...
NO!
THWOOOSH

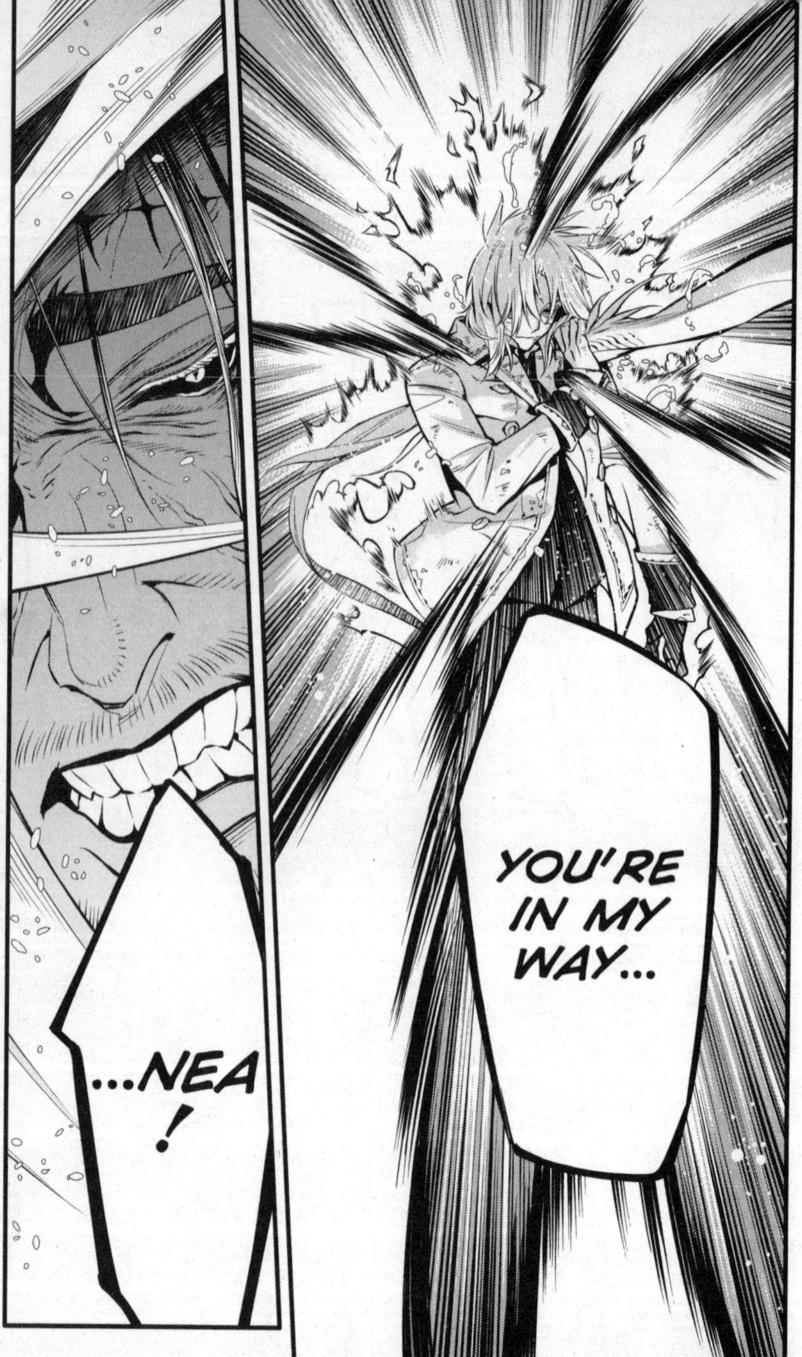
YOU'RE IN MY WAY...
...NEA!

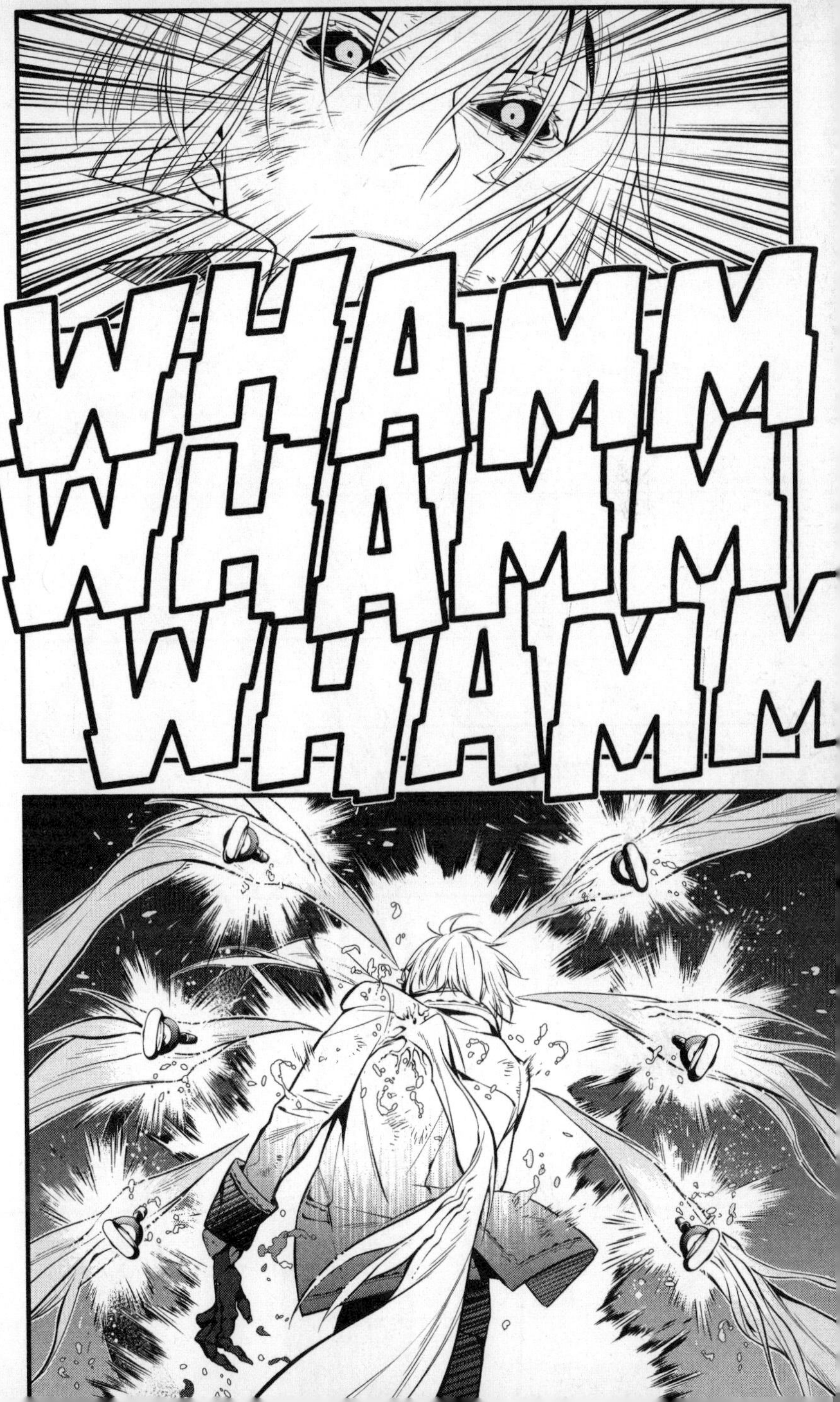
WHAMM
WHAMM
WHAMM

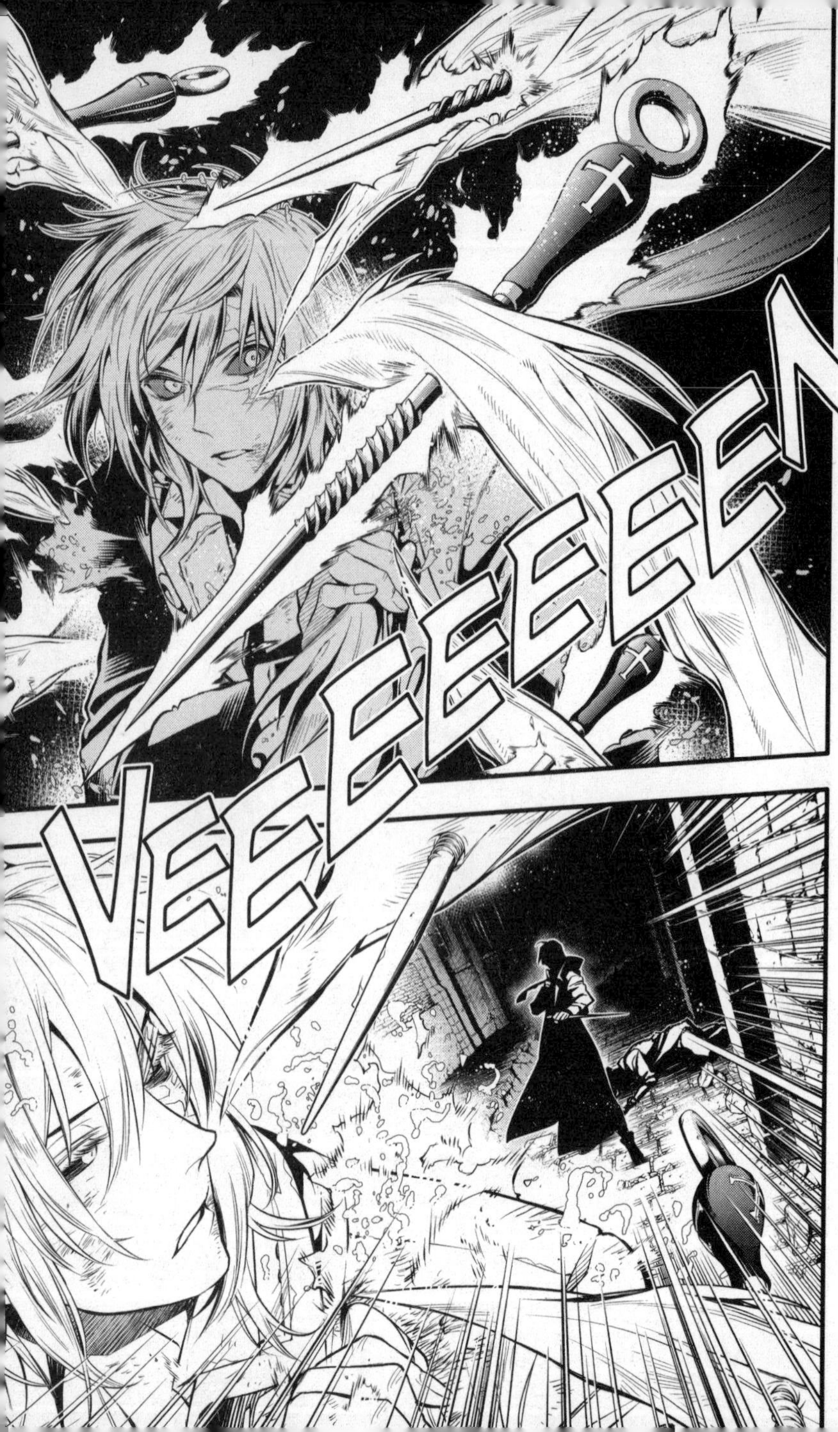
VEEEEEEEEN

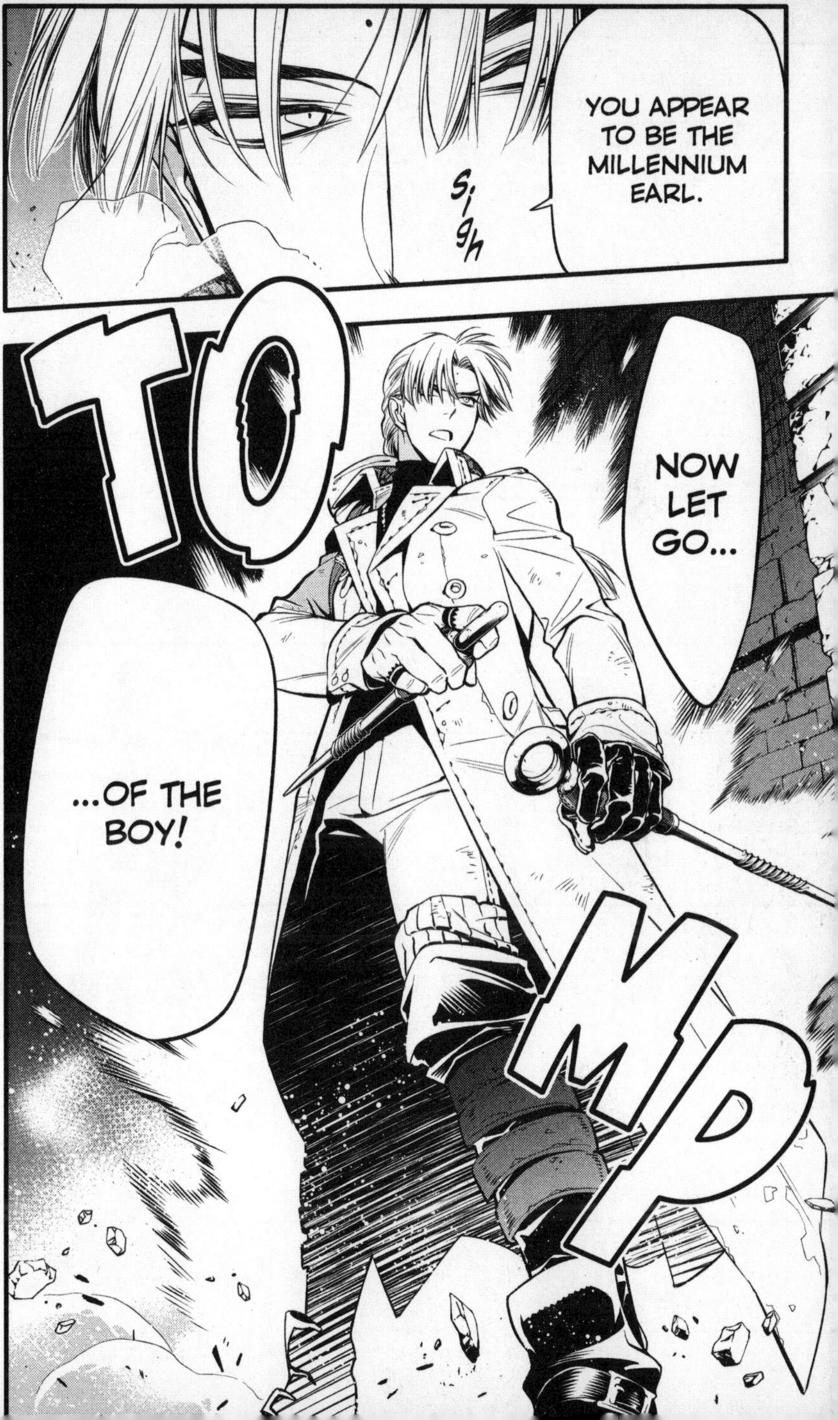
YOU APPEAR TO BE THE MILLENNIUM EARL.
SIGH
NOW LET GO...
...OF THE BOY!
TOMP

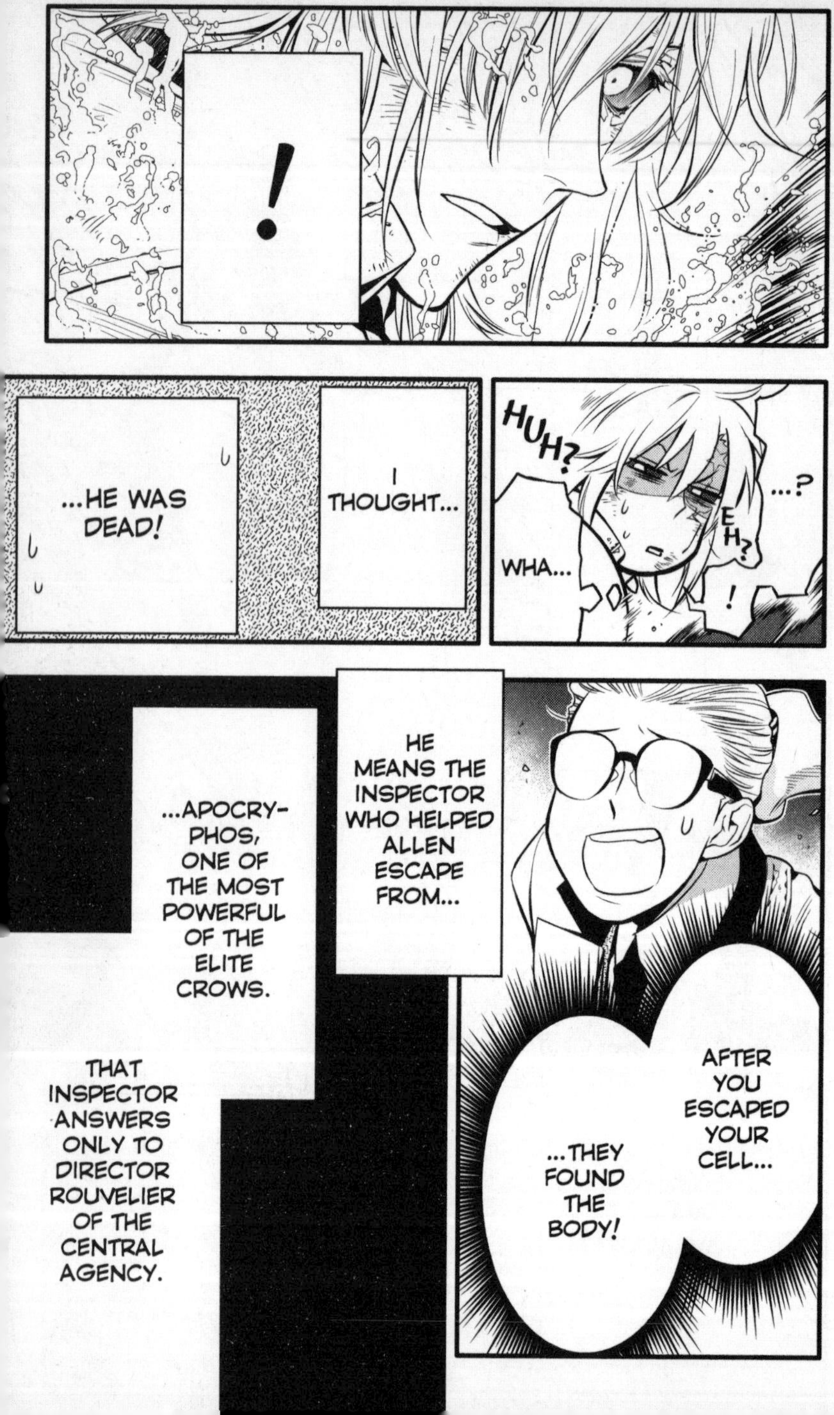
!
...?
EH?
HUH?
WHA...
!
I THOUGHT...
...HE WAS DEAD!
AFTER YOU ESCAPED YOUR CELL...
...THEY FOUND THE BODY!
HE MEANS THE INSPECTOR WHO HELPED ALLEN ESCAPE FROM...
...APOCRYPHOS, ONE OF THE MOST POWERFUL OF THE ELITE CROWS.
THAT INSPECTOR ANSWERS ONLY TO DIRECTOR ROUVELIER OF THE CENTRAL AGENCY.

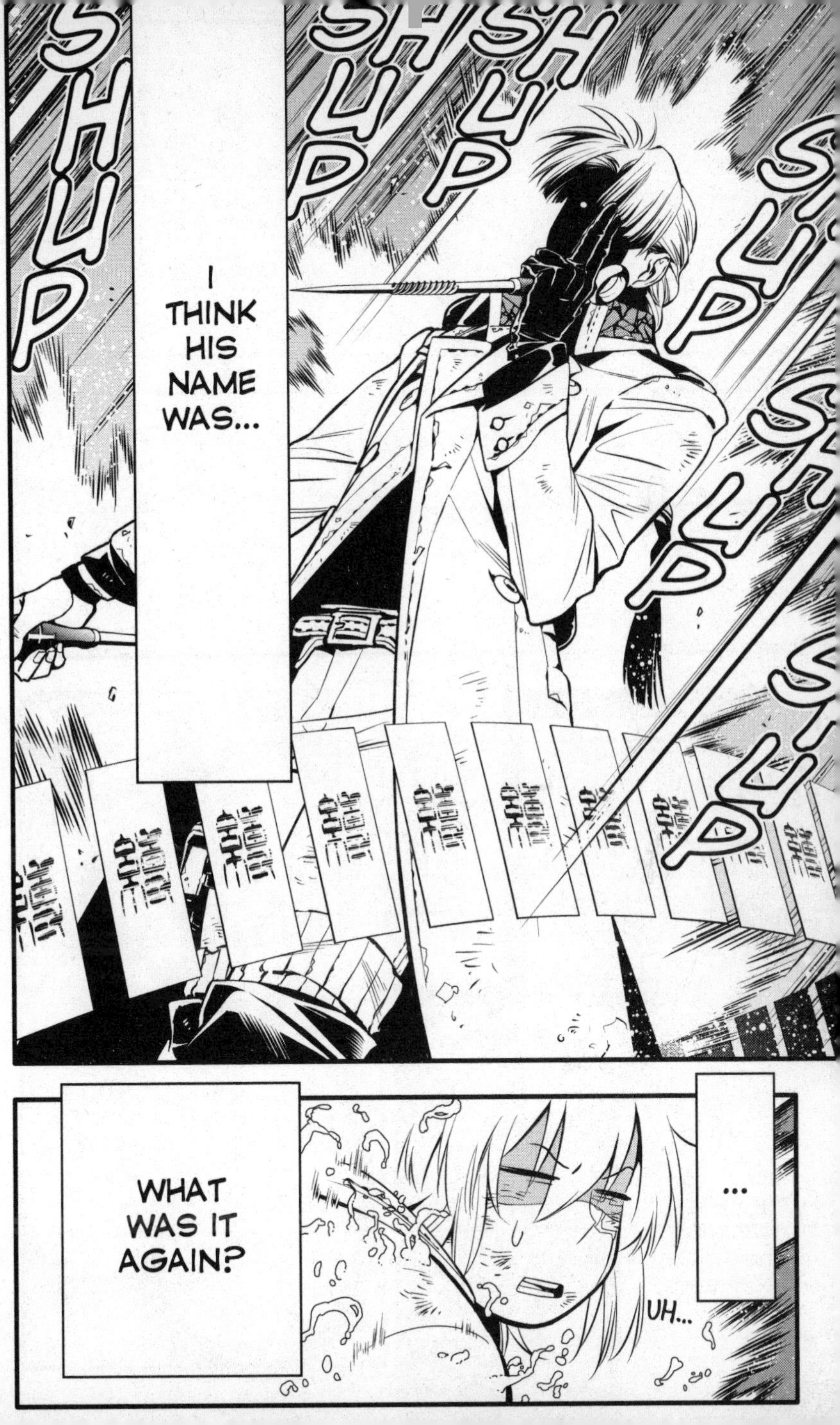
SHUP
SHUP
SHUP
SHUP
SHUP
I THINK HIS NAME WAS...
SHUP
...
UH...
WHAT WAS IT AGAIN?

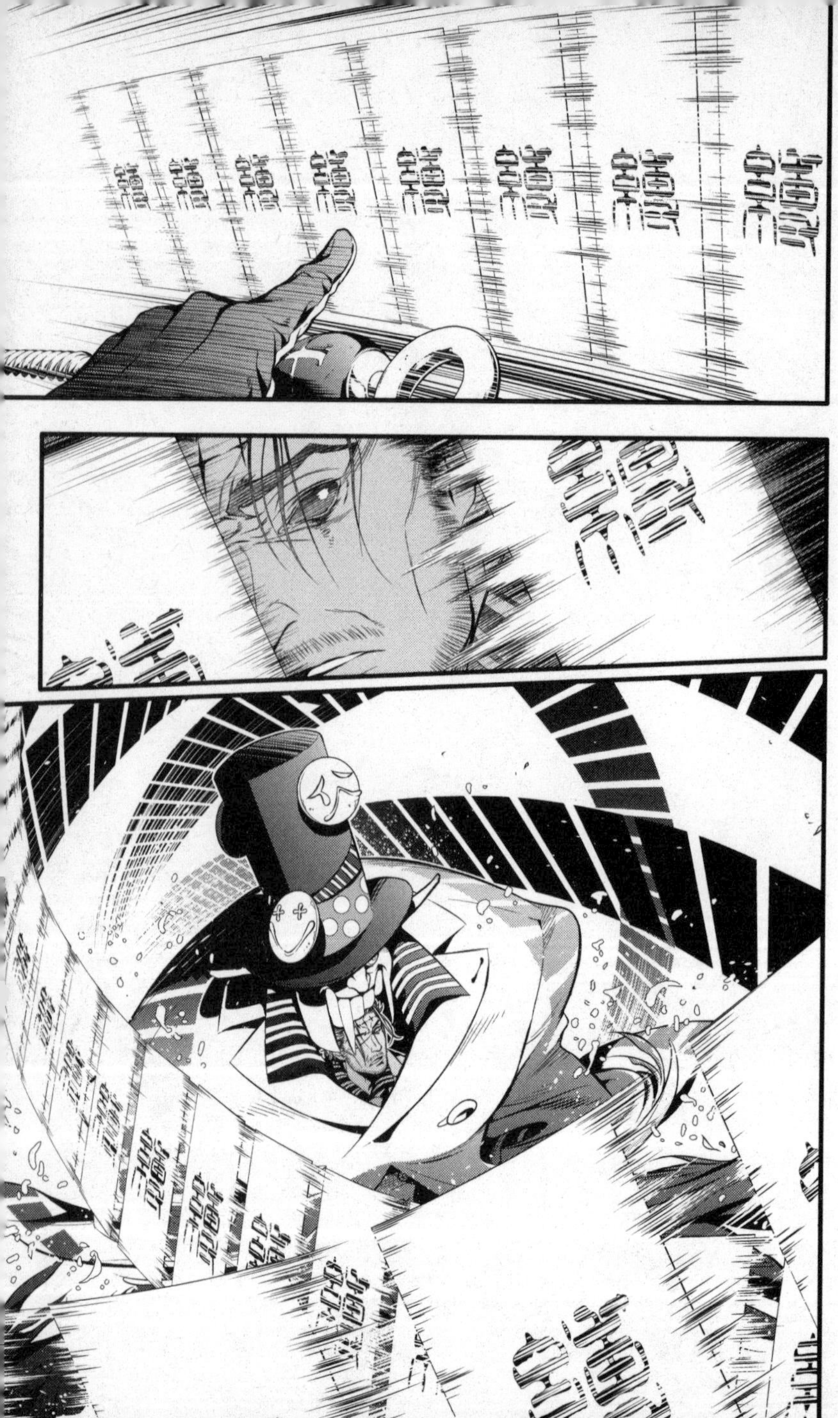

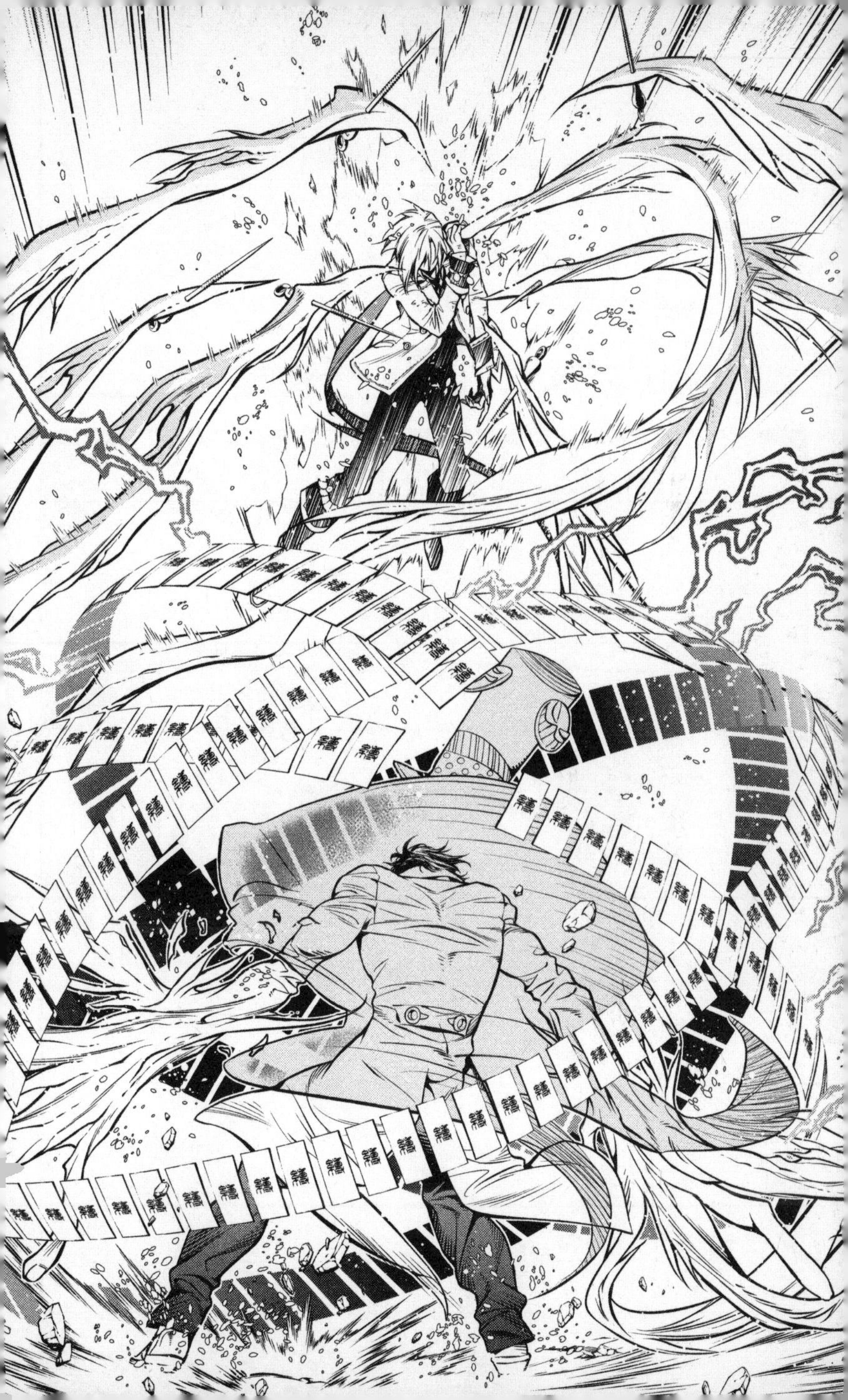

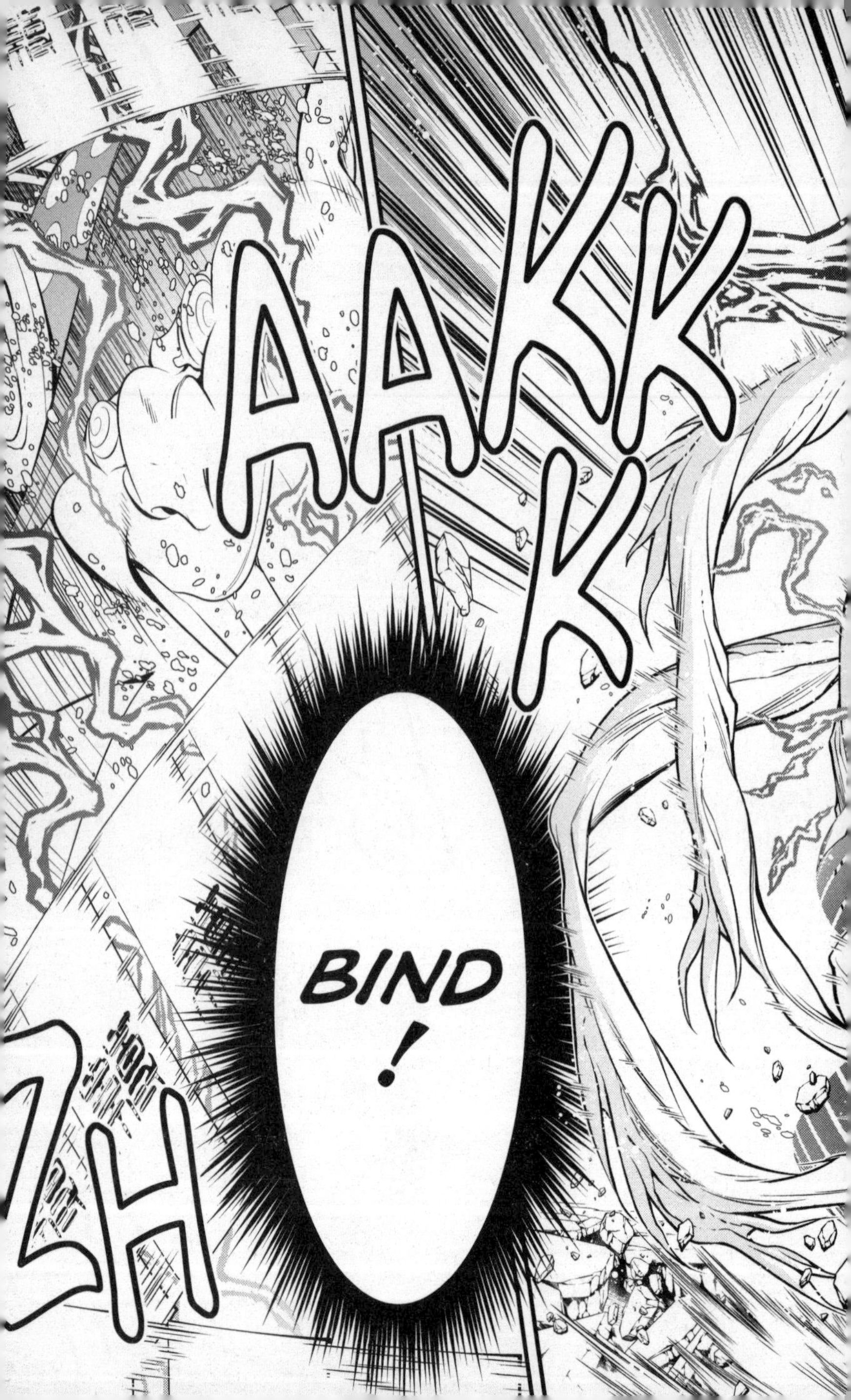
AAKKK
BIND!
ZH

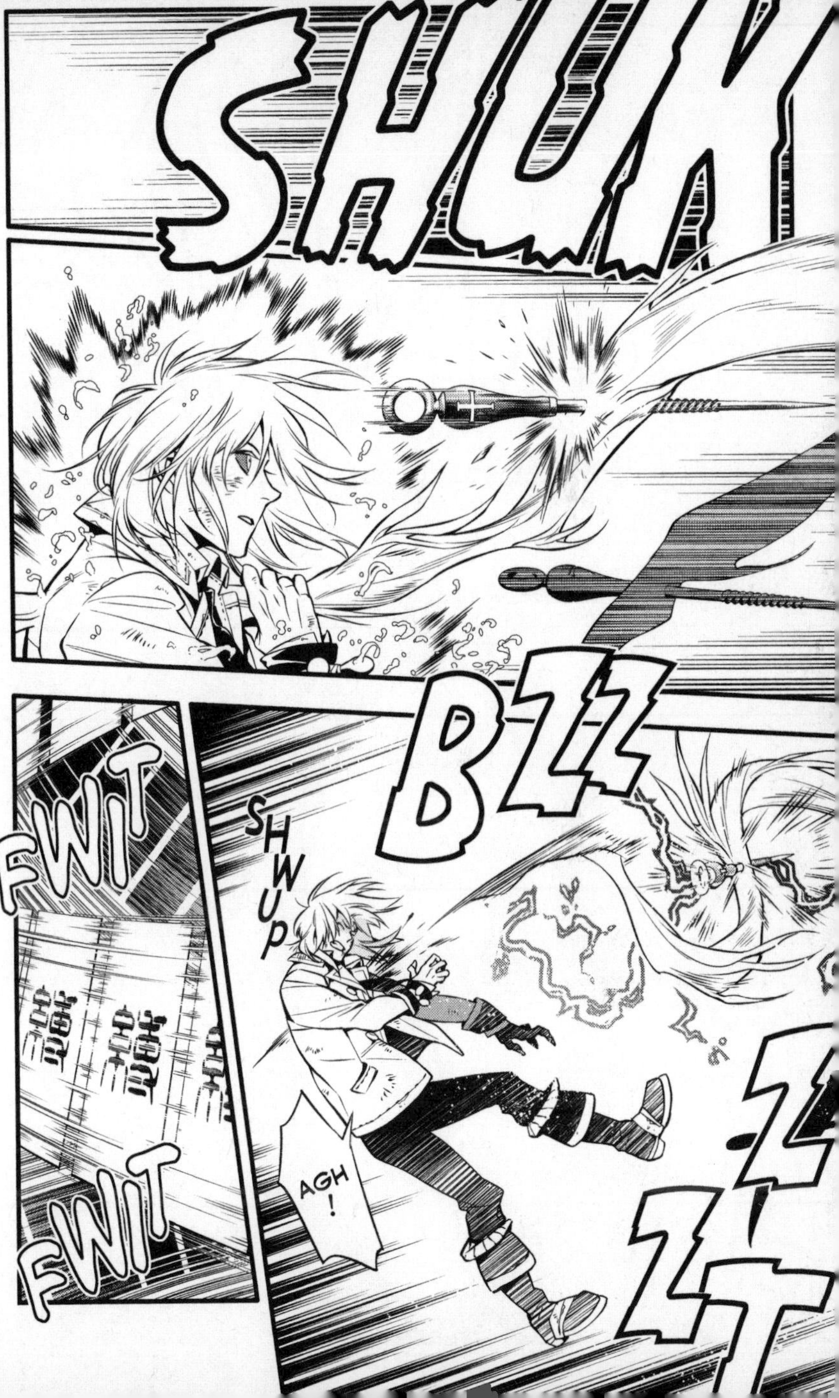
SHUN
BZZ
SHWUP
AGH!
FWIT
FWIT

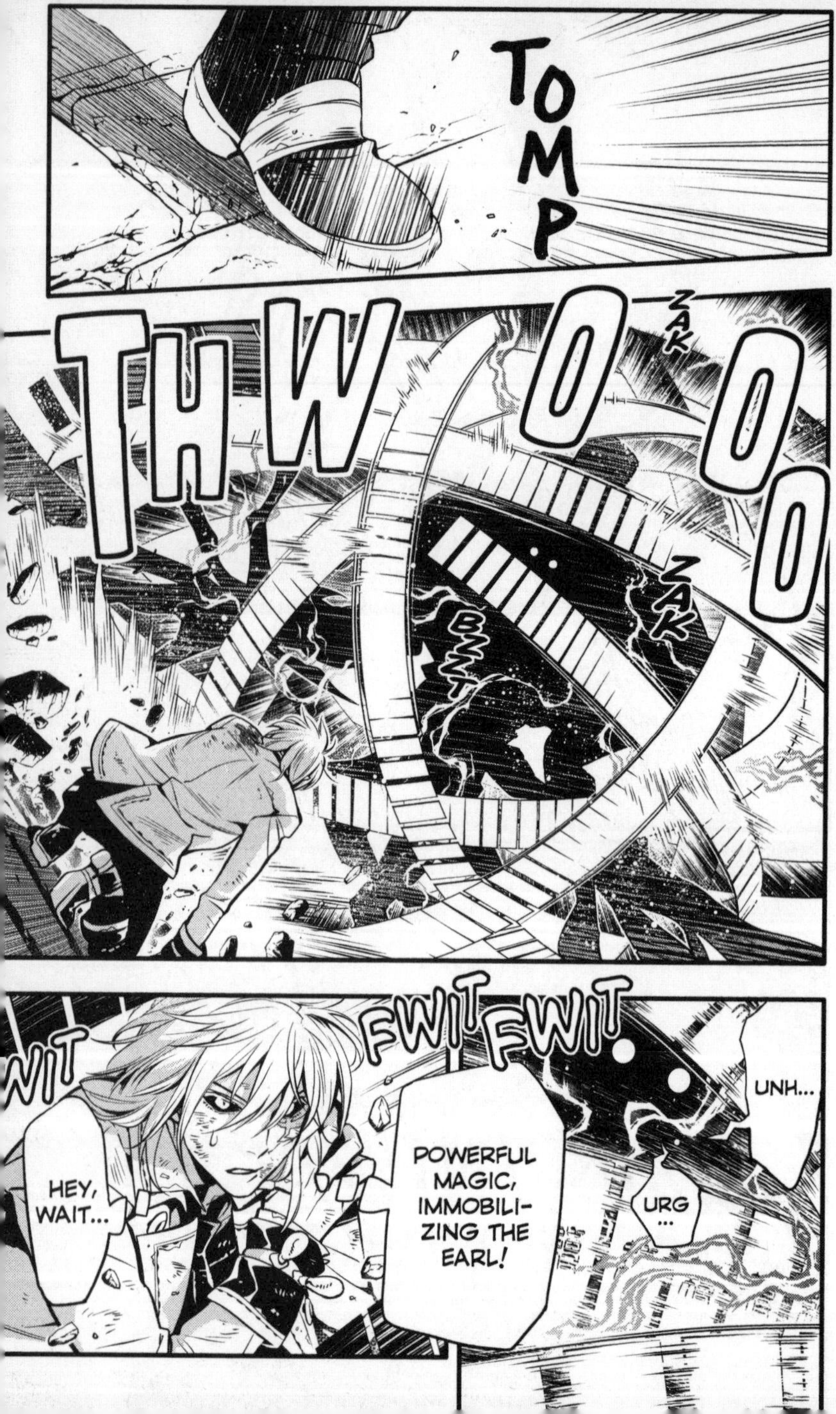
TOMP
THWOOOO
ZAK
ZAK
BZZT
UNH...
URG ...
FWIT FWIT
POWERFUL MAGIC, IMMOBILI-ZING THE EARL!
WIT
HEY, WAIT...

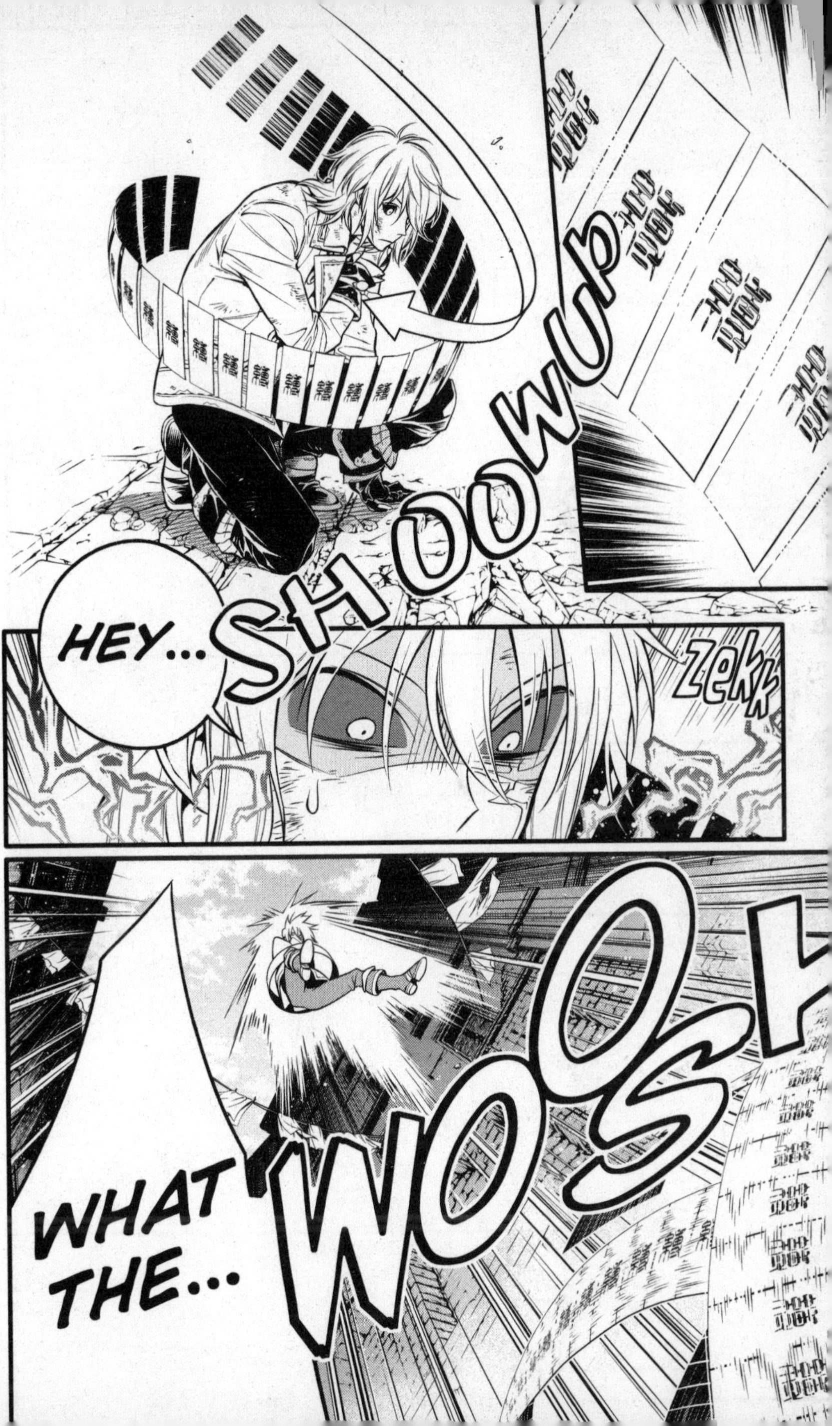
SHOOOWUP
HEY...
ZEKK
WOOOSH
WHAT THE...

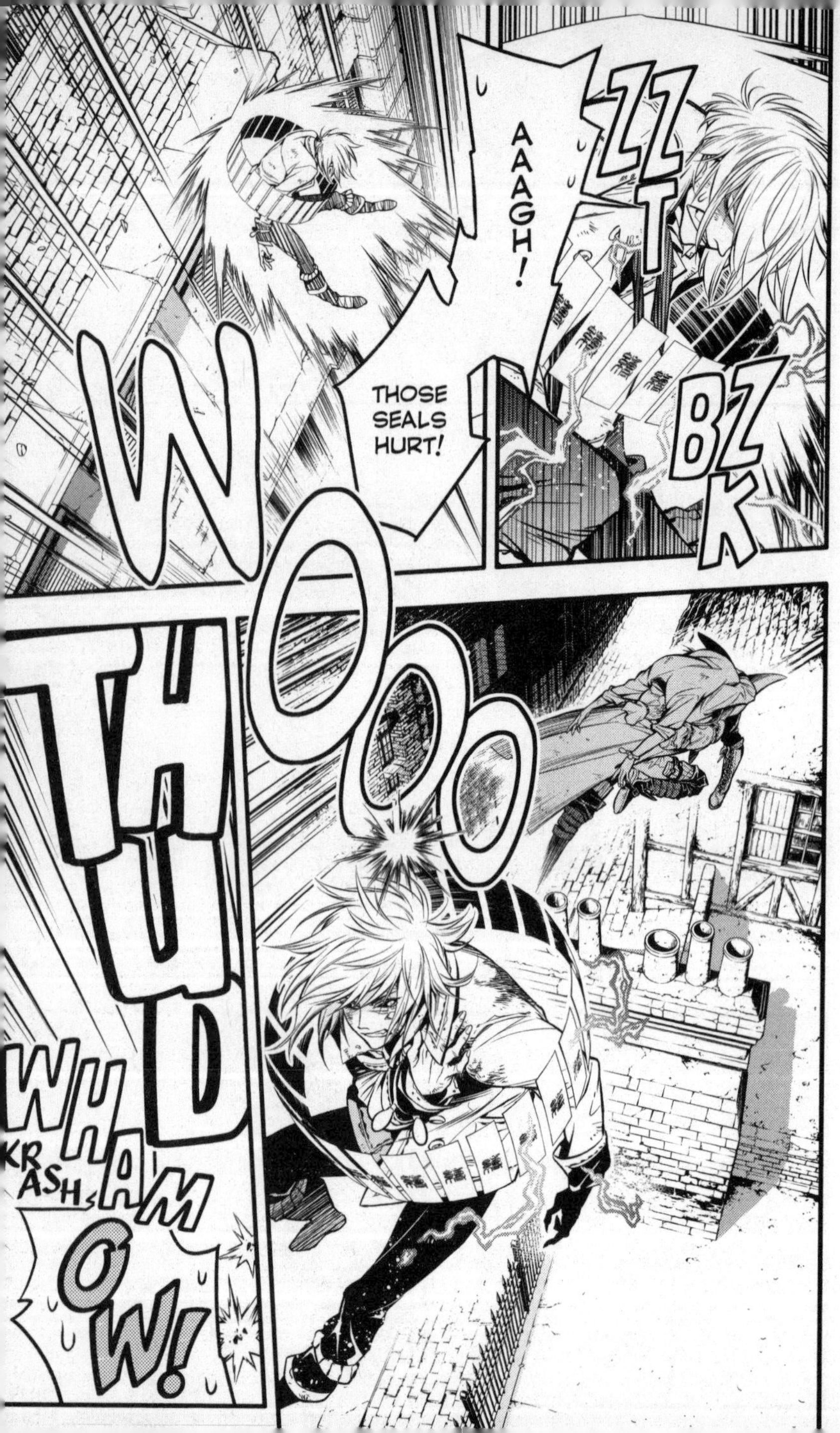
ZZT
AAAGH!
BZK
THOSE SEALS HURT!
WOOOO
THUD
WHAM
KRASH
OW!

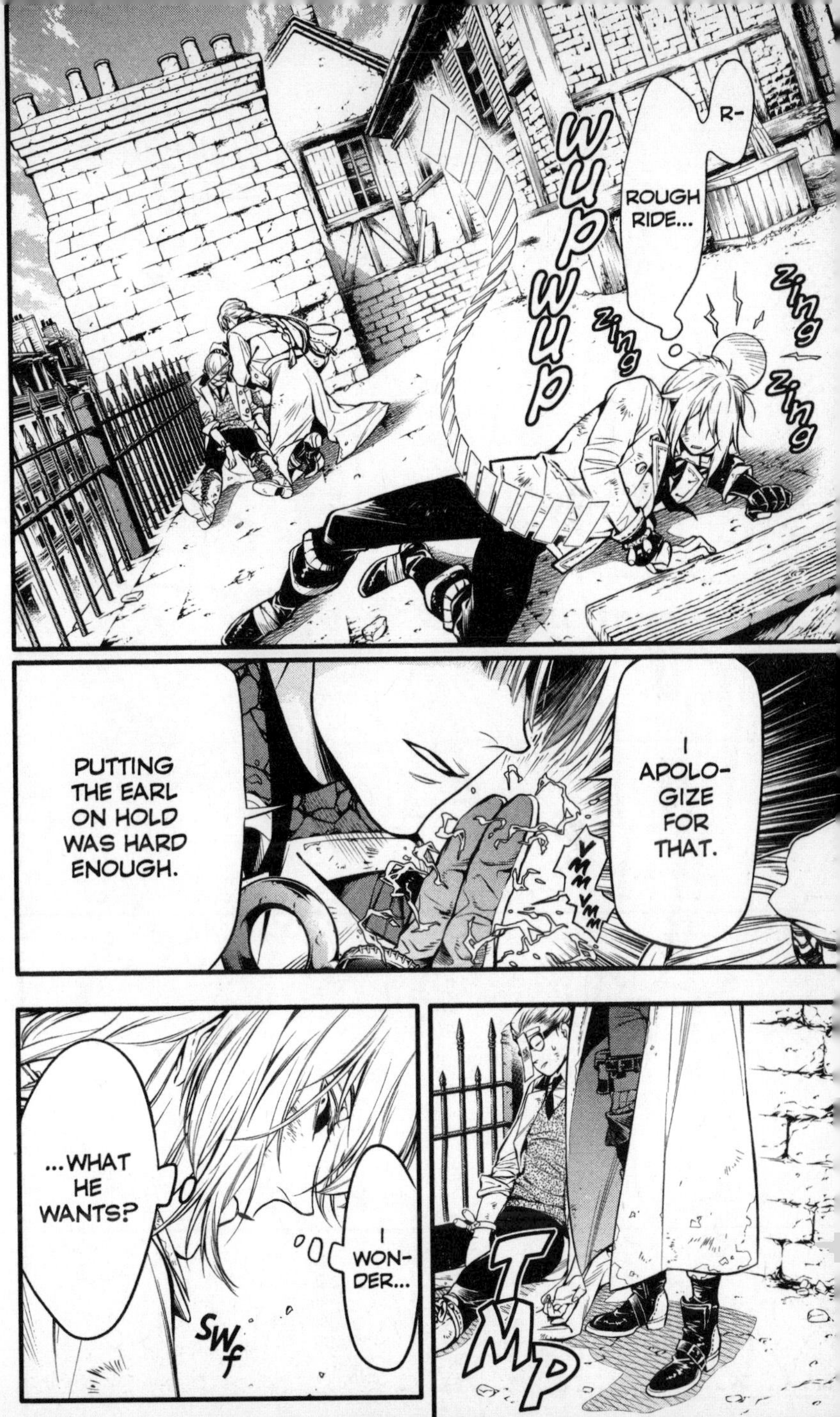
R- ROUGH RIDE...
wupwup
zing
zing zing
I APOLOGIZE FOR THAT.
VMM VMM
PUTTING THE EARL ON HOLD WAS HARD ENOUGH.
TMP
I WONDER...
...WHAT HE WANTS?
SWf

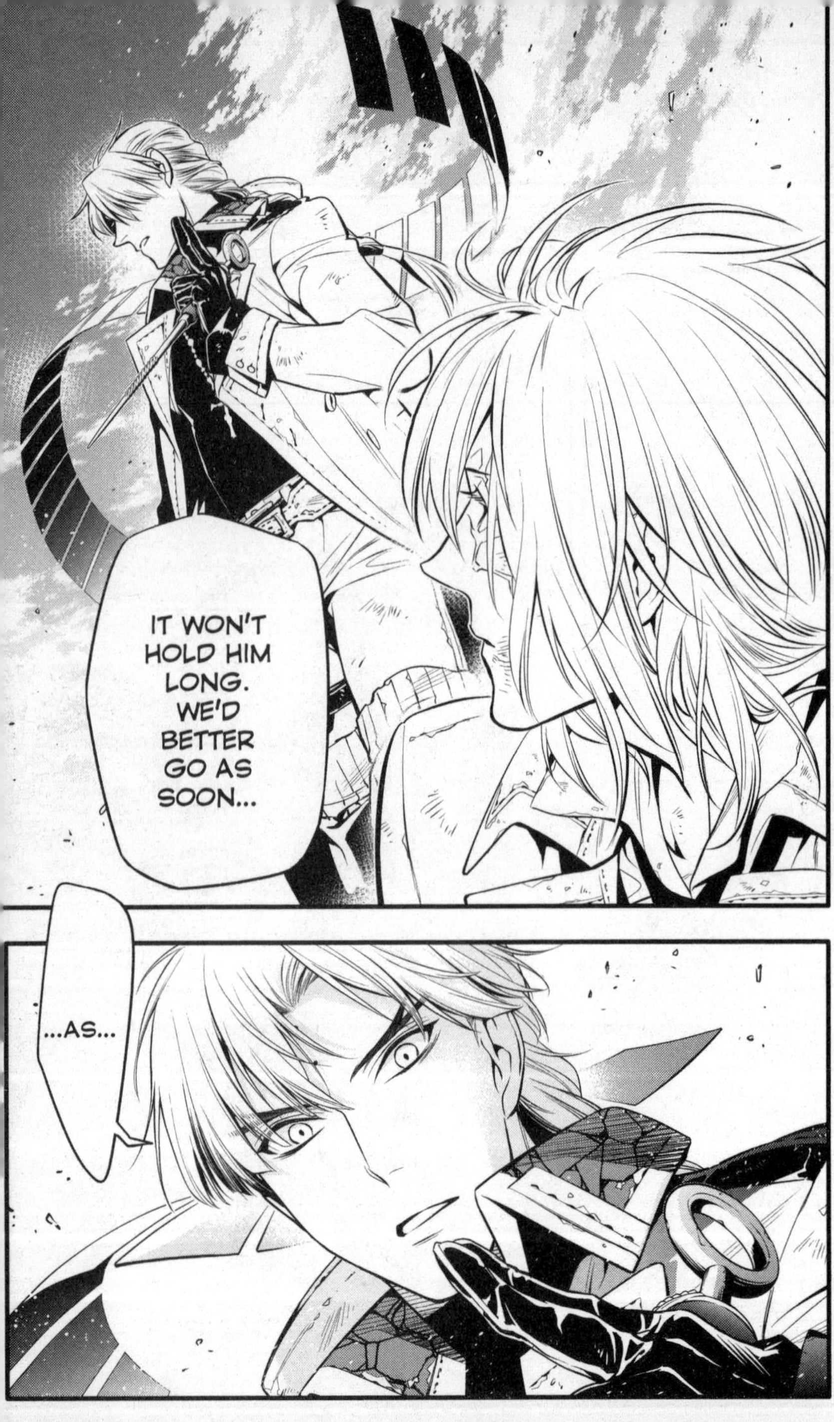
IT WON'T HOLD HIM LONG. WE'D BETTER GO AS SOON...
...AS...

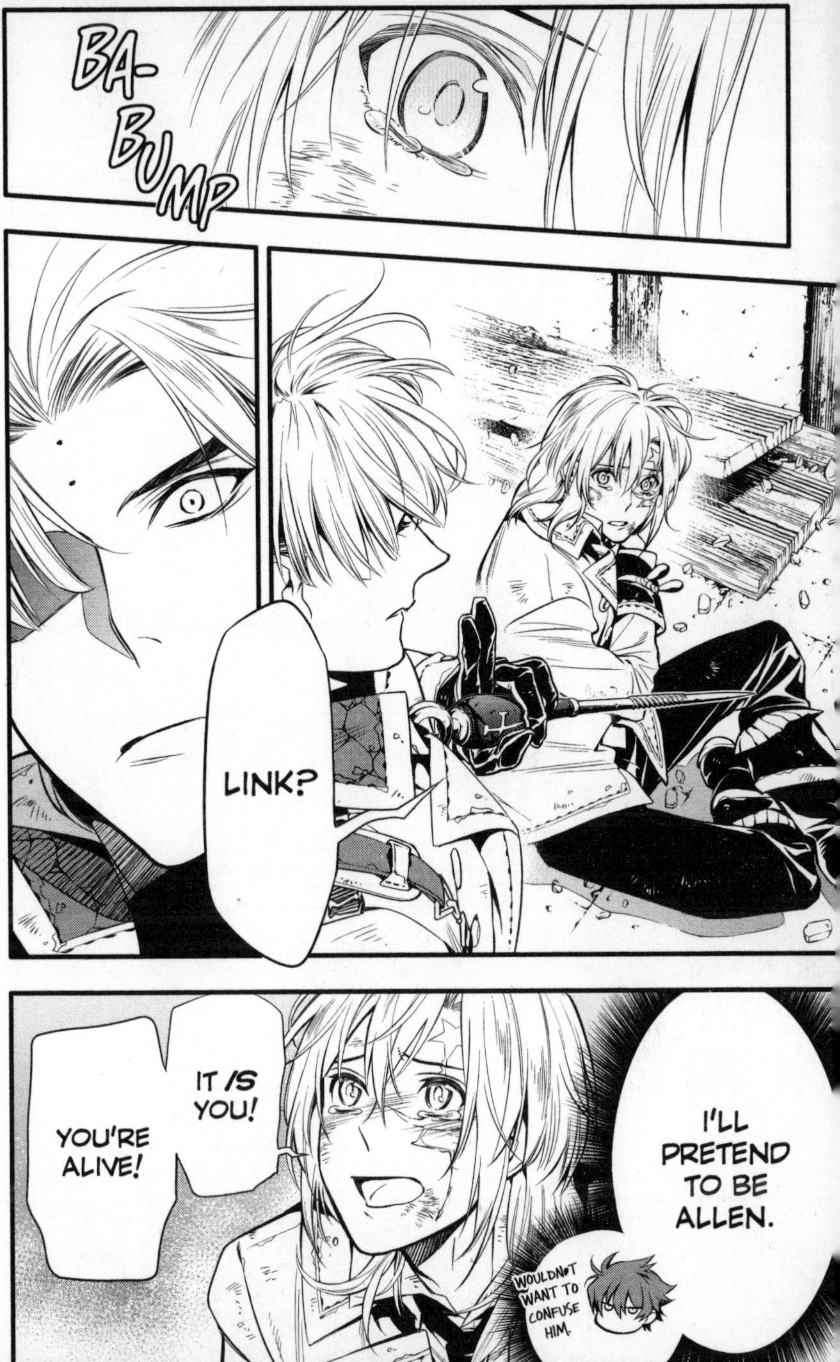
BA-BUMP
LINK?
I'LL PRETEND TO BE ALLEN.
WOULDN'T WANT TO CONFUSE HIM.
IT IS YOU!
YOU'RE ALIVE!

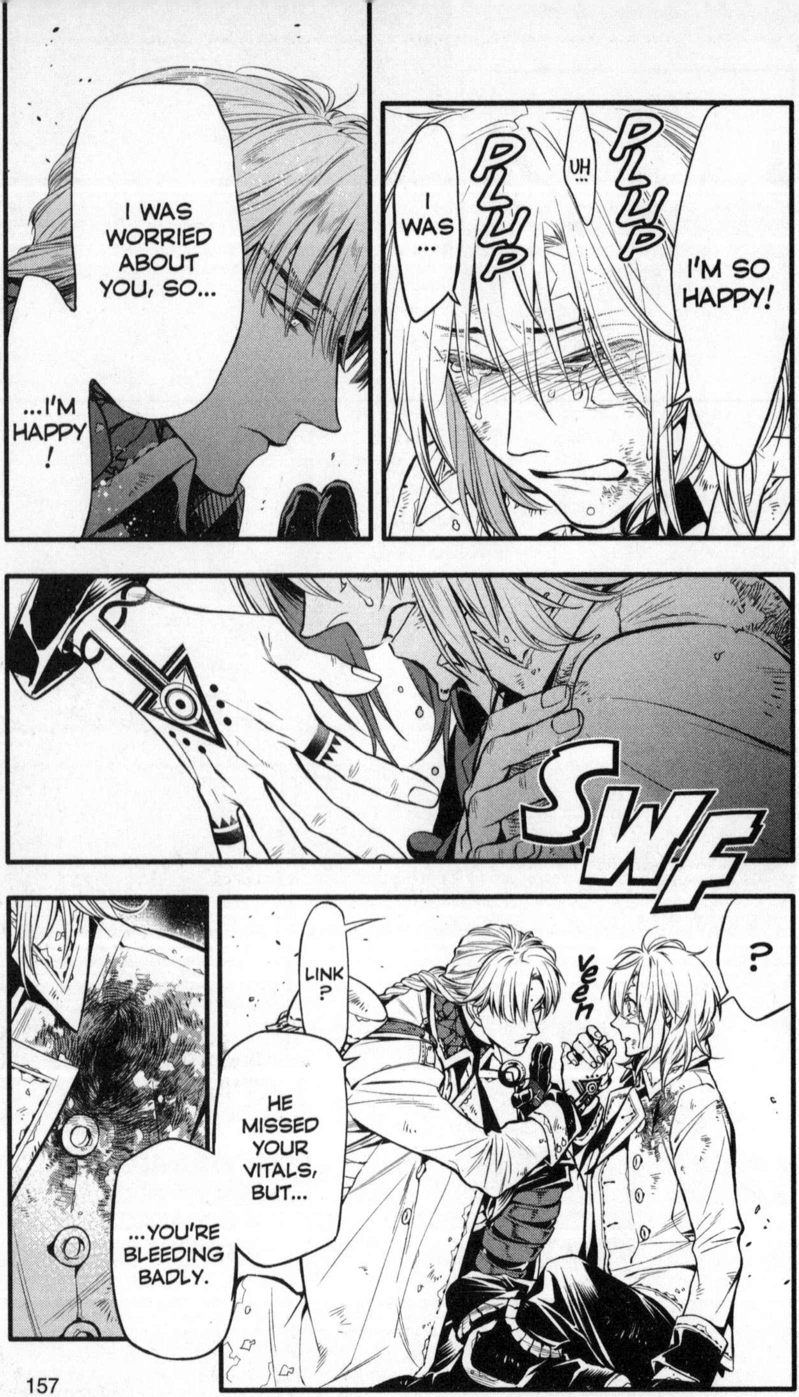
I'M SO HAPPY!
PLUP
UH...
PLUP
I WAS...
I WAS WORRIED ABOUT YOU, SO...
...I'M HAPPY!
SWF
?
veen
LINK?
HE MISSED YOUR VITALS, BUT...
...YOU'RE BLEEDING BADLY.

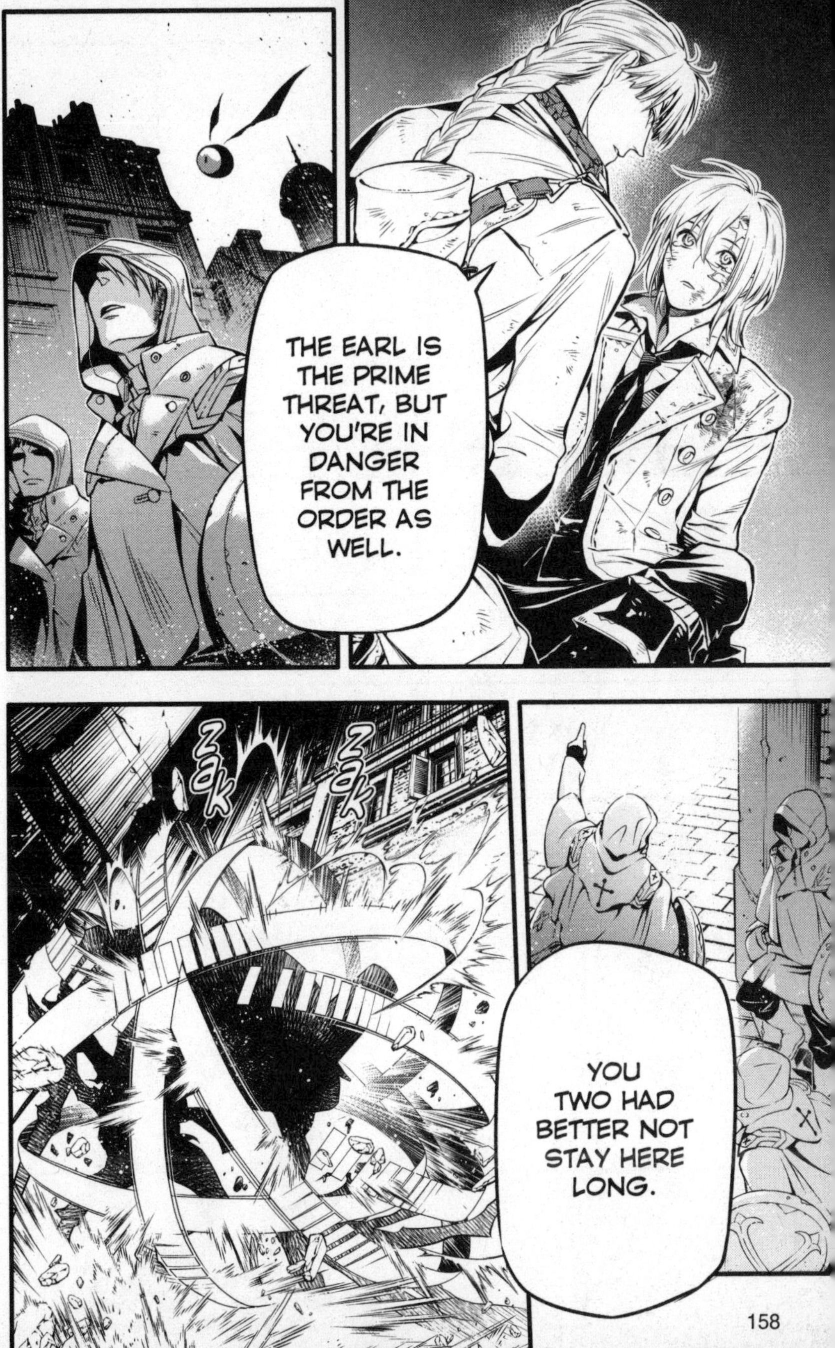
THE EARL IS THE PRIME THREAT, BUT YOU'RE IN DANGER FROM THE ORDER AS WELL.
YOU TWO HAD BETTER NOT STAY HERE LONG.
ZAK
ZAK

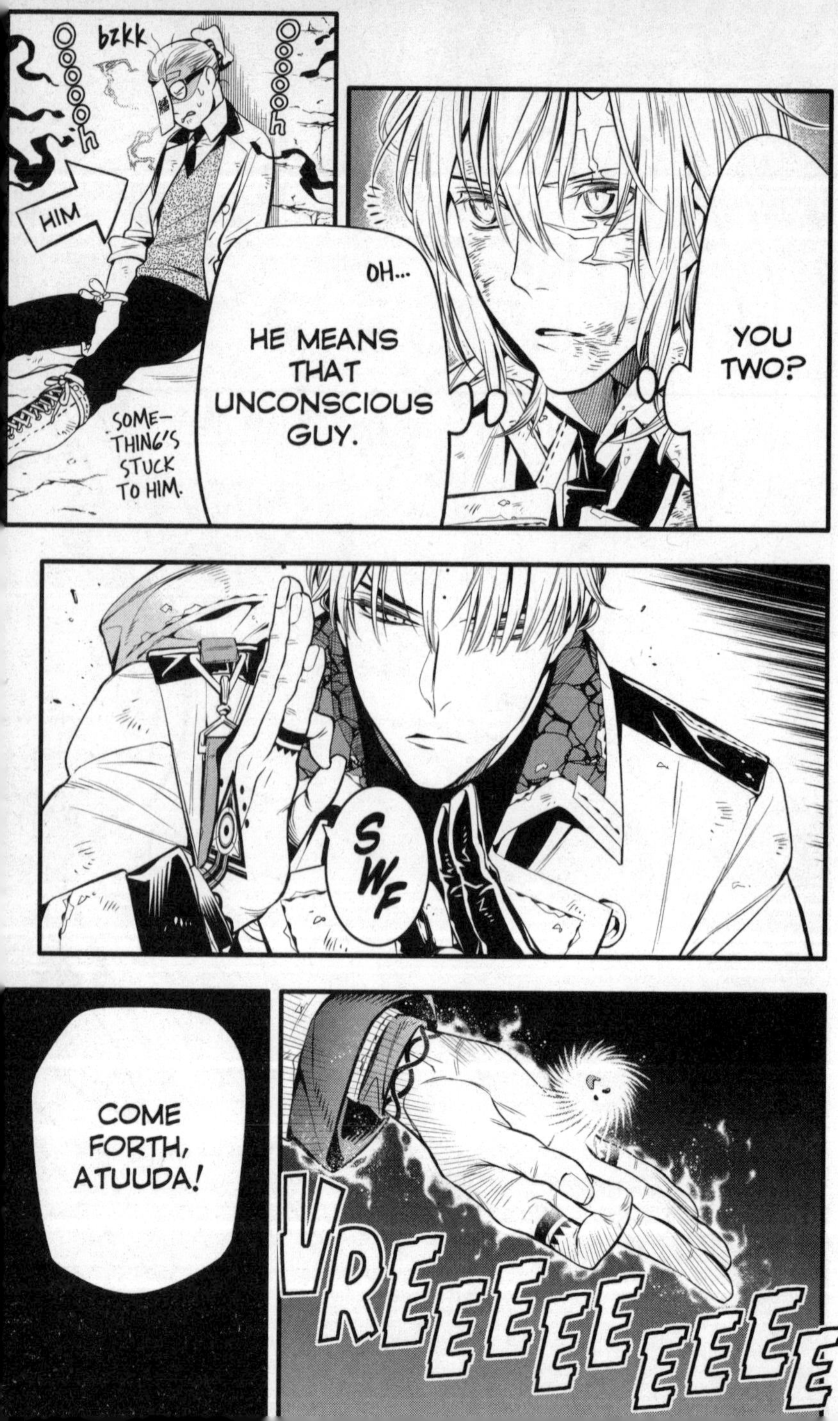
YOU TWO?
OH... HE MEANS THAT UNCONSCIOUS GUY.
Oooooh
bzkk
Oooooh
HIM
SOME-THING'S STUCK TO HIM.
SWF
VREEEEEEEEEEE
COME FORTH, ATUUDA!

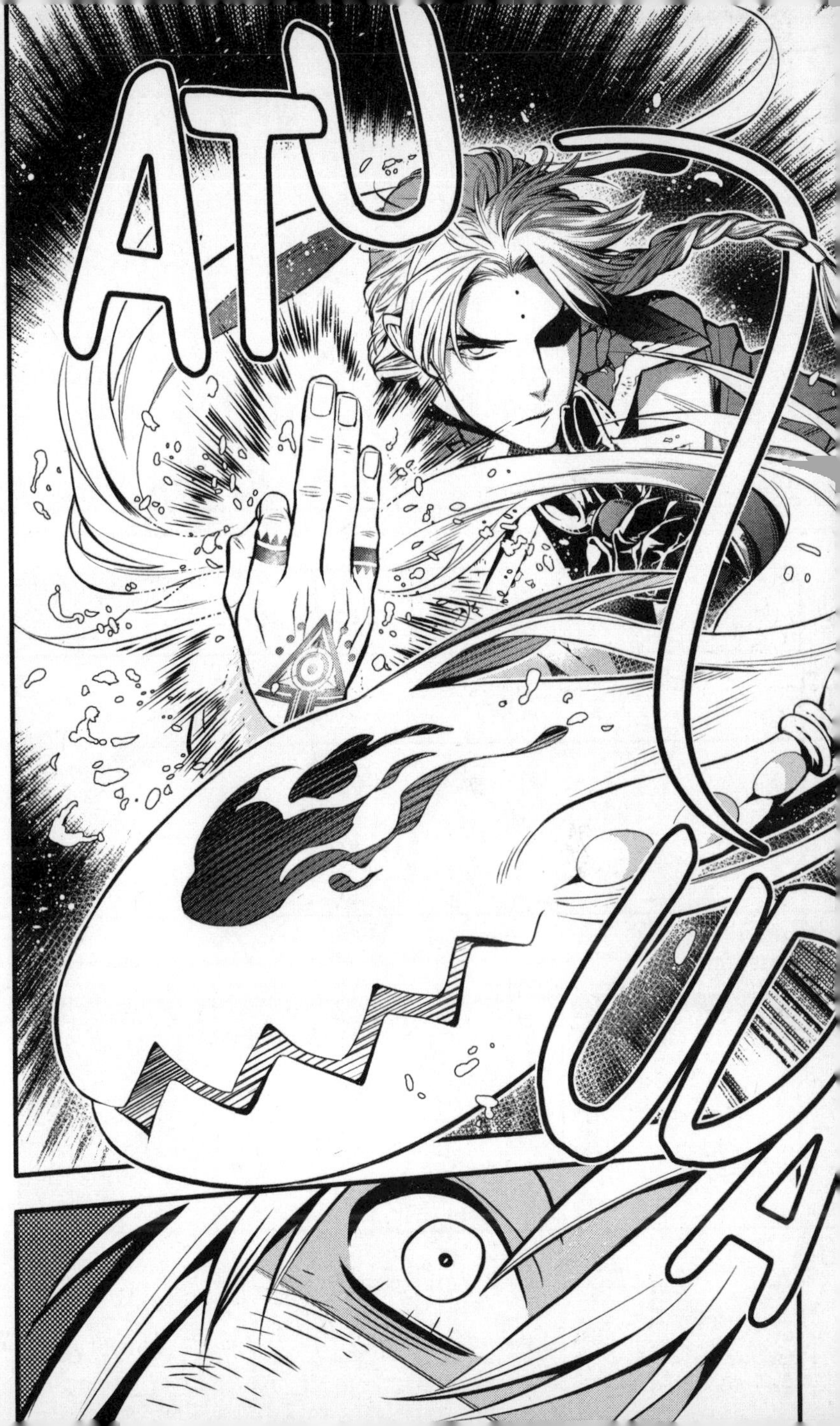
ATUUUA

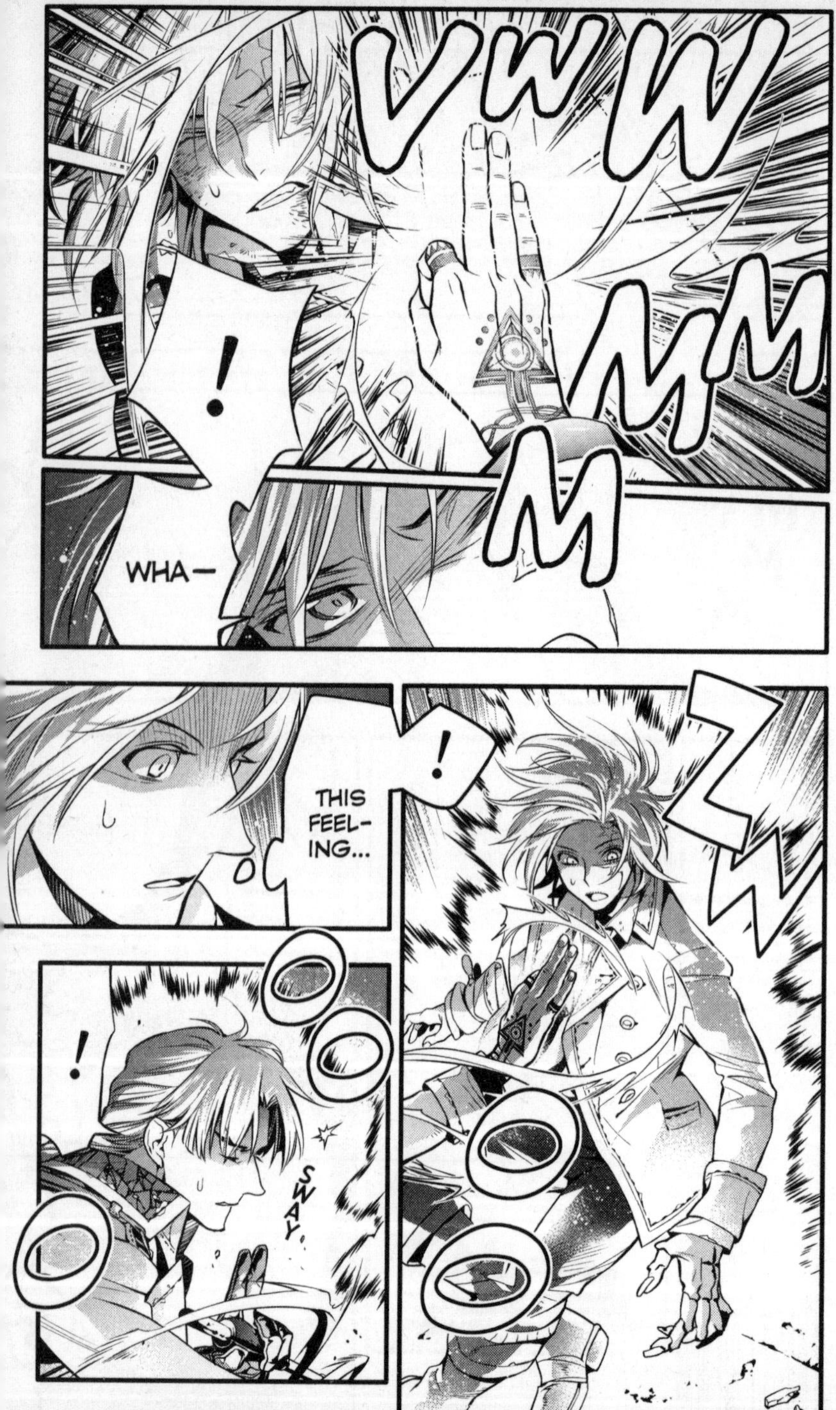
VWW
MMM
M
!
WHA—
ZW
OOOO
!
THIS FEEL-ING...
!
SWAY

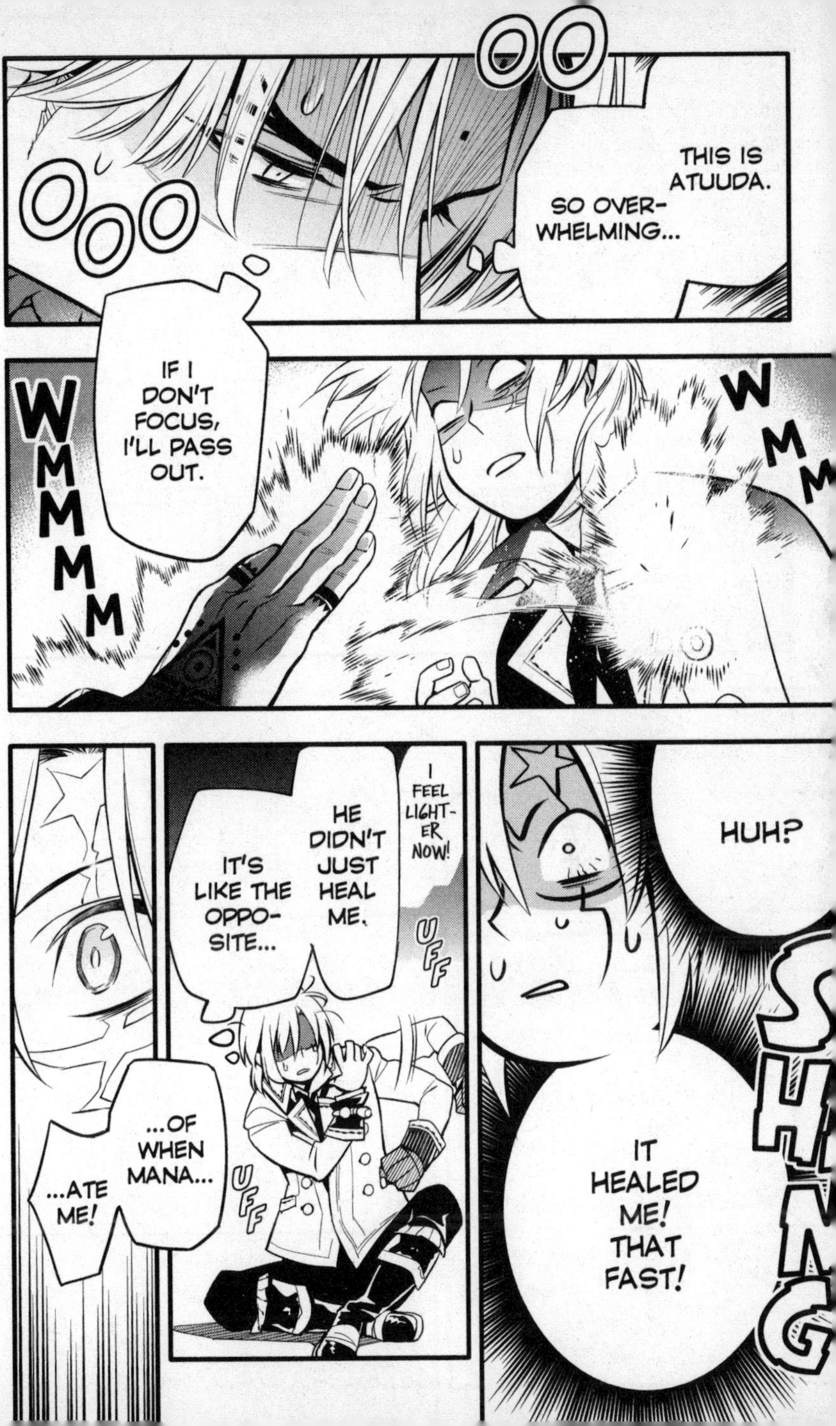
OOO
THIS IS ATUUDA.
SO OVER-WHELMING...
OOO
IF I DON'T FOCUS, I'LL PASS OUT.
WMM
WMMMMM
HUH?
IT HEALED ME! THAT FAST!
SHING
I FEEL LIGHT-ER NOW!
HE DIDN'T JUST HEAL ME.
IT'S LIKE THE OPPO-SITE...
UFF
UFF
...OF WHEN MANA...
...ATE ME!

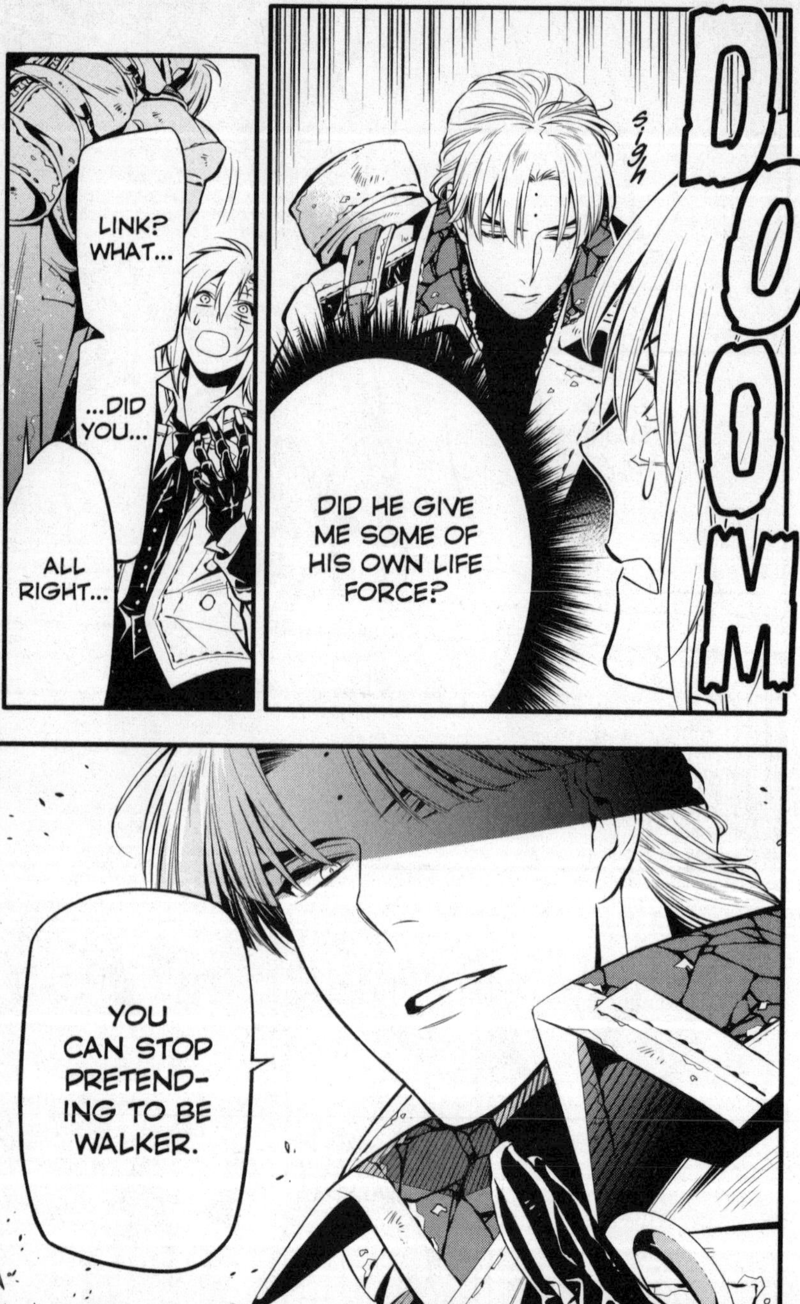
DOOM
SIGH
DID HE GIVE ME SOME OF HIS OWN LIFE FORCE?
LINK? WHAT...
...DID YOU...
ALL RIGHT...
YOU CAN STOP PRETEND-ING TO BE WALKER.

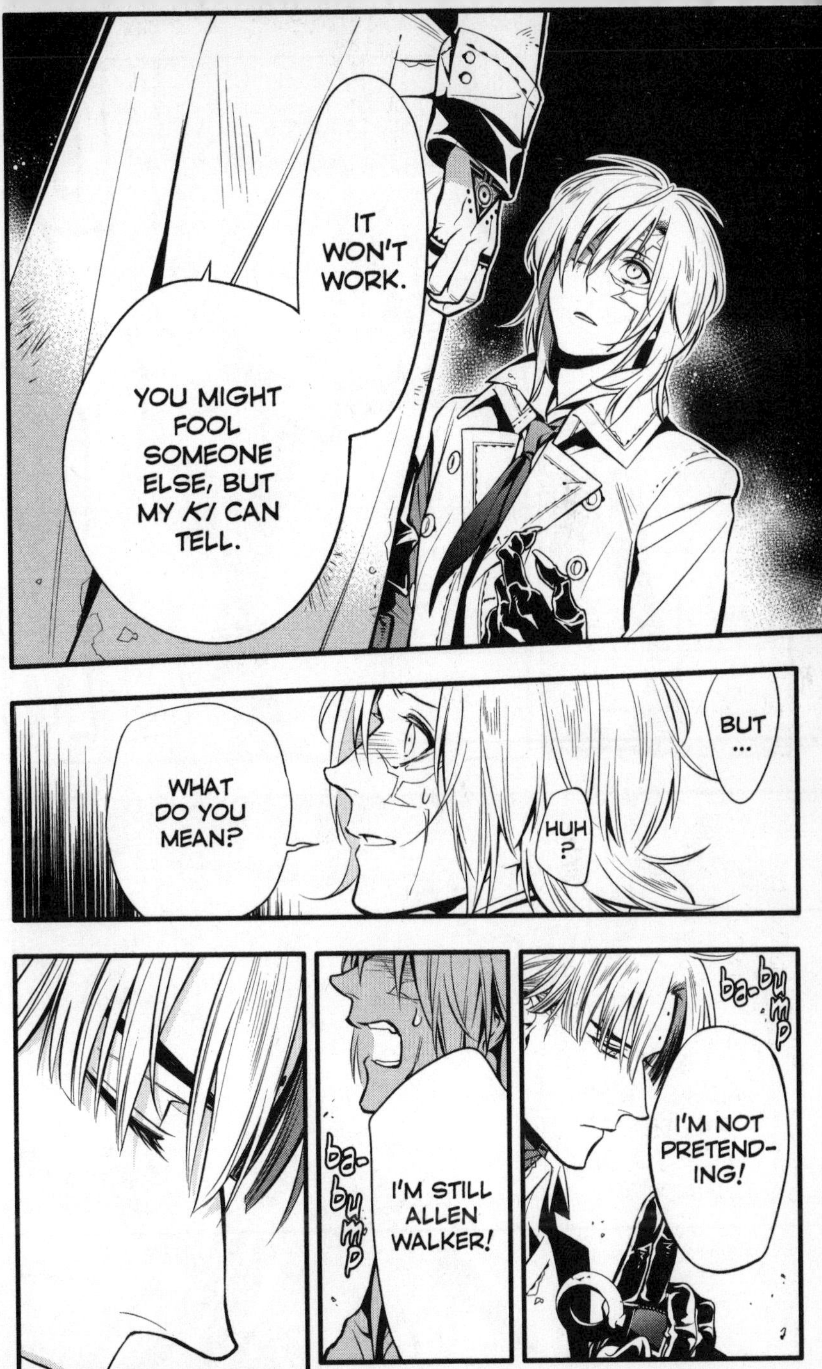
IT WON'T WORK.
YOU MIGHT FOOL SOMEONE ELSE, BUT MY *KI* CAN TELL.
BUT ...
HUH?
WHAT DO YOU MEAN?
ba-bump
I'M NOT PRETENDING!
ba-bump
I'M STILL ALLEN WALKER!

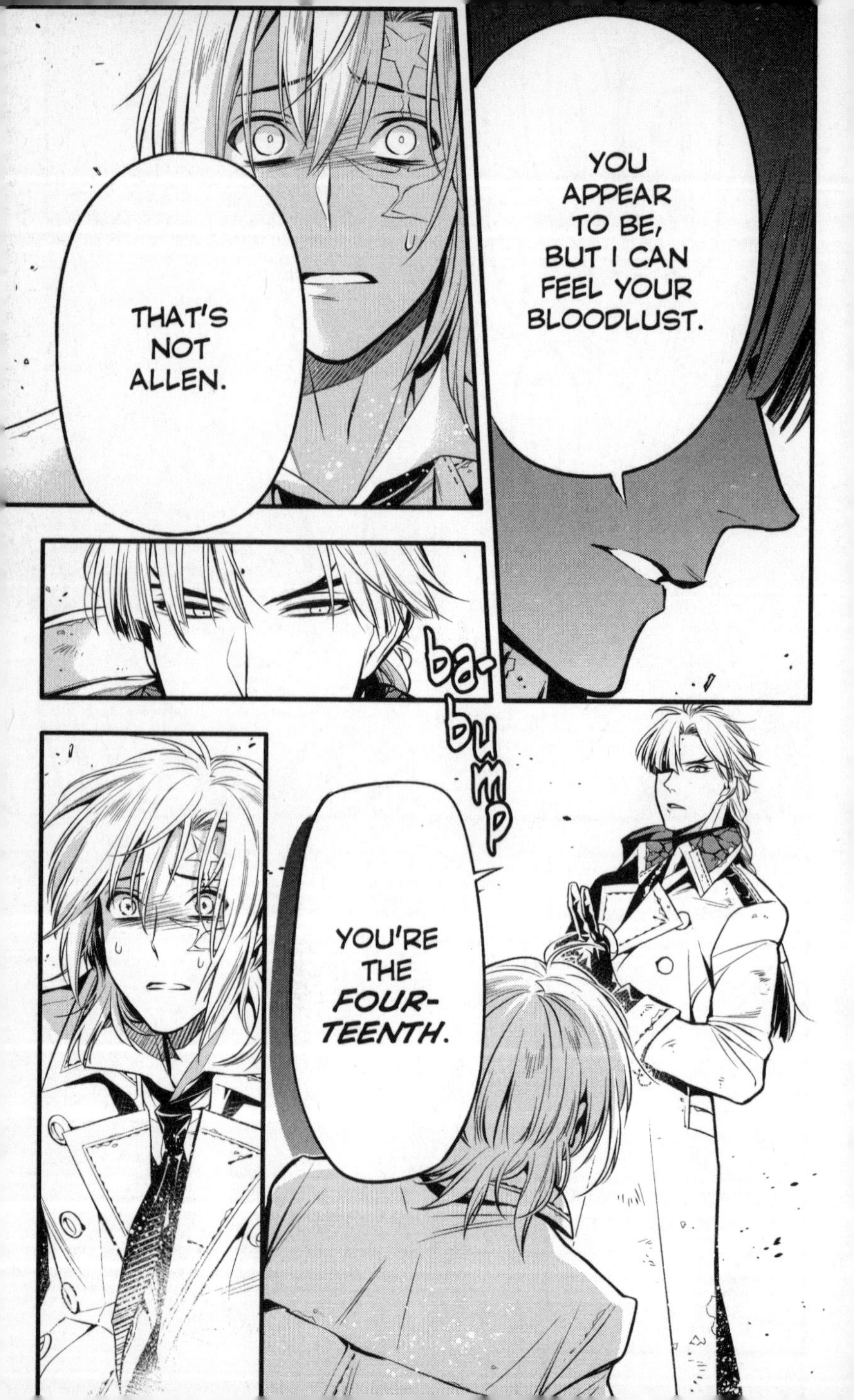
YOU APPEAR TO BE, BUT I CAN FEEL YOUR BLOODLUST.
THAT'S NOT ALLEN.
ba-bump
YOU'RE THE *FOURTEENTH*.

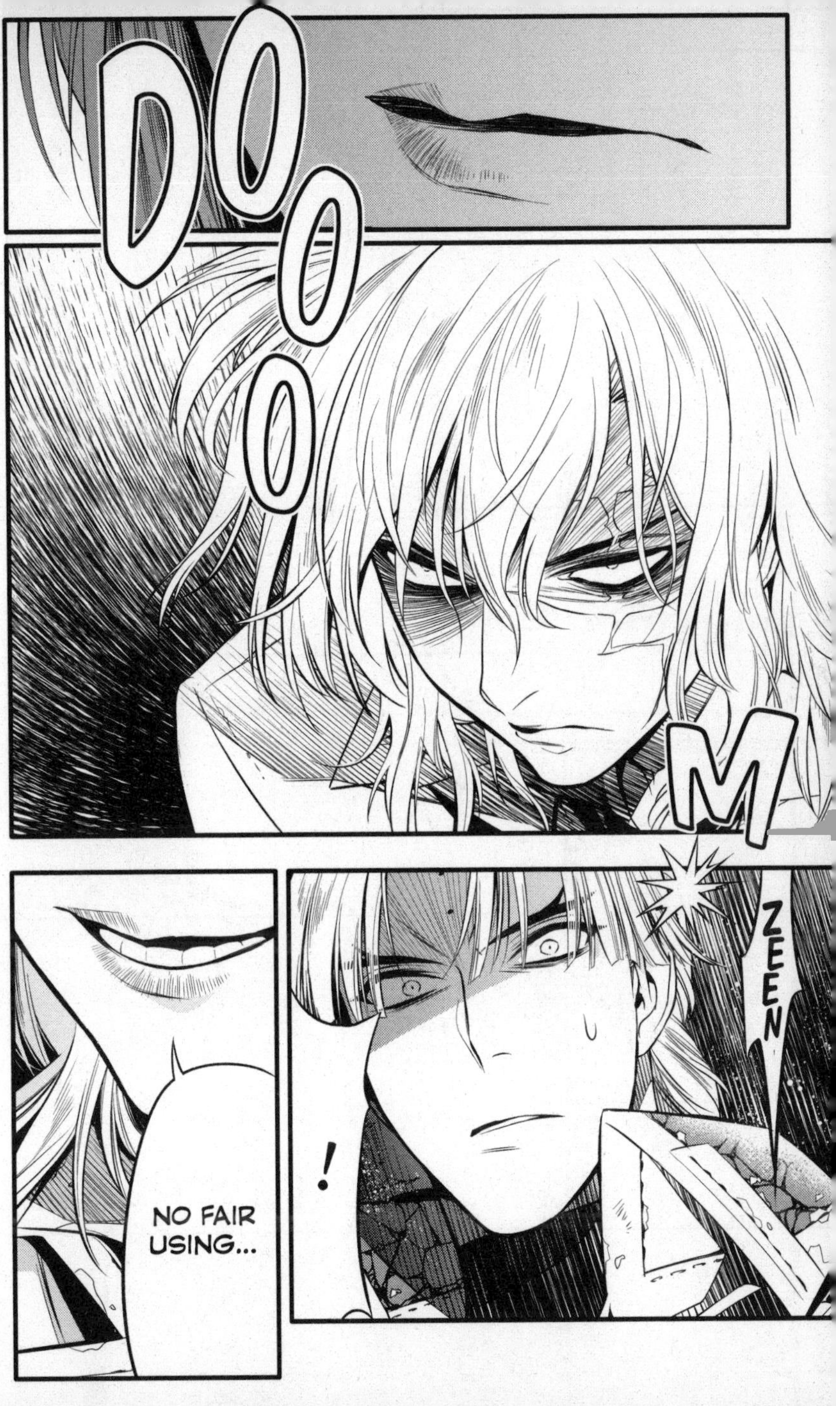
DOOOOM
ZEEN
!
NO FAIR USING...

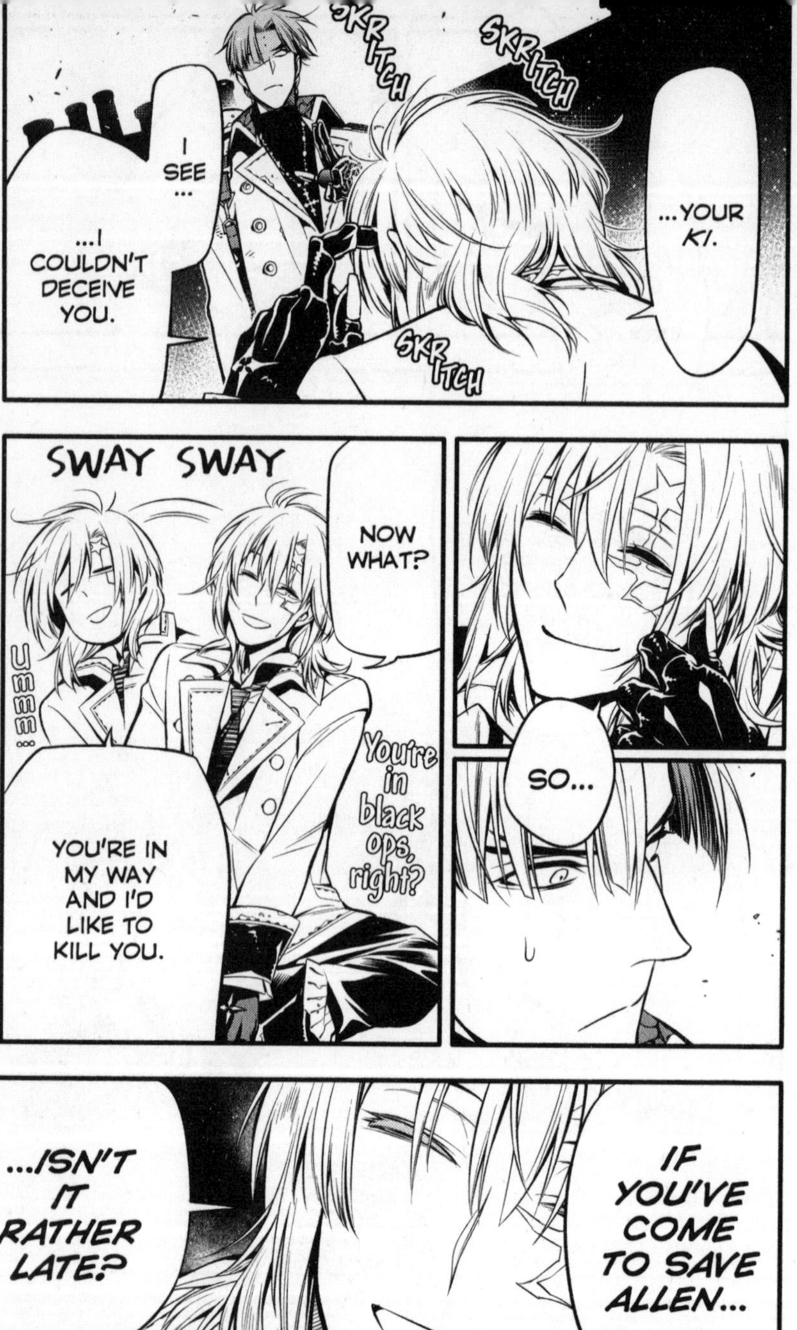
...YOUR KI.
SKRITCH
SKRITCH
I SEE...
...I COULDN'T DECEIVE YOU.
SKRITCH
SO...
SWAY SWAY
NOW WHAT?
You're in black ops, right?
Ummm...
YOU'RE IN MY WAY AND I'D LIKE TO KILL YOU.
IF YOU'VE COME TO SAVE ALLEN...
...ISN'T IT RATHER LATE?

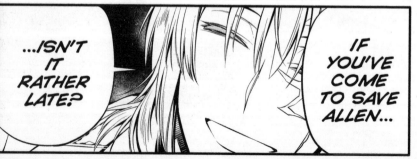

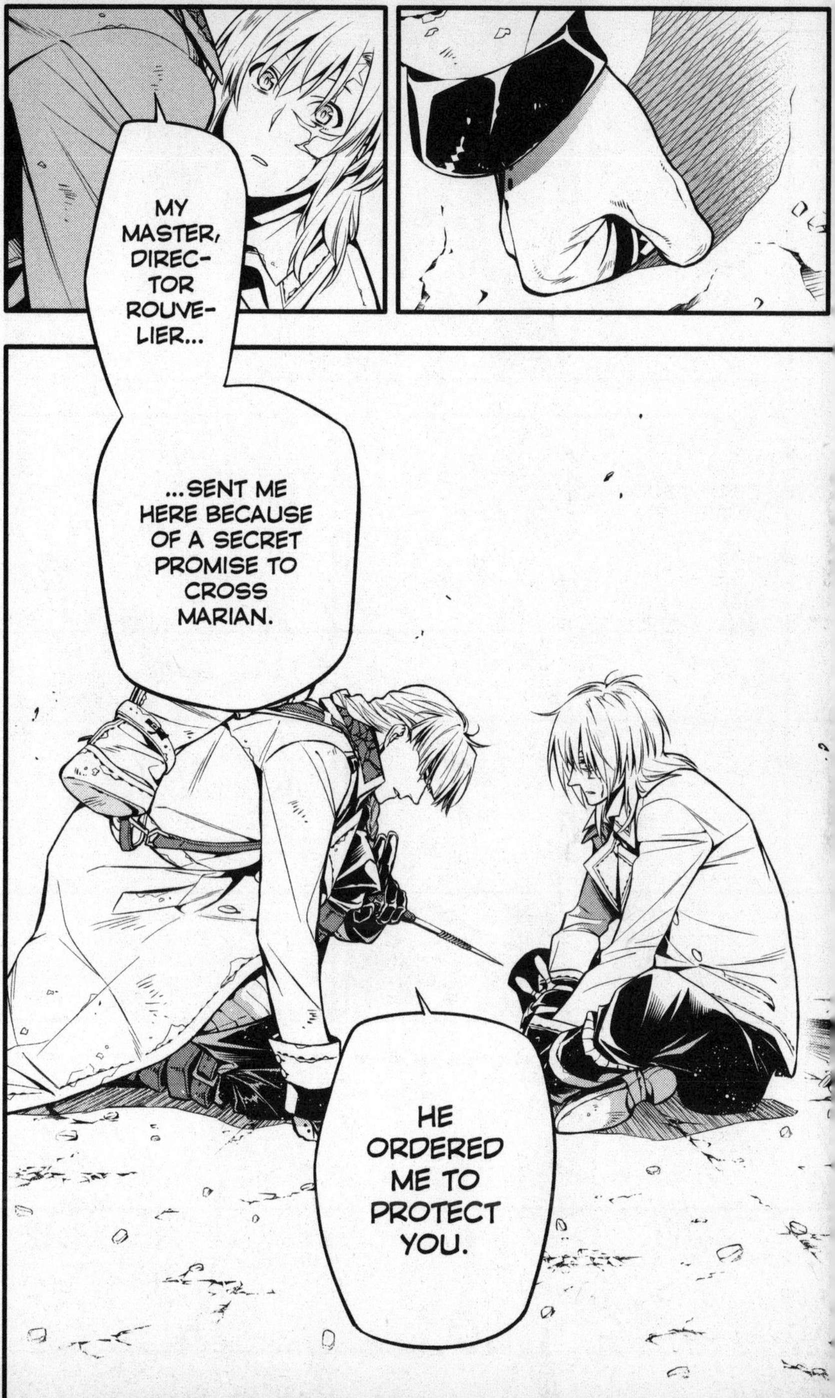
MY MASTER, DIRECTOR ROUVELIER...
...SENT ME HERE BECAUSE OF A SECRET PROMISE TO CROSS MARIAN.
HE ORDERED ME TO PROTECT YOU.

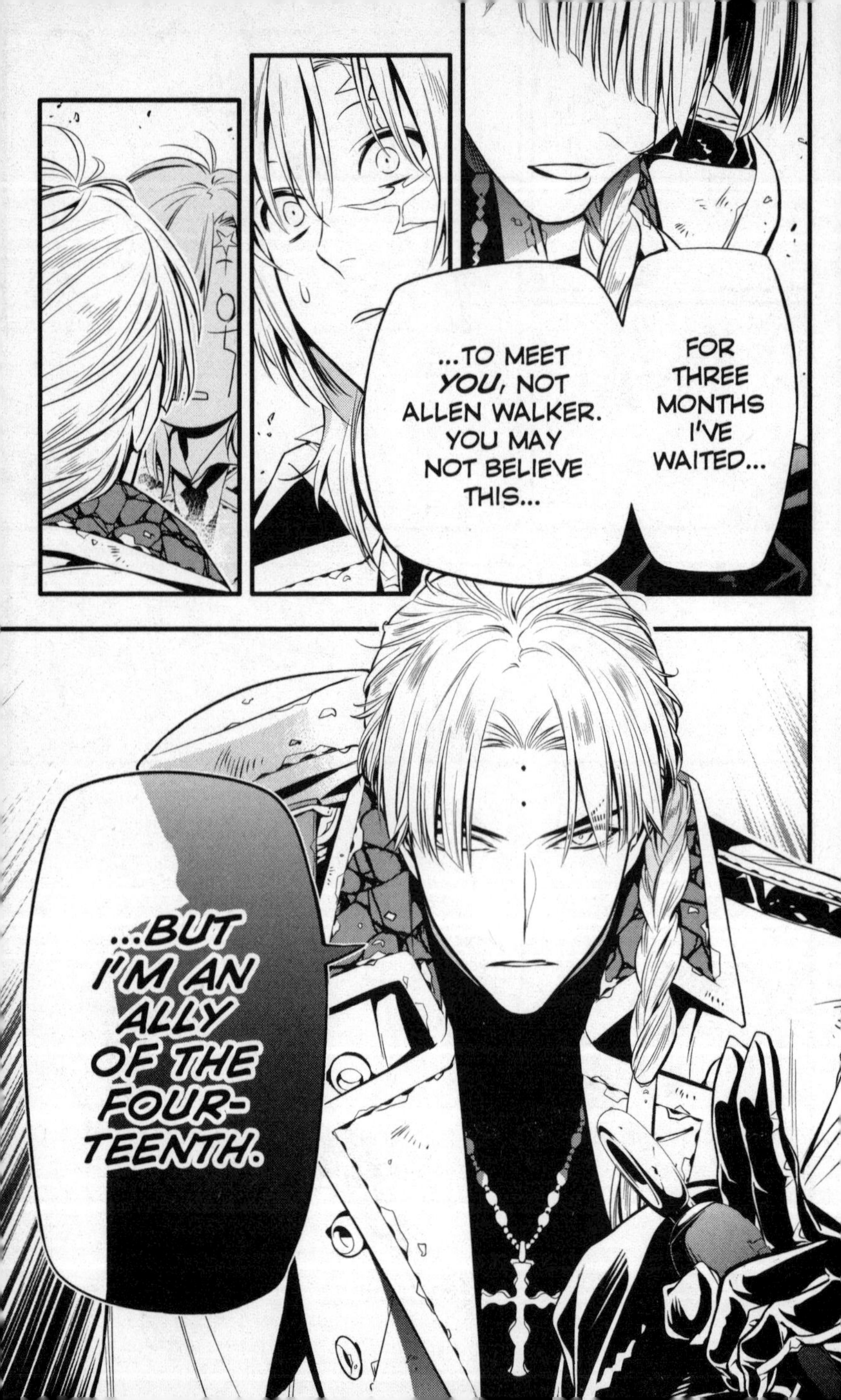
FOR THREE MONTHS I'VE WAITED...
...TO MEET *YOU*, NOT ALLEN WALKER. YOU MAY NOT BELIEVE THIS...
...BUT I'M AN ALLY OF THE FOUR-TEENTH.

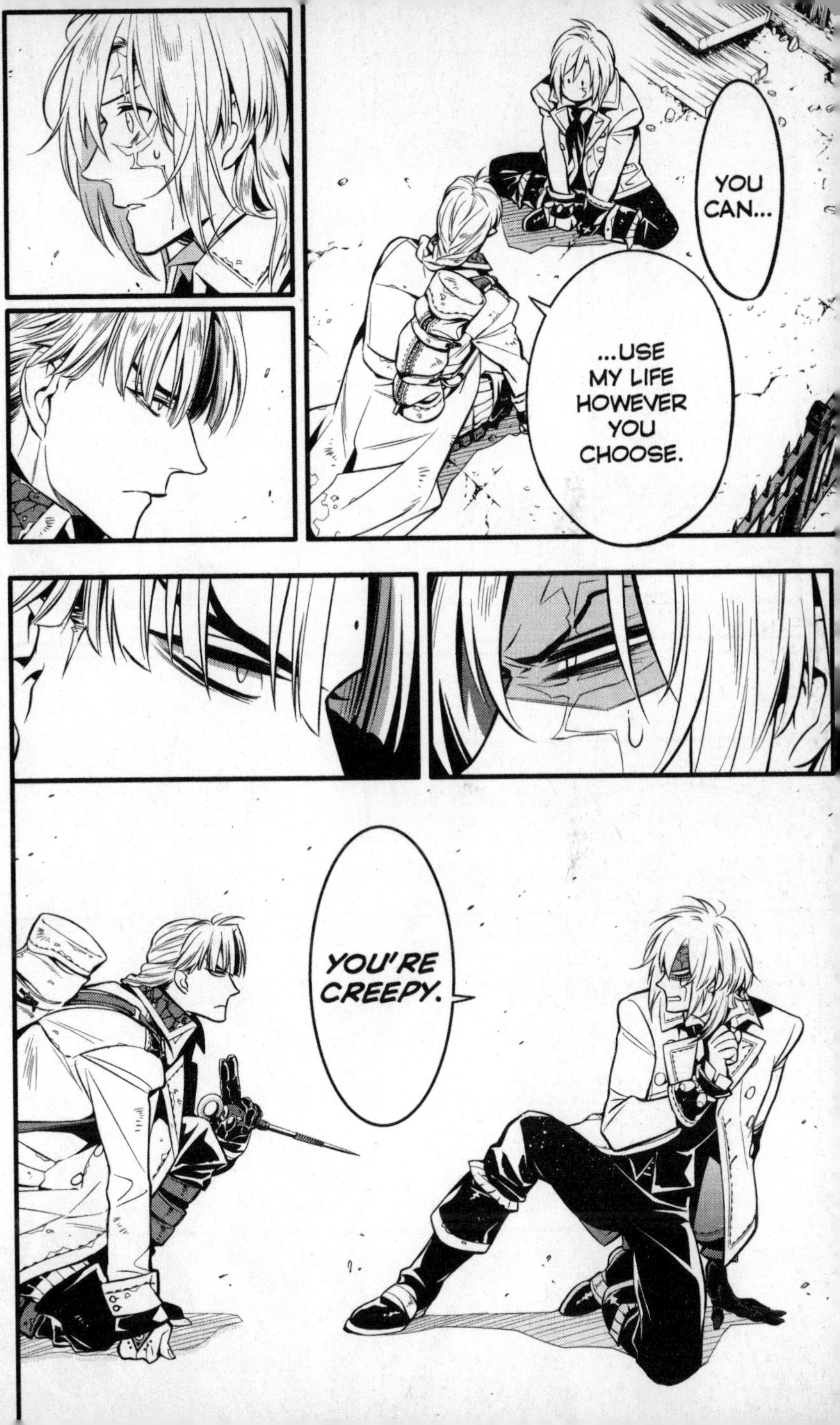
YOU CAN...
...USE MY LIFE HOWEVER YOU CHOOSE.
YOU'RE CREEPY.

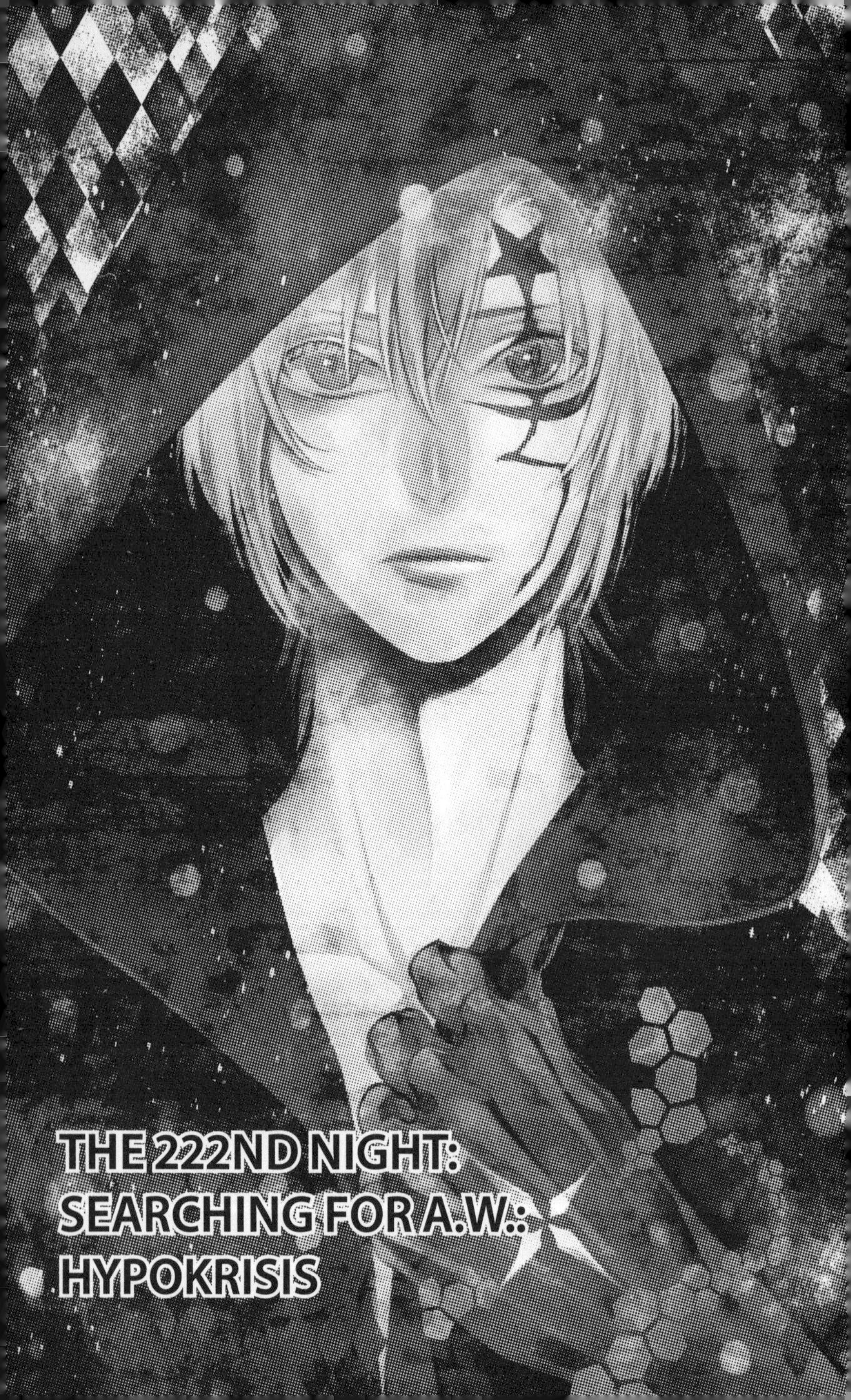
THE 222ND NIGHT:
SEARCHING FOR A.W.:
HYPOKRISIS

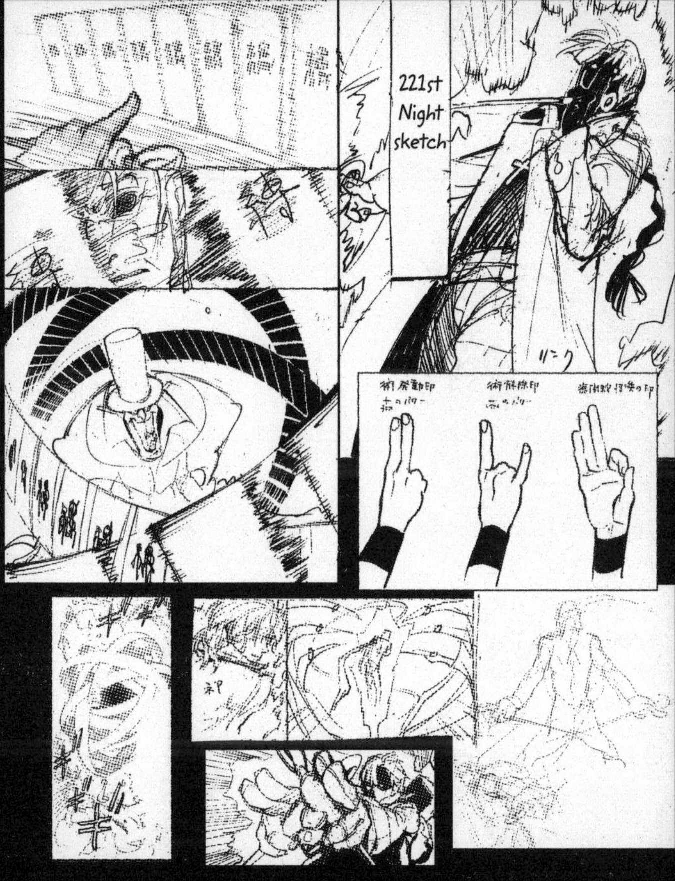
221st Night sketch
リンク
術発動印
術解除印

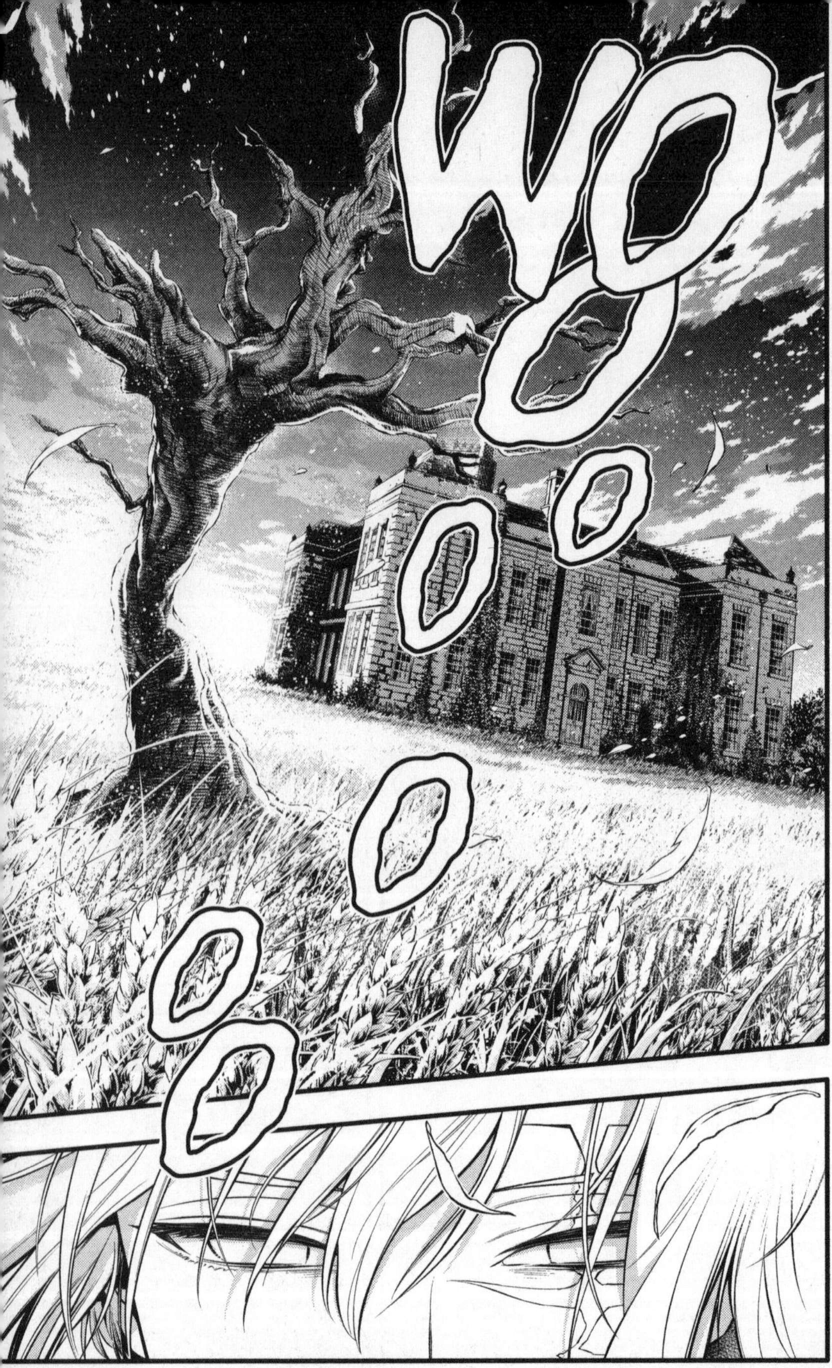
WOOOOOOO

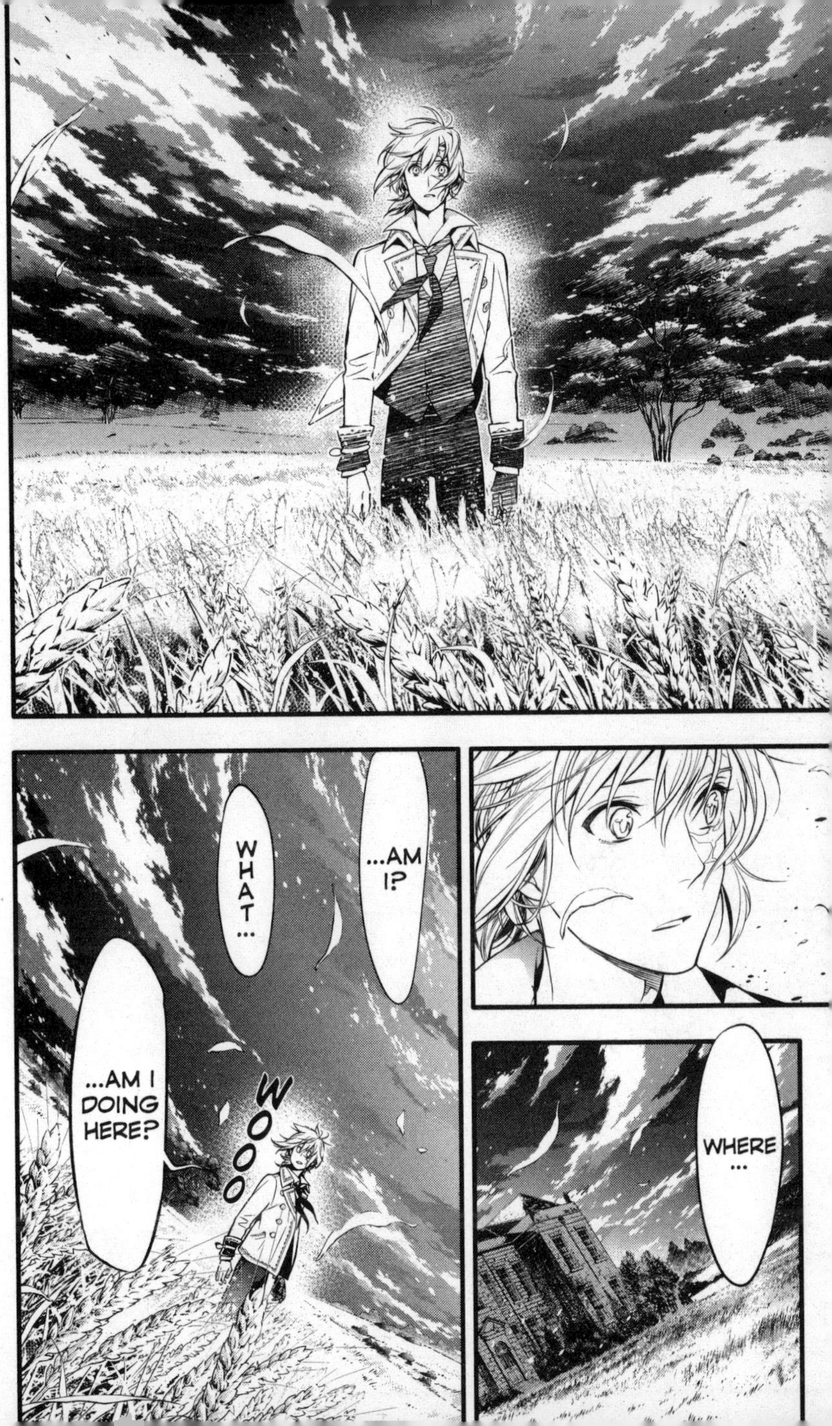
WHERE...
...AM I?
WHAT...
...AM I DOING HERE?
WOOOO

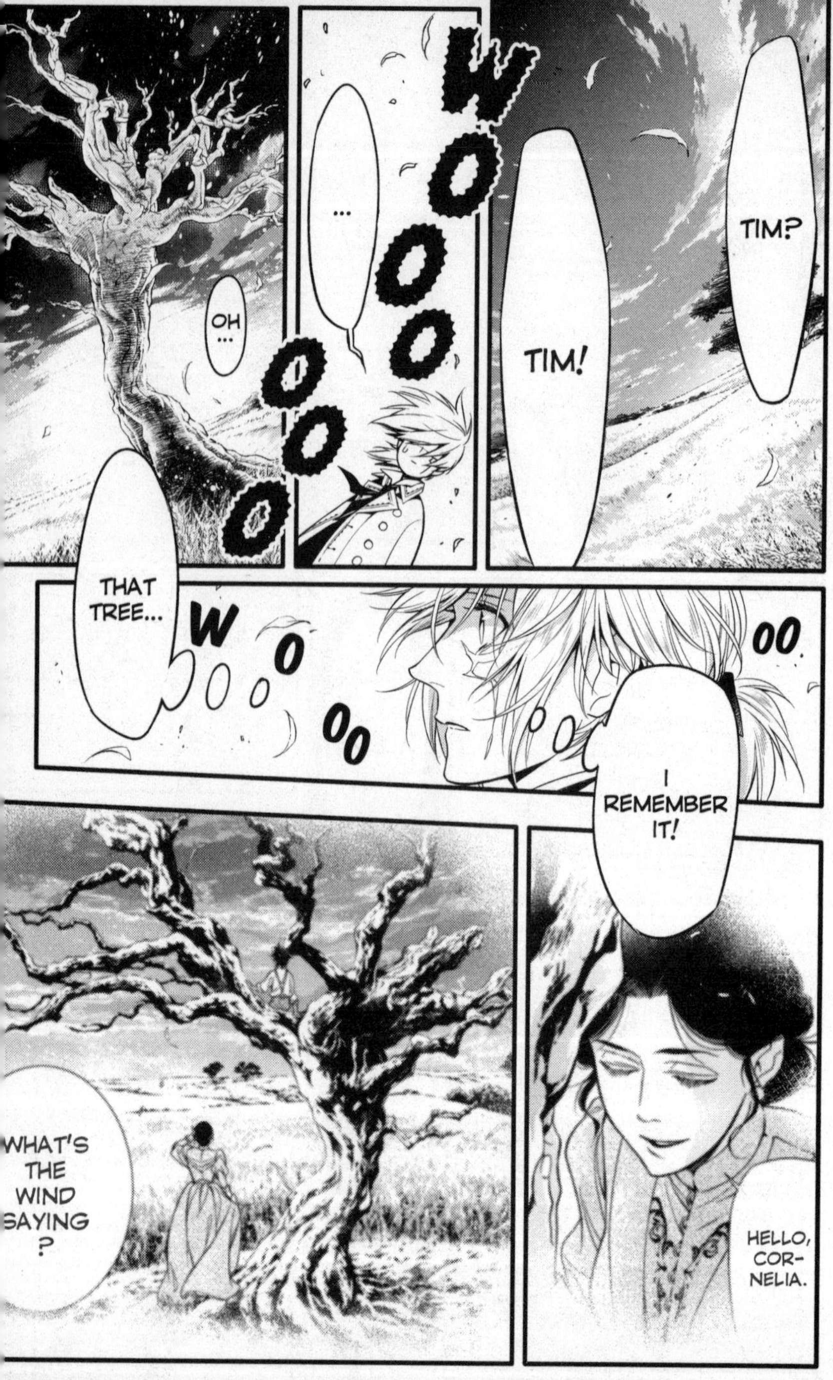
TIM?
TIM!
WOOOOOOO
...
OH ...
THAT TREE...
WOOOOOOOO
I REMEMBER IT!
HELLO, COR-NELIA.
WHAT'S THE WIND SAYING?

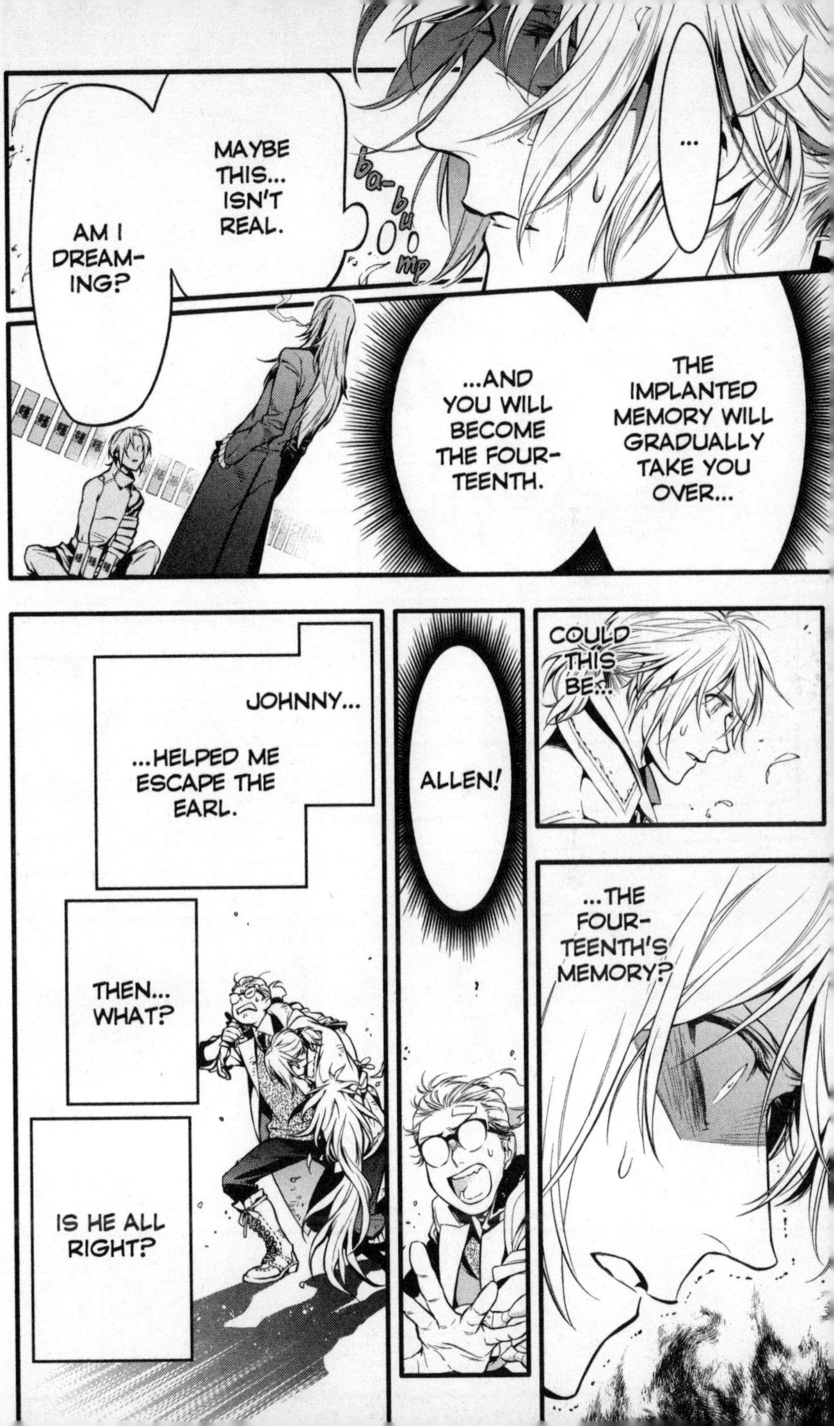
...
MAYBE THIS... ISN'T REAL.
AM I DREAM-ING?
THE IMPLANTED MEMORY WILL GRADUALLY TAKE YOU OVER...
...AND YOU WILL BECOME THE FOUR-TEENTH.
COULD THIS BE...
...THE FOUR-TEENTH'S MEMORY?
ALLEN!
JOHNNY...
...HELPED ME ESCAPE THE EARL.
THEN... WHAT?
IS HE ALL RIGHT?

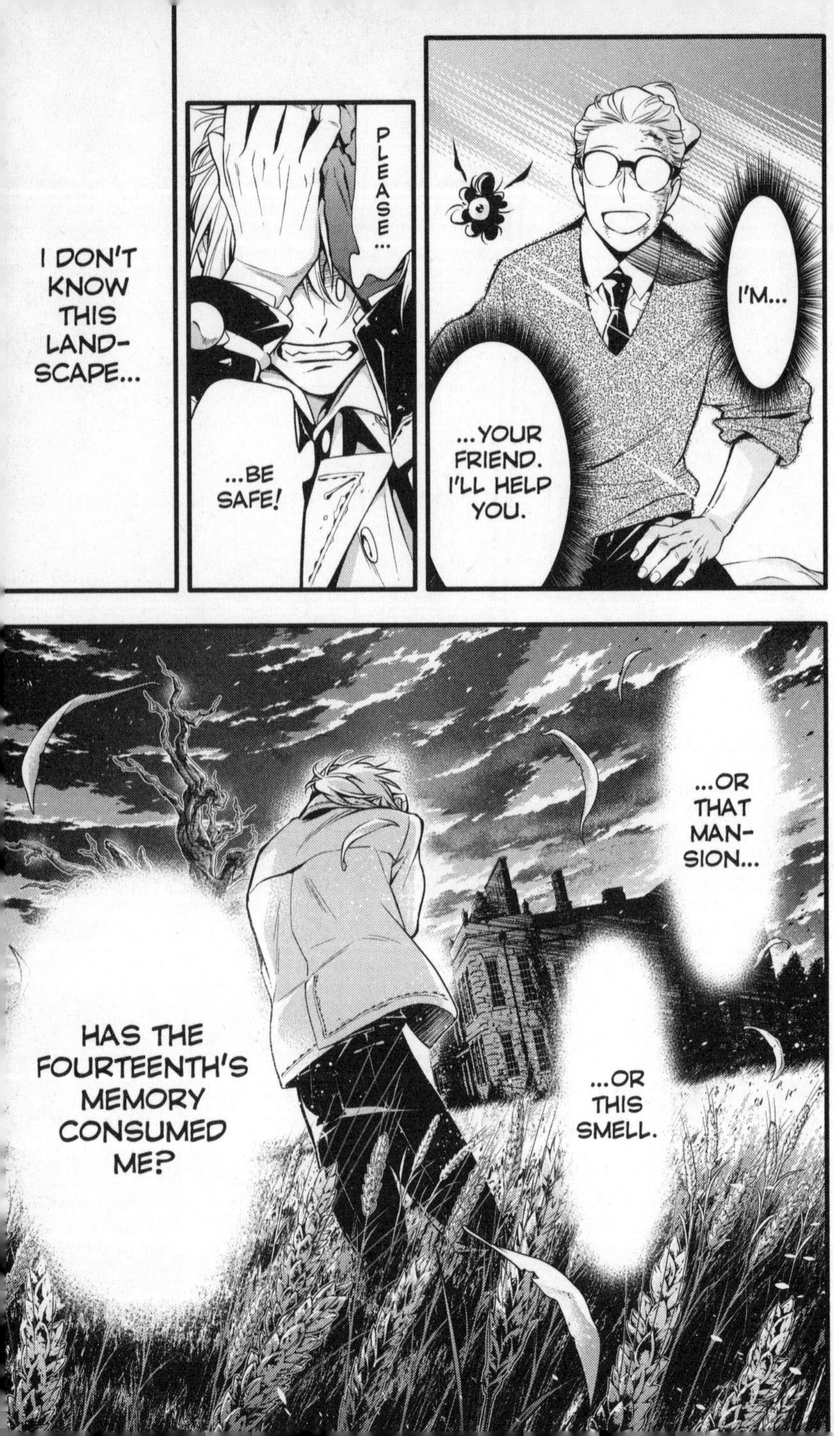
I'M...
...YOUR FRIEND. I'LL HELP YOU.
PLEASE...
...BE SAFE!
I DON'T KNOW THIS LAND-SCAPE...
...OR THAT MAN-SION...
...OR THIS SMELL.
HAS THE FOURTEENTH'S MEMORY CONSUMED ME?

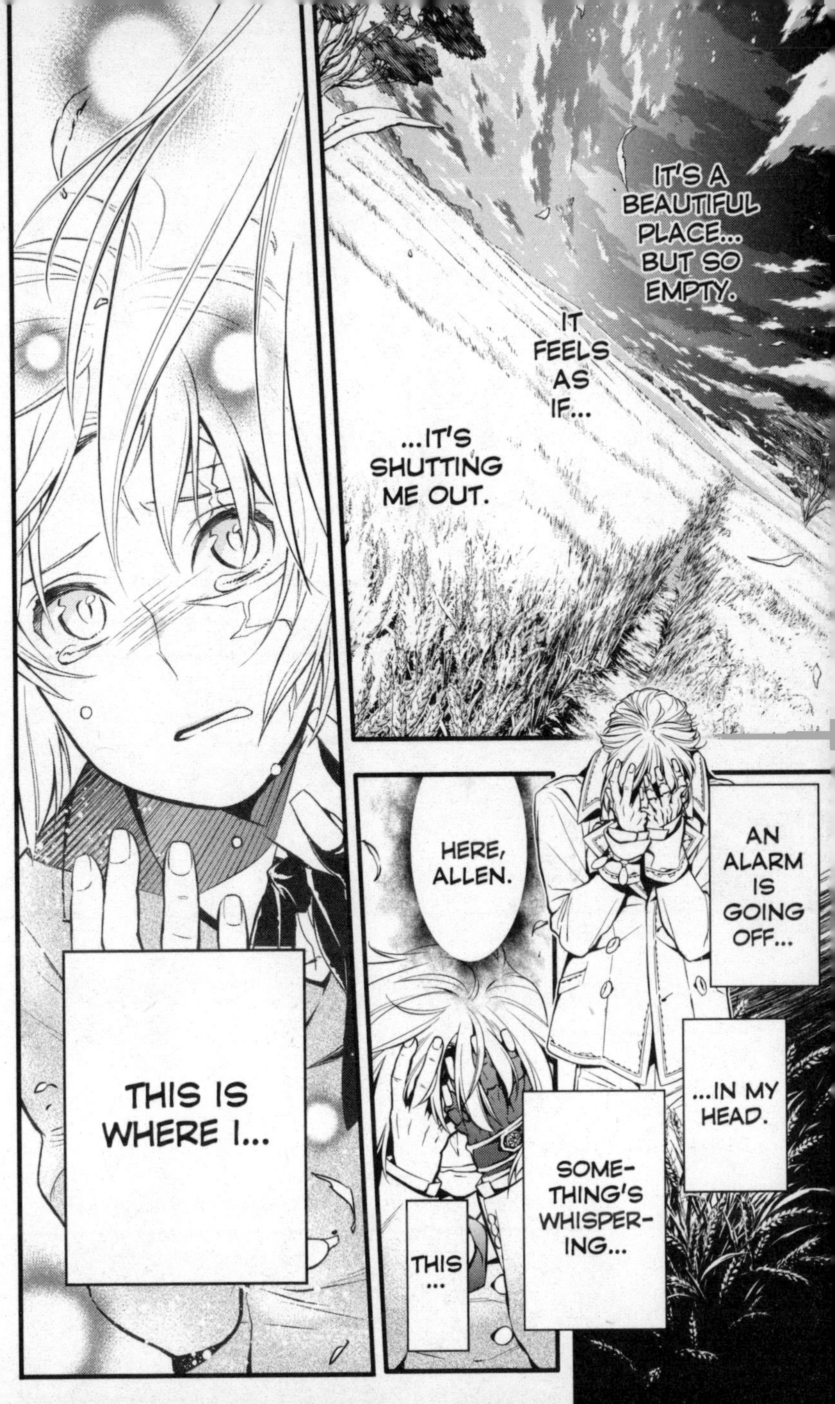
IT'S A BEAUTIFUL PLACE... BUT SO EMPTY.
IT FEELS AS IF...
...IT'S SHUTTING ME OUT.
AN ALARM IS GOING OFF...
...IN MY HEAD.
SOME-THING'S WHISPER-ING...
HERE, ALLEN.
THIS...
THIS IS WHERE I...

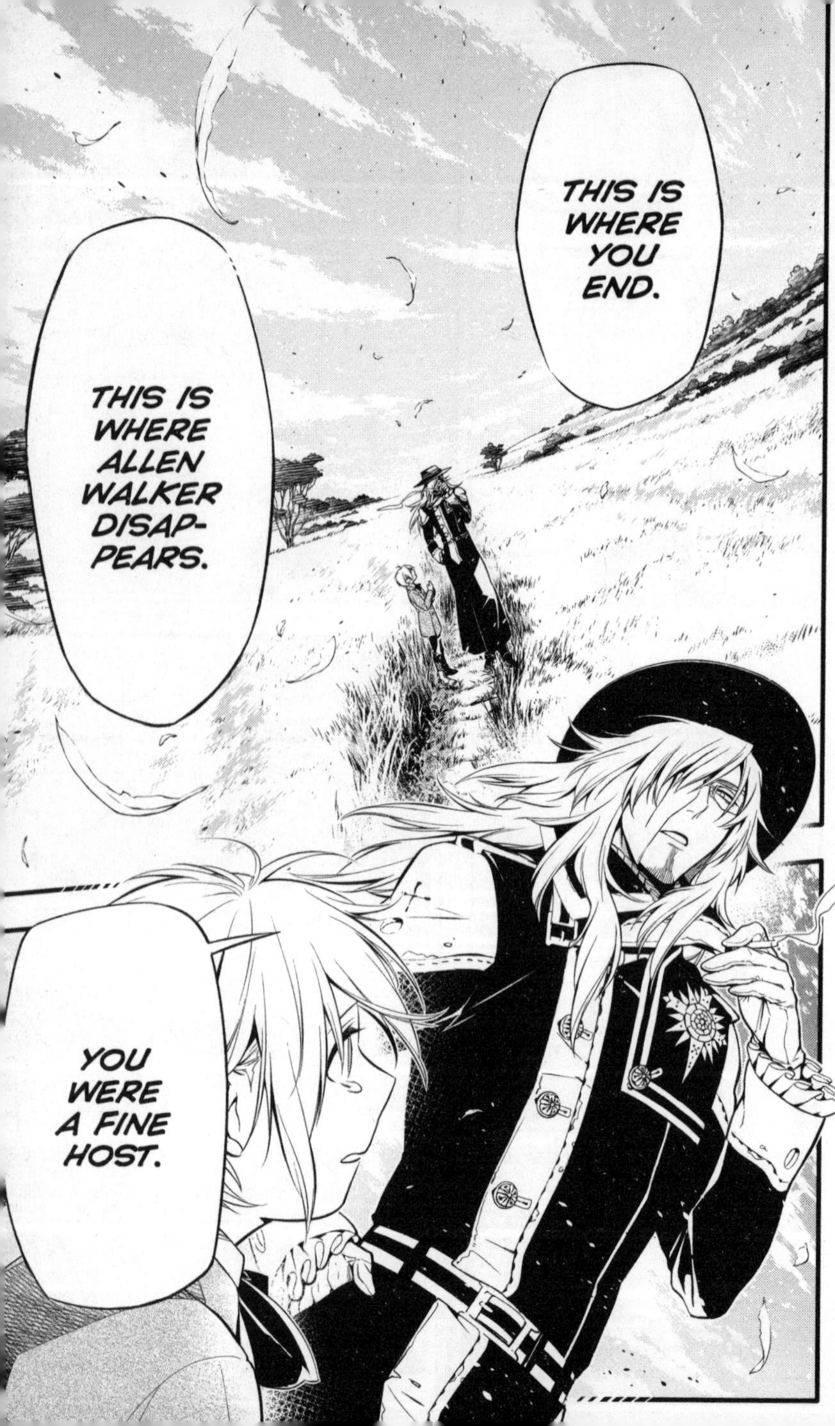
THIS IS WHERE YOU END.
THIS IS WHERE ALLEN WALKER DISAP-PEARS.
YOU WERE A FINE HOST.

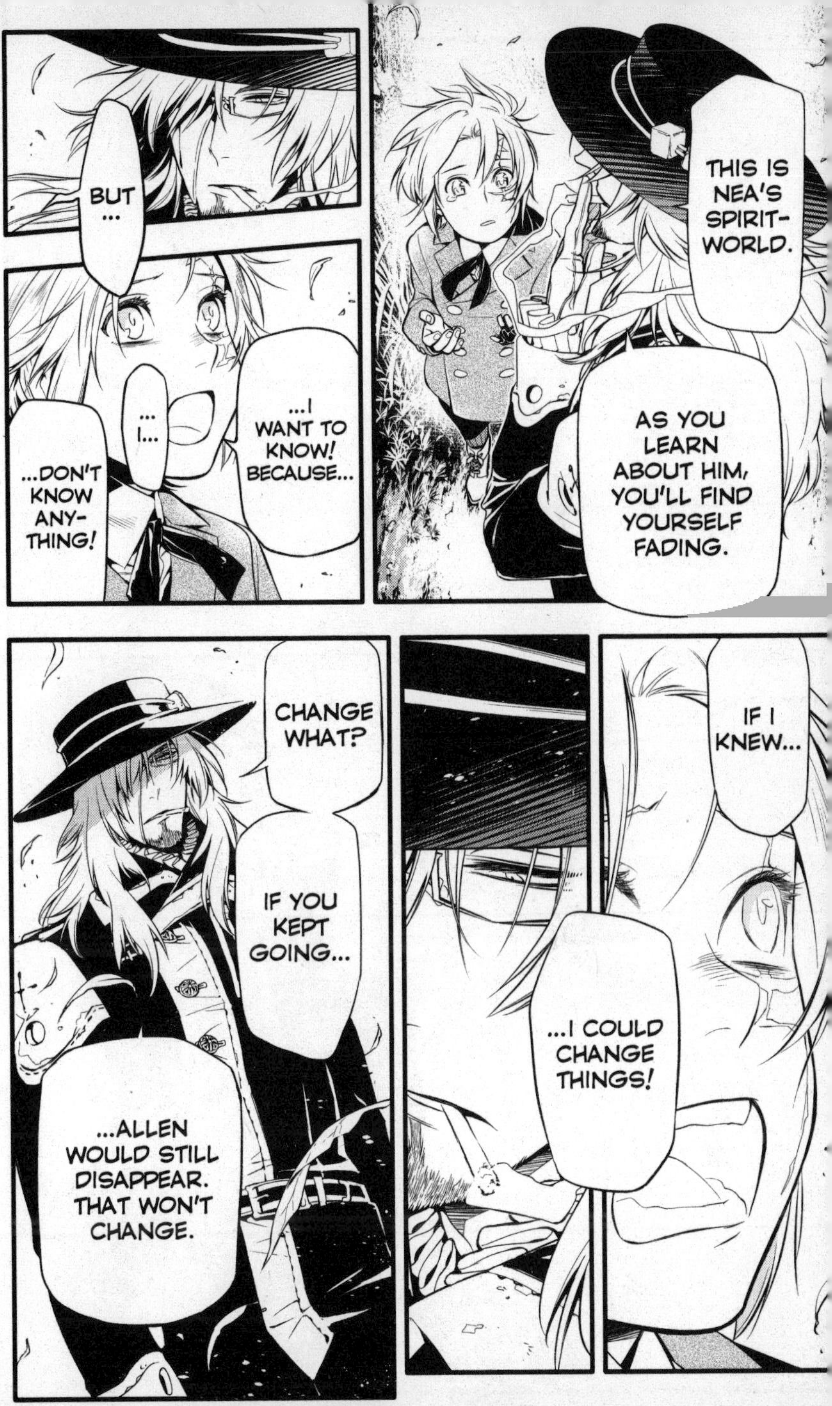
THIS IS NEA'S SPIRIT-WORLD.
AS YOU LEARN ABOUT HIM, YOU'LL FIND YOURSELF FADING.
BUT ...
...I WANT TO KNOW! BECAUSE...
... I...
...DON'T KNOW ANY-THING!
IF I KNEW...
...I COULD CHANGE THINGS!
CHANGE WHAT?
IF YOU KEPT GOING...
...ALLEN WOULD STILL DISAPPEAR. THAT WON'T CHANGE.

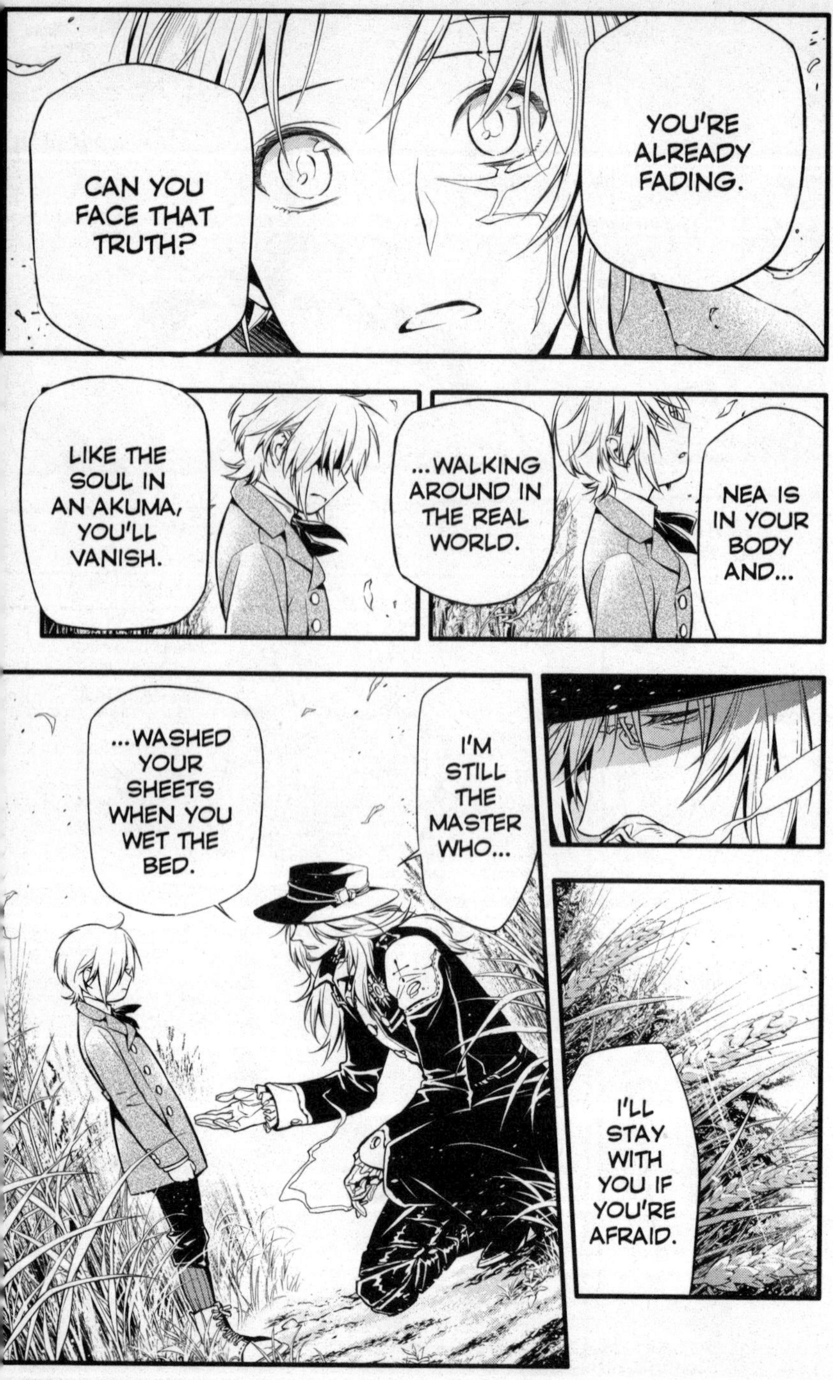
YOU'RE ALREADY FADING.
CAN YOU FACE THAT TRUTH?
NEA IS IN YOUR BODY AND...
...WALKING AROUND IN THE REAL WORLD.
LIKE THE SOUL IN AN AKUMA, YOU'LL VANISH.
I'LL STAY WITH YOU IF YOU'RE AFRAID.
I'M STILL THE MASTER WHO...
...WASHED YOUR SHEETS WHEN YOU WET THE BED.

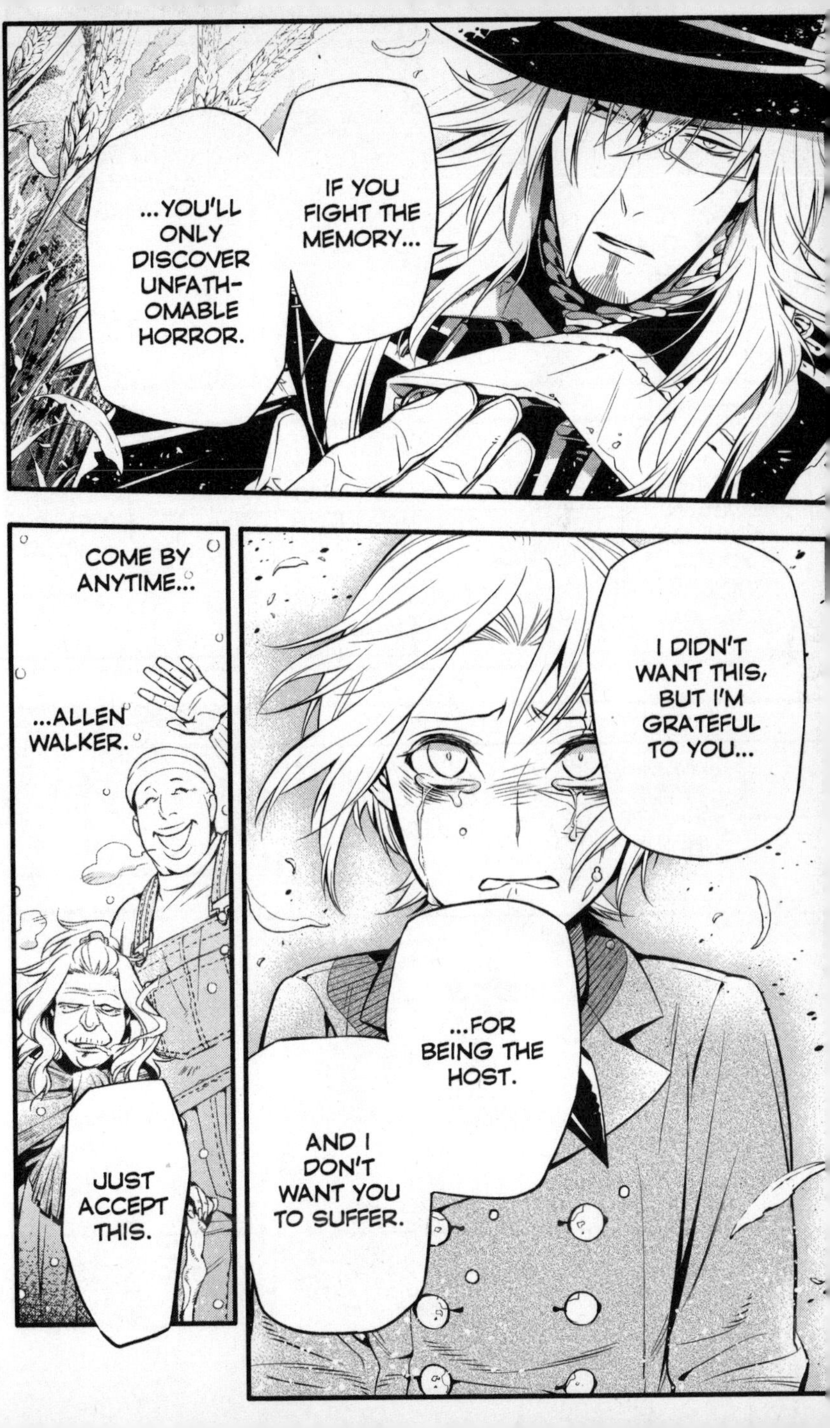
IF YOU FIGHT THE MEMORY...
...YOU'LL ONLY DISCOVER UNFATHOMABLE HORROR.
I DIDN'T WANT THIS, BUT I'M GRATEFUL TO YOU...
...FOR BEING THE HOST.
AND I DON'T WANT YOU TO SUFFER.
COME BY ANYTIME...
...ALLEN WALKER.
JUST ACCEPT THIS.

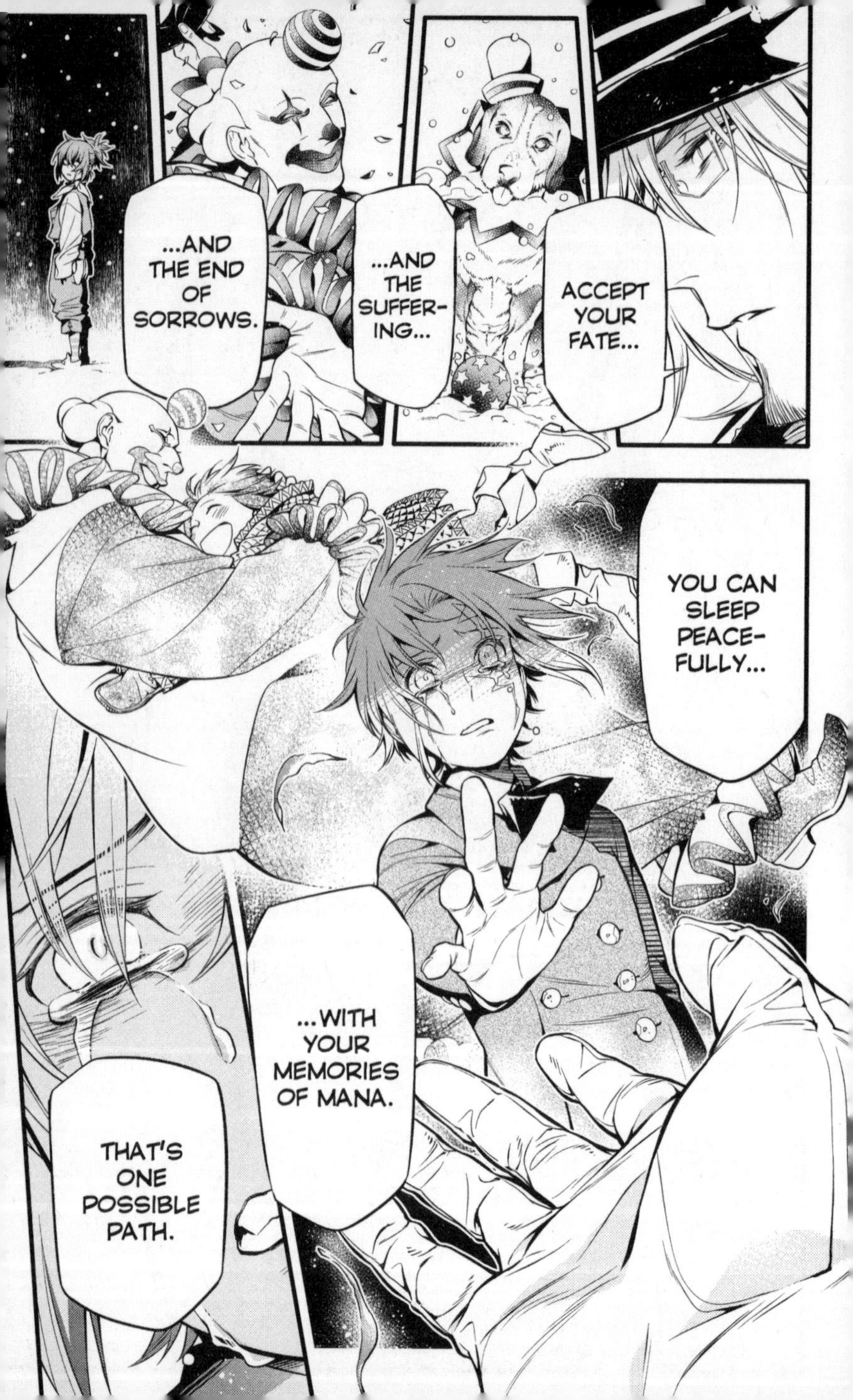
ACCEPT YOUR FATE...
...AND THE SUFFER-ING...
...AND THE END OF SORROWS.
YOU CAN SLEEP PEACE-FULLY...
...WITH YOUR MEMORIES OF MANA.
THAT'S ONE POSSIBLE PATH.

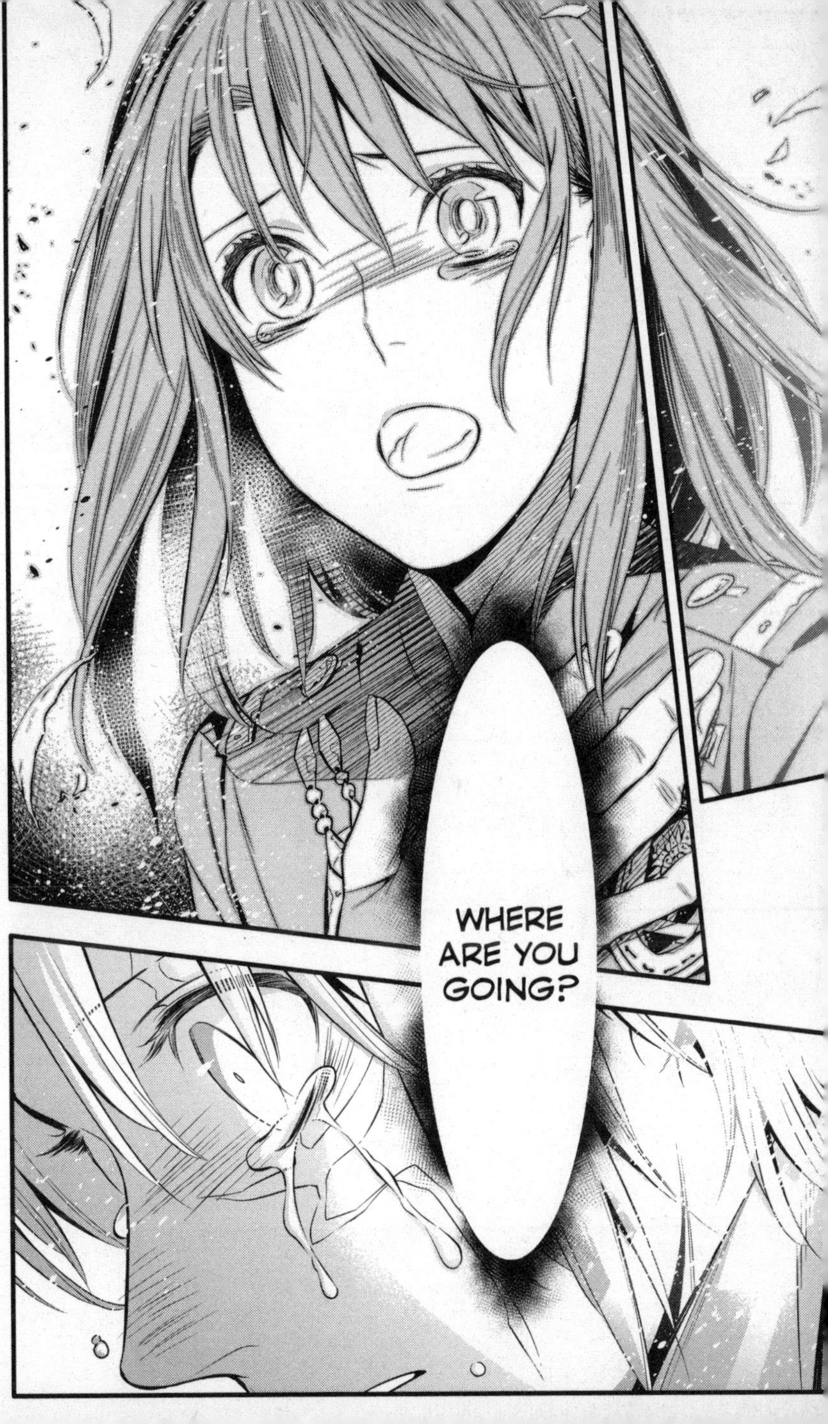
WHERE ARE YOU GOING?

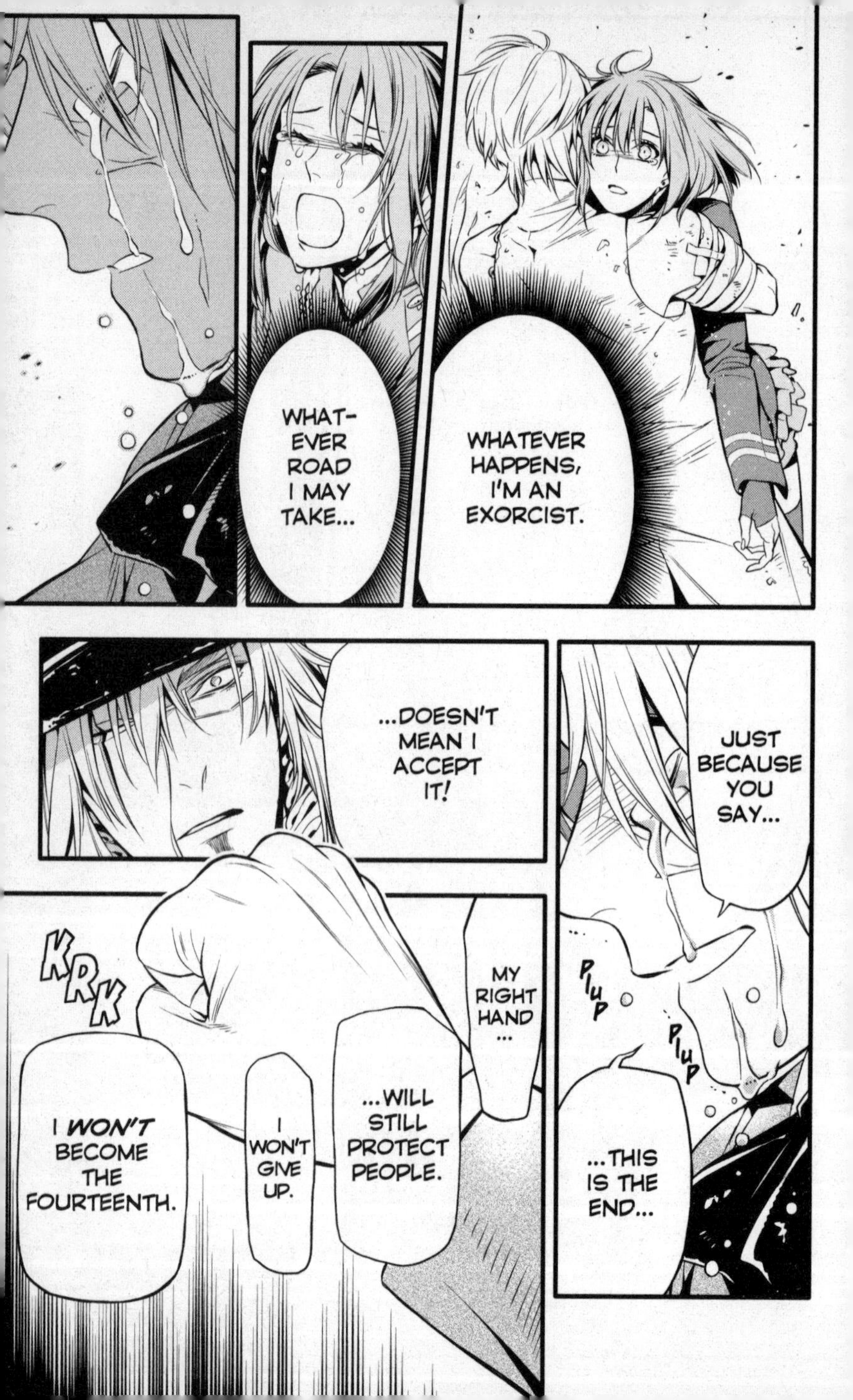
WHATEVER HAPPENS, I'M AN EXORCIST.
WHAT-EVER ROAD I MAY TAKE...
JUST BECAUSE YOU SAY...
PLIUP
PLIUP
...THIS IS THE END...
...DOESN'T MEAN I ACCEPT IT!
MY RIGHT HAND ...
...WILL STILL PROTECT PEOPLE.
I WON'T GIVE UP.
KRK
I *WON'T* BECOME THE FOURTEENTH.

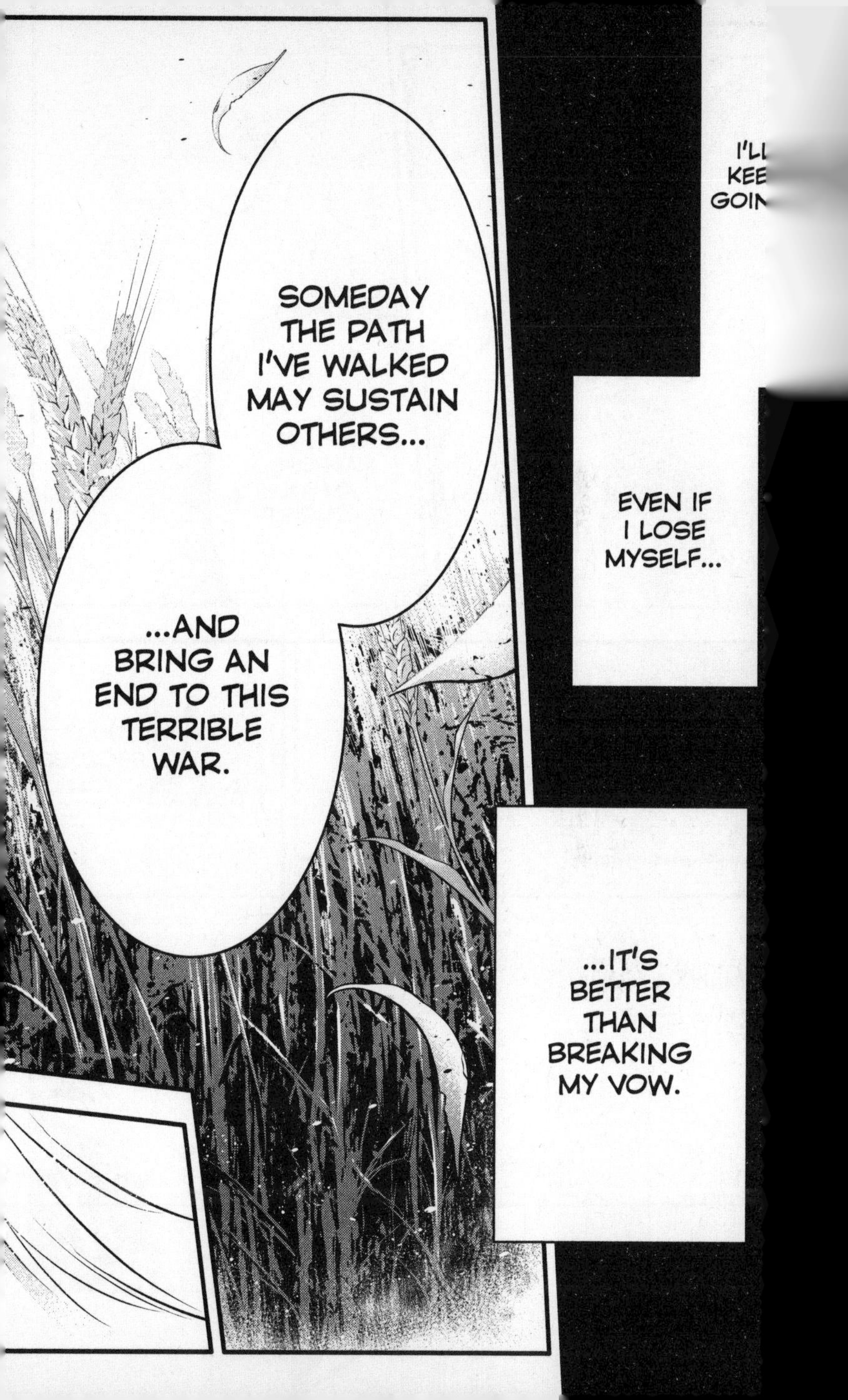
I'LL KEE GOIN
EVEN IF I LOSE MYSELF...
...IT'S BETTER THAN BREAKING MY VOW.
SOMEDAY THE PATH I'VE WALKED MAY SUSTAIN OTHERS...
...AND BRING AN END TO THIS TERRIBLE WAR.

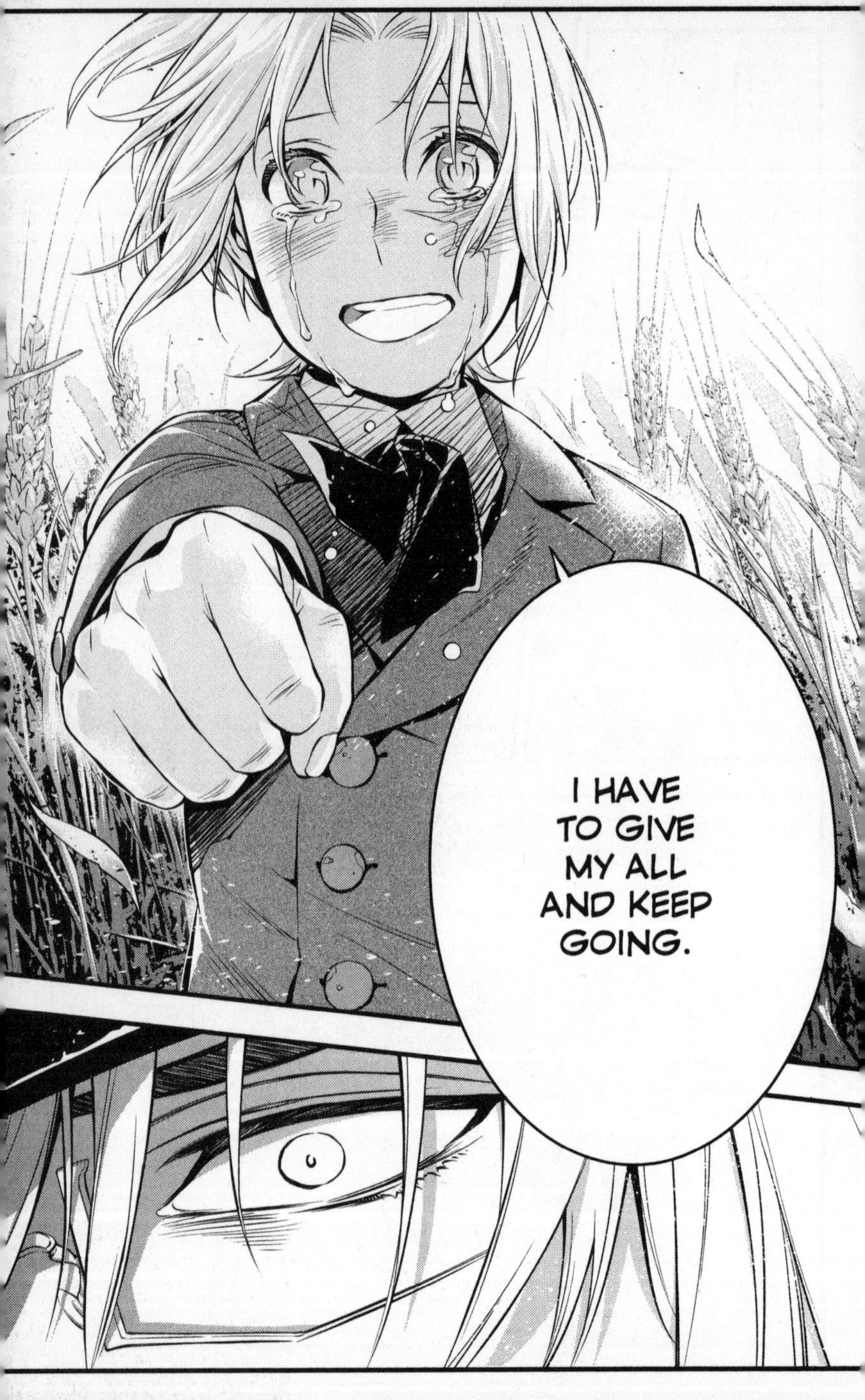
I HAVE TO GIVE MY ALL AND KEEP GOING.

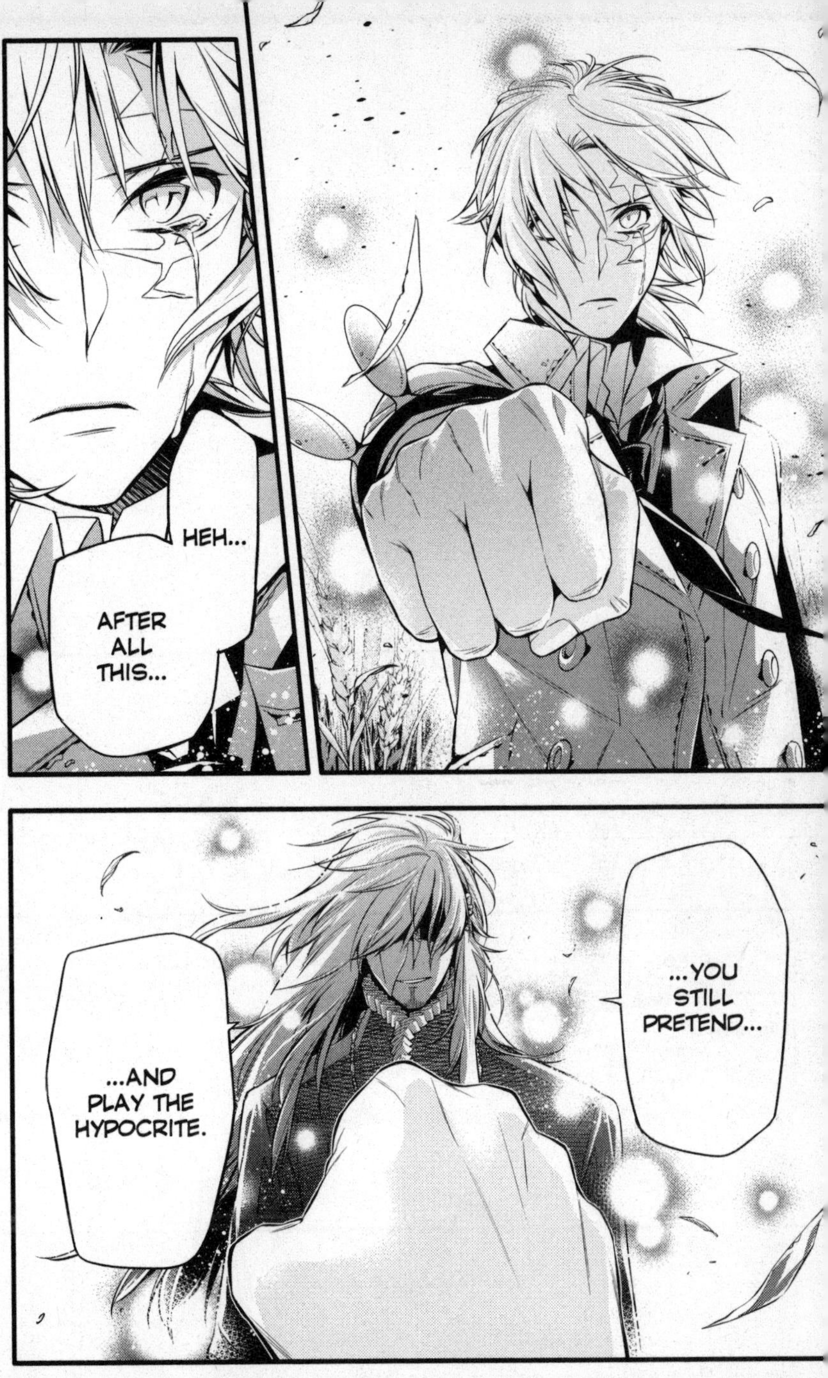
HEH...
AFTER ALL THIS...
...YOU STILL PRETEND...
...AND PLAY THE HYPOCRITE.

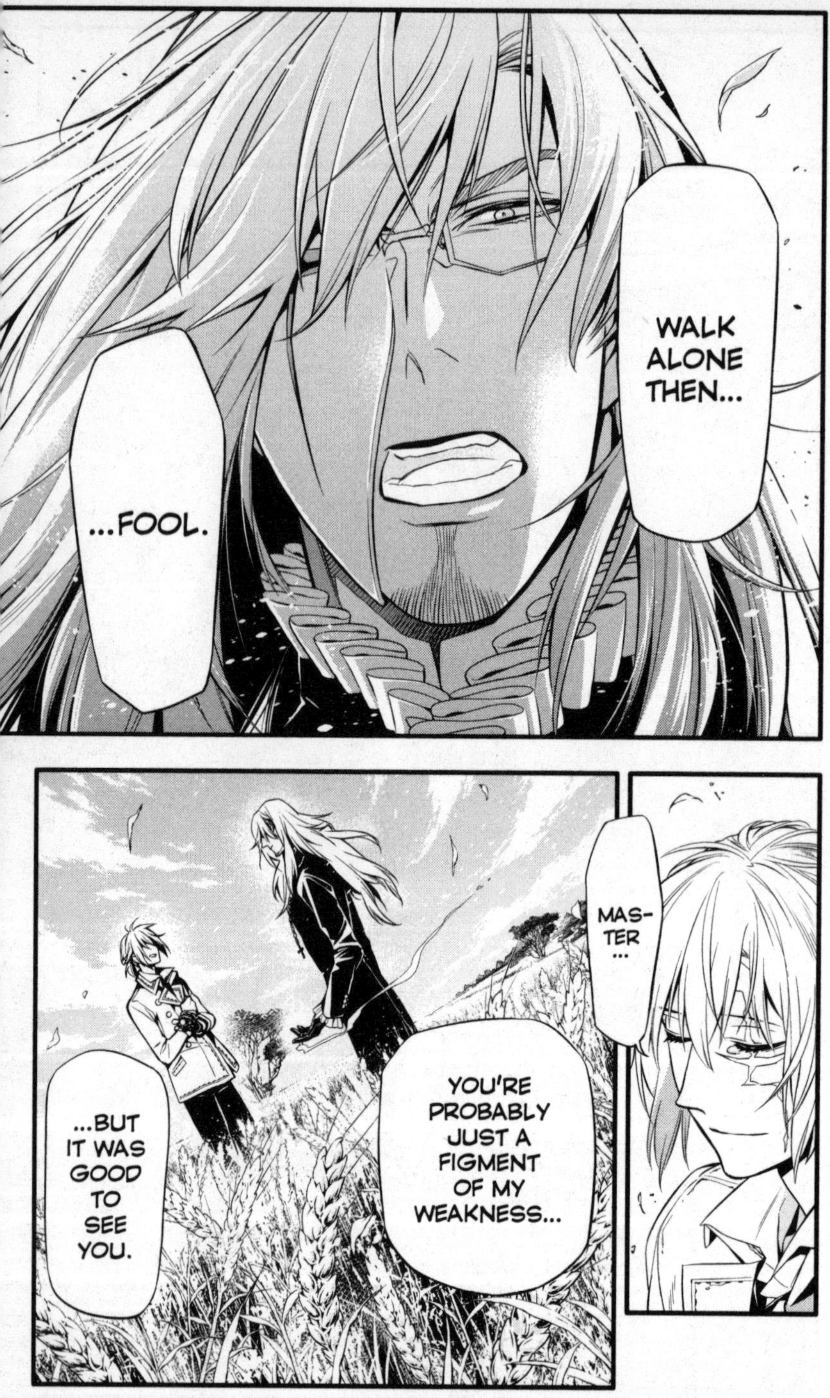
WALK ALONE THEN...
...FOOL.
MAS-TER...
YOU'RE PROBABLY JUST A FIGMENT OF MY WEAKNESS...
...BUT IT WAS GOOD TO SEE YOU.

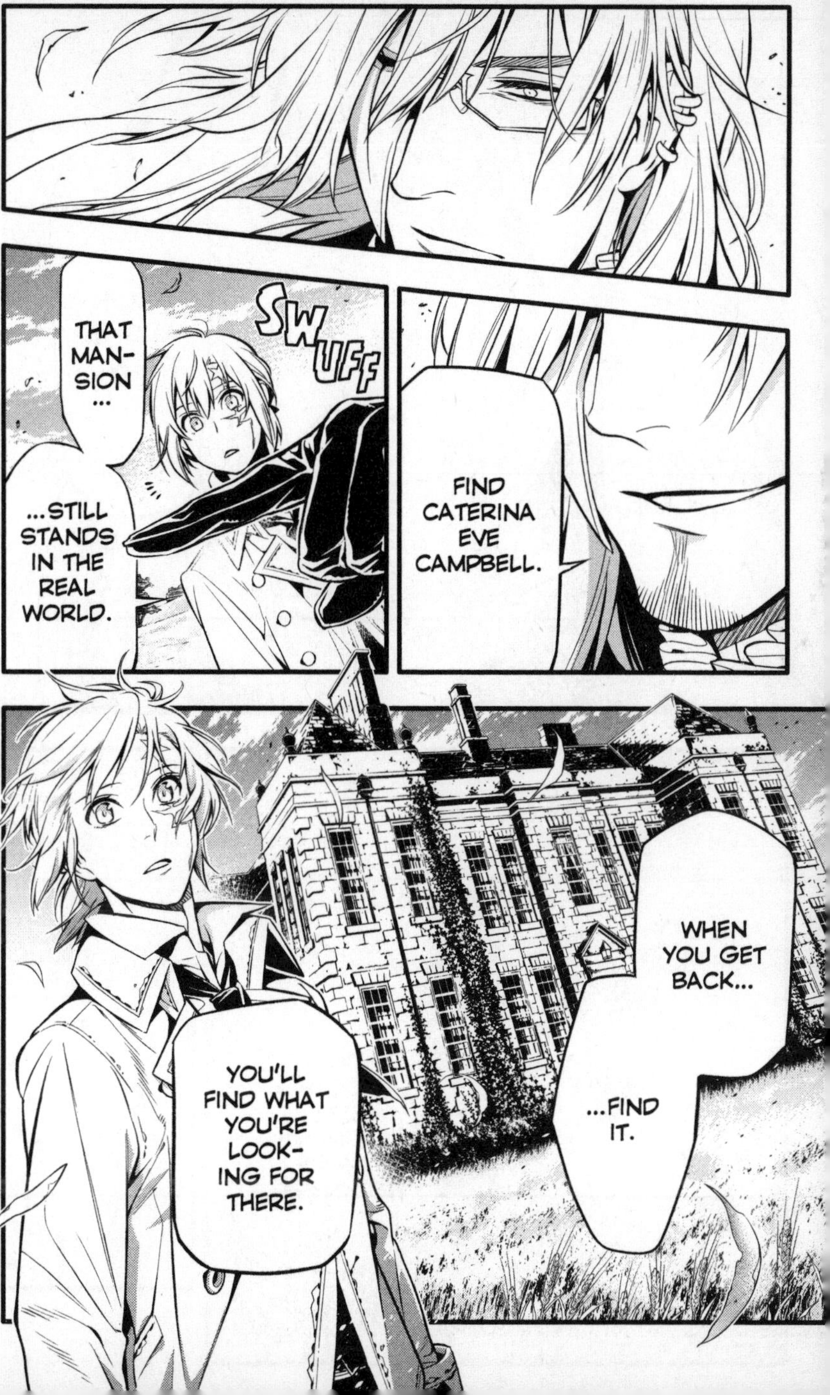
FIND CATERINA EVE CAMPBELL.
THAT MAN-SION...
SWUFF
...STILL STANDS IN THE REAL WORLD.
WHEN YOU GET BACK...
...FIND IT.
YOU'LL FIND WHAT YOU'RE LOOK-ING FOR THERE.

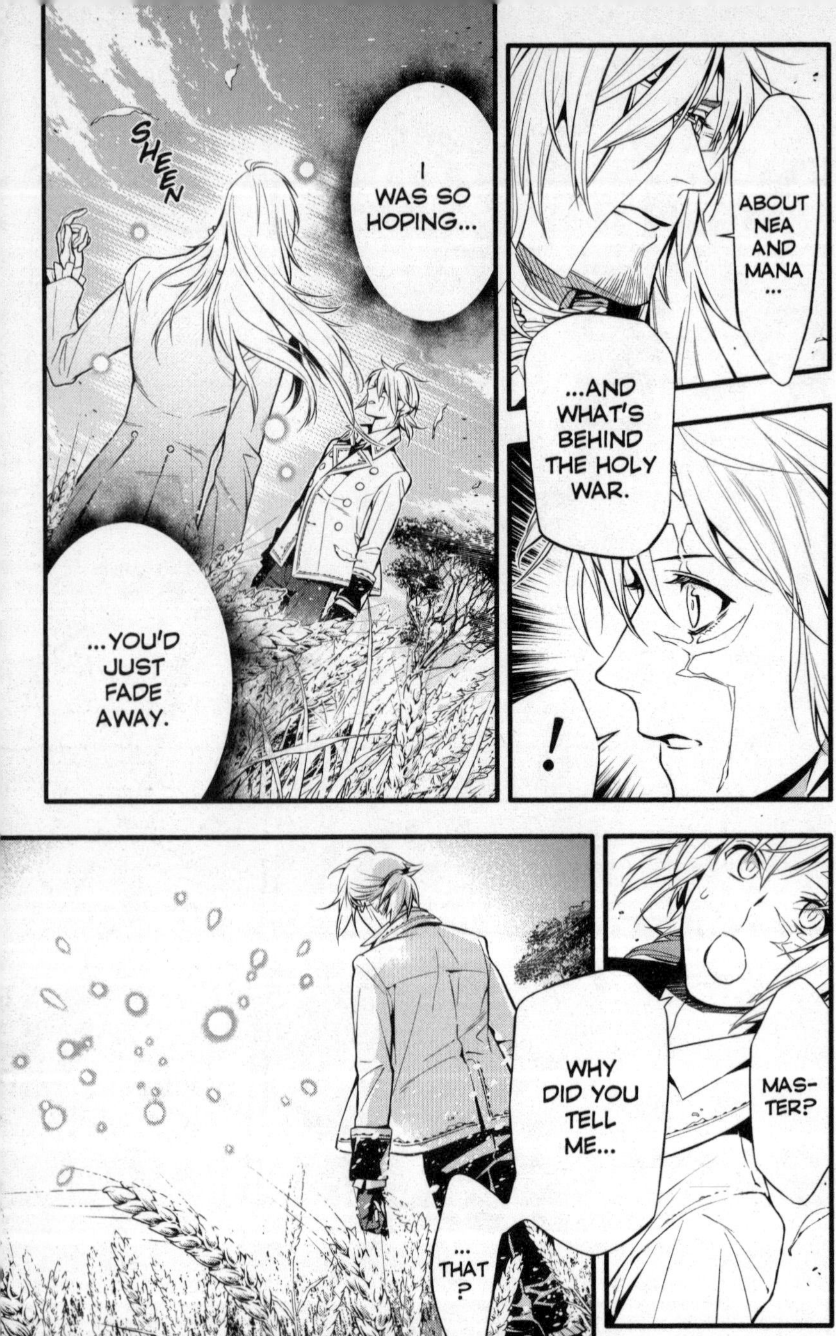
ABOUT NEA AND MANA...
...AND WHAT'S BEHIND THE HOLY WAR.
!
SHEEN
I WAS SO HOPING...
...YOU'D JUST FADE AWAY.
MAS-TER?
WHY DID YOU TELL ME...
...THAT?

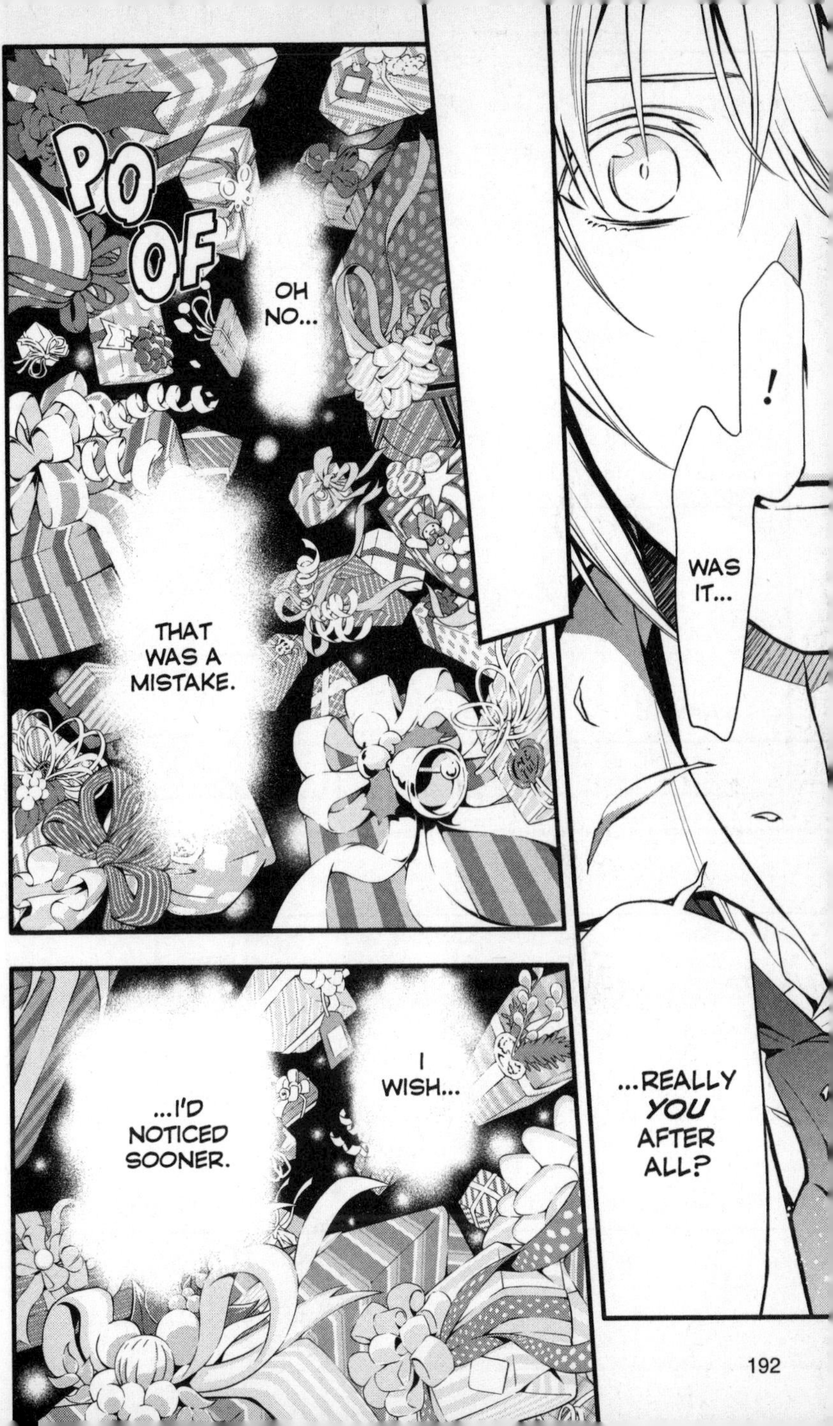
!
WAS IT...
...REALLY *YOU* AFTER ALL?
POOF
OH NO...
THAT WAS A MISTAKE.
I WISH...
...I'D NOTICED SOONER.

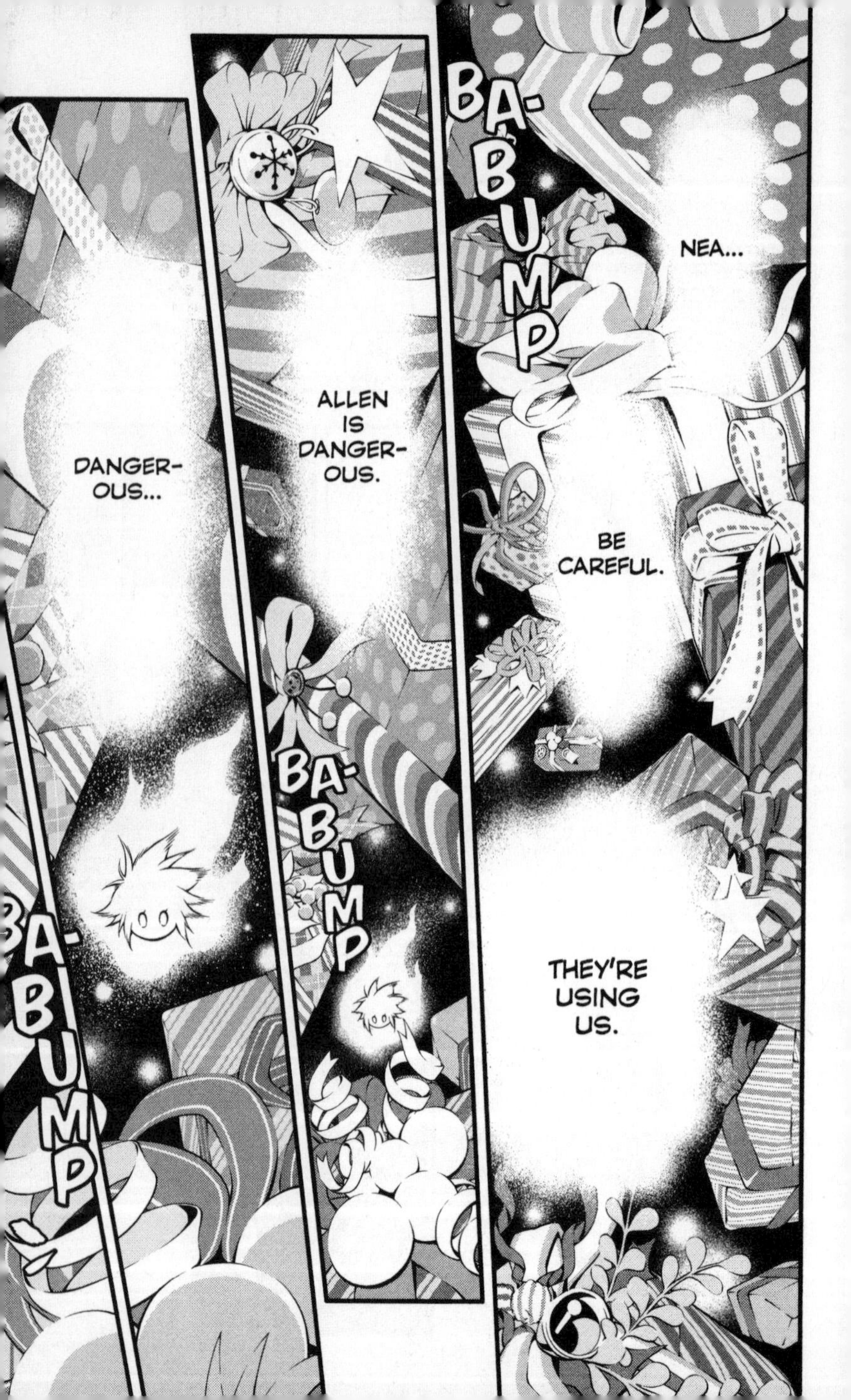
BA-BUMP
NEA...
BE CAREFUL.
THEY'RE USING US.
ALLEN IS DANGEROUS.
BA-BUMP
DANGEROUS...
BA-BUMP

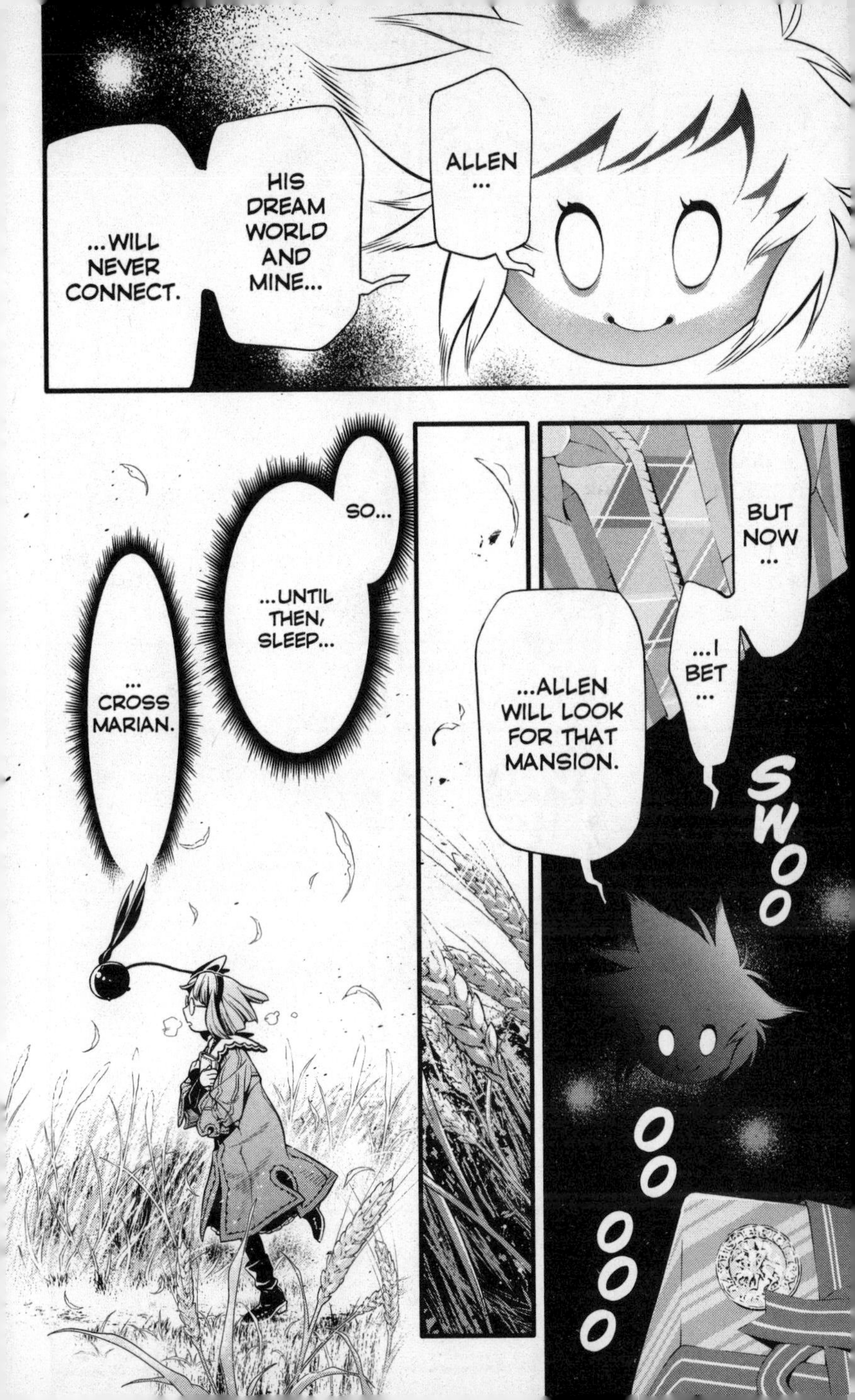
ALLEN...
HIS DREAM WORLD AND MINE...
...WILL NEVER CONNECT.
BUT NOW...
...I BET...
...ALLEN WILL LOOK FOR THAT MANSION.
SWOOOOOOO
SO...
...UNTIL THEN, SLEEP...
...CROSS MARIAN.

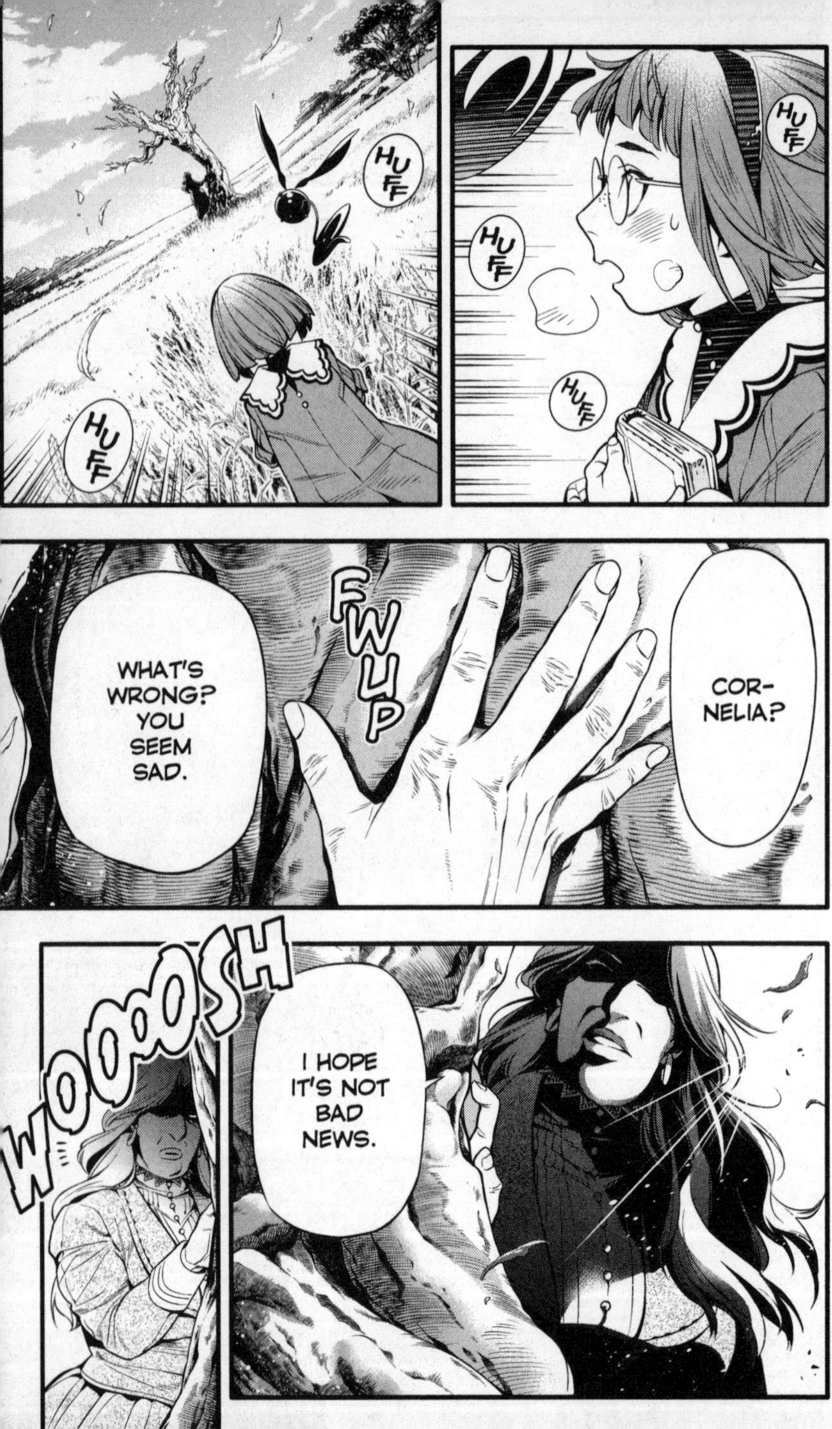
HUFF
HUFF
HUFF
HUFF
HUFF
COR-NELIA?
FWUP
WHAT'S WRONG? YOU SEEM SAD.
I HOPE IT'S NOT BAD NEWS.
WOOOOSH

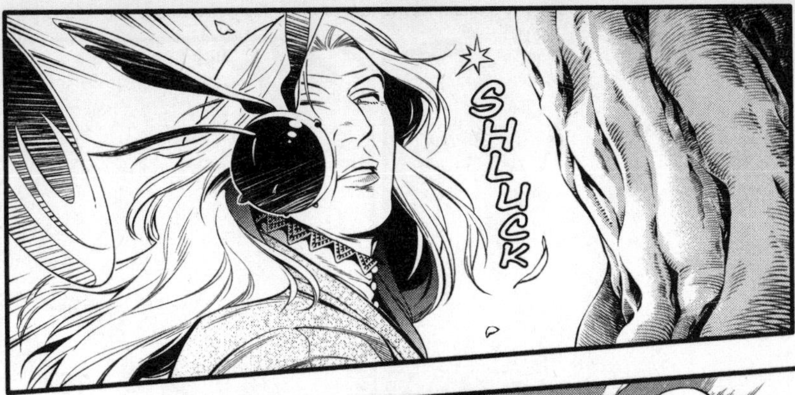
SHLUCK

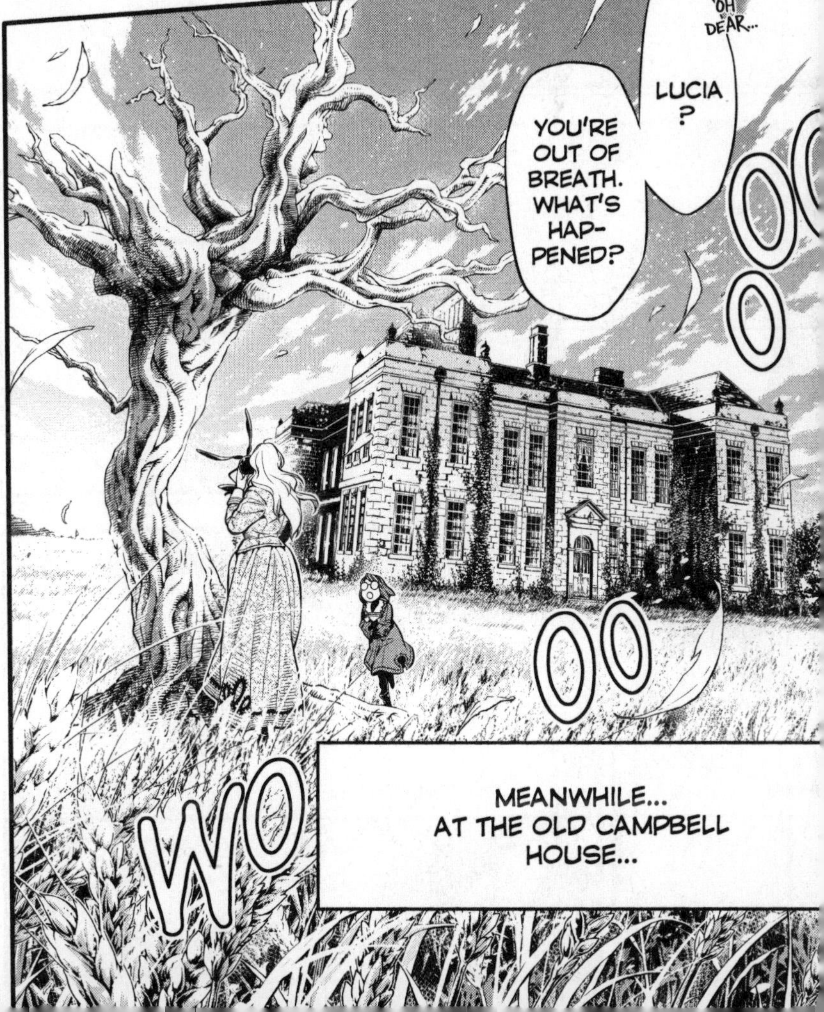
OH DEAR...
LUCIA?
YOU'RE OUT OF BREATH. WHAT'S HAP-PENED?
MEANWHILE... AT THE OLD CAMPBELL HOUSE...
WOOOOOO

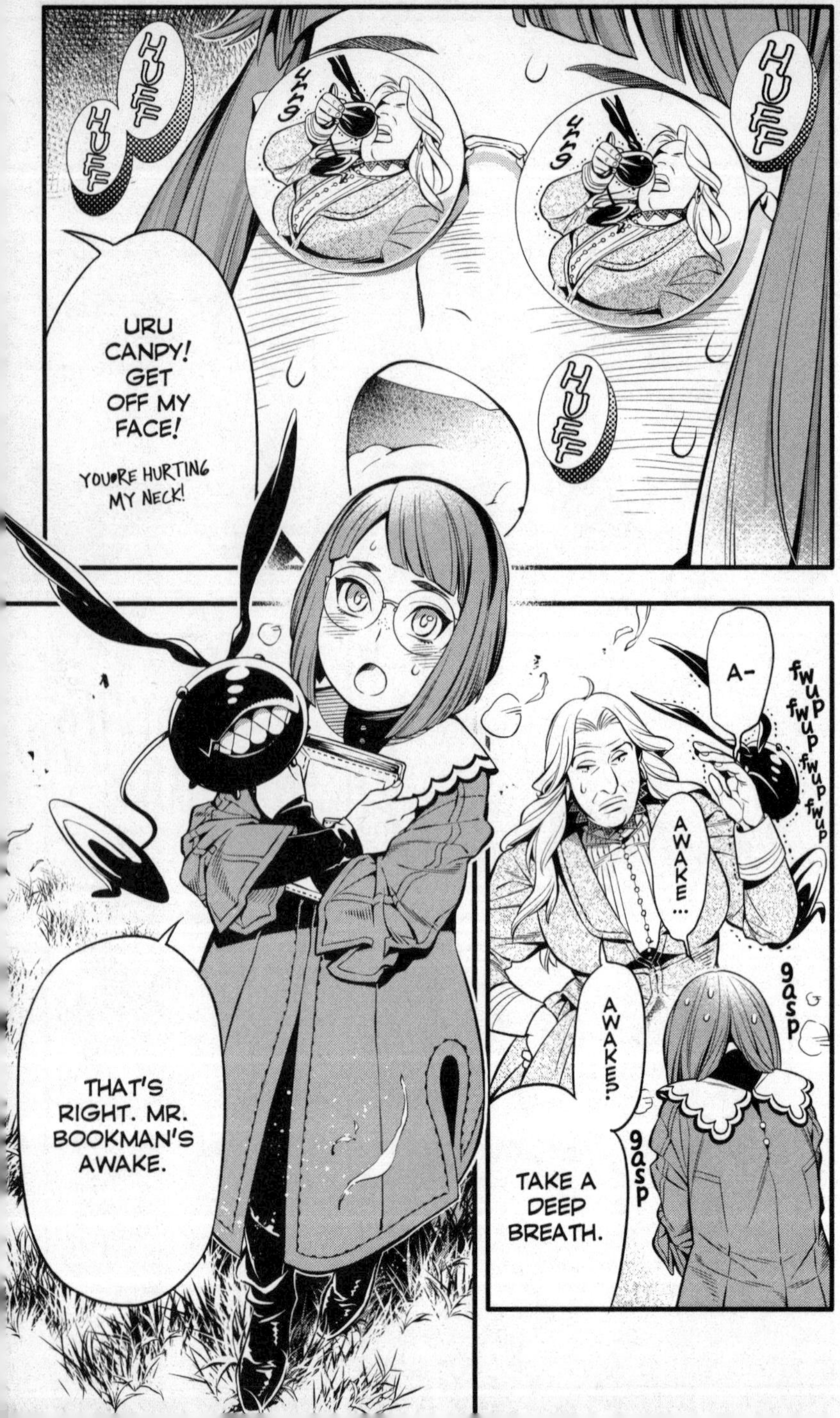
HUFF
urrg
urrg
HUFF
HUFF
URU CANPY! GET OFF MY FACE!
YOU'RE HURTING MY NECK!
HUFF
A-
fwup fwup fwup fwup fwup
AWAKE...
AWAKE?
gasp
TAKE A DEEP BREATH.
gasp
THAT'S RIGHT. MR. BOOKMAN'S AWAKE.

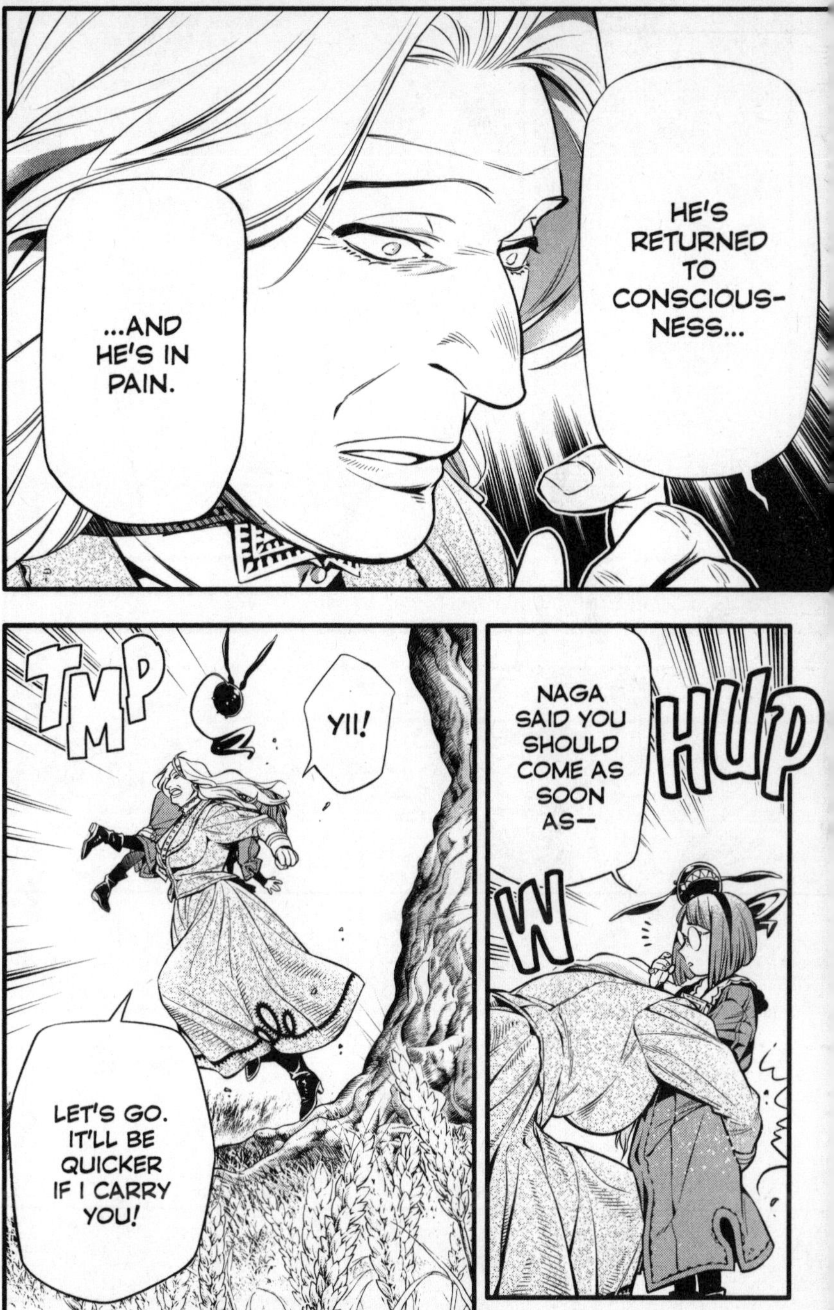
HE'S RETURNED TO CONSCIOUS-NESS...
...AND HE'S IN PAIN.
NAGA SAID YOU SHOULD COME AS SOON AS—
HUP
W
TMP
YII!
LET'S GO. IT'LL BE QUICKER IF I CARRY YOU!

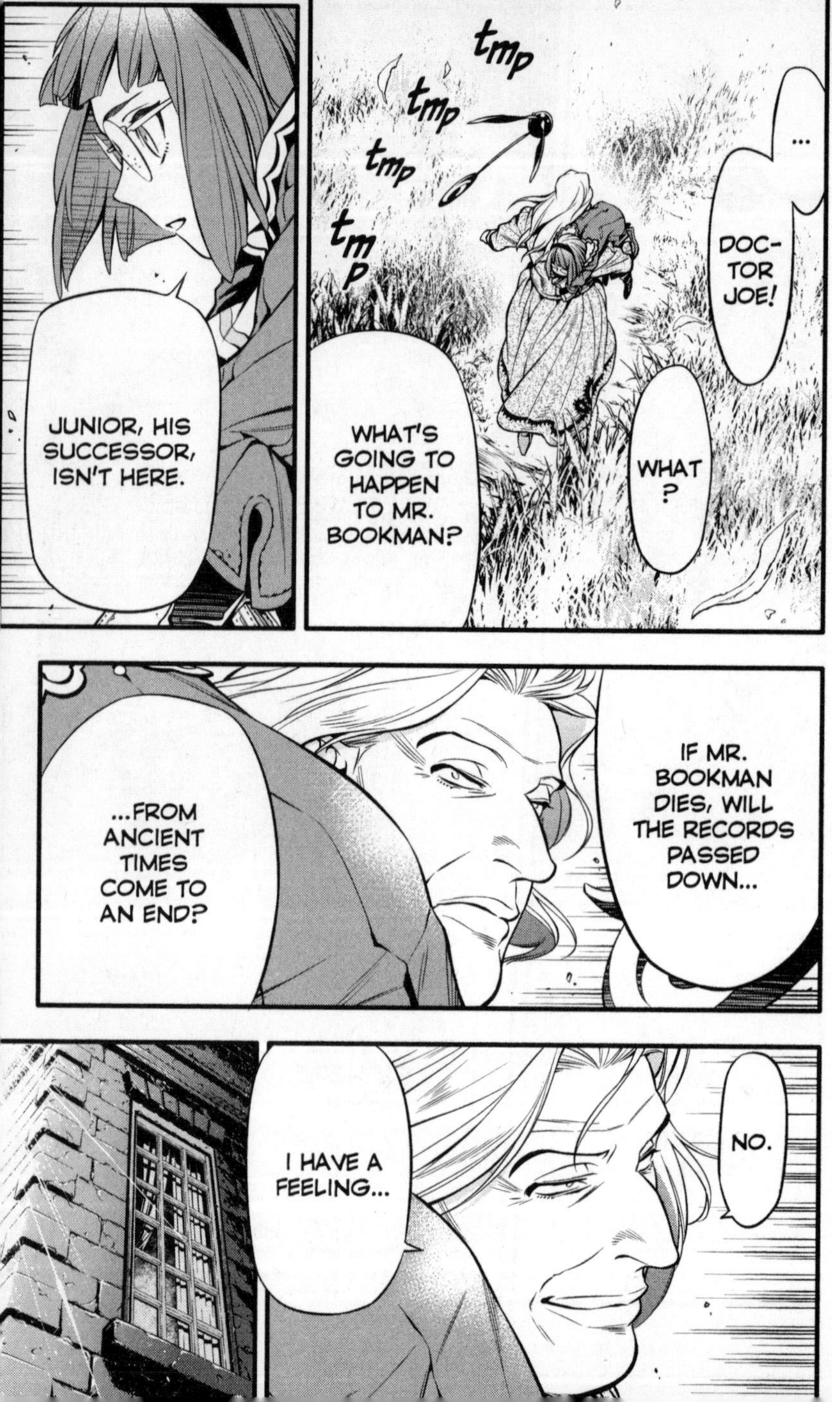
tmp
tmp
tmp
tmp
...
DOCTOR JOE!
WHAT?
WHAT'S GOING TO HAPPEN TO MR. BOOKMAN?
JUNIOR, HIS SUCCESSOR, ISN'T HERE.
IF MR. BOOKMAN DIES, WILL THE RECORDS PASSED DOWN...
...FROM ANCIENT TIMES COME TO AN END?
NO.
I HAVE A FEELING...

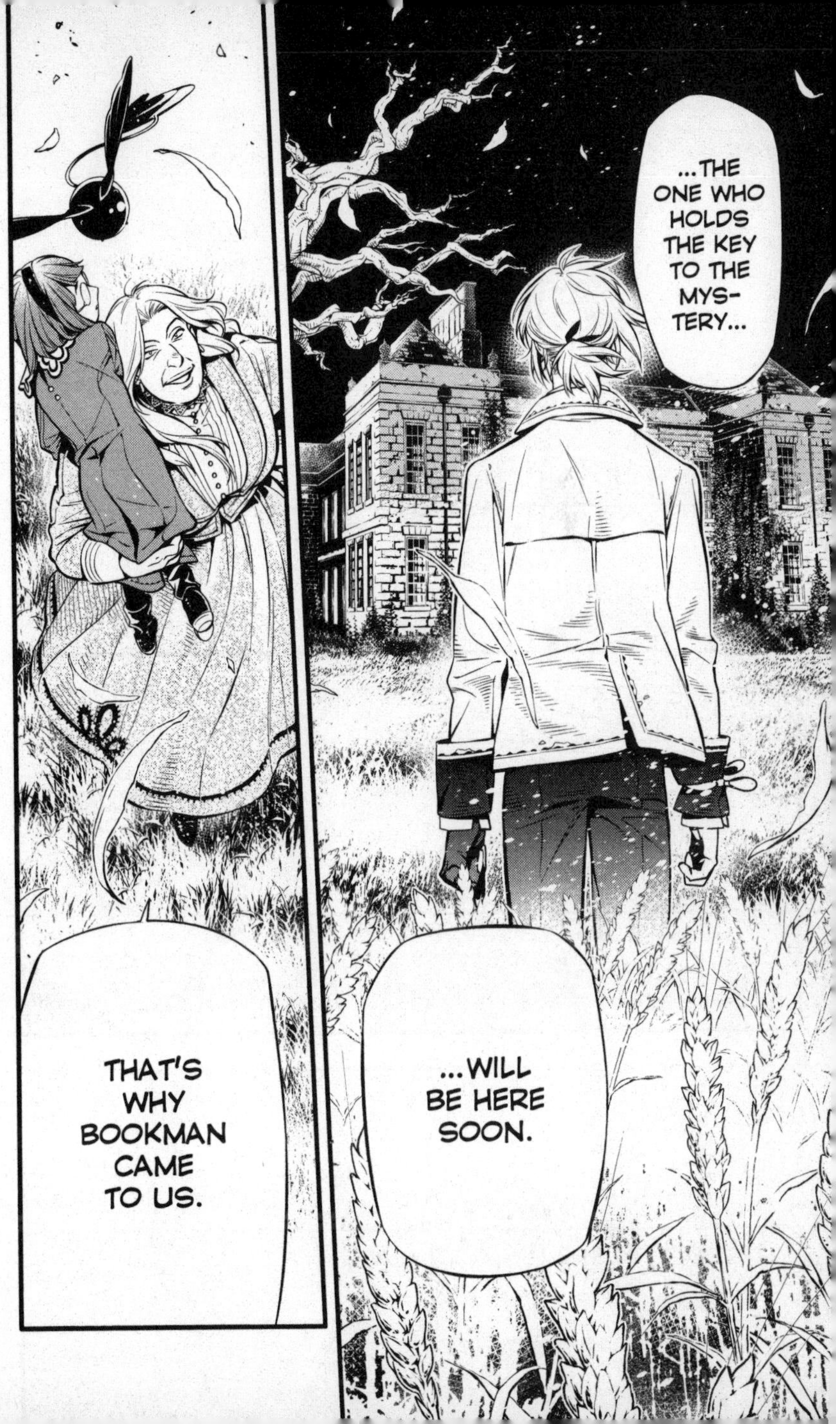
...THE ONE WHO HOLDS THE KEY TO THE MYSTERY...
...WILL BE HERE SOON.
THAT'S WHY BOOKMAN CAME TO US.

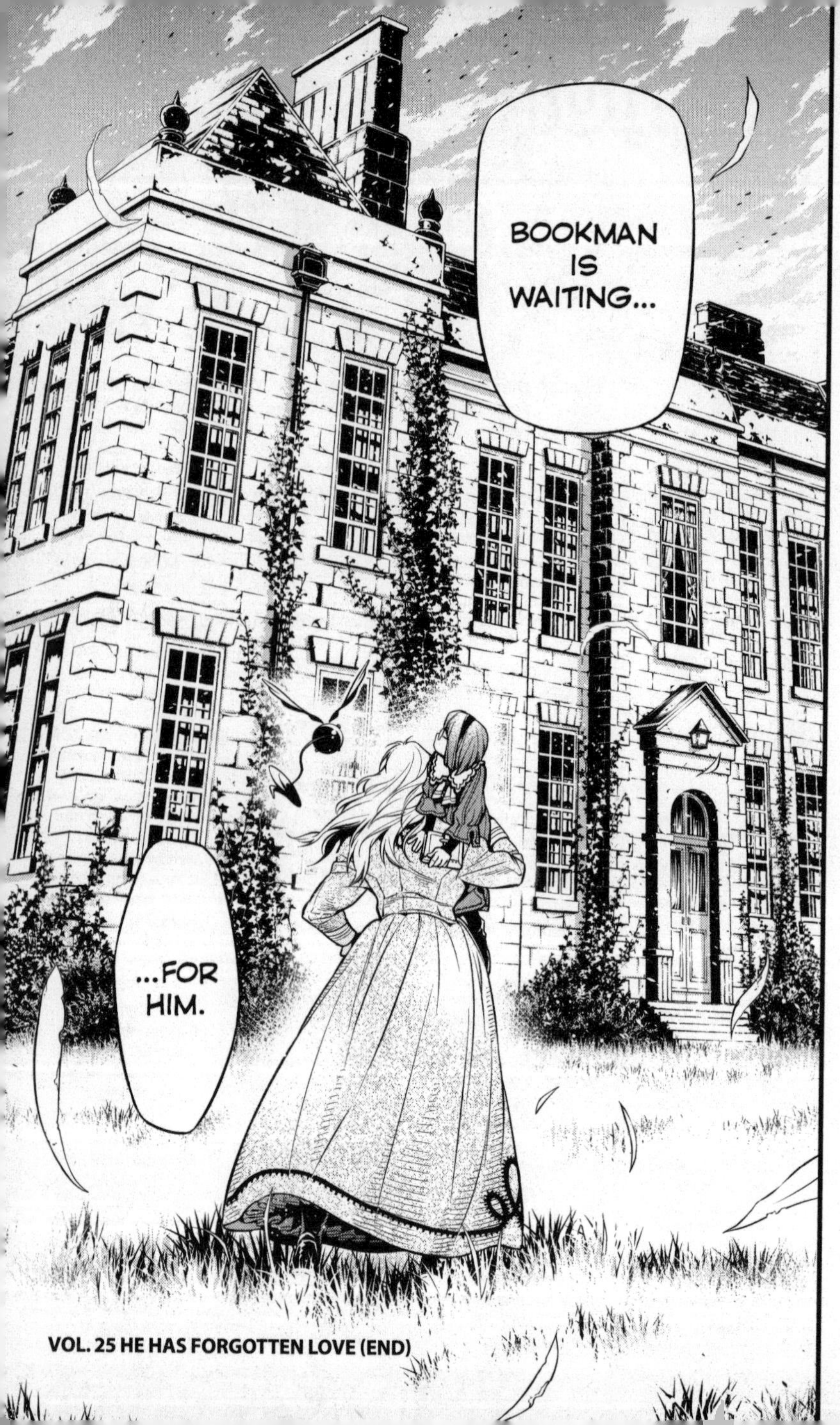
BOOKMAN IS WAITING...
...FOR HIM.

VOL. 25 HE HAS FORGOTTEN LOVE (END)

KOMUI'S DISCUSSION ROOM

PARTICIPANTS
LENALEE (LENA)
TIMOTHY (TIMO)
MIRANDA (MIRA)
KRORY (KRO)
SECTION LEADER REEVER (REEVER)

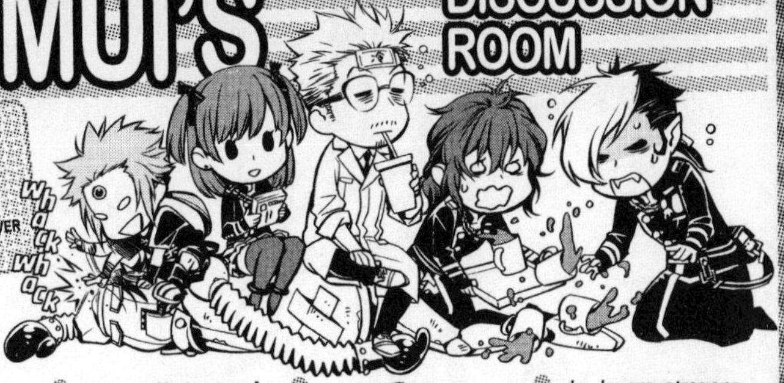
Whack whack

READ THIS WAY

Lena: Good evening. This is Big Brother's discussion room. But he isn't available so this time some members of the Black Order are filling in! You pulled an all-nighter, Section Leader Reever, so I apologize for this. Big Bro has gone off somewhere.

Reever: Don't worry about it. I sort of expected this.

Timo: I'm going to answer every question!

Kro: Th-this is my first discussion room! I'm so nervous!

Mira: Is it all r-r-right for me to p-p-p-participate in such an important event?

Lena: Last time, we went on so long that the editor and designer had a hard time, so this time we'll be brief. *(Striking a determined pose)*

Q: Timothy recently joined the Order. Who is he close to?

Timo: A question for me right off the bat! Hmm... I must be popular!

Mira: Timothy bonded with everyone in the Order rather quickly. It's amazing. I still don't feel comfortable talking to most of the people here.

Kro: But he cried the first time he met me.

Timo: Because I thought you were a vampire! You're scary looking! But now I think you're pretty cool for an old man. Especially when you fight!

Kro: Don't call me an old man.

Reever: Timothy, when you play tag with Emilia, stop running around in the Science Section. You always break bottles of chemicals. Some of that stuff is dangerous.

Timo: But it's the best place to hide!

Lena: You often spend snack time with Allen and the Inspector.

Timo: Yeah, that way I get to see Timcanpy eat. And the sweets Link makes are really good. But don't tell the chef. He's always mad at me and scares me.

Reever: That's because you're too picky. He plans menus with your health in mind and expects you to clean your plate. Otherwise, you'll end up a smelly grownup like Jiji.

Timo: I don't want that! If I'm smelly like Jiji, I won't be popular!

Q: Since moving to the new headquarters, what happened to the Gatekeeper and Number 65?

Reever: The Gatekeeper couldn't move and had fulfilled his role, so we dismantled him along with the old headquarters. He was an interesting guy though! We turned part of him into a monument that now graces the Science Section.

Lena: Chief Peck said he hears strange groans coming from it at night. Is that just his imagination?

Reever: I think...he must be...mistaken.

Mira & Kro: *(Really?)*

Reever: As for Number 65, we couldn't move him either, so Jiji is currently making Number 66. He says he wants it to be able to deal with Komlin. Now others have gotten involved. I warned him and now he's really racking up development costs. But keep this a secret. If the Chief or Barrows find out, they won't be happy.

Lena: *(Assumes the secret will get out but says nothing.)*

Mira: H-how did you move Hevlaska from the old headquarters to the new one? I've been wondering about that. Hevlaska is so big, it must've been really hard.

(cont'd)

Kro:
Yes, the difficulties must have presented a great challenge.

Reever:
Ha ha ha! You'd think so, right? Hevlaska is the guardian of Innocence and the Accommodator of the Cube and usually really big, but when necessary we can put her inside the Cube. Then she's small enough (six cubic centimeters) to fit in your hand. General Tiedoll kept close watch over her and carried her to the new headquarters himself.

Timo:
Six centimeters? Whoa! That's tiny! She can be that small? A huge thing like her?

Kro:
A person can fit in such a small box? (horrified)

Lena:
Hevlaska told me that once her body decayed so drastically that only her soul was left. The physical appearance that we see is created by the light of Innocence.

Mira:
Oh... Hevlaska has been in the Order for over a hundred years.

Kro:
She's not made of flesh. That's why she can fit in the

Cube. But she must have been lonely.

Timo:
I don't get it. It sounds like moving her was easy!

Q At the beginning of the Komuitan Arc in volume 16, Krory was unconscious. So why was he in chains?

Kro:
It's all rather hazy, but I think that monster-girl tied me up. My wounds from the fight at the Ark were still oozing. She forced me to take Komuitan D when I was immobilized by chains and pain. Th-that was frightening.

Reever:
I'd rather not remember that night.

Lena:
Allen says he's refused to take a bath with General Zokalo ever since.

Mira:
After everyone returned to normal, the Chief chased Kanda all over the place. What happened that night?

Lena:
...

Q Why doesn't Kanda cut his hair? Has he just never thought of it? How long does Lenalee intend to grow her hair?

Mira:
Kanda and Lenalee have such pretty hair! I'm envious! (sigh)

Timo:
One time I saw Kanda use a regular bar of soap on his hair and body. When I tried it, my hair was gooey the next day, but his was super smooth!

Lena:
Kanda has potent regenerative powers that quickly restore his damaged hair. Don't do what he does.

Mira:
Tee hee hee! Timothy, it bothered you that Emilia said Kanda's "Asian beauty" was cool.

Timo:
No, it didn't! (blushing)

Lena:
I'm thinking about growing my hair like before. I suppose Kanda doesn't cut his because he just isn't interested in it. His hair has always been long. I doubt he's ever thought about changing it.

Reever:
The Order has its own barber, but Kanda is an elite member who goes on long missions frequently and probably rarely bothers to care for his hair. If his hair got hacked off in battle, he'd probably just leave it that way.

Kro:
I've been on many missions lately and could not care for my hair either, but it feels better when

I tie it back.

Q Does Kanda prefer cats or dogs?

Timo:
Another question about Kanda!

Kro:
The author was surprised that so many people asked this. Why do people want to know?

Reever:
I bet he likes dogs.

Lena:
Dogs. Definitely dogs.

Q Does Krory and Timothy's Parasitic-Type Innocence make them eat like Allen?

Kro:
Well, I do eat more than the average person, but Akuma blood is very filling.

Timo:
Old man, what's that stuff I always see you drinking out of a bottle? An energy drink?

Mira:
It has Akuma blood in it. Chomesuke told him he should always keep some on hand.

Timo:
Chomesuke?

Reever:
Timothy, you eat too many snacks. You eat them like Allen eats food. You should eat more vegetables or you'll end up like Jiji.

(cont'd)

Timo:
Aw, man! Shut up! *(plugging his ears)* I was the biggest eater in the orphanage! I can eat as much as any grownup here! Besides Allen.

Reever:
I suspect that Allen is obsessed with food and money because he was deprived as a child. He says it's because his Innocence is parasitic, but maybe it's partly his upbringing too.

Lena:
One time Allen told me his favorite thing about headquarters was being able to eat as much as he wanted for free.

Mira:
He even said that if Jerry were a girl, he'd marry him! Tee hee... He's so cute!

Q: Has Allen ever considered dyeing his white hair or wished that he had a particular hair color?

Timo:
He said he dyed it once, but it went back to white, so he gave up.

Lena:
Allen said that?

Timo:
Yeah. My hair was originally brown, but when I activated my Tsukikami, it turned blue. It was embarrassing. People started staring at me wherever I went.

Then Allen said his hair used to be brown. He was embarrassed because of all the stares and didn't like it, so he was always hiding his hair. But Lenalee and Section Leader Reever and everybody at the Order treated him normal, so he worried about it less and less as long as he had everyone at Home. So he's not embarrassed anymore. And he said Timcanpy doesn't worry about it anymore either. What's wrong, guys?

Reever, Lena, Miranda, Kro:
(weeping)

Q: How much do the members of the Science Section make?

Reever:
(sobbing) We make about as much as the average office worker. It's low pay considering the conditions, but once you get in, you get awesome research facilities and a budget that's unheard of anywhere else. With benefits like that, we don't worry about the pay so much. And the Order provides food and lodging.

Kro:
But everyone in the Science Section is sleep-deprived, which makes them look frightful and

bloodshot.

Lena:
They're either working or passed out on the floor. *(worried)*

Q: When Miranda goes on missions alone, how does she kill Akuma?

Mira:
M-m-m-m-me?

Kro:
You can do it, Miranda!

Mira:
My Time Record provides logistical support. I, um, can't kill an Akuma by myself. Sorry!

Reever:
That's right. I doubt we'll ever send her on a solo mission. At present, the Time Record can't destroy Akuma, but her ability to control time is extremely rare and useful. Her support is very helpful to Exorcists fighting on the front lines. Timothy, you won't be going on solo missions either.

Timo:
Huuuh?

Lena:
Someone will have to be around to protect your body when you activate and leave it!

Q: Does Lavi have spare eyepatches?

Reever:
Lots of them. Since he joined the Order, we make them for him.

Kro:
He even wears them in the bath.

Don't they get moldy?

Reever:
Don't worry. The Science Section makes quick-drying, bacteria-resistant, anti-odor eyepatches!

Q: Is Director Rouvelier married?

Reever:
I think he used to be, but he doesn't wear a ring. I don't mix with him socially so I'm not really sure. But he's a member of the Rouvelier family, which has followed the tradition of the Lady Saint, so he was probably expected to marry and have kids when he came of age.

Q: Does the Order have a school?

Lena:
There's no school, but I had a private tutor. Timothy's is Emilia.

Timo:
Emilia and Master Cloud are really strict! You had private tutors too, Lenalee? Were your master and teacher strict?

Lena:
The general who was my master died when I was little. I don't remember well, but my tutor was strict. At first, it was just me by myself. Then Kanda came and when I got a little older Section Leader Reever and Rob oversaw my studies.

(cont'd)

READ THIS WAY

Mira:
How awesome to have members of the Science Section for teachers! *(glowing)*

Reever:
That really takes me back! So much happened, like Curly trespassing and causing all sorts of trouble!

Lena:
I loved it when you'd pat me when I answered a question correctly. General Tiedoll's art lessons and Marie's music lessons were fun too! But Kanda hated them. I wish we could all study together again someday.

Timo:
Blegh! Study more?

Reever:
Timothy, you need to work on your writing. The handwriting in your reports is so sloppy I can't read it! How about having Krory teach you? He has the best hand of all the Exorcists.

Lena:
Come to think of it, didn't you teach Allen sometimes?

Kro:
Y-yes. *(blushing)* Despite his appearance, Allen had no gift for reading and writing. Before coming to the Order, he thought he could get by without writing and neglected it. But the Inspector got angry at him every time he did a report or paperwork, so we practiced together in our free time.

Timo:
Didn't Allen have a tutor?

Mira:
He traveled a lot before he came to the Order and has lots of worldly wisdom. He was a big help when I was looking for a job.

Kro:
And he taught me a great deal about living in the outside world.

Lena:
Allen and Lavi have a lot of that sort of experience. It must be hard for them to stay in one place instead of moving around all the time. One time I told Allen I was jealous of him. He gave me a stern look and said he was desperately poor and dirty because he could never take a bath.

Timo:
I'm jealous too! He didn't have strict teachers!

Reever:
Well, he may not have had teachers, but General Cross Marian was hard on him in other ways. He has that to thank for his survival skills. But his reports are filled with grammatical errors. Study enough for both of you, Timothy!

Timo:
Why should I carry him?

Mira:
I hope Allen is getting enough baths since he left the Order.

Kro:
And Lavi. I'm worried.

Timo:
I wanna swim with Timcanpy in the bath again!

Reever:
And I wanna see Allen giving Tim a good scrub again. He said Tim's golden color made him hungry. He was so fascinated by it that he neglected to wash himself. He used to laugh about how the grime came off and his fangs would get shiny when he used one of Chef Jerry's pot cleaners! He looked so happy! Allen... *(crying)*

Kro:
I suppose Allen wanted to take that pot cleaner with him. *(crying)*

Timo:
Timcanpy was so shiny you didn't even need a lamp!

Lena:
So that's why Allen's baths took so long?

⑧ What special abilities are required to enter the Black Order?

Reever:
You just have to be healthy. You can study once you're in. After all, the Order is shorthanded! So join up!

Lena:
I said we'd be briefer this time, but I think we've rambled on too long. *(laughing)*

Timo:
It was fun! Let's do it again sometime!

Kro:
All this talk has made me thirsty.

Mira:
Right. I'll go make tea.

Reever:
Thanks for all the questions! We couldn't address all of them today, so we'll do some more next time! Now I've got to go find Curly. *(standing unsteadily)*

Timo:
Me too! Me too!

Reever:
I'll take you when you learn to eat your meals without being so picky.

Lena:
Besides, Timothy, Emilia is coming for you soon.

Kro:
Study first, play later.

Timo:
Urrrgh!

(End)

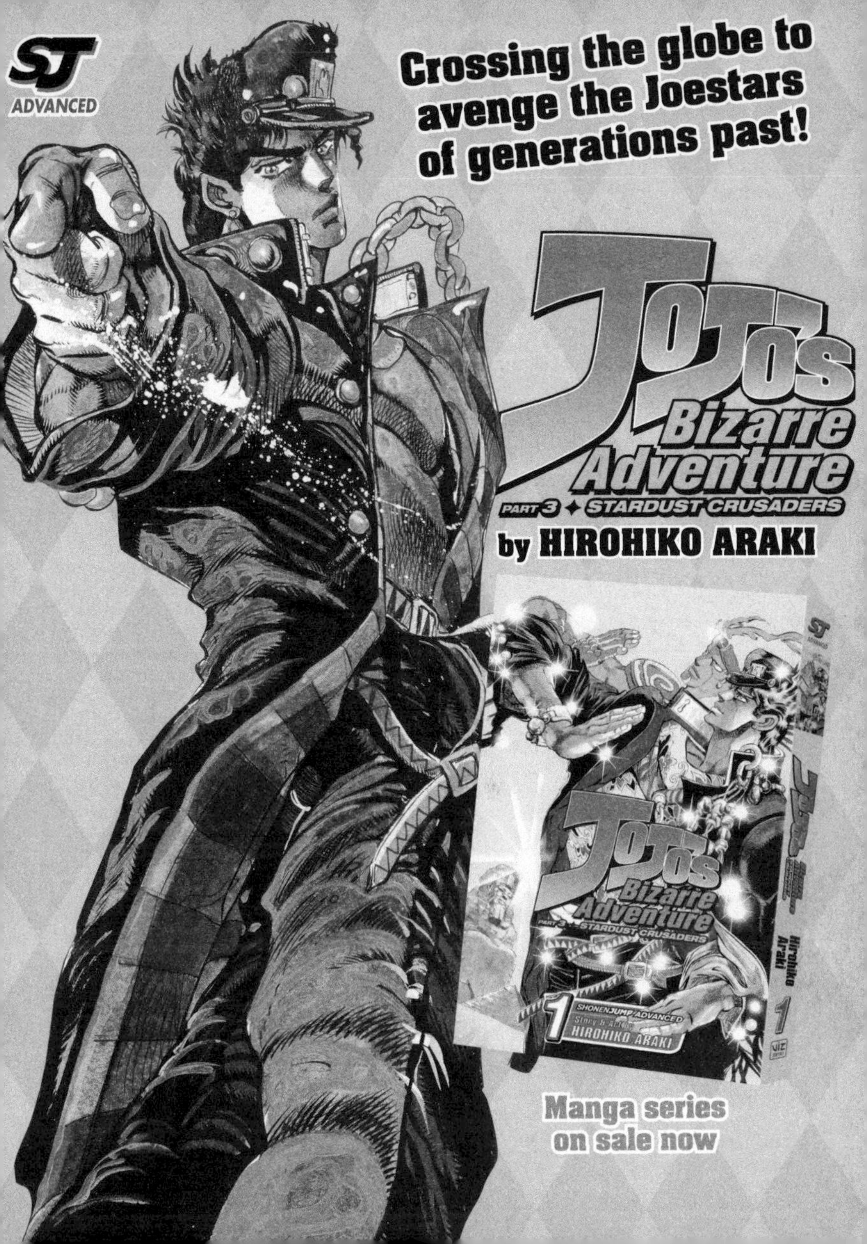
SJ ADVANCED
Crossing the globe to avenge the Joestars of generations past!
JoJo's Bizarre Adventure
PART 3 ✦ STARDUST CRUSADERS
by HIROHIKO ARAKI
Manga series on sale now

Black ✤ Clover

STORY & ART BY YŪKI TABATA

Asta is a young boy who dreams of becoming the greatest mage in the kingdom. Only one problem—he can't use any magic! Luckily for Asta, he receives the incredibly rare five-leaf clover grimoire that gives him the power of anti-magic. Can someone who can't use magic really become the Wizard King? One thing's for sure—Asta will never give up!

You're Reading in the Wrong Direction!!

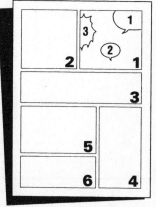

Whoops! Guess what? You're starting at the wrong end of the comic!

It's true! In keeping with the original Japanese format, **D.Gray-man** is meant to be read from right to left, starting in the upper-right corner.

Unlike English, which is read from left to right, Japanese is read from right to left, meaning action, sound effects and word-balloon order are completely reversed… something which can make readers unfamiliar with Japanese feel pretty backwards themselves. For this reason, manga or Japanese comics published in the U.S. in English have sometimes been published "flopped"–that is, printed in exact reverse order, as though seen from the other side of a mirror.

By flopping pages, U.S. publishers can avoid confusing readers, but the compromise is not without its downside. For one thing, a character in a flopped manga series who once wore in the original Japanese version a T-shirt emblazoned with "M A Y" (as in "the merry month of") now wears one which reads "Y A M"! Additionally, many manga creators in Japan are themselves unhappy with the process, as some feel the mirror-imaging of their art skews their original intentions.

We are proud to bring you Katsura Hoshino's **D.Gray-man** in the original unflopped format. For now, though, turn to the other side of the book and let the adventure begin…!

—Editor